Marketing

Second Edition

by Sarah White

ALPHA

A member of Penguin Group (USA) Inc.

International Standard Book Number: 1-59257-135-2
Library of Congress Catalog Card Number: 2003110662

05 04 03 8 7 6 5 4 3 2 1

Interpretation of the printing code: The rightmost number of the first series of numbers is the year of the book's printing; the rightmost number of the second series of numbers is the number of the book's printing. For example, a printing code of 03-1 shows that the first printing occurred in 2003.

Printed in the United States of America

Publisher: *Marie Butler-Knight*
Product Manager: *Phil Kitchel*
Senior Managing Editor: *Jennifer Chisholm*
Senior Acquisitions Editor: *Renee Wilmeth*
Development Editor: *Jennifer Moore*
Production Editor: *Billy Fields*
Copy Editor: *Michael Dietsch*
Illustrator: *Chris Eliopoulos*
Cover/Book Designer: *Trina Wurst*
Indexer: *Tonya Heard*
Layout/Proofreading: *Karen A. Gill, Mary Hunt, Ayanna Lacey*

Contents at a Glance

Appendixes

Contents

Foreword

Any book that bills itself as an idiot's guide to anything immediately catches my eye and attention. I am a certified idiot about a broad range of topics and subjects. It is, as *Dilbert's* Scott Adams assures us, the way of modern life. "Everyone is an idiot about something," he comforts.

My list of areas of idiocy would make a Neo-Rennaisance person blanch. I know absolutely or next to nothing—or just enough to embarrass myself to the point of entering the federal witness protection program and subjecting myself to plastic surgery—about the following topics:

Pre-Columbian architecture

The music of Henri Dutilleux

The Taft-Hartley Act

Comedia dell arte

Deficit spending

The economy of Nicaragua

The declention of Latin verbs

The repair of any mechanical devise more complex than your basic wedge

The levels of British Peerage

Planetary mechanics

The twelve cranial nerves

Quantum mechanics

The laws of thermodynamics

The congress of Vienna

The human immune system

Why gentlemen prefer blondes

Why any parent allows a male child to live through teenhood

This list is not inclusive.

Fortunately for me and others like me, there are people like Sarah White, who not only know what I don't, but who are willing and able to go to the bother of decoding the arcanery of their trade, craft, or profession so that those of us who don't know what they do know can begin to grasp (a) that we don't; and (b) that we might be better off if we did.

White has done a great job of both convincing me that every entrepreneur and small business person, regardless of how small the business or clever the entrepreneur's ideas, needs to be marketing smart to succeed in today's high speed, ultra-competitive business environment, and that I can manage a successful marketing program without an army of high priced professionals who wear suits I could never afford and lunch in places with names I can't pronounce.

Here's a guarantee: If you are a small business person hoping to become a large business person—or just a more successful business person—and you follow White's guidelines for creating and executing a marketing plan, and you don't see an improvement in your business results … I guarantee that you aren't just unknowledgeable but you are actually an idiot. But of course, that's not going to happen.

Why? Because following Sarah White's advice is not only possible, it's easy and mostly foolproof. I say "mostly" because as anyone who works with the public or has ever watched *America's Funniest Home Videos* can tell you, nothing is foolproof. But I know for a fact that those of you reading this book are considerably sharper than those people on *America's Funniest Home Videos*. You did, after all, buy this book—or are standing there in that book store contemplating said purchase—which strongly suggests a superior IQ and a destiny replete with fame, fortune, international travel and many, many of those tropical libations with umbrellas in them.

There can be no question that marketing is an important key to your future. There are too many products and services—none nearly as good as yours, of course—competing for your would-be customers' attention. Marketing, done intelligently, in a focused, precise manner, will open that window of attention, interest, and curiosity that you desperately need to begin the process of establishing a long and fruitful relationship with the clients and customers we both know you can serve long and well.

Marketing is about opportunity—winning an opportunity to prove the worth of your product or service. What Sarah White brings to the table is sage and practical advice for winning that opportunity. As she says, "People don't buy products. They buy solutions to problems." You hold the solution to the "how-to-get-in-front-of-the-buyers" problem in you hands. The rest, of course, is up to you.

—Ron Zemke

President of Performance Research Associates, senior editor, *Training* Magazine, and co-author of the best-selling *Knock Your Socks Off* books on customer service.

Introduction

Who are you? A manager of marketing in a small business, the owner of a startup enterprise, communications director for the Society for the Preservation of Belly Button Lint? Whatever. No matter your job title, I think you all have in common your limited resources for marketing and your unlimited interest in getting the job done—and done right.

If you are who I think you are, you're frustrated with business books that don't speak your language. Marketing texts are too often academic, or their focus is too much toward middle management. The U.S. government calls any business with less than 50 employees "small." Many of you don't plan to ever get that big. Too much marketing advice is off the mark for you.

On the shelf with the academic texts you'll find pep talks in paperback, the motivational how-to books that give you good ideas but no way to organize them into meaningful activity. That's where this book steps in.

The Complete Idiot's Guide to Marketing, Second Edition, is just that. It's not just an introductory course, it's a system that's rational, results-oriented, and downright doable—I know because I've used it. For 12 years I directed my own marketing communication firm. I served clients in wholesale, retail, and professional services. I sold that business, worked for others, and then returned to consulting as a home-based "soloist." The experiences of the clients and friends I served along the way make up the substance of this book.

This book will lead you through an understanding of marketing's core concepts, the development of advertising executions for print, broadcast, and online media, and the management of related activities, like sales and publicity. We'll explore the territory taught in business schools, but minus the lectures, homework, or term papers (unless you feel like writing a marketing plan, that is). I've boiled a complex subject down to just the concepts worth knowing, presented simply enough for Complete Idiots to comprehend.

Nobody said everyone in a business school marketing program is brilliant. This stuff is more like rock 'n' roll than rocket science. You learn your licks, have some fun, get creative, and hopefully get some attention.

How to Use This Book

This book is divided into six parts. The sequence is designed to unfold for you the basis of your marketing decisions and then guide you through the execution of whatever you decide to do.

In **Part 1, "Getting Started,"** I'll skip the b-school curriculum and go straight to what works. I'll introduce you to our example businesses and sketch out the framework on which marketing programs are built.

In **Part 2, "Your Marketing Environment,"** I'll introduce the importance of *people* to your business. You need to know who's buying and why—and who's competing with you for the sale. A look at market research will explain how you can find out the answer to these questions and more. You'll discover that I'm a big believer in using target marketing to attract prospects and in building solid relationships with them once they become customers.

Part 3, "Your Marketing Mix: Product, Price, Place, and Promotion," takes on the "Four Ps" (and if you don't know what that means, you need this part!).

Issues relating to the sales of tangible products, intangible services, and social causes are presented in detail. One chapter is devoted to pricing for value.

I devote two chapters to talking about "place"—one for location issues and one for distribution (getting the goods from Point A to Point Z).

I finish off this section with a look at the heart of that last P, "promotions." Here you'll find tried-and-true techniques for designing successful sales promotions.

So far, my focus has been on pure marketing, the knowledge that should lead to wise strategy decisions in every part of your business. With the hope that my advice has been helpful so far and you've gotten your business ready for the results of increased marketing, we'll move on.

In **Part 4, "Getting the Word Out: Advertising and Publicity,"** we get down to the nitty-gritty of advertising planning and execution. You'll find out the importance of branding and learn how to develop creative messages that support your brand strategy. I'll show you how you can tell which magazines, radio stations, or other media give you the best bang for your advertising buck. Not with sweeping generalizations, but a formula you can use anytime, anywhere, to put competing media options into perspective. Following that, you'll find chapters on the merits of each medium: print, direct mail, broadcast, and online advertising. We'll talk about publicity and how to use it effectively. Finally, I wrap up this section with some low-cost and no-cost promotional techniques specifically designed for those stubborn situations when the usual techniques don't apply.

Part 5, "Here's a Part You Can't Pass Up! (Selling Techniques the Professionals Use)," is time for a break. We'll turn our backs on advertising for a short time and work on the skills needed to turn leads into loyal customers. You'll learn the secrets used car salesmen know, and when and where to forget them. And service providers, you'll find a special chapter on selling professional services—a pet topic of mine.

Finally in **Part 6,** we arrive where most marketing books start out: **"Building Your Marketing Plan."** Follow along as we perform a business review, and then craft a strategic marketing plan and document it in writing. And then I'll bring it all home with a final reminder: Start over at the beginning. Like washing the dishes, marketing is never done.

A Note on the Second Edition

If marketing is never done, neither is writing about it. For this second edition, I've revisited every page, every paragraph, blending in my more-recently gained experiences and perspectives.

"So what's new?" you might ask? Two themes surfaced as one chapter led to the next.

One theme is the importance of target marketing; it's almost a moral imperative to me. Share with the people who care, and leave the rest alone. Don't be a spammer or a junk mailer. Good marketing happens when you solve real problems for a specific group *and* behave like a good neighbor and citizen.

And that leads to my second theme: ethics. As marketers we exert our influence over human behavior in order to accomplish organizational goals. (Or, we get people to buy stuff.) When we do it well, we have real power over other people. Anyone who undertakes marketing must wield this power for good and not for evil. Do nothing you wouldn't be proud to tell your mother.

Signs You'll Encounter Along the Route

As you read along, you'll whiz by four different kinds of boxes. If you think of marketing your business or services as a journey, these are the miniature billboards you'll see along the way:

What?

Build your vocabulary with marketing terms defined in this box.

Pitfall

This box provides warnings. Avoid mistakes others have made!

Mentor

This box gives you perspectives from professionals who have gone through the marketing process and have insights to share.

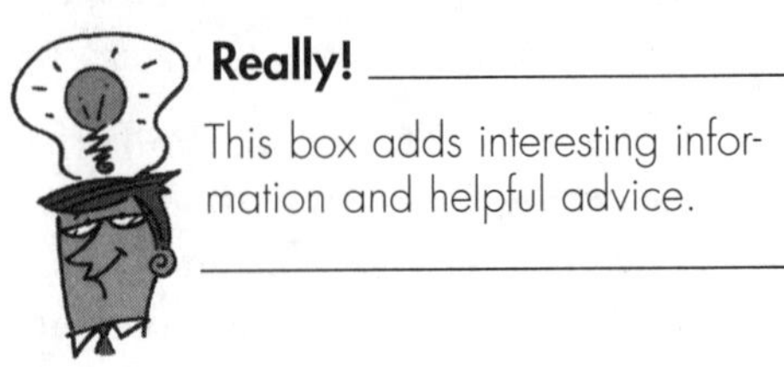

Really!

This box adds interesting information and helpful advice.

Now go spread the word!

Acknowledgments

Numerous people deserve my thanks for their contributions to this book. There will surely be some I forget and will be apologizing to by the time you read this. Foremost, of course, thanks are due the husband who provided a comfortable B&B for my personal benefit so that I might keep at my keyboard. Thank you, Jim.

I'd also like to thank Mike Knight and the good people of Third Wave Research, my part-time employer, a purveyor of demographic research and market intelligence. Check out our articles and self-serve tools on Microsoft's bCentral. (Just go to www.bcentral.com and type my name in the search field. You'll find us.) One of the parts of my job I most enjoy is my correspondence with our bCentral tool users, small business people like yourself who share their quandaries and questions with me by e-mail. Thank you all.

Many thanks also to John Woods at CWL Publishing Enterprises, who initially asked me to write the first edition of this book in 1996 and was kind enough to give me the opportunity to update it for this second edition. Thank you to Jennifer and Michael and all the hardworking people who put the "book" in Alpha Books.

Every client I've assisted, every business "buddy" who shared a tale or trusted my advice, has earned my gratitude for the opportunity to learn and to serve. You've given me the parts of my work that I love best—sharing in the excitement of my clients' projects, applying craftsmanship to their execution, and enjoying the personal relationships that form in the process.

This paragraph goes out to the business people who allowed me to profile their marketing activities. To Robin Woods Sumner of A Life of Faith Dolls, to Anita Hecht of Life History Services, to Fritz Findley and Ava Olsen of Charlee Bear Farms, thanks for permitting me to peek behind the scenes of your operations and experience the exhilaration of your growth. You each set an example I'm proud to share. To the others who appear in this book as portions of composite identities, thank you for bringing your ingredients to the mix.

My thanks to Lynn Jahn, professor of Entrepreneurial Marketing at the Jon Pappajohn Entrepreneurial Center at the University of Iowa for her thoughtful critique of the first edition.

I'd like to thank my marketing mentor Ray Olderman for sharing his insights and acting as a sounding board for mine. In recognition of his deep experience, I tapped Ray to contribute Chapter 11 on social marketing, without which this book would not be complete.

To you, the reader, go my closing thanks: You could be reading a Michael Crichton novel instead. That you chose this book is a testament to your own initiative. Your reward will come when you discover that marketing, once you get past the mystery, is a lot of fun. I hope you'll find this choice of reading material explains and entertains.

Trademarks

Part 1

Getting Started

People usually pick up books on marketing when they feel a pain in the biz. Either sales are slipping, competitors are opening up shop down the block, or your key sales rep just left with your entire client list in his pocket. You need some new customers, buddy.

People don't worry too much about marketing when things are going great. They generally worry about filling orders, finding staff, or getting a computer system that can keep up with the volume. Marketing is the least of their problems.

But not yours. If you picked up this book, odds are you're staring a down cycle in the face. It takes two things to get customers: It takes marketing—with its planning, research, and advertising strategies—and it also takes selling. Plain old "asking for the order."

This book will help you do both. To start, let's explore what marketing is and how the professionals go about doing it.

Chapter 1

Solutions for Sale: What Marketing Is Really All About

In This Chapter

- What marketing is
- What people buy
- Why people buy
- How to get started with your own marketing program

You've been involved in marketing from the day you first begged your parents for something you saw advertised on TV. That early experience—how you thought your life would be better if you had that toy, that cereal, or those shoes—was part of the complex activity that makes up the buying exchange. As an adult, you're participating in the buying exchange in a much deeper way, and it's time you knew more about what's going on. My purpose in this book is to pull back the curtain to reveal what experts have found going on in the marketplace.

It seems like a dry place to start, but we just about have to begin with a vocabulary lesson. We can't talk about new ideas until we have some words in common to describe them.

What Is Marketing Anyway?

Marketing is the process of creating a product and then planning and carrying out the pricing, promotion, and placement of that product to stimulate buying exchanges in which both seller and buyer profit in some way. Got that? Of course not. It's simply too big an idea to swallow whole. Instead, let's look at the parts. An example will help, so let's meet the first of the businesses profiled in this book.

Kalika's Juice Cart: Marketing at Its Most Basic

Kalika is new to this country. She's turned to entrepreneurship to create a job opportunity. She owns a lemonade stand, or more precisely a juice cart. She tows a cabin on wheels down to the local university campus every day and serves juice drinks and smoothies to students.

I bring up Kalika and her juice cart to introduce you to one of the most fundamental ways to understand marketing. There are a number of activities involved. To get a handle on them, we break down the activities into the marketing mix or "Four Ps." These are *Product*, *Price*, *Promotion*, and *Place* (or distribution). As a manager of marketing activity, you need to study each area and formulate a strategy for your situation. (In Chapter 3, we'll look closer at these "Four Ps" and the unofficial "Fifth P," *People*—the customers, competitors, employees, and suppliers who influence and are influenced by the "Four Ps.")

Kalika's Marketing Mix

How is Kalika engaged in marketing? First, she's selected a family of *products* she knows something about and believes that students want. Second, she's arrived at a *price* for those products, based on the costs for her materials, her cart, and the value she puts on her time. She *promotes* her wares with brightly colored signs and menu boards around the cart. If she were a little more sophisticated, she might create promotional strategies like buy-one-get-one-free coupons, multiple-purchase discount cards, or business-card drawings.

She begins the act of *placing* her product by maneuvering her cart into position in the morning. With that ungainly drive, she brings the factory to the store and the store to the customer.

See how the "Four Ps" add up to the first part of that definition of marketing? Kalika has created a product and planned and carried out the pricing, promotion, and placement of that product.

Okay now, what was the last part of that marketing definition? "… to stimulate buying exchanges in which both buyer and seller profit in some way." If both aren't profiting, one or the other will hesitate before repeating the experience.

Really!

The term *product* to a marketer is an umbrella unfurled to cover not just tangible products but also services and even ideas. Think about how your hairdresser convinces you to buy a new shampoo or how your appliance retailer suggests you sign up for the extended service program. "Product" is whatever you offer that has value to your audience. Because services are as important as products, often more so, I like to use the word *offering* because it covers the whole enchilada.

Kalika and her customers both feel happy with the buying exchange at the juice stand. Her customers satisfy their thirst. Kalika satisfies her profit objectives, going home with lighter fruit baskets and a heavier cash drawer. Both parties of the exchange look forward to repeating the experience soon and often.

That's a peek at the "Four Ps" of Kalika's marketing mix. Now let's take a squint at the Fifth P, "People."

People Part 1: Suppliers and Staff Make a Distribution Channel

In most cases a product flows from a manufacturer through a supplier to a retailer and finally to a consumer. Kalika takes care of all that herself. She is a one-woman *distribution channel.* Kalika the *manufacturer* cuts fruit and then blends to order with skill and speed. Kalika the *supplier* sees to it that raw materials are on hand in bulk, and supplies such as napkins and cups are also at the ready. Kalika the *retailer* gets the cart to where the customers are. Kalika the *sales clerk* discusses menu options with prospects, helping them decide what sizes and flavors will satisfy their thirst, and then exchanges her product for her customer's cash. She even provides support after the sale, mostly filling requests for more ice or a napkin. That's Kalika's world—no employees, no subcontractors, just a handful of relationships with fruit distributors and grocery stores.

What?

Distribution channels are all about getting the product to the customers. We'll take up this subject when we get to Part 3 of this book.

What?

Audience, or **target market,** means the universe of potential customers for your product or service. You'll also hear this group of people called customers, clients, prospects, or a market segment. It means the people you want to know about you.

Pitfall

Audiences—and competitors—are people, and people change. Your product or service offering must evolve to meet the changing needs and whims of your audience and stay one step ahead of competitors' changing offerings.

People Part 2: Competitors and Customers

Peopling Kalika's world are *competitors* and *customers.* Competitors we'll talk about when we get to Chapter 8. Her customers are the students, faculty, and staff who come her way. The people who make up Kalika's audience are a diverse lot, but they all have at least one thing in common: They all value a health-conscious snack, and they all habitually pass through the campus commons where Kalika parks her cart.

Your *audience*, or *target market*, is the universe of potential customers for your product or service. I use the word *audience* more often, and there's a reason. It reminds me that life is like theater. As a marketer, you're like an actor trying to please and entertain. You need your audience to believe in who you are and what you're offering.

Let's move on to another important marketing fundamental: What, and why, do people buy?

What People Buy

What did you buy when you picked up this book? Twenty-six ounces of paper covered in ink? Yes and no. What you bought was a solution to a problem, packaged as advice printed on pages.

There's a marketing cliché that goes, "People don't buy drill bits; they buy holes." Here's the point: People don't actually buy products or services per se. They buy the benefits they expect to derive from those products or services. Said another way, they buy solutions to problems.

Maslow's Hierarchy of Needs

The problems you help people solve might be critical to survival, or they might be the fluffiest of whims. Marketers see these problems arranged as hierarchical steps, following the research of Abraham Maslow. This famous psychologist developed his theory to describe what motivates people to behave in certain ways.

Maslow suggested that people have different types of needs, and that these needs can be arranged in a kind of hierarchy, beginning with basic physiological needs (food and water). People will seek to fulfill these basic needs before moving on to the next level of the hierarchy.

Once physiological needs are met, we can move on to concern for our shelter. With shelter secured, we begin to feel our social needs (the need to interact with others). When we have others to interact with, we feel the need for esteem (to be liked by others). Finally, with those needs met, we can concern ourselves with self-actualization (the need to fully express ourselves physically, mentally, and spiritually). The mission of marketers is to provide people with offerings that fill needs at every level, helping people climb that pyramid toward happiness.

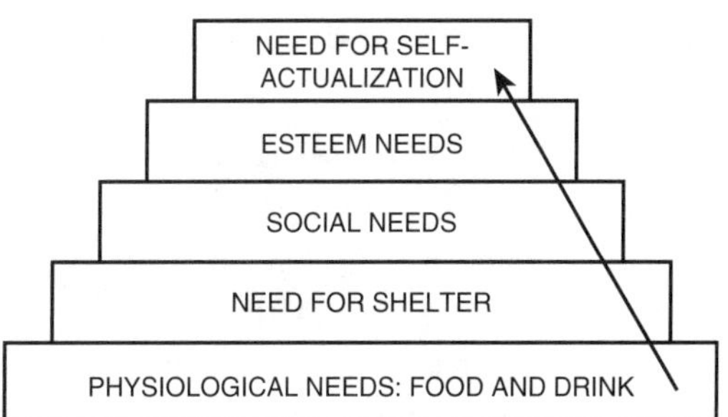

Maslow's Hierarchy of Needs. As each level of needs is fulfilled, we move up to the next level.

Some purchases are meant to satisfy very base level needs. A night in a motel when you've been camping in the rain fills a need that's pretty low on Maslow's pyramid. At the top of the pyramid are less need-driven purchases. A gift of candy for a loved one might be driven by a complex assortment of Maslow's needs. On many levels, that candy provides different solutions to different problems.

Really!

Can Maslow's Hierarchy of Needs be applied to businesses as well as people? Naturally. Businesses' first needs are for the basics of inventory (something to stock the shelves) and shelter (somewhere to put the shelves). With basic needs met, higher needs can be addressed. The search begins first for customers—any customers—and then for better customers who can help the business climb the pyramid toward the ultimate goals of longevity and profitability. If you sell to businesses, you can design offerings that fill needs at any level, from janitorial services (maintaining the shelter) to executive career coaching. Purchase behavior is remarkably consistent with Maslow's pyramid, both for consumers and business buyers.

Pitfall

The "wish lists" in our heads are the rationale behind target marketing and the source of efficiency or waste in advertising budgets. There's not much point in promoting your offering to people who don't have it "on their list." They want what they want. Inducing them to want what they don't want takes a bigger budget and can sometimes border on the immoral.

Mentor

The First Rule of Marketing: People don't buy products (or services); they buy solutions to problems. If you forget this, you leave yourself vulnerable to others who have not. If this is the only thing you glean from the entire book, you will have gotten your money's worth (but there's lots more here, as well).

Your Wish List

We're all walking around with lists in our heads, things we know we need, and things we think would be nice to have. My list right now has "four C batteries, an oil change, some stonewashed black jeans, and some annual vaccinations for my dog." There's more, but you get the idea. An individual's "wish list" is affected by his or her demographics, psychological makeup, and life stage. These factors are surprisingly accurate predictors of needs and desires—but more about that in Chapter 7.

Everything starts with a felt need. Something in you says, "I have a problem …," "I want …," or "I need …."

That something prods you to look for ways to satisfy your craving. The rational side of you comes out and chooses among alternatives. You make a purchase. You use a product. It actually helps you solve your problem or perform some task, and you're satisfied. Or maybe it doesn't work like you thought it would. In that case, you may be grouchily looking for an alternative product to solve that problem. In any case, what motivates you to buy a product or service is some need, usually associated with a problem, and you're looking for a solution.

Why People Buy

Why did you buy this book? Because your boat is leaking. "Marketing is a function of pain," one of my mentors taught me, and I've never forgotten it. You bought this book because you were thinking about a problem that you believe is related to how you market your business.

We buy what we buy because we have hopes the offering will solve problems, fill needs, and take us one step higher up that Maslovian pyramid.

Another Side of Buying Behavior: Self-Expression

We buy to cross items off that "wish list" we carry around, but we buy for other reasons as well. One powerful motivator of buying behavior is the desire for self-expression.

We live in a consumer society, and we show each other who we are by what we have and wear and drive. We start this behavior when we're just kids. Some of us copy the identities of people we admire. Others use our purchases to project what unique individuals we are. We quickly learn that brand names confer status or "cool" that becomes ours when we carry that brand. Because kids are relatively unsophisticated about this, marketing to youth is a very hot (and controversial) topic. But more about that in Chapter 7, too.

As we grow up we continue to use purchasing for self-expression. We buy to display our identities with props and tools and toys that accessorize our hobbies and interests, like cameras, skis, and boating gear.

Young or old, we buy just to enjoy the experience of buying. After all, "the customer is king," and for a moment, wallet in hand, we are the center of a special little universe whether we're 9 or 90.

Now, let's look at buying behavior from the specific perspective of marketers.

How Marketers See Buying Behavior: The Quest for Value

If you make it to Chapter 4, you're going to hear a lot more about value and "the Four Utilities." It's a concept that meshes with the "Four Ps" to help you understand how your offering has value to buyers, and how you can increase that value.

We can describe the formula for value by saying that all customers are looking for a product that …

- Performs as anticipated in form and function.
- Is offered at a place or delivered in a manner that's convenient.
- Is available in a timely fashion.
- Is easy to take possession of at a price that seems fair.

When they find it, they'll probably buy it because it satisfies their need for functionality, availability, and ease of possession.

What?

Value is the benefit that customers receive in terms of their need for functionality, availability, and ease of possession in relation to the price they pay. When a product or service has the appropriate mix of benefits at a reasonable price, the customer will deem it "a good value."

Mentor

Compare the value you offer to the value offered by your competitors. Use the "four utilities" to describe both. Consider the performance of your product, your time and place of offering it, and your payment terms and guarantees. Now consider theirs. How do you stack up?

Think about your purchase of this book. Because it follows the *Complete Idiot's Guide* formula, you can anticipate how it will perform. You probably bought it at a retail or online bookstore, at a time and place that met your need for convenience. Was the price fair? At over 60 words to the penny, I hope so. Compare the price of the book to the price of a marketing seminar, and the relationship of price to benefits seems like a pretty good bargain.

As for ease of possession—unless you picked me up at a yard sale, you might have used cash, check, or charge, whichever met your need at the moment.

The relative emphasis buyers put on these different dimensions is the equation we call *value*. The buyer chooses a specific product or service because he or she finds it to be a superior value to similar offerings. The performance of your product, your time and place of offering it, and your payment terms and guarantees are all things you can tinker with. The right balance will make your offering more valuable than your competitors'.

What's the Value of Bob's Bottomless Boats?

Let's meet our flagship business example.

Out on the highway north of town, where the lake lies so close to the road you can toss your gum out the window and see a carp rise to catch it, sits Bob's Bottomless Boats. You know you're getting close when you see Bob's sign. A vintage 23-foot Chris-Craft cruises high in the air, supported by a slender signpost. If you walk under it, you'll see that, yes, it's bottomless.

Bottomless boats? What's going on here?

Marketing.

No, Bob doesn't really sell bottomless boats. The name is Bob's way of advertising his market position. Bob carries boats of all kinds, from kayaks to cruisers. More boats than any of his competitors. For most purposes, Bob's inventory is—you guessed it—bottomless.

Bob's doesn't just buy and sell boats. Bob's has both a product and a service offering. Bob's rents boats by the hour, day, or week, right off the marina behind the store. Plus, Bob's offers classes in paddle-sport skills. You can get an introduction to sea kayaking, take a mini-course in small engine repair, or earn your master's certificate as a whitewater guide. Instruction is a key to Bob's value. Bob's classes have proved an excellent customer benefit and a sales technique.

What?

A **key customer benefit** is the main reason someone would buy your product over another. There must be some compelling reason, some promised solution to a perceived problem, that comes to mind before other possible benefits. That key benefit may vary from one market segment to the next; it may even be what differentiates the segments you market to.

At Bob's you can test-drive a few models, rent your favorites for a longer trial, and then buy the boat of your dreams. Or you can just drop in and learn a heck of a lot from the staff, no purchase required. That pretty much sums up Bob's *key customer benefit.*

Water enthusiasts of every description can find something at Bob's Bottomless Boats, from a fishing lure to a yacht. There's only one product line he doesn't carry—personal watercraft. "For personal reasons," he explains if asked.

Bob's Bottomless Boats appeals to a broad audience, and sometimes that's a problem. Power boaters aren't that popular with the paddle-sports crowd. The fishermen grump about the motor boaters, who grump about the pesky sailboarders, and so on. Pitches that appeal to one type of boat customer might turn off another. For this reason, market segmentation is a big component of his marketing plan. (You guessed it—more about that in Chapter 7.)

Bob's a successful businessman. He must be doing something right. Let's look at his business through the lens of marketing and see what makes the fish bite.

Bob's Marketing Strategies

What about competition? Bob's doesn't face much, just the three or four other boat dealers in the area, plus the sporting goods stores, the mail-order catalogs, and the second-hand market (all those boats parked in front yards with "Make An Offer" signs taped on the hull). But Bob doesn't worry about these guys—he's the 800-pound gorilla in their playground. You ask him whom he competes with, and he says "Television. Video games. Anything that keeps people sitting on their patooties." Bob's competitive strategy is to get those patooties off the sofa and into a boat. He promotes water sports so that the market just keeps on growing. His store—and his competitors'—reap the benefit.

How did Bob's Bottomless Boats get to be an 800-pound gorilla? Bob's actually started out as Bill's Boats. (Bill is Bob's brother.) Bill was big into kayaks in college but that was the 1970s—you couldn't get a kayak or its special paddle in the Midwest for love or money.

You see, United Parcel Service (UPS) only allowed shipments with total dimensions of fewer than 78 inches. That meant paddles and boats could only be shipped by common carrier, an expensive proposition. The established boat retailers, big into motor sports, wouldn't take the risk on a truckload of "that weird paddle stuff."

When Bill found himself up the creek without a paddle, he discovered a niche market and a business opportunity. He ordered up a truckload of boats and paddles and quickly sold them to friends and neighbors. Delighted, he ordered up another. And another—and got himself a retail location. "Bill's Boats" was born.

Bill's student customers grew and graduated. Their boating interests evolved. Bill's business, still stuck in the '70s, began to leak.

Then Bill's brother Bob blew into town. He'd managed a car dealership and had some ideas he thought would transfer to the boat business. Bob added more products to meet new demand, even (gasp!) adding motorboats and accessories. The inventory became "bottomless." With Bob's strategic vision, it was anchors aweigh for the newly renamed Bob's Bottomless Boats.

Bob offers value to his customers in more ways than Bill's Boats did. The boats still perform as anticipated, whether you buy a Chris-Craft or a kayak. But now you'll find a wider range of forms and functions, and you'll find them available at a time and place that's convenient—a huge retail complex right on the water. There's even an indoor "paddling pond" for winter classes and test-drives.

Bob's also gone crazy making the boats easy to take possession of. He offers financing packages with attractive interest and no money down. He'll hold deliveries until the spring and store boats in the fall. By focusing on why people buy, Bob helps people sell themselves on boats and boating. His marketing smarts are carrying him on a tide of success.

Come On In, the Water's Fine

If you work with this book the way I hope you will, you'll soon understand what marketing techniques might do for you. The examples and anecdotes I use are just jumping-off points. I promise you'll get some ideas about what you ought to try next. You might find yourself fine-tuning some advertising, or you might send your marketing in for a complete overhaul. Whatever your next idea, don't hesitate to try it—dive in! If you like creativity, psychology, and helping people find solutions to problems, then you probably have a knack for marketing. You'll do fine.

> **Pitfall**
>
> How do you feel about marketing? Tell the truth now. Good marketing doesn't come from half-hearted efforts. Marketing's a bit like swimming. If you fear the water or you don't keep kicking, you're likely to sink. Some people are very uncomfortable with the marketing function. Others take to it like a duck to water. If even thinking about marketing makes your skin crawl, delegate your responsibility and give this book to someone else.

Start building the habit of marketing into your daily routines right now. Begin by monitoring what you're already doing. (Use the various worksheets coming up to help you.) Analyze your marketing in light of what you're learning as you read this book. Then create strategies that reach for your goals. Easier said than done? Here's a reassuring thought to get you going.

Nobody dies from a bad marketing program. People get unhappy. Bosses read the riot act when sales goals go unmet, when good products lie unsold, and when money is spent on products that don't sell. People even get fired, go bankrupt, or lose momentum that may have taken years to develop—but they don't die. My point is this: Don't be afraid to experiment a little. The person who never tries anything loses the opportunity to succeed as well as the chance to fail.

The Least You Need to Know

- Marketing involves creating a product, pricing it, distributing it, and promoting it so that both buyer and seller profit from the exchange.
- People don't buy products; they buy solutions to problems.
- People's purchases are motivated by needs ranging from basic survival to self-actualization, depending on how far they've climbed "Maslow's pyramid."
- People look for products and services that meet their definition of value, a balance of form and functionality, availability, and ease of possession.
- Start keeping track of what marketing action you're taking and what is happening as a result.

Chapter 2

Tell Me a Story: Marketing Techniques in Action

In This Chapter

- Why "doing" should precede "planning" (gasp!)
- Key Technique #1: Promoting the end result
- Key Technique #2: Separating yourself from the competition
- Key Technique #3: Anticipating change
- Key Technique #4: Becoming a valued resource
- Key Technique #5: Always doing something new
- Putting techniques into action

When I began working in marketing, a fresh faced and optimistic youth, I placed great faith in planning. I took as my motto "Analyze, strategize, create!" from the teachings of David Ogilvy, one of the most outstanding advertising men of the twentieth century. It's the marketing equivalent of "ready, aim, fire."

I believed that good marketing resulted from an orderly process that involved getting all the information on the table and then working with it to design orderly hierarchies of objectives, strategies, goals, and tactics until every last detail was nailed down. Then, and only then, I believed, could marketing take place that would actually move a business toward its goals. Anything else was willy-nilly, haphazard, amateurish.

Ah, youth.

Now some 20 years have gone by, and I've changed my view. Or more accurately, I've admitted the truth. Nobody plans. At least not like that. People have hopes; they do things they believe will bring those hopes to pass. But the process of articulating those hopes and figuring out what to do is much more haphazard than I wanted to believe at 25.

Planning for Today

If I were still that innocent "ad gal," I would be writing about planning processes. I'd be telling you how to analyze, strategize, and maybe then, if all goes well, create. No longer. Today I believe you should have a plan, but I know perfectly well that "planning" is not the place you're going to start, at least not "planning" in the way advertising agencies and marketing firms talk about it. Too much is going on in your world. A new competitor has opened next door. A key employee is leaking information every time your supplier's delivery driver stops in. The Internet is stealing your customers, or some giant big-box store is.

You can't retreat to some lofty height to look down on your little world and mentally move the pieces around the playing board until you like the result. Who's got the time for that? You're looking for something you can do *today*. So that's where we'll start. Let's go inside some businesses and see what marketing techniques are on the menu.

Mentor

Is there a time and place for "Ready, Fire, Aim"? You bet! Sometimes it's wise to check your firepower before you take aim at your most critical target. That's why I've moved away from recommending a stringent planning process before beginning to take marketing action. I say, start taking action right away. Pay close attention to what that action achieves and what it costs in money, time, and other resources (like credibility). Now you're ready to plan.

A Smorgasbord of Techniques

The following business profiles are a mix of real businesses and fictionalized composites based on the experiences of the clients I've counseled over the years. I'm telling you this now so that, if you go looking for one of them, you don't hate me if you discover it doesn't exist. Of course, I'd like to use all real-world examples, but that's not practical. People have a funny way of not wanting to reveal the inner workings of their marketing plans. Something about competitors. Go figure. I'm going to ask you to trust that these vignettes reflect actual experiences.

Five businesses demonstrate five successful marketing techniques. (There are certainly more than five possible techniques, but that's plenty for now.) I'll introduce the businesses and the techniques they represent. These businesses will reappear in upcoming chapters, so pay attention.

Promoting the End Result: Kai Miaka, Musician at Large

When I met Kai, he was the ringleader of a hot little bar band, and he came to me for some marketing pieces—package design for his band's new CD, a direct-mail piece to go to college music booking agents, that sort of thing. Over time I've watched Kai's business acumen grow sharp and his talents find their niche. He's added "guitar teacher," "jingle writer," "voice talent," and even "talent agent" to his repertoire. That's a lot of balls to juggle.

Marketing for a fellow like Kai means a careful balancing act. Market too much and he could over-sell his capacity to produce. Market too little and he could find himself with no customers at all. Marketing presents a dilemma for Kai, but that doesn't mean he can ignore it entirely. Business, like grass, has a funny way of drying up if you don't water the ground from time to time.

Kai sets a "floor" to his marketing activity. Even when he's busy, he makes sure of three things:

1. He has the marketing literature he needs to project the right image.
2. He keeps his service lines separate but equal, applying some attention to each on a regular basis. As a result, he keeps his project portfolio balanced.
3. He maintains a calendar and faithfully consults it, so he doesn't end up "a day late and a dollar short" when it comes to marketing. Each of Kai's service lines has its own cycles. If Kai ignored that basic fact, his marketing activities would likely fall out of step and soon falter.

When business starts to slow down, Kai ratchets up his activity and voilà! He's soon back up to speed.

Kai sets a "ceiling" for his marketing activity as well. When he gets busy, he maximizes the opportunity for profit by raising his rates. No, he doesn't jack up prices on existing clients; he just starts quoting a slightly higher figure when asked about new work, no matter which of his talents is on offer. As a result, Kai's business activities have grown steadily more profitable over time.

Let's take a quick peek at Kai's customer base. His service lines appeal to several different markets. Kai's band performs for crowds of dance-happy college kids. They make up the customers for tickets and CD purchases. But the real customer Kai promotes the band to is booking agents—the people who schedule gigs for clubs, taverns, fraternities and sororities, college functions, and so on. Because of Kai's connections with these bookers, he's able to help other people get gigs, too—that's where his role as "talent agent" comes in.

Mentor

Each of Kai's service lines has its own cycle. If Kai misses the fall talent-booking feeding frenzy, his band will have fewer college gigs. Likewise, music teaching follows a cycle of its own, with new sign-ups heaviest in September, January, and May. Is there a seasonality to your product or service offering?

What?

A **service line** (or a product line) is a category of services or products you offer. If all you make is rubber bands, you have one product and one product line. If, like Kai, you sell several different things, or sell them to several different categories of buyers, you have product or service lines. Each may require its own marketing tactics.

Next, "guitar teacher." That one came about easily, as people who heard the band came to Kai and said, "Teach me to play like that, man!"

And finally, Kai's talents as a songwriter and his mellifluous voice led him to the advertising business. I don't know who first tapped him to write and sing commercials, but those early contacts with advertising types have led to a lucrative sideline.

Now having a lot of talents is both a blessing and a curse. By working in so many areas, Kai insulates himself from downturns in any one sector. But he also makes a lot of work for himself keeping track of so many different types of customers and prospects. He simplifies the problem by keeping in mind one specific marketing technique: *Promote the end result.*

People don't really want guitar lessons; they want to play guitar! Bookers don't really want negotiations; they want hassle-free profitable musical events. Advertising guys don't want recording sessions; they want finished great-sounding commercials. Kai makes sure all his marketing messages emphasize the satisfying end result. With that as his guiding principle, he's kept a focused, easy-to-execute marketing program going for years.

Separating Yourself from the Competition: A Life of Faith Dolls and Accessories

Are you familiar with the American Girls doll collection? If not, you don't know any 10-year-old girls. This line of historically accurate dolls and accessories is coveted by girls and respected by parents and grandparents who appreciate the quality and attention to detail throughout the line. Each doll is a character from a story. Each doll's product line includes a book series, plus dresses and accessories drawn from the books' story lines.

Why am I telling you about American Girls? Because A Life of Faith Dolls exist to compete with them. Sandy Shelton of Mission City Press, a Christian publishing company, followed the popularity of the American Girls Collection and saw an opportunity. The publisher teamed up with doll designer Robin Woods Sumners who had also been following the American Girls phenomenon closely. The two brought their talents and resources together to create a collection like American Girls but with a twist—a firm foundation in Christian faith.

In 1998, Mission City Press had arranged to update a classic children's series, first published in 1868—the "Elsie Dinsmore" books. (They outsold Louisa May Alcott's *Little Women* when first published.) The potential for an offering similar to American Girls was evident from the start. In 2002, Sandy Shelton set out to accomplish that vision. But while she knew publishing, she recognized that doll-making was beyond her expertise. She found and partnered with Robin, who became responsible for the design and production of lovely dolls and costumes drawing on the characters and activities in the stories. Mission City Press has created a website around "A Life of Faith," full of fun resources for history-related study and play. Lacking the marketing budget behind American Girls, the company has worked the "faith" angle to get the word out about their products. A Life of Faith is a direct-mail operation. Their main promotional tools are printed catalogs and the website. The company attends doll hobby shows and uses direct mail and online advertising to connect with customers.

Robin and Sandy's marketing is competitor-focused. Their job is to get you to think of their products in the same category as American Girls—high-quality, solidly made, very desirable girls' toys. Then they present you with a reason to do business with them instead of their competitors. The difference is the Christian faith message inherent in A Life of Faith's dolls. If that is a value you share, you're in their target market. Their marketing technique: *Separate yourself from your competition.*

A Life of Faith Dolls' offering is in many ways quite similar to their competitors. A doll is a doll. The company's advantage lies in the reasons they've created for customers to do business with them instead of competitors. In this case, it isn't faster results, easier procedures, or better guarantees. It's the component of teaching spiritual values that have been designed into the product offering. What unique advantage can you design into your offering?

CAUTION

Pitfall

Robin and Sandy have taken a calculated chance in choosing to focus on faith. They have consciously chosen a small niche market within the large consumer market for dolls. This limits the upside potential for the business—A Life of Faith Dolls will probably never match American Girls in sales. And that's fine with them. What about you? Fail to make calculated choices of your own, and you risk trying to be all things to all people … rarely a successful strategy. What compelling reason to do business with you sets you apart from your competition?

Anticipating Change: University Credit Union

Credit unions are like banks, except for one thing—the members are the owners. Because they are cooperatively owned by their members, credit unions operate with a different mission. A credit union's goal is not to generate profits for shareholders, but to cover costs and return excess profits to members in the form of shares (dividends) or expanded services offerings.

The credit union movement took off during the Depression, when bank failures led communities to band together and form their own financial institutions. Back then, federal regulations dictated that only groups sharing a common bond, like employees of one company or members of a certain church, could form a credit union. That regulatory environment loosened in the 1980s and 1990s, making credit union membership an option to anyone living near one. That move really heated up the competition for new customers. Now credit unions could compete with banks and even with each other.

Where there's competition, there's marketing activity. But here, credit unions faced a double whammy. They lacked experience at marketing; few even had a marketer on staff when the rules changed. Plus, credit unions (unlike other financial institutions) retained their mission to return excess profits to their members. That means maintaining the lowest possible cost of operations—in other words: *Limited marketing budgets.* Credit union marketers must compete with the bigger budgets and deeper past experience of bank marketing departments.

Cary Ralston came to University Credit Union from a marketing position with a bank. She brought her experience but had to adapt to the limited funds for marketing in her new position. University Credit Union (UCU) had been around for decades serving the students, faculty, and staff of a major university; it is one of the largest credit unions in town, with over 80,000 members. Cary manages a staff of two.

The marketing department of UCU pursues twin strategies of recruiting new members and retaining current ones. The latter is important because students tend to move their accounts away when they graduate. UCU works hard to hang onto those accounts, as graduating students are just entering their best years as customers of financial services. After years of bouncing checks and living lean, they're about to get jobs and start buying cars, houses, and other big-ticket items.

Cary and her marketing department must never lose sight of the intense competition they face. Other financial institutions are always implementing new strategies, and UCU must respond in kind or lose market share. Cary's key marketing technique: *Anticipate change.*

Aggressive competitors, new technology, changes in the regulatory environment—any and all could threaten the status quo if UCU neglected to anticipate change. To insulate against the impact of change, UCU constantly looks for new products and services to offer and uses a variety of marketing methods to promote them. Not so long ago, offering online services was the "next big thing," and UCU was right there at the forefront since students are naturally *early adopters* of technological solutions. Every day, Cary must focus on knowing what tomorrow's competitive advantage will be.

What?

Early adopters are people who are by nature optimistic and open-minded. They're often eager to try new products and services that might make their lives better. Early adopters are important to the success of new products because their acceptance tends to be catching. Once early adopters start buying your offering, you're well on your way to growing sales.

Becoming a Valued Resource: Life History Services

Anita Hecht is the founder and sole proprietor of Life History Services, a personal-history business dedicated to preserving individual, family, business, and organizational histories in video, audio, print, and digital formats.

Personal-history businesses like Anita's are popping up all over the country. More people are getting interested in securing help to preserve their memories in forms such as photography, audio and video recordings, scrapbooks, collections of family stories, and published books. At the same time, technology such as short-run printing, DVDs, and the Internet is expanding the possibilities for creating and distributing

Pitfall

Pity the poor fool who sells a product or service that nobody knows they want. Businesses like Life History Services, which have to create awareness of their product category before they can begin to create desire to own it, have a tough row to hoe. If you're in this situation, marketing will take up more of your budget, and take longer to show results.

those memories. As a result, there is a growing business opportunity for professional services related to memory preservation.

If you've seen "Creative Memories" products or attended a scrapbooking party, you've encountered the "do-it-yourself" end of the spectrum. Anita's business occupies the other end of that spectrum, where families pay thousands of dollars for a high level of service and high-quality archival final products.

Life History Services faces a marketing challenge that's all too common. Anita's target market is barely aware such a service even exists. So she has to start with education—helping people understand how recording their memories gives family members a unique heirloom. That means long sales cycles, with families sometimes taking years to consider the concept before finally signing a contract with Anita.

One way Anita coped with this challenge was through affiliation with a professional organization. She was one of the earliest members to join the recently formed Association of Personal Historians. This organization works hard to raise the visibility of personal history work to lift the burden of education from individual members. It also acts as a clearinghouse for marketing ideas, as members exchange tales of their efforts, what worked and what didn't, through an active e-mail list.

Anita, like many of the association's members, works hard to get the word out in her community. She actively pursues publicity. She speaks to groups such as retirement centers, writers' groups, churches, estate planners, and service clubs. Typically, her presentation begins with explaining why recording one's personal history is important. Then she talks about methods and processes, always suggesting that one could do this by oneself but that professional assistance like she offers has many advantages.

Anita pursues a marketing technique of *becoming a valued resource.* She's found through experience that she has two sources of clients: people who want to record their own life stories, and people who want to contract Anita's services for an elderly family member. In both cases, lots of information helps make the sale.

Many of the first type of prospects, those who want to record their own history, follow the same path: first they attempt to do it themselves. But they soon get bogged down, finding it more difficult and time consuming than anticipated. Now, convinced that it should be done, they turn to Anita for help.

Many of the second type of prospects, those who wish the service for a family member, need help convincing the elderly relative that the process is worthwhile. "My story wouldn't interest anybody!" is the typical reaction. Anita provides testimonials, samples, and articles that help change that belief.

Anita's marketing technique, while slow to work, results in satisfying long-term relationships with families. If you are selling a professional service, like Anita is, this technique will likely work well for you. How can you help your clients do things faster, better, less expensively? As a valued resource, you get another opportunity to sell something every time a client comes back to you for help.

Always Something New: Bob's Bottomless Boats

In the previous chapter, we met Bob and his business, Bob's Bottomless Boats. He's got a boatload of inventory and he's got a marketing challenge: how to be all things to all people. By focusing on why people buy, he's been able to add services and products that keep some very different types of boating enthusiasts coming back for more. Services like rental, instruction, storage, and delivery make up part of that equation. Products that range from lightweight kayaks to boats big enough to be second homes keep Bob's Bottomless Boats an interesting place to drop in and browse what's new.

Bob's key marketing technique: *Keep adding something new.* Bob's suite of services and products just keeps growing. Every time he adds something new to the line, he creates an opportunity to make more sales. There are four advantages (at least!) to this strategy:

- The new offerings attract customers who were looking for that very thing.
- The new offering produces repeat sales from existing customers, who discover they want that thing.
- Bob can create special package offers by combining the new offering with something that was already on offer.
- Bob can use that new offering as a "hook" for an ad campaign or a round of press releases, thus stimulating sales through increased awareness of his business.

Retailers like Bob find this marketing technique very effective, but demanding. Those last two advantages add up to heavy usage of advertising for sales promotions, with big budgets to match. If your business has a strong emphasis on *products,* and the resources to invest in advertising, this technique should work for you.

Really!

For retailers, developing new products is relatively easy; it's just a matter of altering or adding to the merchandise assortment in the store. Successful retailers have a talent for finding new products that fit well with existing assortments, adding excitement that helps move old merchandise as well as new. For manufacturers, developing new products is more difficult. Despite the difficulties or research and development, they must keep new products in the works or risk sales decline as current products reach the end of their life cycles. Developing new products can be resource-intensive but highly rewarding in the long term. For more on this, see Chapter 9.

Putting the Techniques into Action

First, credit where credit is due. I'd like to recognize the work of Bob Leduc and Janet Attard of Business Know How, advisors whose thoughts on marketing techniques have influenced mine. You can find more of their thinking at www.businessknowhow.com, if as they say, "God's willin' and the creek don't rise."

The five techniques listed in this chapter are by no means the only items on the marketing menu. You could be exploiting seasonality, or maximizing package design to increase perceived value, or focusing on special promotions to generate excitement, just to name a few.

Do any of these techniques look like they might give your sales a boost? Do any seem consistent with actions you're already taking? Jot down your ideas, using the following worksheet. When you're done, rank the techniques in order of their relevancy to your situation. Keep this worksheet handy as you read (or just browse) the upcoming chapters. In Part 6 of this book, I'll show you how to use this and other worksheets to build your marketing plan.

In the meantime, start doing something—just about anything! Keep track of what you did and what happened as a result. And keep studying marketing basics … by moving on to the next chapter.

Key Marketing Techniques at Work in My Business

Key Technique	This would work for me because ...	Ranking
Promoting the end result	________________	
Separating yourself from the competition	________________	
Anticipating change		
Becoming a valued resource	________________	
Always something new	________________	

The Least You Need to Know

- You should have a marketing plan, but "planning" is not the place to start. Action is.
- Consider using marketing techniques like promoting the end result, separating yourself from the competition, anticipating change, becoming a valued resource, or adding something new.
- Examine the marketing actions you're already taking—how do these actions align with the marketing techniques described in this chapter?

Chapter 3

A Marketing Workhorse Revisited: The "Four Ps" Plus One

In This Chapter

- What's a marketing mix?
- Products and their life cycles
- The relationship between price and value
- Location and distribution are marketing strategies
- Diverse activities come together to make "promotions"
- Why "People" is the most important P

You met the "Four Ps" and the all-important "Fifth P" briefly in Chapter 1. Now we're going to look at these elements in a little more detail. They are at the heart of creating those exchanges that get your offerings to customers and their money to you.

Marketing professors have been using the "Four Ps" for 50-plus years, and yet look around. The world of products and services has gotten much more sophisticated. Where half a dozen hair-coloring products from two main suppliers once served a mass market, we now have many more hair care companies offering dozens of different versions of their products.

So why study a model built to describe one mass market when most of us are engaged in much more targeted activities? Because it still works.

I'll update the old "Four Ps" where I feel a need. "Place" these days can include the Internet. "Product" is more likely to be about services. "Price" hasn't changed much, but "Promotions" has grown some online avenues. And then there's that important new P, "People"—the customers, competitors, employees, and suppliers who inhabit the world described by the "Four Ps." People are integral to the activity of marketing, a fact we should never forget. That's why I've declared "People" the unofficial "Fifth P."

The term "marketing" covers a complex set of interdependent activities. We use the "Four Ps" to break that set of activities into components we can look at individually. Then, once we understand the components, we can see how they interact to make up the whole marketing function.

Four Ingredients Make Up the Marketing Mix

The "Four Ps" make up the *marketing mix*, the components of marketing that are under your—the marketer's—control. You can't do a thing about the weather, but you can control the "Four Ps."

What?

The **marketing mix** is the combination of activities that make up your approach to your marketing. It is a blend of strategies regarding the "Four Ps" of Products, Places, Prices, and Promotions. These four elements are under a marketer's control. Marketers have begun to include "people" in the marketing mix because customer behavior is also a key element of marketing strategy.

Remember Kalika and her juice cart from Chapter 1? She's a good one to demonstrate the marketing mix. Kalika has developed a product line—fruit juices—and offers them at a price she establishes by balancing greed and reason. She chooses a place for distributing the product—the college commons—and promotes her line in a few simple ways, like signage and cheerful selling technique. Her presence in the cart keeps her close to the people she serves. That's how she's chosen to mix the elements of marketing strategy.

Really!

Are you marketing's next Julia Child? Cooking up the right marketing mix for your business requires an approach like hers. Set out your ingredients—your thoughts about the "Four Ps" at work in your business—have a glass of wine, and let your creativity emerge. Taste the results. Adapt your recipe and decide what works best for you. Blending the "Four Ps," like adapting a recipe to your own tastes, will result in marketing techniques adapted to your unique situation.

What Is Your Product?

The word "product" covers a lot more than the obvious tangible, physical articles available for sale. A product can be a service, like dry-cleaning or management consulting. A product can also be a concept you would like an audience to believe. You might be selling support for a person, place, event, organization, or idea.

Your product will most likely be a combination of tangible items, services, and beliefs. That is why I like to use the word *offering*. What you offer customers will almost certainly contain elements of each. A haircut is a product, but it results from the service of cutting hair. A political candidate is in many ways a product, promising to function in a way that solves problems for you if you elect him or her to office. Nonprofit agencies sell feelings, asking us to support activities that make us feel good about doing good. Each of these examples represents a different offering someone is asking an audience to buy or buy into.

The product also includes its packaging and the customer service policies that back it up. For retailers, choice of product is key in creating an appealing merchandise assortment. For all businesses, product life cycles must be taken into account.

What?

The **product life cycle** begins with Introduction (the product launch) and moves on to a Growth phase if the introduction was successful. A growing product will reach a Mature phase that can end in months or endure for decades. Most products will eventually enter a final stage of Decline. At this stage there's a risk that unless the product is phased out or rejuvenated, it will sap resources.

"Turn, Turn, Turn"—The Product Life Cycle

As a marketer, you must understand something about the life cycle of your products. Most products (and product categories) will pass from Introduction through Growth, Maturity, and Decline. Marketers cannot ignore this. You need products in different phases of the *product life cycle* to ensure against one product going bad and turning your whole operation sour. If one product is slipping in popularity, you need to have something else in the pipeline.

Sometimes a declining product can be reintroduced and enjoy a second go-round. In Malcolm Gladwell's *The Tipping Point* (2000, Little, Brown and Co.), he describes an unexpected product rebirth. As he tells it, sales of Hush Puppies shoes were down to 30,000 pairs a year in 1994. In 1995, 430,000 pairs were sold. Why the increase? Hip young New Yorkers began wearing the shoes to hip youth clubs in Manhattan. In 1996, the company sold over 1.7 million pairs of Hush Puppies. Good thing the company hadn't followed through on plans to "kill the puppies" back in 1994!

How do you develop new products? Are there innovations you can bring to current products, to make them "new and improved"?

New and Improved! Some Product Strategies

Following are just a few of the issues that can affect product strategies. See Chapter 9 for more on this topic.

- **Improve functionality.** What features of your product do your customers find important? How does your offering compare to your competitors'? Maybe there are features you can add to products that will transfer into real customer benefit. The manufacturer who developed the self-cleaning kitty litter box broke new ground with new product features.
- **Add convenience.** What specifics do you know about the demographics and lifestyles of your customers? Tailor products to fit them better. This can be as simple as selling soup in individual-serving cans for singles or toilet paper in 6-roll packs for big families.
- **Find new uses.** There's one thing that never changes in marketing—you always have to adapt to change! Try finding new uses for old products, like the guy who thought of marketing Arm and Hammer baking soda as a refrigerator deodorizer.

Mentor

Think about these three issues: improved functionality, convenience, and expanded uses in relation to your current products. Do you see opportunities for new or improved product offerings?

Product Strategies in Action

In the previous chapter, several businesses were introduced. How do product strategies affect these businesses? Kai Miaka deals with product issues each time his band releases a new CD and a new package must be designed for it. A Life of Faith Dolls and Bob's Bottomless Boats are both adding new products to their merchandise assortments with every new season. By doing so, they keep current customers coming back to see what's new—and making purchases as a result. New products almost always require some advertising support. If you emphasize new products in your marketing mix, be sure to put some money in your promotions budget to get the word out.

Pitfall

Never forget our First Rule of Marketing (and if this isn't familiar, see Chapter 1): People don't buy products; they buy solutions to problems. If your product offering fails to evolve, solving customer needs as those needs evolve, you put your business at risk. Carefully consider the product life cycle of your offerings. For those that are mature, look for ways to freshen or improve them to stave off decline.

What's Price Got to Do with It?

"Price" is the amount of money or other consideration that is exchanged for a product offering. "Price" is a quantifiable way of measuring the value customers place on the product. For effective marketing, you need more than a price on your product. You need a pricing strategy.

Some people, and maybe your boss is among them, don't believe price is a marketing issue. They believe price is a result of accounting for the cost of materials, overhead, and profit goals slated for a particular product. These people are wrong. Pricing policies that don't take market realities into consideration can lead to disaster.

The price you ask exerts an influence over your whole operation, from your customers' perception of your value to the amount you take home in your check. An effective pricing strategy is the result of good strategic thinking.

Value is the key to pricing, not just what the product costs to make, but also what quality is delivered at what cost. The price you ask affects the image of the product. Under-pricing a product that delivers premium value can be as destructive as over-pricing a low-value item. You have to communicate value to your audience so strongly that price seems reasonable in relation to the product.

Pricing for profit is a big facet of your business, one of the most critical decisions you'll ever make, and make, and make again. We'll take a closer look at pricing issues in Chapter 12.

A Life of Faith Dolls uses pricing to establish the value of the dolls and accessories they offer. By setting their prices near that of comparable American Girls dolls, they persuade potential buyers that these dolls will be of comparable quality and desirability.

When Is "Place" Not a Place?

Place can mean a lot of things to a marketer—location, or distribution, or virtual sites in cyberspace. If you're a retailer, Place might really mean "place" to you. Is your store located in a convenient, attractive location? Are you open the hours customers like to shop? If so, then you've got *place strategy* under control.

What?

A **place strategy** to a marketer means getting the right goods in the right quantity to the right place, for the lowest possible cost, without sacrificing customer service. "Place" can mean a retail location, a distribution system, or an online presence—or all of the above.

Very few of us, however, actually do business through one location. Even small retailers have websites that expand their reach beyond their storefronts. If you're a consultant, perhaps your work takes place at your clients' offices rather than your own. If you run a pizza delivery service, your "place of business" is customers' doorways. When we talk about "Place," we're really talking about all the aspects of getting products to end users.

A successful place strategy satisfies each of these requirements:

Getting the right goods … has been achieved through product development.

… *in the right quantity to the right place* … is internal, an operational issue affected by how well you can predict demand and get inventory to where that demand is.

… *for the lowest possible cost* … means the distribution strategy, or the efficiency and effectiveness in how you actually move products from your place to your customers.

… *without sacrificing customer service.* If the place where customers can take possession of the offering is out of the way or complicated, you have negatively affected the value of your offering.

Up and Down the Distribution Channels

For most businesses, the *P* in *Place* is actually a *D* for *distribution.* In this situation, a "Place" strategy will concern what market area you're willing to serve, how you dispatch your resources to serve it, or how you make use of others to create a *distribution channel.*

A distribution channel is just a fancy name for the way in which a product or service gets from its point of origin to its final destination, the person or business that uses it. Typically, a product moves from manufacturer to wholesaler to retailer to consumer. You might be involved in any of these stages, and you could certainly be involved in more than one.

A business can *pull* a product through the distribution channel by creating demand at the end user level, or it can *push* a product through by giving wholesalers and retailers special incentives to sell that product or service. Both strategies focus on leveraging distribution as the "Place" P in the marketing mix.

A company that uses home sales, like Tupperware Parties or Creative Memories, is combining wholesaler and retailer into one independent sales agent. They've taken the "place" aspect right into America's homes, shortening the distribution channel and increasing price efficiencies by cutting out middlemen.

Everyone downstream from you in your distribution channel is your customer. To get a product successfully from factory floor to end user, a lot of people along the way have to believe in its merits. No matter whom you're talking to, wherever he might be in the channel, he's looking for solutions to problems. Offer them, and you've got the start of a mutually beneficial relationship.

Chapter 13 is devoted to understanding distribution issues.

Really!

The World Wide Web is one of the most fascinating "Place" phenomena to come along. The virtual shopping malls, online retailers, and auction sites have changed the world for many people. People who are too busy, too tied to the home, or simply too frail to get around easily have found a brave new world literally at their fingertips. An Ipsos-Reid survey in 2002 found that 72 percent of the U.S. population goes online at least once a month. Another survey by Jupiter Research in early 2003 predicted that retail spending online would grow at a rate of 21 percent each year through 2007 and found that nearly a third of all retail spending is influenced by the Internet.

Place Strategies in Action

For a business with lots of customers like University Credit Union, convenient locations offer a chance to stand out from competitors. The credit union adds several branches each year, following trends among their members carefully to figure out where new branches should go.

Life History Services is by its nature a "Flying Dutchman" of a business. It doesn't matter where Anita lives because she travels nationally to deliver her service. Anita's early projects for families in far-flung locations have led through word of mouth to more business in those and other cities. She travels several months of the year to conduct interviews where her clients are most comfortable—in their homes. Her business "Place" strategy involves trying to schedule work trips for maximum productivity and to get her out of her Wisconsin home base in winter.

For University Credit Union and Life History Services, "Place" is about delivering the offering at a location that meets customers' needs for convenience.

Promote the Damn Thing!

Your marketing mix wouldn't add up to much if it didn't include some good old-fashioned promotions. If you're going to develop a product, put a price on it, and bring it to market, you'd better put some work into promoting the damn thing.

Promotions in this context means more than the contests and giveaways you probably think of when I use that word. To a marketer, the Promotion "P" includes all aspects of marketing communications, from planning the advertising campaign to training the sales staff to designing the gimmicks and gimme's that boost sluggish customers' desire to buy. It's all aimed at helping the prospect realize a need and then triumphing over other similar offerings when the prospect goes out to fill that need. Part 4 and Part 5 of this book are devoted to giving you the skills needed to promote your product, whether it's a candidate, concept, or can of pop.

Promotion's "Three-Legged Stool"

There are three classifications of activities that come under the heading of Promotion: advertising, selling, and sales promotions. Think of it as the three-legged stool that Promotions sit on.

What?

Media outlets are the newspapers, magazines, billboards, television stations, and other vehicles available for you to purchase commercial space or time. Read more about media outlets in Part 4 of this book.

Advertising, the first leg of that stool, encompasses the planning and development of advertising strategies and then the creation and placement of the advertising messages themselves. Advertising is a way of mass selling. It's only useful if you have a large enough market wanting to hear about your offering, and if there are *media outlets* (i.e., newspapers, television stations, radio, and so on) available that reach the market.

Advertising doesn't work alone. It is only one part of the promotional process, creating the environment in which more targeted selling can take place. Advertising contributes to the success of sales people, developing prospects and creating awareness and interest. It works both early in the sales process by helping to stimulate desire, and also at the end of the process by helping the purchaser feel happy about his choice.

Really!

Don't overlook publicity, an activity that is related to but distinct from "advertising." An article in *The Wall Street Journal* or a spot on *Oprah!* can cause your business to take off. The key to getting good publicity is to find something about your business and the product or service it offers that is truly newsworthy and then find the right media to tell your story. Print and television editors are always on the lookout for newsworthy stories that would interest their readers or viewers.

Selling makes up the second leg of that stool. Advertising brings in prospects. Salespeople use their skills to turn prospects into trial buyers and trial buyers into repeat customers. There are a number of skills involved in sales, from understanding human behavior and the selling process to knowing how to motivate yourself when you'd rather be out fishing. If you're smart, your promotional strategy will include plans for developing these skills in yourself and your staff. We'll look closer at the sales activity in Part 5.

The third leg of the stool under Promotions is *sales promotions*. Sales promotions are the short-term strategies marketers come up with to give customers incentives to buy. When you use coupons from your local quick-lube station or dry cleaner, or you drop your business card in a bowl to enter a drawing, you're responding to a sales promotion.

Sales promotions are tools that produce results quickly but without lasting impact. When the promotion ends, its effect tapers off quickly and sales will return to previous expectations. Sales promotions are common in some industries and rare in others. Professional service providers, such as lawyers or accountants, are not likely to engage in two-for-one offers or business card drawings. Retailers, on the other hand, are likely to use sales promotions often.

Promotions in Action

For University Credit Union and Bob's Bottomless Boats, promotions are a dominant part of the marketing mix. That's because these businesses have an ongoing need to communicate with their audiences (because competition is intense) and because those audiences can be reached efficiently through local newspapers and local television (both appeal to a broad consumer audience in a relatively confined geographic area). Don't be surprised to find more about these businesses in Part 4, when we take up the topic of advertising.

For our other example businesses, like Kalika and her juice cart, Kai the musician, and Anita's history business, promotional activity is less dominant in the mix. For A Life of Faith, promotion takes place only in the most strategic bursts, at hobby shows and through direct mail drops. These businesses can't ignore promotions—no one can—but their marketing mix will have a different emphasis.

Pitfall

Don't engage in sales promotions for the wrong reasons. There are three good reasons to engage in a sales promotion: to temporarily increase sales, to create a sense of urgency, or to produce temporary excitement. A promotion can do any or all these things, depending on how it's designed. Resist the temptation to use promotions for other reasons, such as to hurt a competitor. Customers can start to feel jerked around if promotions are used haphazardly or for the wrong reasons.

It's the People, Period.

Marketing is psychology applied to the arena of business. For that reason, psychology—an understanding of people and why they do what they do—is critical to anyone who wants to be a success in marketing. Or to succeed in the world, for that matter. Want to be happier? Less stressed? Better able to influence others, more savvy about their influence on you? Get more money, friends, power? Study psychology, baby. (Check out the books in the *Complete Idiot's Guide* series covering personal enrichment—you'll find almost everything you need to know.) Only through understanding human behavior can we hope to meet the marketplace and have a clue what's going on.

In the world of the marketer, people fall into four groups:

- Your staff team
- Your suppliers
- Your customers
- Your competitors

Obviously "customers" are the group of most interest to marketers. But the other groups are key as well. If the staff aren't persuaded of the benefits of a product, or aren't informed of a promotional campaign underway, they can unintentionally undermine your best efforts. Suppliers and competitors can cause you hell if you don't understand what they're doing and what motivates their actions. As marketers we must be close students of the people all around us.

There's a dark side to this. We study, we gain knowledge, and we gain expertise at using it. Marketers use psychology to manipulate people to produce behaviors, like purchasing a specific brand or voting for a specific candidate.

With our knowledge of persuasive techniques, we have power that we can use for good or for evil. Let me say right now, please use your influence over people to accomplish good things for good reasons. If you're selling gas-guzzling monster trucks, cut it out. If you're promoting fake weight-loss pills, shame on you. Please find something better to do.

CAUTION

Pitfall

Marketers use psychology to induce desired behaviors in people. Encouraging behaviors that are not healthy for people or the planet is a bad idea. That's how we marketers got the reputation for being hucksters and snake oil salesmen, and we're still trying to live that down. Adhere to my simple two-part moral formula and I think you'll be okay. Ready, marketeers? Raise your hand and recite the oath: First, cause no harm; and second, do nothing you wouldn't want to tell your mother.

"People" is where the new thinking in marketing is happening these days. Theories and techniques are growing around concepts like one-to-one marketing and permission selling. The rise of management practices like customer relationship management (CRM) reflects the importance of people in the marketing process. These concepts will be covered in Chapter 5.

In any of our example businesses, there would be no business without people! No music students for Kai, no boaters for Bob. No people to tell their life stories to Anita, nobody to log on to University Credit Union's online services, no grandmas to buy dolls from A Life of Faith for little girls who'll someday study music, buy a boat, or join a credit union.

People are so important that Part 2 is devoted to the marketing environment and getting to know the people in it.

Right now, use the following worksheet to record your thoughts about the "Four Ps plus one" in your marketing mix. Jot down any strengths and weaknesses that come to mind as you think about each "P" in the mix. Then, as in Chapter 2's worksheet, rank each item in order of its significance in your current situation.

Marketing Mix at Work in My Business

"P"	Strength	Ranking	Weakness	Ranking
Product	________	___________	________	_______
Price	________	___________	________	_______
Place	________	___________	________	_______
Promotions	________	___________	________	_______
People	________	___________	________	_______

The Least You Need to Know

- Product, Price, Place, and Promotion are the four elements of the marketing mix that combine to attract and sell offerings to customers.
- To maximize your product strategy, think about your products' place in their life cycle, the benefits each segment of users receives from the offering, and what innovations might keep your offering "new and improved."
- Your prices should be based on more than just costs plus profit margin.
- The successful place strategy will get the right goods, in the right quantity, to the right place, for the lowest possible cost, without sacrificing customer service.
- Promotional activities include advertising, personal selling, and sales promotions (short-term incentives).
- People, including staff, suppliers, customers, and competitors, are critical to good marketing and deserve study so that you can understand and influence their behavior.

Part 2 Your Marketing Environment

Where are you going, what are you doing, and who are you doing it with? (Sounds like your mother talking, doesn't it?) Let's talk about the crowd you're running with. Who are your customers and why? What are they really buying from you? Who are your competitors? What makes you think you're right?

When you were 18, you marketed yourself to your widening circle of friends on pure instinct. You tailored who you were to their ideal, whether that meant hanging around with a cigarette in your mouth or leading the track team. The same thing is going on for you today, only now the circle is your marketing environment and how you respond is called "positioning."

My next goal is to make you understand what's going on around you the way your mother wished you could at 18. And if I'm successful, you'll be able to choose responses that are healthy for you and your business—just what your mother would have wanted.

Chapter 4

Develop Your Customer's Imagination

In This Chapter

- Understanding the "Four Utilities" of form/function, place, time, and ease of use
- Visiting the Customer Value Pyramid of product, service, and price
- Exploring the internal and external influences on the buying exchange
- Developing customer imagination

Many a time in the past two decades, I've participated in client conferences like the one I'm about to describe, where my goal has been to help my clients see things from their customers' perspective. This time, let's imagine you're my partner, and you're sitting in on the discussion.

We're at Hearthstone Bookstore, Inn, and Café, a local independent bookstore (and more), gathered in the room where the book clubs meet. It's cozy here, but that's an illusion. It might as well be the war room of a military campaign. Never mind the cups of good coffee in front of us, the gentle music in the background, and the beautiful art on the walls. We may feel insulated by the rows of books around us, but we're at the mercy of every consumer's whim and competitor's whammy. What's our best defense? To take cover inside the minds of the shoppers out there in the aisles. We're pursuing a strategy called *customer imagination.*

Our purpose is to find and study clusters of good customers. We're going to find out what they're looking for, and that doesn't mean what books. We're going to get inside their heads until we know every cultural value, every secret motivation, every perception and nuance that affects their decision about where to go, what to buy, and what value to place on that exchange.

Some of this information is already lurking in our software, recorded at the point of sale. More of it flows toward us via predictable channels: our customer comment book, the observations of our sales staff, and the results of our occasional customer surveys. But the most important factors may never surface this way. We must also go scouting for the information our customers don't even know about themselves.

Get to Know Your Customers Inside and Out

Customers may have no clue why they choose one item over another. Asking them will only reveal why they think they do what they do. The real reasons may be entirely different. A purchase is the culmination of a complex set of behaviors. That's where customer imagination comes into play—that sixth sense that helps you empathize with customers.

Many businesses pursue market research to find out why customers buy, among other goals. Research is useful for learning the expectations your customers bring to the purchase process. When you get to Chapter 6, you'll find out I've grudgingly become a believer in research.

What?

Customer imagination is an intuitive understanding of target customers' needs and wants, giving one a "sixth sense" for presenting an offering in a way that makes it more appealing than competitors' offerings.

If you think about performing research on customers, you'll come to the obvious question: What questions should I ask? The answer in a nutshell: questions about their perceptions of value and the factors that influence their purchase decisions. In this chapter, we'll look closely at these perceptions and factors. The more you learn about your customers' inner psychology and the outer influences on their behavior, the better your customer imagination will become.

The "Four Utilities": Vehicles of Customer Value

I learned about the *Four Utilities* from my colleague John, who has helped me refine my understanding of marketing. He brings them into nearly every conversation. My attention tends to wander when people try to teach me things. By the third time he brought them up, I began to think of "John's Four Utilities" like a quartet of sporty little trucks.

And they are like little trucks in a way, durable concepts that help you break the complexity of customer needs down into chunks of information you can haul back to headquarters and process.

Let's test-drive the "Four Utilities." The theory goes like this: People value things not for what they are, but for how they can use them. They value services that either help them do something or help them do it better. They value a product for the task it accomplishes, whether it's bringing TV channels into the living room or making water into coffee. The usefulness of a product or service is what gives it value to people. All this is really just another way of saying that we buy things because they help us solve problems. The "Four Utilities" just help us refine this idea.

There are four types of usefulness: *form/function*, *time*, *place*, and *ease of possession*. Taken together, these dimensions make up a product or service's value, or utility, to you, to me, to anyone. Your offering may not necessarily deliver a top-notch utility in each dimension. Even Bob's Bottomless Boats can't deliver a custom boat with the same ease of possession (that is, reasonable price) and timeliness as it can a standard floor model.

There's always some trade-off in these utilities. For example, giving customers a low price might mean they have to wait longer for delivery. Still, understanding the "Four Utilities" will help you focus on how you can use the other "four" concepts I've been writing about, the "Four Ps." The "Four Utilities" provide hints into how you can attract and retain customers, and they help you figure out ways you can add customer value to your offerings.

What?

The "**Four Utilities**" are a way of understanding value from the perspective of the customer. What people always value are the benefits they expect to derive from a purchase. Form/function, time, place, and ease of possession are all forms of utility that a company can add to its offering to enhance its value to a customer.

Form/Function: A Minivan or a Miata?

What physical and tangible elements about your offer make it more useful to the customer? How it looks, how it performs, how carefully it's made? These are aspects of its *form/function utility*.

It would be simpler if we could just talk about "form," but form and function are two sides of the same coin. A hunting jacket's camouflage design gives it a particular form, and that form is necessary for the product to perform its function. A coffee maker's function is to turn two ingredients into brew, and that dictates a lot about its form, from the capacity of its water reservoir to the durability of its heating mechanism.

What?

Form/function utility includes the tangible aspects of a product or service. This utility includes aesthetics, durability, ease of use, and so on. In services, it includes the cleanliness, comfort, and atmosphere of the place where the services are rendered along with the courtesy and competence of those delivering the services.

Time for an example. For our bookstore client, the *form/function utility* derives not so much from the books themselves (*Wind in the Willows* is the same book on our shelves or on a competitor's) but from the selection we choose to carry. The nature of that carefully chosen inventory is an important point of differentiation from other bookstores.

Think about the form and function utility of the products or services you offer. Does this give you ideas for improvement? Write them down.

Place: The Dealership or the Den?

Where is your product or service delivered? That's where you'll find *place utility*.

This concept looks like the Place component of the "Four Ps" hanging around with some new friends. How is this different? In the "Four Ps," we looked at how place affects your internal operations. In the "Four Utilities," we look at how place can add or subtract value for your customer.

Place utility is often achieved through distribution, with strategies that run the gamut from home-delivery to mega-mall. In retail, choosing a location has a big impact on your business. Our bookstore friends have a downtown location that is charming but not very convenient in terms of parking. To offset that negative, they've included a café and a playful children's "oasis" where entertainers frequently perform. There's even a bed-and-breakfast upstairs, each room decorated in a literary theme. The owners have created a wonderful ambiance throughout their establishment that encourages families to come and linger. They've maximized the *place utility* of their offering by selling atmosphere along with books.

What?

Place utility is about where the product or service is delivered. If it's a retail establishment, customers should have easy access to it. Mail order companies deliver place utility by making it easy to shop at home and then have purchases delivered to your front door. All this has value to customers, and they are willing to pay for it.

How are place issues affecting your business? Is the place where you operate easy to get to? Do you deliver? Take the place utility for a test run and see whether there are opportunities to add value to your offerings by, for example, making it easier for customers to get to your location or by making goods available in more places, or by overnight delivery.

High-Speed Maneuvers: The Time Utility

For many people the *time utility* outweighs others in importance. Most people are so busy they'd gladly pay extra for a twenty-fifth hour in the day. Because that is impossible, they look for efficiencies in how they use time, and that affects a lot of the purchases made.

Some offerings have a time utility inherent in their nature. Christmas trees are an inherently timely product. What you pay $30 for on December 15, you can probably get for less on December 24 and for free the day after.

To other offerings, time utility is added by design. Example: Wal-Mart's original concept leveraged the place utility. The company built the biggest stores and filled them with a huge amount of bargain-priced stuff, and people rolled up for the perceived value. Only one problem with the equation—the big stores take a lot of time to negotiate, a disadvantage if you're a busy person out to pick up just one or two specific items. To attract the hurried-and-focused customer segment, Wal-Mart began building "convenience stores" a quarter of the previous size. By tracking the most frequently purchased items at their full-size stores, Wal-Mart's managers know just what items to stock in the convenience stores. Now they're working both "place" and "time" to create even more value for customers.

What?

Time utility involves making offerings available when customers want them. This includes being open when people want to shop and having products in stock when customers want them. If a vendor does not have what customers want when they want it, this diminishes the value of that vendor's offerings in the eyes of customers.

To leverage time and place utility, our booksellers place bestsellers and periodicals nearest the café, and arrange for that aisle to remain open for business all hours the café is open.

Ease of Possession: Great Utility, No Money Down

This utility is a little harder to see at first. It's not parked out front on the lot like the form of the product, the place it's found, or the time it's found there. *Ease of possession utility* has to do with pricing, payments, and warranties—in short, the ways you and your competitors make it easy (or difficult) for customers to buy your offerings. Yes, this is the price component of the "Four Ps" seen from a different angle.

What?

Ease of possession utility has to do with pricing, payments, and warranties. It involves making it easy for customers to take possession of an offering and be assured it will work or that the company will fix it if something goes wrong. Such assurance has value to customers and can make one company's offerings more attractive than another's.

Making transfer of ownership as easy as possible for customers adds value to your offering. Accepting credit cards is one common way to increase ease of possession. That's why even the artisans selling at craft fairs have credit card processing equipment. A potential patron's spontaneous desire to buy mustn't be cooled by complicated negotiations over payment.

Special sales and payment terms make possession easier for those who are on the verge of a purchase decision and need a reason to tip them over the edge. When you see "No money down and no payments 'til March," you're seeing the possession utility at work.

Offer your customers a "take it home and see if you like it" policy, and you'll alleviate some of their anxiety. Provide an opportunity to see that the product functions as expected, and you've made possession less risky—and easier—for customers.

For the proprietors at Hearthstone Bookstore, Inn, and Café, ease of possession offers some interesting opportunities for market smarts. The owners use a promotional program to increase ease of possession by adding an incentive to buy. They've created a program where they save your purchase receipts, and when your book purchases total $500, you get a free night upstairs in their inn (a $135 value, equal to a 25 percent discount on each book you purchased).

Circling the Wagons: Summarizing the "Four Utilities"

What do you do with your "Four Utilities," now that you've got them circled in the driveway? Study the load they're carrying. These are all aspects of product or service offering that are under your control. Take advantage of the opportunities they present. Whatever you're selling, these are ways to increase its value to customers, and in a tough competitive environment, developing marketing strategies around the "Four Utilities" can help you achieve your goals.

The Customer Value Pyramid

Now drive those "Four Utilities" over to the Customer Value Pyramid and do a little sightseeing. (All right already, I see I've gotten about all the mileage I can out of that metaphor.) We'll leave the "Four Utilities" for now and move on to another marketing construct.

The Customer Value Pyramid is a tool for understanding what customers are really looking for. This theory holds that customers hope to find an appropriate mix of these elements:

- Product quality (fitness for use)
- Service quality (reliability)
- Reasonable price (value in relation to service and product quality)

Customers perceive value when they find that each element meets or exceeds their expectations.

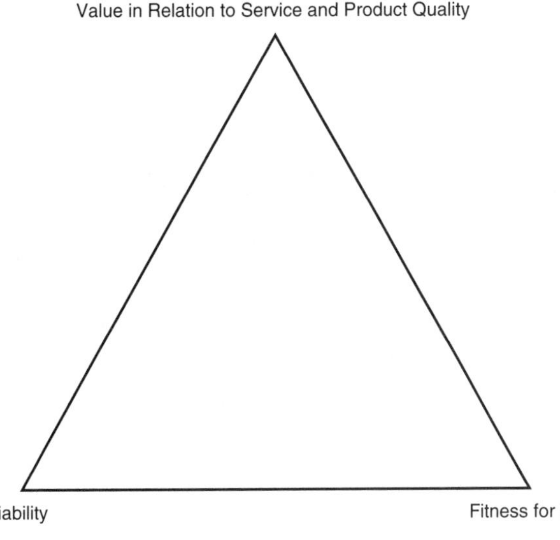

The Customer Value Pyramid. Your objective is to blend these items in a way that attracts customers and makes a profit for you.

Product quality derives from fitness for use—its form/function utility, in other words. A product must solve the problem that sent a person looking to make a purchase—and better still if it solves other problems as well. Let's say your coffee maker is broken and you go to buy a new one. Any model on the market will solve your obvious problem, lack of a way to ingest caffeine. However, the coffee maker you buy has a feature your old coffee maker didn't: brackets for under-cabinet mounting. You hadn't thought about needing more counter space until you saw the option and, voilà, now your kitchen is roomier! And you are mighty satisfied with the coffee maker you purchased. The product's fitness for use exceeded your expectations by filling a need you didn't know you had.

Service quality is about reliability. A product should work in just the manner it was promised to perform, and for the duration promised. If it wears out sooner than expected or turns out to be more difficult to operate, the customer will be disappointed.

Product and service quality create the base of the pyramid and support the price point. The price may be high or low in relative dollars. Now you're asking, "How are services and products related? Aren't we either in product-based or service-based businesses?" Not exactly. Think of it like this: Your product is the deliverable, tangible result of your work. Maybe it's the manuscript from the writer, the flowers from the florist, or the mental health attained after hours passed with a shrink. Your "service" is the experience of being involved in that exchange. If you were a psychiatrist, would you interrupt your client mid-sentence to say, "That's the end of our session?" Of course not. That would be poor service quality!

I could belabor the point, but I think you see what I'm saying. You must meet or exceed customers' expectations of both the product and service. Only then can they decide what value to place on your offering—that is, what price they're willing to pay.

CAUTION

Pitfall

Establishing value when selling a service is tricky. Because your customers don't have anything to touch or test-drive, as a service provider, you have to find other ways to communicate the value of your offering. A high fee is a profitable way to project the image, "I'm good at what I do."

Hearthstone Bookstore, Inn, and Café walks a careful line to establish its value in terms of service and product quality. The store is not warehouse-sized, so the book buyer must choose what products to carry with strategic precision. Her policy: Consistently carry all New York Times best-sellers, the latest literary lions, a decent assortment of culture, art, and decor books, and an excellent collection of classic and modern children's stories. That meets the expectations of just about everyone who enters the store (an urban demographic mix of students and professionals).

The bookstore adds value to their product selection with their exceptional service. The store is happy to order any book for a customer, and at no extra charge will mail or even hand-deliver the book the moment it arrives. Many patrons live or work within a few blocks, so hand-delivery is practical and has the side-benefit of increasing the number of contacts between customer and staff.

The store commands a higher price for its books than suburban mega-stores—and the customers are fine with that.

Mentor

Reliability is another way of saying we as consumers like the things in our world to behave predictably. You don't mind if batteries run out of juice, or pens run out of ink, if they last about as long as the other batteries or pens you've used. If either disappointed you, you'd change brands—not your expectations of reliability.

How Consumers Think

I've become a believer in research, although it was a tough sell. More about that coming up. For now, let me remind you—to understand internal and external influences on customers, you will need to perform research. Your gut instincts will tell you something, but research will tell you more.

Really!

Market research objectives vary. Customers can be researched to yield profiles of market segments by demographic, geographic, or even psychographic (mental traits and lifestyle choices that express behavior, attitudes, and social values) factors. You can also make it your objective to understand beliefs surrounding the purchase process or external influences on the target buyer. Any and all research objectives will add to the pool of knowledge that guides your customer imagination.

If you don't dig for influences on buyer behaviors, what are you doing instead? Probably just copying your competitors, going along with the general flow of things, and not understanding half of what happens in your buying exchanges.

"Purchase Committees" Influence the Buying Exchange

A purchase happens when someone perceives a need, has the ability to buy, and finds an offering that meets or exceeds his or her expectations of reliability and fitness for use and is offered at a reasonable price. A committee of six people is involved in every purchase decision, even if all six are inside one head. These are

- **The Initiator.** The one who first says "I want" or "I need."
- **The Influencer.** The one who discovers ways to satisfy the want or need.

- **The Decider.** The one who chooses which alternative will best satisfy the need.
- **The Buyer.** The one who engages in the purchase transaction.
- **The Consumer.** The one who uses the product.
- **The Evaluator.** The one who later is able to say the product did or didn't satisfy the need.

Different types of products face different *purchase committees*. Let's take one example: summer camps. The initiator might be a child who says, "I want to ride horses this summer." That child's parents become influencers, as they collect brochures and discuss different possibilities, including riding lessons and riding camps. Hopefully, the decider will be the child, who will be allowed to choose which camp to attend. The buyer is the parent who fills out the registration form and signs the check. The consumer is the child, who actually goes to the camp. The evaluator might be the parents, or of course, the horse!

What?

The **purchase committee** consists of one to six people, each perceiving the buying exchange in a different way. These six are the initiator, the influencer, the decider, the buyer, the consumer, and the evaluator.

You can affect purchase behavior by choosing to exert your influence on any one member of this committee, several of them, or all. Let your imagination and creative insight decide your approach.

A tip: Don't underestimate the importance of the evaluator! He's the one who'll give out positive or negative reviews about the purchase. If buyer's remorse sets in, it's the evaluator who's affected most. And that can hurt you.

Buyer's remorse is the dread that a purchase was a mistake. The larger the financial outlay, the more likely it is that buyer's remorse will occur. This disease most often afflicts people who fear change, who dread making decisions, or who have a concern about the value of the offering purchased.

To combat buyer's remorse, give your customer plenty of support throughout the sales process. Be thorough in exploring concerns, and consistently stress benefits of the offering that address those concerns. If you do your job well, the evaluator will be "vaccinated" against buyer's remorse.

External Influences on Buyers

We've been talking about internal influences on buyers—the "voices in their heads" that affect their buying exchanges. But there are voices outside their heads as well. These are the external influences on buyers.

To talk about external influences, we need a couple of terms. The first one is *norms*. Norms are the rules of conduct that groups develop to determine what behaviors are acceptable in that group. The norm that says "Well-rounded individuals should be able to play a musical instrument" is what dictates the need for Kai Miaka's music lessons. Underlying social norms are *values*, the deeply held beliefs of the members of the group. Values give direction to norms—no norm exists that is not in harmony with an underlying value. It's the value that says, "I want to be a well-rounded individual," that drives the norm of taking music lessons.

What?

Norms are rules of behavior: What's okay to do in a particular social context? **Values** are the deeply held beliefs that give norms direction. (These cultural values are not to be confused with monetary value, or the relationship of price to benefits delivered.)

Norms and values are the currency of the external influences on buyers. Those who follow the rules are rewarded; those who break them are punished, or at least excluded from the group.

Important external influences on purchase behavior include culture, social class, reference groups, and families. We'll look briefly at each.

- **Customers' culture.** Culture is the matrix of values, attitudes, beliefs, ideas, and symbols that serve as acceptable tools for members of a specific group. We all belong to more than one cultural group: ethnic, religious, economic, and geographic, just for starters. These groups affect our tastes and desires. One economic group might prefer beer, while another might choose martinis instead.
- **Social class.** We have the potential for mobility—up or down—by our choices in aspiration, recreational habits, and even physical appearance. One way we exercise our mobility is by the products and services we buy. If, as a marketer, you can position a product as "upscale" (appropriate to upward mobility), you can add significant value to the product.

Mentor

Regional and ethnic groups have different taste preferences. A snack food manufacturer found Midwesterners like "cool ranch" flavor, while Southwesterners prefer jalapeños. The changing ethnicity of America is bringing sweeping change to cultural influences on buying behavior.

Culture and social class are mass phenomena, affecting large groups within the population. The other external influences on buyers take place on a more personal scale.

- **Reference groups.** Each of us is surrounded by groups of people who influence our attitudes and behaviors. Our families, friends, and co-workers make up our most intimate reference groups. Others are less personal but just as influential on us. For example, our professional organizations or the religious congregations we belong to often help to shape our attitudes and beliefs.

  We buy what we buy not just to please ourselves but also to influence others' opinions of us. This is not too important where private products are concerned—the things we buy that others don't see, like deodorant or shampoo. But with public products, especially those like cars and clothes that project our culture and social class, the influence of our reference groups is extremely important.

- **Family.** We each belong to two families—the immediate one we live with, and the extended family of relatives who surround us with their influence on our lives and buying behaviors. These families each have a life cycle that influences our individual values and habits. By understanding your best customers' families and their life stages, you can predict their needs and develop offerings geared to serve them.

All these external forces influence buying behaviors. As you try to understand why your customers buy what they do, remember this: Research external influences around your customers. Seek insights into the relative weight of culture, class, reference groups, and family influences on your customers.

Your customers might be any or all of the players in a distribution channel. Each is under all the influences talked about in this chapter. The distributor as a customer has different needs from the end user, and so does the retailer. Each may come from a different culture, bringing different attributes and motivations to the buying exchange. If you ran a microbrewery, you'd need to apply customer imagination to understand the trucker who hauls the beer, the tavern that stocks the beer, and the people who drink the beer. Study of buyer behavior applies to each stage in the distribution channel.

Really!

We each play multiple roles in our lives. We buy the products and services that make the right props for those roles. When we move into new or unfamiliar roles, our reference group becomes more than usually important. We rely on them to show us how to behave, just as freshmen in high school look up to seniors for appropriate behavior. For a case study, watch the advertising directed to new mothers or first-time homebuyers, both examples of people transitioning into new roles.

How to Develop "Customer Imagination"

What goes into customer imagination? It is a relentless pursuit of a deep, intuitive knowledge of your customers. Survey questions and formal research can only go so far; we do our most creative work when we understand the audience so completely we develop a "sixth sense" of their needs. How can one learn this skill? There are three phases to the learning process.

1. **Description.** Before you can do anything, you must know who the target marketing audience is. Describe the market you plan to serve by asking: Who will buy? When? How? Where will they make their purchase? How often? How do they perceive the Four Utilities and the Customer Value Pyramid as they pursue solutions to their problems?

2. **Understanding.** Now add what you've learned about the buying exchange, and you'll begin to develop empathy for your market. What factors are affecting the buying exchange? Think about the purchase committee—the initiator, the influencer, the decider, the buyer, the consumer, and the evaluator. How is your customer experiencing each of these roles, as he or she shops with you or your competitor? How are the influences of culture, class, reference group, and family at work?

3. **Prediction.** When you've built an accurate, multidimensional portrait of the people in your market, you will begin to experience customer imagination. Ideas will come for product or service innovations. You will find ways not just to serve customers, but to delight them. Because your thinking is grounded in solid understanding, your intuition will steer you toward effective marketing strategies.

Mentor

Customer imagination requires one thing above all: time to think. You can review research reports and compare features with competitors all you want. But when you've finished with that, the real work is just beginning. Sit back and allow your mind to wander over the field of information you've just created. You'll discover the best potential marketing strategies when you're in a relaxed creative state, aware of the forest and the trees, exploring the terrain, not spinning your wheels in the mud.

Having customer imagination could be compared to having a talent for playing host. Anticipating guests' needs, stimulating and delighting them, and showing them a good time without placing demands are skills that develop loyal bonds, if not of friendship, of customer loyalty.

The Least You Need to Know

- The Four Utilities (form/function, time, place, and ease of possession) are aspects of your offering that allow you to stand out from the competition.
- Customers hope to find an appropriate mix of product quality (fitness for use) and service quality (reliability); the customer's perception of these elements drives his or her perception of an offering's value.
- Influences on the buying process come from the needs of the six-member "purchase committee" and from the culture, social class, reference groups, and families surrounding that "purchase committee."
- Customer imagination is the key to delivering solutions of good value.

Chapter 5

Customer Information: Use What You Know!

In This Chapter

- One-to-one marketing: The goal is share of customer
- The tools of one-to-one marketing: permissions and touch points
- CRM: a marketing approach and a software solution
- Using customer information requires technology

Over in the conference room at University Credit Union, the marketing people are sitting across the table from the "IT" guy. He's the one from Information Technology, the one they go to for a mailing list of members living near the newest branch or a count of students using the online-banking website. Marketing and IT have faced off over this conference table before. The relationship is sometimes an uneasy one. After all, from the IT guy's point of view, his job is to support the people in operations by tracking member account data. "It's nice that member data is useful to Marketing," the IT guy thinks, "but that's not what we're here for."

For Cary, UCU's marketing director, IT's perception of Marketing has got to change. So once again, she launches into her explanation of the importance of customer information to the marketing function.

It goes like this.

It's a proven fact that it is cheaper and easier to sell new offerings to current customers than it is to recruit new customers. Sales to current customers are more profitable because it takes less money and time to reach them than to reach strangers in hopes of making a sale. To get those increased profits, to experience that reduced cost and effort of selling, you need one thing: customer information.

Mentor

If you have only a few dollars to spend on marketing, concentrate your efforts on current customers. Since customers who use more of your products or services tend to build strong relationships with you, it makes sense to devote your resources to converting low-volume purchasers into loyal high-volume purchasers who either buy more frequently or buy more of different items you offer.

What?

Touch points are the moments when an individual has a personal interaction with someone or something representing your business. When someone stops by your trade show booth, that's a touch point. When someone dials your phone number and reaches an automated voice response system, that's one, too. A touch point is an opportunity to either delight or disappoint an individual.

Customer Information Is Key

Increased profitability makes up the first part of Cary's argument, but she has a second point to get across. Leaning forward to emphasize her words, she continues.

With customer information you can differentiate your customers on the basis of their purchasing behavior, as well as other traits such as their demographic attributes and their life stages. This serves you well, in that it helps you perform market research to predict their likely purchase needs, and it helps you predict and analyze trends. But it also serves your audience well. You provide better customer service when you have accurate information available to you at every customer *touch point*. By focusing on touch points, you influence your audience's perceptions of your business.

Accurate information lets you use what you know about certain customers who show potential to become better customers. You can flag them for special follow-up or target special offerings to them based on the products or services they're using now.

How marketers market has been changing over the past few years, and the big change is this: leveraging the value of customer information.

New buzzwords have sprung up to describe this big marketing idea. We now throw around phrases like touch points, one-to-one marketing, permission-based marketing, and customer relationship management

(CRM). You'll be familiar with these terms and—I hope—sold on using these techniques by the time you finish reading this chapter.

Big Idea: The Goal Is Share of Customer

In 1993, Don Peppers and Martha Rogers wrote a book that broke new ground in the field of marketing. That book, *The One to One Future*, presented a manifesto for how companies can increase profits by selling more things to fewer people. Their key insight? Instead of concentrating on how to reach an ever-larger number of new customers, the focus should be on keeping customers longer and getting more transactions from each of them over time.

The thinking behind their book—and their one-to-one marketing strategy—is straightforward, and it led directly to this moment, with Cary and the IT guy squaring off across the table. To emphasize her point, Cary asks everyone at the table to envision a customer's lifetime stream of needs from their credit union.

Members typically enroll in University Credit Union when they arrive on campus as freshmen. Their needs are for checking accounts, credit cards, and student loans. For some, there will be auto loans as well.

Then the students graduate and move into the working world. If the credit union can keep these customers, there will come a string of mortgages and lines of credit. These members start families and begin savings programs for their children's education. They take out loans for bigger houses and bigger cars. Many begin saving for retirement.

As life's parade passes the teller windows, the credit union's members will be met with the products and services they need from cradle to retirement condo. That, in a nutshell, is the *share of customer* approach to marketing.

Cary wants to launch a new marketing program aimed at increasing share of customer. To her, this is more than just a new ad campaign. It's a whole new philosophy, recognizing that members enrolled as students can and should be members for life. Her goal in calling this meeting between the Marketing and IT departments is to gain the cooperation she needs, so she can steer her marketing efforts in this new direction: building share of customer with one-to-one marketing. But Cary's success

What?

The **share of customer** approach to marketing means that you don't focus on a single offering and try to sell it to as many customers as possible—you focus on addressing a larger share of each customer's needs over the long term.

relies on more than just getting access to the customer information. One-to-one marketing can only be truly effective if it takes into account two things:

- We must consider each customer as an individual with a lifetime stream of needs and desires.
- We must collaborate with that customer if we are going to participate in that lifetime stream of purchases.

Collaborating with the customer has become a technique, and it's been given a name: *permission marketing*.

Permission Marketing

Peppers and Rogers' one-to-one marketing strategy led to subsequent eye-opening observations, including Seth Godin's popular book, *Permission Marketing: Turning Strangers into Friends, and Friends into Customers.* The basic idea of *permission marketing* is very simple. Consumers are constantly filtering out most marketing messages, but are actively looking for others related to their needs and desires of the moment. (That would be the "wish list" we discussed in Chapter 1.) As marketers, we seek not to intrude on individuals with unwanted messages, but to engage in a dialogue with consumers who give us permission. If what we offer matches reasonably well with what's on their "wish lists," that dialogue develops into a relationship that grows stronger over time.

Permission marketing implies directing messages to those who are open to them and leaving the rest of the world in peace. Permission marketing absolutely requires getting and maintaining permission to exchange messages with potential customers, one to one. "You can't build a one-to-one relationship with a customer unless the customer explicitly agrees to the process," says Godin.

> **What?**
>
> **Permission marketing** means obtaining permission from a prospect or customer before directing marketing efforts toward them. Permission, properly gained and used, benefits both the consumer and the marketer.

Permission marketing benefits both the consumer and the marketer. Consumers get the information they need to make purchase decisions, and marketers get the efficiency of directing their efforts toward those most likely to buy.

The goal of permission marketing is to move those who've consented to the process along a continuum from strangers to friends to customers. To do this you engage in learning about each other. You don't spew information at a prospect—like any good relationship, you let the give and take of your conversations guide you. As a marketer, you need to have a "curriculum" ready to teach your prospects about you and your offerings, as their curiosity draws them closer to you. But you don't force that curriculum on your new friends. You respond to each offered permission with another lesson in the benefits of your offering.

Moments of contact, whether initiated by the prospective customer or by the marketer, are the touch points in the customer relationship. Each is an opportunity to strengthen that individual's feelings of trust, comfort, and loyalty in relation to the offering and the institution that offers it.

At University Credit Union, Cary's got plans that make the cooperation of the IT guy a must. She wants to analyze current account information to create profiles of graduating students' typical needs. She then plans to solicit permission from individuals in highly defined target segments, to offer them messages about products or services that her analysis indicates they're likely to want. That means capturing each response to the survey and then tracking every subsequent customer touch point, record by record. That's a lot of demand on the database.

Mentor

The goal of permission marketing is to get invited to engage in learning about each other. If the marketing messages you send have been invited, if they are relevant and personal, they will cut through the clutter and increase the recipient's knowledge about you and the benefits of your products or services.

Back in that meeting, Cary's practically pounding the table with her shoe as she makes her case. Accurate information tracking is necessary if she's going to know the permission or "opt-in" status of any one individual customer or prospect at any given moment. Accurate customer records will drive every step of the marketing approach that Cary envisions. With IT's help, she can do it.

Every Touch Point Is an Opportunity to Gain or Lose Permission

Every touch point is a moment of truth. Handle it skillfully, and that customer interaction becomes an opportunity for personal follow-up, or to make a recommendation based on products and services that individual is using now. You can use customer touch points to cross-sell, to reward loyalty, and to stave off buyer's remorse with a well-chosen word in praise of a purchase decision.

Cross-selling is a useful technique to increase share of customer. At UCU, Cary's marketing plans include training the tellers and customer service representatives in cross-selling techniques. With customer information at their fingertips, they can easily see what products and services a customer isn't using but could be, judging by life stage and demographics.

Pitfall

Permission marketing, when conducted online, is called "opt-in" marketing. An opt-in is a very basic level of permission, gained when a website visitor clicks a selection box to indicate willingness to receive messages on specified topics. But too many marketers run too far too fast with opt-ins. Permission is not flexible. It's too easy to misjudge a prospect's interests, attitudes, or perceived relationship with you. Using opt-in status to send a message like "Since you like X, you'll probably be interested in Y" is not permission marketing!

How can you use touch points to increase your share of customer? Educate customers about the wide range of products and services beyond those they already use. You can mix techniques like sales promotions and personal selling to keep your customers learning the curriculum you've designed for them. Use each touch point to share information about different products and services, to the extent you have been given permission!

Every time you (or anyone associated with your operation, right down to the delivery driver) have contact with a customer, it's an opportunity to make that relationship warmer or colder. The bookstore that delivers orders in person (mentioned in the last chapter) presents an example of maintaining a warm relationship by maximizing customer touch points. You can call it a bold new technique or a back-to-basics movement—just don't call it late for dinner. Make the most of every customer touch point as an opportunity to learn and to share.

What Is Customer Relationship Management (CRM) and What Do I Do with It?

Customer relationship management (most often just called CRM) is a straightforward idea: Put together what you know about your customers and use it. For some, CRM is a way to market to customers more efficiently. For others, it is a way of automating the operational functions of sales, marketing, and customer service. It's a no-brainer that customer data can be used to retain customers and increase profits. The question is really, how? In the bad old days, businesses used file cards. Now, spreadsheets and databases automate customer record-keeping. Dedicated *CRM software* has emerged that reaches far beyond what those record-keeping methods can do.

We'll break down our discussion of CRM by the two different ways you can look at it—marketing and operations.

Marketing-Oriented CRM

If your business is like many of those I counsel, the data you have about your customers are scattered across your company. Some information is in the billing software, while other information is in sales people's contact management systems. Some important information may be stored nowhere other than in key individual's brains. The point of CRM is to get that data together, and then to get it "speaking" to you.

What?

CRM software functions as a central location for all of your customer data—sales records, contact information, prospect lists, and more. CRM can improve operations by helping to predict demand for certain products. CRM can help marketers time promotions and customer touch points to arrive just as customers are likely to buy again.

Jim Novo, in his book *Drilling Down*, says, "Marketing with customer data is a highly evolved and valuable conversation." He explains that customer data "speaks" by sharing three key facts:

- Who purchased *recently*
- Who purchased *frequently*
- Who has spent the most *money* in total

These three keys add up to a powerful model for predicting who will be your best customers in the future. Your primary goal is to monitor recency of purchases, frequency of purchases, and money spent. As a marketer, you need access to the data that will support that goal.

The basics customer information you're tracking—recency, frequency, monetary value—provides the foundation for a marketing approach built on CRM. What you build on that foundation can be a cottage or a castle. Let's take it to the next level.

All the customers who score high on recency, frequency, monetary value are by definition your best customers. Now, let's mine that data to describe a best customer profile. Do these purchasers have other traits in common? What are they?

Try pinpointing your customers on a map. Do they share geographic characteristics? Try grouping them by age, gender, income level, or life stage. Do clusters appear? Look at the purchase habits within those clusters. Are patterns taking shape?

This type of customer profile analysis generates insights that are invaluable to a marketer. You can use this information to make your marketing tactics more successful. You can purchase better direct mail lists, choose more efficient media buys, or decide where to locate your next store. Whatever your marketing challenges, a foundation of customer information leads to better strategic choices.

Marketing-oriented CRM seeks to make the most of the potential in customer touch points. Touch points are often initiated by the customer. The touch point can arise at any moment, without notice. Anyone providing customer service should have immediate access to accurate information about each previous communication with any individual customer. The data brought together by a CRM database is just the tool a customer service provider needs to turn touch points into successful long-term customer relationships.

CAUTION

Pitfall

When is "CRM" not "CRM"? Depends on who's talking. To a marketer, "CRM" generally means the whole philosophical approach of managing relationships customer by customer—one-to-one marketing, in other words. To a technical type, the term "CRM" more often refers to the software that supports the marketer's idea of CRM. When you get in a conversation about CRM, make sure you're all talking about the same thing!

Hearthstone provides an example. Katy, who runs the books to their new owners, reviews each customer's profile before leaving the shop. If the opportunity arises, she makes suggestions about other books the customer might enjoy. Just like Amazon, but pleasantly personal! It's thorough tracking of customer data that allows this business's marketers to manage the complex mix of customers and prospects for the bookstore, the inn, and the café.

To summarize—the point of CRM from a marketing perspective, is to

- Help you draw best-customer profiles, to guide marketing tactics.
- To make detailed customer information available to anyone who needs it, at any customer touch point.

Operations-Oriented CRM

Small businesses have a distinct advantage when it comes to implementing CRM. There's been a lot of grumbling from large enterprises over CRM, and it all boils down to "It cost us a fortune, and now we can't get people to use it." The biggest challenges for larger businesses are integration of "legacy data" (the records in the billing software, or on the file cards, or whatever) and low adoption rates by the people expected to use the system.

With smaller businesses, both issues are less problematic. In a small business, there is simply less legacy data to bring into the new system. It's easier to upgrade 200 records than 20,000. Plus in smaller workplaces, there tends to be a different attitude toward change. Small businesses tend to run lean and mean, with the result that individuals are generally more eager for changes that allow them to do their work more efficiently.

Does your operation justify a full-blown CRM software installation? Many businesses don't. Kalika's juice cart has no need to track who purchased recently or frequently or spent a lot of money in total. When hunger and hot sun combine, smoothies sell themselves.

Pitfall

Does a very small business need a CRM system? Maybe yes, maybe no. A micro-retailer like Kalika with her juice cart has very little need for the operational benefits of CRM. She doesn't use marketing tactics that require customer profiling, and she manages her customer touch points just fine by simply using her head. If you serve a fairly small customer base and see your customers nearly every day, you can probably do without CRM. In almost every other situation, I would say "better safe than sorry"—get some kind of CRM system in place.

For many businesses, including the majority of our examples from Chapter 2, a database and a spreadsheet program can do the job of CRM software. (That is if the marketer knows how to use both and takes the time to do it!)

Kai Miaka (the musician) and Anita (Life History Services) use simple contact manager software to approximate CRM. A Life of Faith Dolls uses a system designed for mail order businesses. University Credit Union will make the leap to CRM software when the dust settles from that meeting between Marketing and IT. Bob's Bottomless Boats has been using CRM software for years.

Do you need CRM? You need the approach, whether or not you need the software. If you are looking to goose your business into a growth phase, implementing CRM and the software to support it is a good way to go. To find systems suited to your needs, you could start with "CRM" and a search engine. But that may be a little too much like diving in among sharks for your tastes. Ask around among your business associates. What software do they use to perform CRM? Expect to hear names like Peoplesoft and Salesforce.com. Microsoft has a product designed for smaller businesses named Customer Manager. You might start out reading about these, if you're heading toward CRM.

Using Customer Information Means Using Technology

CRM is in many ways an old idea in new clothing—database marketing. Often it seems the excitement in marketing work comes from reaching new markets and getting new customers. But as I hope I've shown in this chapter, great profit potential can be found by turning to your existing customers. The people in your database have an awareness of your offerings, a positive (hopefully) perception of your business, and a potentially loyal relationship with you.

You know more about these people than you do about the general public you reach through mass marketing. With your knowledge of them and their knowledge of you, it only makes sense to focus on them.

Each business faces a decision whether it makes sense to allocate part of its marketing budget to creating, maintaining, and using a customer database for one-to-one marketing. As long as you're committed to technology to support that database, why not see how far you can take the computer as your partner in CRM?

Online marketing lends itself to automated solutions. In the online world, an opt-in equals permission to share a relationship. Computer scripts can take it from there.

Mentor

Sophisticated database functions make one-to-one marketing possible. You can sort that database and use specialized printing to deliver mail pieces that are customized right down to the individual recipient, a technique called variable printing. (I promise there will be more about this when we examine target marketing and using direct mail in upcoming chapters.)

One example of one-to-one marketing based on permissions is the *cascading response sequence*, a series of touches triggered by customer-driven events. The cascading response sequence can be driven entirely automatically, using e-mail auto-responders.

If there's one message you should've gotten by now, it's this: You've got to have some technology in place to manage customer information. You can't use the information you've got if you don't have it stored where you can get to it, in the right format, when and where you need it. The flaw with the old box of file cards was the format. You can't automate a search and sort routine on a box of papers. You can't drive auto-responders with a few sheets of address label masters.

Customer data must be kept in a format that's sophisticated enough to support two activities: sifting that data for insight, and making the relevant data available to stimulate and respond to customer touch points.

The Least You Need to Know

- One-to-one marketing shifts the focus from mass market share to share of individual customers over their lifetimes.
- The tools of one-to-one marketing are permissions and touch points.
- Customer Relationship Management (CRM) is a marketing approach and a software solution.
- Using customer information requires technology; this can be as simple as a spreadsheet and a database, or as complex as an enterprise-wide dedicated CRM software application.

Chapter 6

Use Market Research to Guide You

In This Chapter

- How market research helps you understand your customers and choose marketing techniques
- What research can reveal about your audience
- Types of research and the types of data they produce
- How to get started—and why

Market research. Lots of people talk about it, but is anybody doing something about it? Ask among your business acquaintances. Has anyone you know used research? The answer you get depends on how you ask the question.

So what's market research all about? Understanding buyer behavior through studying clusters of good customers, examining their purchasing process, their culture, and their motivations, and then using that knowledge to get the most efficient bang for your marketing buck. You get that bang by developing target marketing and positioning strategies. The result will be advertising that is not only creative but amazingly effective.

Few small businesses perform the kind of direct, quantitative research that we think of when we use a term like *market research*, such as questionnaires. But there's more to research than just questionnaires. A trip to the Internet or a glance in the telephone book to count your competitors are research activities. You—and many people like you—have used research techniques in the past and will again in the future.

The analysis of customer information I recommended in Chapter 5 is market research. In this chapter, we'll explore more types of research directed toward customers, and keep riding that horse into the next chapter to develop target marketing strategies based on what you've learned. Survive that ride and you'll be rewarded with a discussion of competitor research in Chapter 8. Yee-haw!

What Is Market Research?

Research is the collection and analysis of data to produce information. Market research is what you do when you come up with an idea but you don't know whether to run with it. That hesitation usually means you are missing some information you need to make a decision. Market research fills the need for information.

Collecting information from customers with a questionnaire is market research. Collecting anecdotal observations about customers from sales and customer service people is market research. Recording and analyzing demographic data about your audience is market research.

Mentor

Are your customers businesses rather than consumers? You'll find that in these chapters I tend to dwell on the consumer population more than the purchaser of goods or services for businesses. People are people whether they're buying for home or business consumption; the same buying behaviors tend to apply. I assure you, market research is just as relevant for business-to-business situations. Some specific techniques you can use for researching your market are discussed in Chapter 8.

Why Do Research?

Research is a way to determine characteristics about your current customers that will enable you to find new ones. Research can help you gather information for new product development or assess the quality of your service. You can use research to test advertising campaigns or to find out how people view you and your competition.

Research can help you answer questions like these:

- How well are you meeting customers' current needs?
- How do your customers perceive your competitors?
- Who are your most likely customers, and what drives their purchase behavior?
- Is your operation—location, hours, and so on—in sync with customers' expectations?

Plus, research can guide specifics of advertising strategy such as:

- Should your marketing feature a price incentive?
- What sales promotion strategies might be effective?
- Should your ads emphasize your company's reputation, the quality of your offering, your price, or what?
- Should you go head-to-head with a competitor, or ignore all competition in your ad messages?

Wouldn't it be useful to know what kind of people your best prospects are, how to use advertising media to reach them, and what lifestyle attributes might dress up your message in ways that appeal to them? Knowledge like that might just lead to spiffier, more effective marketing ploys, and that can lead to some nice changes in lifestyle for yourself.

Mentor

One role for market research is in new product development. You need to know what consumers feel they're not getting now from the products and services on the market. Then design new products and services to fill those needs.

A Little Information Goes a Long Way

A small amount of information about customer preferences, if gathered regularly, will repay the effort many times over. Yes, I know you're running a business and you already have enough to do. I know that suggesting you take time out to do customer research is going to hit you like a request that you do without sleep for the next week. Sorry about that.

I wouldn't be insisting on research if I didn't believe the benefits are huge. The monetary costs can be quite low for a simple do-it-yourself research project, and certainly worth the investment. In my opinion, research—especially research directed toward customers—is essential if you want the business you're running to *stay* in business.

Really!

Market research is what you do when you think, "My gut will tell me if I'm right," and your gut doesn't answer back. Most of the small business people I've dealt with haven't been very thorough about their market research. Most just go on gut feelings alone. And it works, up to a point. They then need to get a little smarter and start playing the game more seriously. Suddenly market information, and the research to get it, becomes a valuable commodity. When you're ready to grow, market research is the way to go.

Understanding Buyers Through Research

To begin with, you need some questions. Scientific research is all about making a hypothesis and then trying to disprove it through testing. Market research is no different. It's a quest for the systematic, objective development of information for making marketing decisions.

What hypothesis comes to mind? You might want to test the performance of your Four Utilities or ask questions that benchmark customers' expectations.

What Questions Should You Ask?

If you understand your customers, you can find clusters of good ones, and you can also look for more nuts who belong in the cluster. So think about what you'd like to ask your best customers and what you'll do with the answers.

Basic customer research should cover the following:

- **Descriptive information:** demographics, information sources, influences
- **How they use products:** buying behavior, usage traits, loyalty to specific brands
- **Customer perceptions:** likes and dislikes, perception of an offering's attributes, benefits and flaws

The simplest technique for directing research toward customers is to conduct a customer survey. This can be as simple as offering a customer comment card near the cash register.

In Chapter 4, I introduced Hearthstone Bookstore, Inn and Café, a business that includes a café and bed-and-breakfast in their operation. Here's an example of a simple customer survey conducted by the café manager. This survey, printed on a smallish card, was presented to each café patron along with the bill.

Thank you for dining at our café.

Your comments are appreciated.

1 = Excellent 2 = Good 3 = Average 4 = Fair 5 = Poor

❑ How was the service?

❑ Were your beverages satisfactory?

❑ Was your food satisfactory?

❑ Did your order arrive promptly?

❑ How do you rate the dollar value?

❑ Please rate your overall experience while at our café.

Other comments:

____

____

Please tell us how you heard of us. Radio? Newspaper? Friends?

____

Have you shopped in our bookstore?

❑ Yes, occasionally ❑ Yes, often ❑ No

Have you or any of your out-of-town guests ever stayed at our bed and breakfast upstairs?

❑ Yes, occasionally ❑ Yes, often ❑ No

With this simple customer survey, it won't be long before the café manager finds out what people think about the food and the establishment. By keeping the completed comment cards attached to the party's bill, and then analyzing them together, she was able to find out which menu items were consistently poorly rated and improve them. By calculating the average score for each question on a weekday versus weekend, she was able to determine whether food or service quality suffered during busy times. That's quite a lot of insight from a simple customer comment card!

> **Pitfall**
>
> Most of us believe that a survey must involve a rigorous process of questionnaire development and sample selection—otherwise the results won't be statistically valid. This is true, up to a point. But don't let it keep you from doing what you can to find out what customers think.

Surveys can be considerably more complex than this example. A full-blown survey project usually involves a rigorous process of questionnaire development and sample selection to be sure the results are statistically valid. Such surveys take more time, effort, and money than this example, of course. My point is this: You can start using research to improve your operation, even if the full-blown version seems beyond your reach.

"Who, What, and Where": Descriptive Information

For U.S. companies, a wealth of descriptive information about consumers is available through U.S. census data and the Consumer Expenditure Survey conducted by the Bureau of Labor Statistics. The Canadian government makes similar information available for that country. You can find this information online (see Appendix C). You have access to some of the same "who, what, and where" data that huge corporations use to understand their customers. (One note of warning—it won't always be free.)

> **What?**
>
> **Demographic** data includes population statistics such as income, gender, age, occupation, and marital status. **Geographic** data is about buying statistics in different parts of the country—north, south, rural, suburban, right down to my side of the street versus your side of the street.

The "who, what, and where" questions deal with *demographic* and *geographic* data and characteristics.

What are demographic characteristics? These are derived from a statistical study of the population, measuring its size, density, distribution, and vital statistics. Typical demographic statistics include age, sex, income, education, marital status, family size, and occupation. Demographic research can tell you how many employed mothers between 25 and 44 holding college degrees prefer minivans to convertibles, or how many Hispanics over age 65 consume non-alcoholic beer.

What are geographic characteristics? Geographics are destiny, purchase-wise. When it comes to where we live, "birds of a feather flock together." People living near each other share surprisingly homogenous demographic and lifestyle characteristics. Several major market research vendors use geographics plus demographics to predict consumer attitudes and spending patterns. Any customer list (say, *yours*) can be analyzed by geographics. That data can be used to buy mailing lists or to locate advertising media that reach other geographies with similar characteristics. These "look-alike locales" can be a productive source of new customers very like your own current customer base. One of the most common uses of geographic data is in selecting which advertising media you'll use.

"Why" Characteristics: The Murky Waters of Psychographics

Geographics and demographics will only take you so far in developing customer imagination. Although they give you a rough sketch of the buyer, *psychographic* characteristics are just as helpful, filling in the details that let you really imagine what goes on inside buyers' heads. "Psychographics" is a rather unscientific term coined to describe individuals' mental traits and lifestyle choices that express their behaviors, attitudes, and social values.

Psychographic research studies the activities, interests, and opinions of the individuals who make up a market. Psychographics attempt to provide a quantitative analysis of self-concept. This helps us see the market as a person to be addressed, with character traits and human strengths and failings. This can be very helpful when it comes to creating appealing advertising. Such data are usually collected by giving consumers a set of statements with which to agree or disagree.

The catch with psychographic research is that it is expensive and difficult to do on your own. To get statistically accurate samples, you would have to survey a large number of people. Luckily, you don't have to do that. The information is available (at a price) from major market research vendors. To find them, enter "psychographics" in your favorite search engine.

These companies study the consumer marketplace, using demographic, geographic, and psychographic attributes to describe the population. They maintain databases of households with these attributes attached to each record. These companies rent out this data in the form of mailing or telemarketing lists. You can order a list, using any combination of demographic, geographic, or psychographic attributes as sort criteria.

You could order a list of consumer households in your geographic area and match it against your customer list to discover psychographic attributes about your own customers. You could use that information to rent lists of prospects who match the attributes of your own best customers. But more—much more!—about that in later chapters.

What?

Psychographics attempt to provide a quantitative analysis of self-concept by focusing on customers' lifestyles: their activities, interests, and opinions. "Real" social scientists discount psychographics (not statistically reliable enough), but marketers find the concept quite effective in target marketing.

Mentor

The problem with psychographic research is the cost and difficulty of conducting it. You can purchase this data. But first, check with your trade association or other industry sources to see whether psychographic surveys may already be available describing your customers. It will likely cost you less than dealing with the data vendors.

Techniques for Research

Every research project revolves around three key issues. Regardless of the product class or the problems at hand, research will involve (1) the consumer, (2) the product, and (3) the competition. You need to find out what consumers need and want, and you need to know how your product measures up against the competition when it comes to satisfying those needs and wants.

Really!

Consumer research falls into three categories. First, you can ask questions that help you describe consumers by learning their demographics, geographics, usage traits, information sources, and influences. Second, you can learn about their processes as consumers. These questions probe consumers' buying behavior and degrees of loyalty to products and brands. Third, you can study consumer perceptions, discovering likes and dislikes, and perception of products attributes, benefits, and flaws. Taken in this order, your line of questioning will help you arrive at customer imagination.

Techniques for research can be *qualitative*, meaning open-ended in nature, or *quantitative*, meaning measurable data suitable for statistical analysis. Methods of gathering research can be either *direct*, gathered by you, or *indirect*, found in existing sources.

The following figure suggests how the different types of research fit together.

Types of market research.

	Quantitative	Qualitative
Direct	Example: Questionnaires	Example: Focus Groups
Indirect	Example: Research Reports	Example: Case Studies in Textbooks

Let's assume you have an idea of your information needs, based on the first part of this chapter. Now, how do you respond? Where can help be found? You could start by going out and collecting data; but before starting in this direction, let's consider what data may be available from existing sources.

What?

Qualitative research is anecdotal, open-ended, and feelings-based. In short, it's the right brain of market research. **Quantitative** research, on the other hand, relies on measurable data gathered for statistical analysis, you know, left-brain stuff. Both are necessary to understand a research problem. The qualitative tells you what to ask, and the quantitative tells you what to do with the answers.

Indirect Research: Stalking Data in the Wild

First, you probably have some internal information already. You just need to know where to look for it. Check out your sales data (purchase records, warranty cards, sales force reports) and your previous advertising/promotional plans. Talk with your salespeople. Most importantly, listen to your key customers to gain insights about possible new market opportunities.

Second, look for external information sources. You may find data through these sources:

- The government
- Industry
- The media
- Financial institutions

A great deal of this information is available online, if you know where to look. (A good place to start is the About site. Go to www.about.com and type "Market Research" into the search field.) Or if you need to get some exercise, stroll on over to the library and ask at the reference desk for the *Bureau of the Census Catalog of Publications* and the *Statistical Abstract of the United States*. Government census data is extremely helpful if your product is distributed on a fairly wide scale. When the librarian observes your avid interest in these tomes, he or she will most likely bring other government publications to your attention.

An amazing amount of data about spending patterns is available to you courtesy of your government. The *Consumer Expenditure Survey (C.E.S.)* is a national survey of households designed to represent the total United States consumer population. It surveys consumer behavior and, when considered over time, allows us to understand and predict trends. Data are gathered from households via diaries and interviews. You can find C.E.S. data online, although the data are pretty unwieldy in their raw state. For this reason, third-party vendors have created tools to allow you to examine specific spending categories broken down by a variety of demographic factors. Expect to pay from $50 to $200 for reports; find them by entering "Consumer Expenditure Survey" in your search engine.

Pitfall

There's a problem with relying solely on indirect research: Most of it is somewhat out-of-date when it reaches you. By the time that data have been gathered, analyzed, summarized, and distributed, their hot findings have cooled considerably. Even with the Internet speeding up distribution of findings, there's still too much lag time. Don't rely solely on indirect research; use it as a prelude to your direct research.

Industrial sources are helpful as well. Your specific industry association may have performed research that will help you. Ask that librarian about the Simmons Market Research Bureau publications if you want to dive into the sea of industry data available.

Many trade publications perform research. Specific journals to look at include *Advertising Age*, *Business Week*, *Business Marketing*, *Catalog Age*, *Fortune*, *Forbes*, and the *Wall Street Journal*. Check with the trade journal for your industry as well. Many have information available for you, basically an offshoot of publications analyzing their readership to better market their ad pages. Much of this information is available online, but you may be required to register, subscribe, or otherwise part with some of your money or your precious personal information to get access to it.

Finally, do not pass "GO" without stopping to talk to your banker. (Although I'll be surprised if you collect $200.) Financial institutions have access to all kinds of industry data. Your banker may be worth his weight in gold when it comes to market research.

Direct Research: Growing Your Own

But what if indirect research fails to turn up the answers to your burning questions? Then it's time for direct research. Time to collect data specific to your problems.

In the previous chapter, the marketing director of University Credit Union was laying the groundwork to conduct a customer survey. Her research goal: to create profiles of graduating students' typical needs and, while she's at it, get a sense for how to reach them (what advertising techniques to employ). She plans to segment those students into precisely defined target segments and then employ one-to-one marketing to keep them as members long after they graduate. Her situation suggests a direct quantitative survey be used. She's got a good idea what she wants to know and what she plans to do with the result. This use of the credit union's resources (time and money) can easily be justified.

Mentor

Decision time! You're ready to consider doing a research project when you can answer yes to these questions. Can you afford to do this? (Time, effort, dollars?) Will the data you get be worth the cost? Do you know what you plan to do with the results? If you said no to any of these three, *no go!*

What if your organization lacks the resources of UCU? Look to your trade or professional associations. These groups often conduct direct research drawing on members' experiences. This was the case with the Association of Personal Historians, the trade association Anita Hecht (Life History Services) joined. The organization conducted a survey of members, asking questions about their background, demographics, and use of the association's member services. But there were more questions in that survey designed specifically to help members with marketing. The survey asked about products offered, methods of charging for services, breakdown of types of clients, and demographics (such as income and age) about those clients. Also, the survey asked members about what marketing techniques had worked for them.

It's not hard to see how useful this information is to Anita in marketing her business. If your trade organization doesn't provide information like this, you could encourage it to pursue a similar research project.

Do-It-Yourself Research

Developing a research project requires five steps. Should you be the kind of dedicated do-it-yourselfer who, after replumbing your pipes and reprogramming your database, takes on a survey project or two, this one's for you.

1. **Describe the problem.** Look for answers that will be useful in solving the problem, not simply interesting to know.
2. **Make a hypothesis.** Now propose an answer. Develop a research project to prove or disprove that hypothesis. Check out what sources of information are available. What's already available (indirect research)?
3. **Choose a research technique.** Decide whether your research should be qualitative or quantitative, indirect or direct. You might decide to use a focus group,

or a survey tool like interviews and questionnaires. There is a multitude of research techniques to choose from. A quick look on the Internet or at your local library should give you plenty to think about.

4. **Select the sample.** You'll never be able to include every member of a specific target group in your research, so you must choose a sample instead. How will you make that sample representative of the whole? You could try for a statistically accurate random sample, or go by some less scientific method, like simply asking each customer who enters your store one afternoon to answer a short list of questions.

5. **Collect and analyze the data.** Determine the questions you'll ask and how to phrase them. In order to generate usable answers, put them in a sensible sequence, and then distribute and collect the results.

We flew over a lot of detailed activity in this chapter. If you had time for a leisurely dive into the topic, the design of the survey instrument alone could be the basis for a half-day seminar, if not an entire book.

Conducting research gives you data—but not information. First you must tabulate the responses, totaling them for each question and recording the total as a percentage of the number responding. Then group the tabulated responses into meaningful categories. If half the respondents agree strongly and half disagree just as strongly, with no middle ground, that's meaningful. When you understand *why* they respond that way, you're getting at the real result of market research: new insight into your problem and its solution. That's customer imagination taking shape. And that's the end of this over-simplified five-step process!

> CAUTION
>
> **Pitfall**
>
> Never ask a question if you don't know what you'd do with the answer! Keep your homegrown research projects short and simple.

A great place to start, if you're not ready to dive into research with both feet, is with a key informant interview. Follow the first two steps—describing the problem and making a hypothesis—then go to lunch with somebody who's likely to know more than you about the problem you've described. A good customer, a mentor, your banker—you decide who. Pump that person for everything he knows, and then approach your research question again. You're likely to have a deeper understanding after a few such interviews.

One word of caution here: Never design a marketing research questionnaire without first doing some qualitative research, such as talking with key informants or industry experts. You need as much qualitative insight as you can get about the key issues to be researched before you start drafting the actual survey questionnaire. Otherwise, you are likely to overlook something that is very important to your customers.

Really!

Focus groups are a means of performing qualitative direct research that can be very important if you're not sure what problem to research or what hypothesis to propose. A focus group is a highly structured meeting of people who have been carefully recruited to resemble the audience in question. They are asked, under the guidance of a professional moderator, to focus on a company, issue, or product and speak their minds about it. Often, the group is videotaped or viewed through a one-way mirror. Focus groups are particularly useful when you are trying to understand people's perceptions or depth of feeling (positive or negative). Focus groups must be professionally hosted to yield usable results—expect to pay $5,000 or more.

Get Started by Researching Your Customers

Let's zoom out and take a look at the big picture. The reason we're talking about market research is that it leads to segmentation strategy, which leads to positioning strategy (which are both discussed in Chapter 7), which leads to efficient and effective advertising strategy. In the next two chapters, we'll talk more about customers and competitors, and what you need to know about them before you can enter that strategy zone.

The following worksheet is a starter kit for customer research. Adapt the questions to your situation. The questions in this survey are divided into five areas: media usage, the "Four Utilities," demographics, geographics, and psychographics.

Mentor

Have you ever heard the Groucho Marx quote that goes something like, "I'd never join a club that would have me as a member"? Most of us have that basic insecurity somewhere in our makeup. It's not a bad thing; it's part of what motivates us to improve ourselves. But it does make us afraid to talk to customers. The marketing version of the quote might go something like, "I'd never shop in a store that would have me as a manager." Get over it. Walk right up to a customer and tell him, "I'd like to know what you think!"

Questions for Customers (All Answers Anonymous)

Media Usage Questions

What newspapers do you read?

What radio stations do you listen to?

What TV shows do you watch?

Which magazines do you read?

Name a billboard you remember passing recently (advertiser and/or location).

Where would you expect us to advertise?

Questions Guided by the Customers' Values

Where do you purchase [product/service category]?

What specific [product or service] do you currently purchase?

How often do you make those purchases?

Please rate our service from 1 (best) to 5 (worst):

What services would you like us to offer?

What products would you like us to carry?

Who do you consider to be our competition?

Have you shopped with one of our competitors in the past (3 months) (year) (three years)?

Is our location (convenient) (inconvenient)?

Is our price (low-scale) (high-scale) for what you get?

Would you pay 10 percent more if you felt you were getting 20 percent more value?

Questions to Guide Segmentation Decisions

Demographics

What is your gender? ________ Your age?_______

What is your occupation?

Your household income? (___0–$20k, ___21–40k, ___41–60k, ___60k+)

Your marital status?

Number of members in your immediate family/household?

Do you (rent) (own) your home?

Geographics

Your zip code (home)

Your zip code (work)

Comments

The Least You Need to Know

- Market research can help you understand your consumers and product offering better.
- Research can reveal demographic, geographic, and psychographic characteristics of your audience.
- You can choose a research technique that is direct or indirect and that gathers qualitative or quantitative data.
- Start your research program with your current customers' media usage, demographics, geographics, and psychographic traits.

Chapter 7

No More Mass Markets! Target Your Niche

In This Chapter

- Why segment and target customers
- A target marketing vocabulary lesson
- How attributes combine to define niches
- Pros and cons of following a segmentation strategy

Once upon a time, America was a mass consumer society, depicted in situation comedies like *I Love Lucy* and *The Dick Van Dyke Show* and reflected in the audience that watched those shows. The families that gathered in living rooms around flickering black-and-white TVs were a consumer group so broad and general they were defined by nothing more than their ability to purchase an offering. Marketers didn't trouble with descriptors like geographic location, age, or lifestyle. They simply offered products to viewers who, with their postwar purchasing power, aspired to the lifestyles of the sitcom characters. The viewers purchased the goods and believed they were gaining on the good life by doing so.

Fast-forward half a dozen decades. The days when it made sense to market to a mass audience are just about gone. We're a nation dividing itself into smaller and smaller subcategories, or *market segments.* We want products and services that fit *our* needs, not those of a large mass of people who are a little like us in some ways. This slow but serious tectonic plate shift is changing the entire lay of the land for marketers.

One result is an ever-growing emphasis on segmenting and targeting niche markets.

A Vocabulary Lesson

Whoa, what was that? Three terms just flew by! We're going to throw them around like doubloons at Mardi Gras in this chapter, so let's define them now.

Mentor

Here's the Second Law of Marketing: Not everybody will buy your products. But some will, and they can probably be identified by traits they share—their demographic profile, geographic location, and lifestyle. Your challenge is to identify those traits and then use that knowledge to find look-alikes.

What?

A **market segment** is a group of people who have identifiable similarities. Market segmentation means zeroing in on what traits groups of buyers have in common. **Target marketing** is deciding exactly which segment to market to. A **niche** is another term for a market segment. **Niche marketing** is another way of saying target marketing—that is, picking a segment to market to.

Market Segments

Not everybody will buy your offerings, but a smaller subset of "everybody" will, and those people can be identified by traits they share. Everyone who may buy your product can be divided into small groups referred to as *market segments* or *niches.* We group them by descriptive attributes such as their age, sex, race/ethnicity, and location—their demographic and geographic characteristics. We also group them by behavioral attributes, such as their lifestyle, activities, interests, and opinions—their psychographics. Why do we group them? We pick those segments (or niches) as a tool to help us focus our spending. By choosing a *target marketing* approach, we spend advertising dollars reaching the potential customers most likely to buy our products and services.

Target Marketing

Target marketing means focusing your efforts on those segments most likely to buy your product or service. There are two main reasons we target individual markets rather than mass-market all products to all people.

First, it is simply ineffective to try to persuade everyone to buy the same product. Some people are more likely to buy, and some people are more likely to be profitable as customers. I'll make a wild assumption here and state that your dollars for marketing are limited. Therefore, it makes sense to pursue the easier and more profitable customers first.

> **Pitfall**
>
> Not every identifiable market segment deserves to become a target. The segments you choose to target must be large enough to be profitable, discrete in their characteristics (so you can identify who is and who isn't in the group), and for best results, must be able to be reached selectively through targeted media.

Second, and just as obvious, it is inefficient to spend money on advertising that reaches a mass audience. It is very expensive to advertise in the mass media. (You've heard what those Super Bowl commercial spots cost!) Therefore, it makes sense to pick a target market and advertise in specialized media that targets that same audience. If you can match a niche you'd like to target with one that is reached by specific magazines or cable TV channels, you can avoid wasting money placing message after message in front of people who have no interest in your offering. Say Bob's Bottomless Boats wants to pitch kayaks. They'll spend less and get more for the money by targeting the readers of *Paddle Sports* than the readers of *TV Guide*.

> **Mentor**
>
> Do you market your offering to businesses rather than consumers? Target marketing is just as relevant for businesses, but less complicated, so you'll find that's not our focus here. At the end of this chapter I'll share some thoughts on how you can apply these concepts if you sell "B2B" (as we used to say in the dot-com era).

One Nation, Highly Divisible: Segmentation Variables at Work

Consumers base decisions on all kinds of factors, from rational to emotional—to downright nuts. But you have to start somewhere. Demographics are the simplest place to start. Lifestyle and ethnicity require more subtle understanding, so we'll consider those once we've got the basics under our belts.

The Building Blocks of Segmentation: Demographic Traits

Common demographic statistics include age, sex, race/ethnicity, education, income, occupation, marital status, and family type. The most frequently used for segmentation are income and age, so let's look at those first.

Income data can inform retail location decisions and choices of advertising media. We generally think of this from the upscale side—sellers of luxury goods look for locations and ad vehicles that reach the $100,000-plus income segment. But this works on the downscale side as well. Retailers are rediscovering the purchasing power of lower-income individuals, a niche with targetable needs for good value at lower price points.

Age data is a powerful key to demographic niche markets. This is so popular it has a name: *generational marketing*. The authors of *Rocking the Ages, the Yankelovich Report on Generational Marketing* propose "Members of a generation are linked through the shared life experiences of their formative years." That's a simple statement and a powerful thought. Experiences bond members of a generation together. These shared experiences inform the values of each group as they go through life. Social scientists refer to these generational groups as *cohorts*. The shared values and experiences of a cohort provide the lens through which that group views life. Your cohort is a significant factor in your conception of "the good life" and affects everything from what you consider financial security to what type of music you prefer.

What?

Generational marketing is a strategy based on segmenting niche markets by age. By doing so, marketers reach **cohorts**, groups of individuals of similar age who share values and experiences based on the times in which they came of age. Because first experiences tend to form intense impressions, cohorts are typically defined by the influences on its members during their teen years.

You've no doubt seen generational segments referred to as Youth, Gen Y, Gen X, Baby Boomers, and that horrible catch-all, Matures. Since each of these broad segments can span 20 or more years, marketers break them down into smaller segments. Within "Youth" you'll find "Tweeners" (early adolescents), a special niche between the very young and the turbulent teens. Within "Matures" you'll find many niches with different needs, depending on each individual's health, income, and other factors.

Really!

What's your "Woodstock"? In the 1960s, events like civil rights protests, political assassinations, and the Vietnam War influenced young people. Teens responded with new ideas, attitudes, and beliefs. Some of those teens attended a rainy three-day music festival. Say the word *Woodstock* today and you bring to mind those young people with their rock music, long hair, and rebellious attitudes … now edging toward retirement! For every generation, there's a "Woodstock"—an event that comes to define a specific cohort. As marketers, we use our understanding of cohorts to tailor products and advertising messages to connect with specific niche markets, often by referencing their "Woodstock" in the product design or advertising messages.

Let's talk frankly about generational marketing because there's a dark side here that contributes to the perception that marketers are a species lower than a snake's belly. "Understanding the values of a generation will be a key source of competitive advantage," say the authors of *Rocking the Ages*. But what's good for business can be bad for society.

As marketers we know that by understanding generations, we can connect with customers better, tailoring products and messages to "push buttons" very effectively. But we can use this power in manipulative ways. Tobacco companies misuse generational marketing to promote cigarette use to young people. Why? Because it works. But is it right? I'd rather you use the power of generational marketing for good, not for evil.

How might a businesses target a generational cohort for marketing? A Life of Faith Dolls, the historical doll company, segments its market by age, and more or less by default, generational cohort. Little girls, their parents, and their grandparents are all involved in the appreciation and purchase of A Life of Faith's Elsie Dinsmore and Millie Keith dolls. Grandparents might remember reading the original books, while parents are drawn to the idea of "character-building products." The girls naturally react to the attractions of the products themselves, dolls and stories and things to do that are "like having a best friend from another time." (I'm quoting from the company's catalog.) A Life of Faith Dolls employs different media and different advertising messages to win favor with these three different age groups.

CAUTION

Pitfall

Sex (gender) is so obviously an important attribute in defining target markets that it hardly needs mentioning. However, you should be cautious about targeting only males or only females. You could be engaging in illegal discrimination. As I write this, Curves fitness franchises are being challenged in court on their practice of restricting membership to females only. Granted, it gives them a distinct advantage in the marketplace, but it may well turn out to be discrimination—just like keeping women out of traditionally men-only clubs.

Segmentation by Subtler Factors: Lifestyles and Ethnicity

In the past century, *lifestyles* were more or less dictated by chronological age and income bracket. No longer. Lifestyles are much more flexible now that periods of education, work, and leisure recur at various times in a person's life. A change in a major relationship or a move across country for a job may change a person's lifestyle.

What?

Lifestyles are the result of choices people make in daily life that express their personal behaviors, attitudes, and social values. Lifestyles carry with them predictable purchase behavior. Lifestyles are tied closely to psychographics—some people use the terms interchangeably.

Lifestyles can be identified and targeted as profitable niche markets. Predictable spending patterns accompany lifestyles. When a person's lifestyle changes, big spending takes place to outfit the new lifestyle. Take newlyweds, for example. Newlyweds spend more in the first six months of marriage than a settled homeowner spends in five years. Now that's a niche market worth going after!

When lifestyles change, so do spending patterns. An expectant mom spends to outfit her new baby's nursery; an empty nester spends to refit a child's bedroom for new uses.

It's amazing how the value of customer information increases when a customer is approaching a life-changing event, like a wedding or a child graduating from college. Use your customer imagination to identify these changes as they're about to happen—and tailor offerings to these individuals' emerging needs and desires.

Many people sharing a similar lifestyle will share the same age cohort, but not always! An elderly widower and a Gen X party girl might share a similar purchase pattern of single-roll paper towel packs and meals-for-one made in the microwave, but their lifestyles are very different. Just thought I'd point this out, since those two would need different niche marketing strategies, if you're selling microwavable meals or paper towels.

A Life of Faith Dolls segments its market by lifestyle. The company found that it was getting requests for information and accessories that would turn the dolls into teaching tools for homeschoolers. Homeschooling is definitely a lifestyle choice, with attitudes, social values, and spending patterns associated with it. Many families with deep religious beliefs home-school their children. Homeschoolers need educational materials, curriculum guides—everything school teachers need. Naturally, historically accurate dolls with a story line built on faith appeal to this market. A Life of Faith Dolls promotes its products through conferences and publications that reach people with a home-schooling lifestyle.

As I said before, we're a big nation made up of small niches and we want products and services tailored to our niche's needs. Many of us identify with our ethnic heritage or race as a defining factor in "our" niche. Thus, *race* and *ethnicity* help identity niches for target marketing.

Do not underestimate the buying power of minority consumers. Blacks, Hispanics, and Asian Americans wield significant discretionary income. While Whites continue to account for the majority of consumer spending, their share is dwindling at a rate of 3 to 5 percent per year.

In a flat marketplace, it's smart to find and focus on niches that are growing. Hispanic, Black, and Asian American niches are growing faster than the mainstream population, both in numbers and in purchasing power. Yet these markets have too often been overlooked—and underserved.

Let's take a quick look at the four major racial/ethnic categories tracked by the U.S. Census:

- **Asian Americans.** The most frequent shoppers of all ethnic groups, these are also the most brand-conscious. They almost never go out to shop without a plan, and often rely on the Internet to research purchases before shopping.
- **Hispanics.** Hispanics of any race like to shop as a family, and children have considerable impact on the brands the family buys.
- **Blacks.** The happiest shoppers in the bunch! Blacks are more fashion-conscious than other groups, are willing to travel an hour or more to reach a favorite store, and are more willing to check out new stores, especially if a bargain may be found. Blacks enjoy the activity of shopping, even for mundane items.
- **Whites.** The grumpy bunch. Almost two thirds of Whites report they go shopping only when they absolutely need something, and nearly half dislike browsing. Whites are more likely to make spur-of-the-moment purchases than other groups, but also plan further ahead for expensive items.

What?

As terms, **race** and **ethnicity** are confusing to me, frankly. I think we should use them interchangeably; to me they both point to the countries and gene pools our forebears came from. My dictionary defines race as "a group of people united or classified together based on common history, nationality, or geographic distinction," while "ethnicity" is about "belonging to a religious, national, or cultural group."

Really!

Do you use direct mail to sell products? Take a look at target-marketing to ethnic niches! According to Scarborough Research, Black consumers are more likely to buy based on direct-mail advertisements. For many product categories, the Hispanic and Asian American ethnic groups respond more often to direct-mail offers than Whites do.

I've drawn these "factoids" from an *American Demographics* article in February 2003, which cites the Selig Center for Economic Growth at the University of Georgia. If they've piqued your curiosity, hit the Internet and search on the term "multicultural marketing."

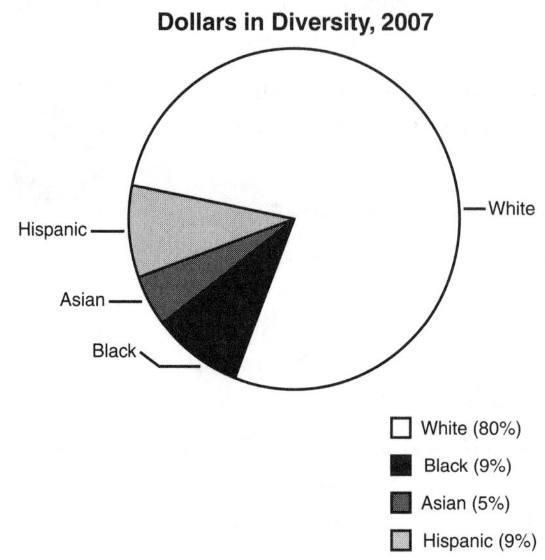

Dollars in Diversity: Black, Asian, and Hispanic buying power is growing. By 2007, these minorities are expected to make up 20 percent of the consumer marketplace. Note: Numbers add up to more than 100 percent because Hispanics may be of any race.

(Source: American Demographics *February 2003, from Selig Center for Economic Growth. The University of Georgia.)*

As the buying power of ethnic/racial minorities increases, it becomes more important for you to understand the differences between these groups in terms of how, when, where, and why they shop. Do your homework. No ethnic group is homogeneous. The Hispanic market, for instance, includes several countries of origin, including both South and Central America. Some Hispanics are foreign-born; others are "Statesiders" by birth. Some are bilingual, but not all. The same holds true among Blacks and Asian Americans. Within each group you'll find cultural distinctions and smaller niches.

The first rule, then, is to look beyond numbers to find out who's who and what they're purchasing. Walk around the ethnic community you want to serve; talk to its leaders and business owners. Use market research techniques to develop customer imagination specific to the population you want to serve.

You've probably heard some of the horror stories of ethnic marketing by groups that failed to do their homework. In the 1970s, Chevy tried to introduce its Nova in Mexico, but no one told the automaker that "No va" means "Won't go" in Spanish. Car sales "didn't go" either.

In 1995, milk producers tried to export the popular "Got milk?" ad campaign to Hispanic communities. However, the initial ads were translated too literally.

Spanish-language ads reading "Are you breast-feeding?" were quickly replaced with more appropriate words and images.

If you decide to address an ethnic market, get your act together first. Here's a checklist to help you guard against embarrassments of your own:

- **Get to know the culture first.** Read ads in ethnic publications, check out the resources of the American Marketing Association, and look for classes in cultural diversity.
- **Learn about your specific offering in your target culture.** Feng shui (designing physical space to promote harmony) is important to Asians—obey its tenets when you lay out a store to serve Asian American customers. Family is central to Hispanics—offer something for all ages in your store.
- **Recognize the diversity within the target niche.** Terms like *Hispanic* and *Asian* can refer to dozens of nationalities, language groups, and cultures. Even within the same niche, differences such as age, income, and lifestyle must be taken into account.

I am very excited about multicultural marketing. We are finally passing beyond the limits of black-or-white thinking. Marketers are finally seeing the rainbow. We're creating offerings tailored to every niche in Roy G. Biv's community. This has got to have some good effects, like, say, a chance for peace, harmony, and a better standard of living for all. (Sing with me now, "We are the world.")

Now back to business.

Segmenting for Business Markets

In this chapter, I've talked mostly in terms of end users as the customers you segment and target. But what about business markets?

People don't stop being people when they arrive at work. Segmentation strategies can be just as useful on the business-to-business side. Business markets can be easier to quantify and target than consumer markets. The main difference, when talking about business markets, is that you use the segmentation characteristics of the organization instead of the individual.

The attributes used for segmentation mirror those of consumer markets. Geographics and demographics are still the best place to start. Geographic traits in this context mean not only where the company is located, but where it considers its territorial boundaries to lie.

For demographic characteristics you will want to study organizational traits, such as a company's age and size (measured in sales or number of employees or square feet of real estate). You will access a wealth of information if the businesses you target fall within a specific NAICS (North American Industry Classification System) code. Business directories (both in book form and on the Internet) can provide the geographic and organizational information you seek.

Joe in purchasing is still more Joe than he is purchasing agent. So your target marketing must also take into account Joe's demographics, lifestyle, and ethnicity.

Mentor

Home-based businesses can be a great niche to serve but a tough one to research. Businesses with four or fewer partners and no paid employees make up about 70 percent of all U.S. businesses. (Source: 2000 U.S. Census.) With so few employees it's a good bet that a larger number of these businesses are home-based. To target this niche, point your browser to your favorite search engine and try "SOHO" (for "**s**mall office/home office") or "Soloist" and you'll find resources to help you understand and serve this niche.

To Segment or Not to Segment

Segmenting requires that you recognize one thing: You cannot, even if you're Bob's Bottomless Boats, be all things to all people. Even Coca-Cola practices target marketing. Why do you think there's Coke, Diet Coke, Cherry Coke, and even Mr. Pibb? The desire to segment the market bubbles out of the recognition of this inescapable fact.

Pitfall

No system is perfect, including market segmentation. There is great diversity within even well-defined market niches. Just ask a roomful of Baby Boomers whether they supported the Vietnam war, if you want to see diversity of opinion. Never assume target marketing is the last word on understanding your customer.

What You Gain from Segmentation

Why do successful marketers practice segmentation strategies? Why emulate them? Because those who do will improve their competitive position and serve their customers better. This results in more units sold and more dollars realized as profit. It seems fairly obvious that if you focus on the areas you can serve the best, you're likely to prosper.

Segmentation is an important step on the journey toward true one-to-one marketing. You can overlay segmentation attributes to define smaller and smaller niches, with greater and greater return on your effort. A Baby Boomer woman of Hispanic heritage who has just become a grandparent represents a consumer unit with foreseeable needs and desires as well as predictable behaviors, attitudes, and motivations. Using your customer imagination, you see a very detailed portrait of this woman; stimulating buying exchanges with her should be easy for you.

Okay, What's the Bad News?

There is a downside to segmentation. Segmenting by generational cohorts, lifestyles, ethnicity—am I recommending you have multiple market segmentation strategies going at all times, just to accommodate these different niches? Well, actually, yes. To the extent you have the resources, multiple strategies combined will bring better results than an undifferentiated mass-marketing strategy.

Without a doubt, there will be increased costs related to market segmentation. Research costs will be greater because you now need to study each market in detail. You will need separate marketing plans, separate ad strategies, maybe even separate products or packages or whatever designed for each niche.

However, in my humble opinion, the increased cost is a risk worth taking. Your dollars are focused on those most likely to buy; that focus brings potential for increased sales. How will you know until you try it? You won't, of course, so try it.

Mentor

Individuals in a market niche share a common perception of value, which can be defined by examining their take on the Four Utilities and the Customer Value Pyramid. (Go back to Chapter 4 if those terms don't sound familiar.)

Segment to Serve—And to Profit

How do you pursue a target market approach? As with any journey, you take it in steps. I'll walk you through it when I get around to it—specifically, in Part 6, when we start building your marketing plan. And if that gets your motor running, check out Appendix B.

For now, here's a peek at the territory we'll be covering. You'll define your market and then pick one or several segments to zero in on. You'll collect information, develop some customer imagination, and then build a marketing plan to address the niche(s) you've chosen. That plan will specify any needed changes to the form/function of your offering, its time/place availability, and its ease of possession. (Hey, did you just see the "Four Utilities" whiz by?)

Sometimes following a segmentation strategy leads to the spin-off of a whole new company. Wisconsin Public Radio creates several programs that interest the "lifelong learner," including a popular "Chapter-A-Day" series of books read aloud, and popular lectures from the University of Wisconsin available on tape. To recoup some of its investment in creating these programs, the radio station created a marketing arm to sell these radio programs on audio-cassette. In a classic segmentation move, it created two catalogs. One targets loyal listeners in Wisconsin, playing up the "support our public radio" angle. The other targets libraries and schools all over the world, with the emphasis on the quality of the educational content, not the provider of that content. The two are run as completely separate companies, with separate sales goals to achieve.

> **Pitfall**
>
> How much segmentation is enough? Too many choices cause confusion for the consumer and wasteful expense for you. Decide where the match between a target market's need and the product or service you offer shows real potential. Remember the principle at the core of the buying exchange: It must be beneficial for both parties.

The moral to this story? Not everybody will buy your offerings, but some subset of them will. Those subsets are more likely to respond to messages and offerings designed specifically to appeal to them. By pitching specific messages to specific niches, you not only serve them better, but you also profit from more of their purchasing power. That's market segmentation in an extremely small nutshell.

> **Really!**
>
> Hey, I'm a nonprofit. How do I make all this work for me? Nonprofit organizations typically have two markets to serve: a client group (those whom it is the organization's mission to serve, be they needy children or endangered animals or whatever) and a donor group (those who share their time, money, or resources to further the organization's mission). These groups can be classified into niches just as consumers can. Target marketing is a key success factor in donor development.

The Least You Need to Know

- In today's consumer marketplace, carefully segmenting and targeting customers is very effective.
- Segmentation involves identifying groups of buyers who have something in common that would make them a target market for products or services.
- Niches can be defined by attributes like age, lifestyle, and ethnic or racial identity.
- Segmentation strategies incur increased costs but more than offset those costs with increased results.

Watch Your Back: Checking Out the Competition

In This Chapter

- Why you care what your competitors are doing
- How to be your own Agent 007
- Using what you've learned to improve your offerings and protect your profits

You need to know what your competitors are up to. It's the second-most important factor driving your business.

Remember, it's not the most important factor—that should be what customers value because that drives what you offer. Maybe it should even come third, because what you want and need out of your professional life ranks pretty high, too. Arguably, though, competitor information by necessity has to come before goals. Competitors can kill dreams, even if those dreams are noble. Watch your back—or as a friend of mine puts it, "Know the sea you swim in."

Identify the Competition

Who are your competitors? I'm certain one name rises to your lips as soon as I ask that question. It's that guy who's always under-bidding you, marking down his goods to five cents under your price, or advertising that he'll honor your coupons as well as his own. You know he's competition, but let's look harder. Get a piece of paper and write down three headings: Current, Potential, and Substitute. Write that guy down under Current, and then add any others who come to mind.

The next area of concentration is the Potential. Are there rumors of new start-up businesses that might compete for a piece of your pie? The Internet has brought new competition to every local business. Maybe a business in another part of the country, or even overseas, is looking at expanding in your area. Might a business in a related field be eyeing your niche as a way to broaden its base of operations? If so, it needs to be placed under the Potential heading. Right, you say. All those things might be going on, and I would never know until it's too late.

Later in this chapter we'll look at ways to uncover potential competitors. For now, write down any potential threats you're aware of, or areas where you feel you could be vulnerable. Here's an example: If there are vacant stores up and down the street from you, those potential new tenants are potential competitors. The fact that you don't control those storefronts makes them a threat.

Mentor

Here's an early warning system for finding potential competitors: Attend venture-capital seminars and business start-up classes. You'll catch wind of possible competitors before they're even open for business.

What about competition from *substitutes?* To imagine substitutes, go back to the First Law of Marketing: People don't buy products; they buy solutions to problems. You don't buy a drill; you buy a hole. You don't buy burglar alarms; you buy home safety. Get the drift? If a person looking for your product might be lured away by a substitute, that's competition you need to be aware of. A burglar alarm salesman might face competition from a breeder of Rottweilers. Either can protect a home. Under the third heading on your page, write down your substitution suspects.

What?

Your **substitute competition** is any business that can fulfill your customer's need—solve his or her problem—using a different kind of product or service from the one you're offering. Substitute competition can be a more virulent threat than current or potential direct competitors.

Current, potential, and substitute competitors are all breathing down your neck. Your success depends on anticipating their actions and making the right response.

Anita Hecht's Life History Services faces a tough competitive picture, which might surprise you given that she's one of only 300 or so people practicing this profession in North America. Her toughest rivalry comes not from current competitors or potential ones, but from substitute products and services. Every "Creative Memories" consultant and every retailer of scrapbooking supplies, every one of dozens of books on journal-keeping and memoir-writing, competes for the dollar of the individuals who choose to preserve their memories. "Do-it-yourselfers" and those who supply them create substitute competition for those who sell professional services. (By putting this book in your hands, we're acting as substitute competition to marketing consultants.)

Mentor

One of the most important things to know about competitors is what your customers think of them. And even more important than that is what your customers think of you in comparison to them. That knowledge might just lead to an opportunity you've overlooked.

Why Knowledge of Your Competitors Matters to You

Knowledge of your competitors matters for a number of reasons. Here are just a few:

- If you're doing business in a flat market, then winning share from competition is your best growth strategy.
- Your competitors, the key benefits they offer, and the market segments they've chosen to pursue all have an impact on you; they influence your positioning (which we'll talk about in depth in Chapter 16).
- Most important of all: Learn from your competition's mistakes!

Studying competitors is an important course of action to take in running your business. Learn from their growth strategies, positioning, and media strategies. Take every opportunity to learn, including observing what they're doing right—not just gloating at their failures.

Really!

My emphasis on studying the competition should not be taken as an invitation to copy someone else's moves. Your competitors are as likely to be your peers as your teachers—don't assume they know more or have already found the right answers! You are both enrolled in the same course in this "business school of life." Your goal as a student is to find fuel for the fires of your own innovations, not formulas for success.

Get Ready to Go "Spying"

It's not really spying—it's really more intelligence gathering by various methods. Let's explore them.

Get Comfortable

The first thing you've got to do is to face your own attitudes about spying. I have met very few people in business whom I would call "unethical." Most of us are forthright, honest people who care about our reputations and our community and would never stoop to gossiping or spying in our personal lives. Why would our values change when we enter the business arena? Still, having values doesn't mean you can't play the game.

> CAUTION
>
> **Pitfall**
>
> Industrial espionage, such as stealing confidential lists or new product designs, is absolutely illegal. So is hiring an insider from a competitor and getting him or her to give you confidential or proprietary information. Using available information is the idea here, not stealing secrets. Please stay on the right side of the law as you pursue competitive information.

I'm not going to suggest you go through your competitor's trash or peer in the window when his accountant is doing the books. But the saying "All's fair in love and war" might stretch to include this situation. Don't you love what you're doing? Wouldn't you fight to defend it? If you're not comfortable with the basic nature of competition, get out now. You'll never survive the rough-and-tumble of business.

As you set out on this mission, remind yourself that competitor research is fair and necessary. Keep a positive attitude. Always be open about your company ties, if asked. Don't pressure the other guy in a way you wouldn't appreciate if the roles were reversed.

Clarify Your Goals

What *exactly* do you hope the knowledge gained will do for you? Will it guide new product development, affect positioning strategies, or assist in setting prices or making advertising plans? Be specific, and you'll save yourself wasted time and effort.

This is a good time to review your budget and deadline expectations for competitor research. Think about the tasks that may be involved and who in your company might be the right people to undertake them. You didn't think this was going to happen without time and effort on somebody's part, did you? Sometimes managers make the mistake of creating "unfunded mandates." Think about what resources can be allocated to this project, and start getting the people involved in the plan.

Make a Commitment to Organized Effort

Will you be doing store visits, interviews, or library research? We'll talk about these and other strategies for information gathering in the section coming up. After you've chosen your spy approach, choose your team and parcel out the tasks.

Think about who's going to maintain the files you create. Who will keep all the information organized and up-to-date?

Your competitor intelligence files will contain *company literature* (product literature and catalogs, website printouts, price lists, and annual reports), *published reports* (SEC filings, news articles, and business school case studies), and your own *internal intelligence* (notes from the salespeople and other staff members, management's observations about competitors strategic plans, and analysis of competitors' products, services, and financial status). Plan for a place to store these files and assign responsibility for keeping them current.

Mentor

If you market your offering to businesses rather than consumers, the recommendations in this chapter do double duty. You can use competitor research techniques to understand your customers as well as your competitors.

Spread the Results of Your Research

Since every area of business is affected, make sure every area stays informed. If you have a financial officer, a personnel manager, a technical supervisor, or quality-control people, make sure they're in the loop. They may have information you need, and they may need to know information you find out elsewhere. Involve them throughout the research process.

The fastest way to build a competitor profile is to involve everyone in your company. Ask individuals to subscribe to competitors' newsletters, go to their seminars, and talk to their peers in other companies. Make discussions of competitors part of staff meetings, and make sure everyone knows that you'd like to hear their observations and insights.

Competitor intelligence must be an ongoing activity, not an occasional one. Articles in the paper, the word on the street—news about your competitors is flowing all around you, so keep your eyes and ears open. It may take several years for a complete competitive picture to take shape in your files. Don't give up if, after a few months, it seems you have learned very little. For best results, intelligence-gathering must become part of your everyday routine.

Successful Sleuthing

When you start looking, you'll find sources of information near and far, obscure and obvious. They fall into two general camps: *published information* and *resource people.*

Published Information

Go to the published sources first; the homework will have you better prepared when you approach your resource people to fine-tune knowledge.

The main disadvantage of published information is that it's never very current. The advantage of the information is that it is accessible and tends to be of a quantifiable, statistical nature—unlike the rumors and gossip picked up from people.

Websites, trade directories, reference works, and periodicals contain valuable information about business and industry, some of it relevant to your business. Before the arrival of the World Wide Web, spying via published information meant skulking around the library. You would sashay up to the librarian and pop the question (no, not that one!). You'd ask, "Where would I find useful information about (fill in the blank)?" Depending on the question, that good person behind the reference desk would likely guide you to one of the following:

- **Atlases and almanacs.** Useful for geographical data such as population statistics for cities or regions, which can help you research competitors customer bases and distribution.
- **Business directories.** These include *Standard & Poor's*, *Dun & Bradstreet*, the *Thomas Register*, and so on. They're useful "snapshots" giving parent/subsidiary relationships, ballpark financial figures, estimates of sales, product and service lines, and so on.
- **Directories of professional associations.** Associations compile and disseminate industry data.
- **Periodical indexes.** Useful for locating business and management journals, which can be a good source for overview or background information.

But then the web came along. Now you can skulk in a vastly larger virtual library. The problem is, it's humongous and, given the state of its indexes, can resemble a library with the card catalog scattered all over the floor. You can look for each of the above resources online; on a good day, you'll find a vast store of useful information.

The collection of online information gets shuffled almost every day, so any resource I mention may be gone by the time you read this. Here's one I suspect will be around as long as the California university system survives. Check out the UCLA Rosenfeld Library of Competitive Intelligence. Here's the URL: www.anderson.ucla.edu/resources/library/libcoint.htm. You'll find resources in three categories: corporate profiles, industry environment, and socio-political environment. That should keep you busy for more than one rainy day.

Mentor

If there's a university near you, ask for the business school, find the marketing professors, and learn what information is stockpiled in their ivory towers. You should find a decent business library. Furthermore, many professors make a bundle of money on the side by consulting for companies, and as a result they have extensive knowledge and industry contacts. Tap the professors to tap into these resources.

Your state and federal government is hard at work collecting the information you need. Try the Bureau of Labor Statistics—you'll find a powerful storehouse of data about employment patterns, manufacturing trends, and more. Your state's Commerce Department is another source of data. The Securities Exchange Commission (SEC) has annual 10K filings and reports to shareholders.

Your local government, from the Chamber of Commerce to the city's economic development officer, deserves your attention as well. Don't forget the courts: liens, bankruptcies, environmental filings, and other court actions are public information.

A great deal of business and industrial information is available (at a price) from major market research vendors like InfoUSA. These vendors collect information on businesses and aggregate it for analysis using classification systems like *SIC* and more recently *NAICS*. You can purchase information on specific businesses including mailing addresses, employment and purchasing patterns, raw materials usage, and more.

What?

The **SIC** (Standard Industrial Classification) code had been the federal government's system of classifying industries in order to collect information about certain categories of business for many years. Trade journals, market researchers, and others used this system of codes to classify business market segments. But America's business activity has evolved considerably since SIC codes were defined. In the late 1990s, that system began to be phased out, and the **NAICS** (North American Industry Classification System) code set came into use. This classification scheme includes substantial revisions in the Retail and Information sectors of the SIC system to better describe economic activity in these sectors. NAICS also provides better comparability in statistics across Canada, the United States, and Mexico.

"Wait a minute," you're saying. "Do you mean businesses like Bob's Bottomless Boats are all plowing through this government data?" Remember, Bob's a smart guy. He took a different route: He found go-betweens. You can, too. If your banker is any good, he or she knows a lot about what data are available and where. Make your first phone call to your bank. For your second phone call, try that marketing professor at the nearest college. Maybe a graduate student is waiting to take you on as a case study or class project. Make your third phone call to your home and tell them you'll be there early. Taking on the bureaucracies might be more pleasant if you're making those calls away from the distractions of the office.

Two other sources of published information deserve your attention: your professional association and the general business press. Almost every industry has a national trade or professional association, and a major portion of its mission is to provide you with information. The magazines or newsletters they publish are just the start. Trade associations also conduct surveys and other types of statistical research. Contact yours and start asking what's available—and if you're not a member of a trade organization, look for one to join.

Many associations organize trade shows or seminars. Go. Pick up product brochures and talk to everyone in sight. These shows provide places for you or your employees to mingle with counterparts from other companies. If you're alert, useful information can be picked up just walking the floor and keeping your ears open. Training seminars also offer a prime opportunity for ethical espionage. The question-and-answer session is a chance to find competitors' weak spots.

By *general business press* I mean the local, regional, and national publications that cover the business scene. This would include *Inc. Magazine*, *Advertising Age*, *Business Marketing*, and regional variations like *Crain's Chicago Business* or *Corporate Report Wisconsin.* Your friend the librarian will help you find publications that are relevant for you, or you can search online for the American Association of Business Publications. The articles in these publications will be a source of information; the reporters who write them are an even better resource. A call or a flattering comment on a recent story, and you might be off and running with your new industrial spy.

Resource People

Competitors are one of your best sources of information about competition. Visit their premises. Take a tour of their production plant and go into stores. Subscribe to their newsletters. You can even attend speeches given by their top executives. Most speakers use examples from their own experience. If you pay attention you'll pick up insights into your competitor's management philosophy. If she's talking about flattening the management structure, that's a clue for you. If she's discussing patent application processes, that's a clue of a different nature.

If she doesn't give you the opportunity to hear her speak, try another angle. Is the company publicly held? Call up and ask for the investor relations department. Watch the information pour in when they think you're considering a stock purchase.

This may seem obvious, but competitors' advertising is a major clue to their strategic strengths and weaknesses. Observe and keep notes on their advertising media choices and creative themes. You'll gain insights into their marketing budgets and strategic thinking. Even the help-wanted ads offer a clue to which firms are growing.

Some of my most reliable resource people are my suppliers. In my industry it's the printers; in yours it might be the produce delivery drivers, the chemical guys, or whoever. They see competitors as often as they see you. Gossip is part of their stock in trade.

Mentor

Customer contact equals an opportunity for insight. Who in your company has contact with customers? Teach them to listen for reports of trouble at the other guy's establishment: complaints about products, price, and service, or reports of high turnover of employees, financial difficulties, problems with suppliers, quality control problems, obsolete technology—I think you get the idea.

Reporters carry news, and that includes information; make them your friends. Be of service. Present yourself as a ready source and you may be called on for commentary. (More about this in the chapter on publicity.) One good turn deserves another. Your availability with a quick quote on deadline could earn you an occasional answer about the business climate across the street.

Bankers, developers, and other members of the financial community are another group of people in the know. Office-space planners and real-estate agents know about comings and goings around town. Most are much too ethical to relay confidential information, but we're all more prone to gossip than we like to admit. General trends, and even quite specific information, can be obtained if you maintain friendly acquaintances with financial types.

But don't forget to look close to home for information! Under your own roof are employees who have parts of the puzzle, even if they don't realize it. Production people may have information from their peers in similar jobs at the competition. Your sales force is always hearing what the other guy has offered. Make time to gather information from the home team.

And last but not least, don't ignore your customers as a source of information about the competition! Consider holding a focus group. Have a moderator probe for attitudes, experiences, and impressions about the other guys.

CAUTION

Pitfall

What if you get caught? Don't be surprised if information gets back to the competition that you've been seeking information on them. That's why it is important that you do nothing unethical. If you've done nothing to be ashamed of, you can answer with a clear conscience, "I'm pursuing information in the best interest of my business." Remain professional in your pursuit of competitor intelligence, and you have nothing to fear!

What Was the Question?

It's hard to get a handle on the competitive environment. Gathering information can put you in the middle of a bunch of trees, looking for a forest. If you're having difficulty making this information meaningful to you, use the following worksheet to clarify your current position.

Start by trying to fill out the worksheet, ranking yourself and your three top competitors on a scale from one to five, with one being "doing a poor job at this," three being "not bad, not great," and five being "excellent." If you feel you just don't know enough to make a good guess, guess what? Now you know exactly what intelligence you're seeking! Look over the information sources available and decide where you're likely to find the most clues. Put on a trench coat and dark glasses—it's time to go sleuthing.

What questions do you want to be asking? Now might not be a bad time to review Chapter 6 on market research. If you're planning to perform some research, include a look at competitors. Kill several birds with that stone. I hope the following questions will get you thinking about the necessary information to learn. You'll probably want to rephrase these questions in order to use them on a competitor survey—I'll leave that detail work to you:

- What territory does the company sell in?
- Who are its prospective customers?
- How does it distribute its products/services?
- What is its price/value position? (Premium, low-cost, in-between?)
- What are its plans for growth? Market expansion? New products?
- Is the company well capitalized? Could it afford to start or survive a price war?
- What is the company's marketing strategy? What creative themes are apparent, what strategies for distributing the advertising message?

Worksheet

Aspects of Competition	Competitor Companies					You
	A	B	C	D	E	
	Rank 1 to 5. 1 = Poor, 5 = Excellent					
Market share	___	___	___	___	___	___
Consumer loyalty	___	___	___	___	___	___
Advertising	___	___	___	___	___	___
Sales force	___	___	___	___	___	___
Distribution	___	___	___	___	___	___
Product quality	___	___	___	___	___	___
Service/warranty	___	___	___	___	___	___
Pricing policies	___	___	___	___	___	___
Technology	___	___	___	___	___	___
Financial strength	___	___	___	___	___	___
Personnel	___	___	___	___	___	___
TOTAL SCORES:	___	___	___	___	___	___

Total the score in each column.

Where are the scores the highest?

Do you see areas in your business where you can correct a weakness?

Notes:

Competitor A name:

Competitor B name:

Competitor C name:

Competitor D name:

Competitor E name:

Using What You've Learned

To use what you've learned, first you have to find out what you've learned. You've collected piles of data. Now you need to turn that into information and absorb it until it becomes knowledge that will guide actions in response. How do you get there from here?

To turn data into action, follow this four-step process.

Step 1: Collect information.

Approach every available or appropriate source.

Step 2: Interpret the information.

One way is to make a list of questions as if you were surveying competitors directly, and then tabulate the answers as you would a market research questionnaire. Look for similarities and for significant differences, too. Review the worksheet in this chapter to get an idea of what questions to put on your list.

Step 3: Evaluate.

Weigh the urgency of the information gained. Decide who in your company will have insights, and who should be involved in planning your next steps. Hold discussions or review sessions; include business advisors as well as key personnel.

Step 4: Respond.

Decide a course of action; make it happen.

Really!

Need a money-saving strategy for responding to competition? Look at the potential for market segmentation. You and your competition are both trying to appeal to the same general market, but something about your offering makes it unique. What is that something? Target the segment of the larger market for whom that unique feature makes a big difference. These are the people most likely to buy from you. A segmentation strategy is an efficient way to keep your marketing budget pared to the bone.

Mind Your "Ps"

The "Four Ps," that is. Consider how you differ from competition as you think about each component. Competitor by competitor, write a short description touching on each P. How is their product or service different from yours? Are there place issues affecting you: location or distribution strategies used by competitors that threaten your success? What pricing strategy are they following? How do their promotions measure up?

What about the unofficial fifth P, People? The customers, competitors, employees, and suppliers who are under the influence of the "Four Ps"? People are an integral part of your competitors' business environment. How do you and your competition compare in terms of your people?

To conclude your description, answer the next questions as best you can from the knowledge gained:

- What is this competitor's key advantage or strength?
- What action is it taking to pursue that strength? How should you react?
- What are its weak points? What is it doing to correct that weakness? In the meantime, how can you exploit that weakness?

The notes you write now, in answer to these questions, will be very useful when we talk about positioning in Chapter 16.

Sample Tactics

Your best tactics will come from your own innovative thinking. But here are a few tried-and-true strategies, to get your thinking started:

- **Take the bypass.** Play up any differences, perceived or real, between you and the competition. Take pricing: If it's perceived as the premium product, maybe you should go for the best-value-on-a-budget position. Make direct comparisons. Show how you're better. Tell your story—point out your benefits that beat the competition. Find your unique difference and spread the word.

  If competitive differences are few, maybe service is the answer. If you both sell dog food, maybe you're the one who'll carry the bag out to the car at no charge. If you find something that matters to a prospective customer, you've got the makings of a strategy that will help make the sale.

- **Pick an under-exploited niche.** Where is there potential to serve a population that competitors have overlooked? It might pay off to review Chapter 7's advice on target marketing after you've researched your competition.
- **Find a management advantage.** Use experience, innovative thinking, and administrative skill to make your organization better than the competition. Maybe computer technology is the secret—networks to increase work group

productivity, or integrated estimating and order-fulfillment software. Look at the different areas of your business and think, "How could tinkering with this system serve my customers better?"

- **Move over: We're coming through.** Direct competition is—well, it's direct. It gets you where you're going in a hurry, although it might not get you a reputation as Mister Nice Guy. Buy a lot of ads and get your message out there. Make yourself look like the Big Man on Campus. Use what you've learned through competitor research to support your position. (Keep in mind, if you adopt this strategy, you're going to need some ammunition to pull it off. You need a real competitive advantage and a big advertising budget.)

The Best Strategy: Rely on Your Strengths

Use these strategies to respond to competition—and watch them use these strategies to respond to you. Build a defensive line against counter-attacks. Where does the bulk of your profit come from? (Go back to Chapter 5's discussion of customer profiling on the basis of recency, frequency, and money spent, if you don't know the answer to that one.) Protect the profitable areas of your business, even if it means withdrawing from some of your more experimental developments. Give proven sellers the support they need to remain profit-generators, whether that means pushing them through advertising or devoting resources to improving their weak features.

> CAUTION
>
> **Pitfall**
>
> Don't overextend yourself responding to competitors' moves, or you'll be letting them drive your business as well as their own.

The Least You Need to Know

- Remember, you are under attack from three sides: your current competitors, potential entrants to the game, and substitute products or services that could lure customers away from your offering.
- Your competitors are your mentors—everything you learn from observing them will help you improve your business.
- Communicate about competition throughout your company and update your competitor files at regular intervals.
- Adopt a competitive strategy that plays to your strengths and protects the most profitable areas of your business.

Part 3 Your Marketing Mix: Product, Price, Place, and Promotion

In this part, I'll show you how to really understand your offering, whether it's product- or service-oriented. How do you create new products? Where are the emerging opportunities? What do service marketers need to know, and what special tips might help those of you in non-profit situations? It's all in this section.

How do you price your product fairly and not lose your shirt? How do you manage the "place" issues of distribution strategies and location decisions? What's your angle on promotions? You'll find chapters devoted to each in the upcoming section.

To the customer, the distinction between each of these "Ps" is meaningless, but from your point of view, each is worthy of special focus. Let's enter the forest and tap into each of these four trees (to keep that syrup analogy flowing).

Chapter 9

Product Strategies

In This Chapter

- Your product's place in the tapestry of commerce
- Issues affecting product strategy
- The impact of product life cycle on product strategy
- The support your product needs to succeed
- Some product strategies to try

I have in my pocket a little round lump of wheat flour, liver, salt, and garlic. It's called a Charlee Bear Treat, and in spite of its humble nature, it's an indispensable part of my daily life.

That lump in my pocket is a product, a bundle of solutions to my dog relationship problems. It's more than a tasty and non-crumbly dog-cracker, just as a BMW is more than transportation. To begin this chapter, let's get specific. What exactly is a product? And why do you need a strategy for yours?

Products: What Are We Really Talking About?

A *product*, at its simplest, can be defined as the tangible thing you buy. It's the milk you picked up on the way home.

Of course, that's just the tip of the iceberg. Above the water line, so to speak, are the tangible features that make up the core product. Under the water line are deeper layers, including the expanded product and the product concept. Let's look closer at each.

Each product has a core set of benefits that make it desirable to its consumers. One thing usually drives their desire for this product above others, and that is the product's key benefit. When you want a ⅜" hole and I sell a ⅜" drill, it's my drill's ability to make your hole exactly that size that you're buying. My product has a tangible feature that delivers satisfaction of your particular need. That's what marketers call the *core product.*

Mentor

For the duration of this chapter, when I say *products,* I mostly mean products (tangible items people buy), not "products and services." I'll be dealing with services at length in Chapter 10.

The *expanded product* is all the stuff that comes with the drill. The expanded product might include the other drill bits packaged with it, the six-month warranty on the motor, and the new cordless rechargeable base. The expanded product is the exact mix that makes this drill package different from the other drills on the market and usually establishes the customer's price/value perception of the offering.

What?

The **core product** is the item itself—the thing that provides the core benefit sought by the buyer. The **expanded product** includes things like extra parts or a warranty—the exact mix of tangible accessories and intangible product support included with that purchase. The **product concept** is the "big idea"—the market niche you want to fill by offering the product.

So what does that leave for the *product concept?* The long-range perspective. The product concept starts with what you imagined at its conception—the customer needs you hoped to satisfy, the empty niche you hoped to fill. It looks beyond the core and expanded product to address your plans for this product throughout its life cycle. The product concept includes the environment of brand and service quality you build *around* your products.

What Product Strategy Is All About

What you put into your products in each of these three aspects makes up product strategy. Take that "need for a ⅜"" hole, meet it with a well-built cordless drill, support it with a brand name and a good warranty, and you have a solid product strategy—if you're a tool manufacturer.

Let's fly up and look at the big picture—the way products (and services) fit together in the marketplace. Imagine you're a traveling salesman and you are just arriving on Planet Earth.

The Marvelous Tapestry of Commerce

All around you, there is a marvelous tapestry of people offering products and services to other people. Businesses are selling things to other businesses. Some of the things are finished goods being sold to distributors who help get them to the end users. And there are other businesses selling raw materials, machinery to help turn raw materials into finished goods, or services like personnel training or bookkeeping services that help businesses turn raw materials into finished goods better.

Mentor

Product strategy is one of the elements in your marketing mix, the ingredients marketers call the "Four Ps." In the chapters coming up, I'll be covering the other Ps: Price, Place, and Promotion. A number of issues affect product strategy, and I'll explore them in a minute.

Meanwhile, retail businesses are taking the products and services assembled out of all that and selling them to end users. I'd call them *consumers*, but not everybody who buys something consumes it—just ask the moms who buy gummi worms and bubble-gum tape for their children.

These offerings are of three basic types: convenience, shopping, and specialty products. Why do you care which of these categories your product fits into? Because that affects product strategy. You should manage a convenience product much differently than you do a specialty product. What marketing strategies do these categories suggest?

- **Convenience products.** To fit the definition of a convenience product, an item must be 1) inexpensive, 2) needed regularly, and 3) easily replaced by a substitute. If you sell a convenience product, distribution is the key to your health. Focus your product strategy on making your offering available in more places, at more times of the day.
- **Shopping products.** Shopping products are typically those that project an image of ourselves to others, like our clothes and accessories, but aren't such a major investment as a specialty product. Shopping products have easily recognized differences that project "cachet," like brand names, or are important for

other reasons. Focus your product strategy on keeping your product quality high. Design your marketing programs to project the right brand image.

- **Specialty products.** Specialty products are the ones consumers hope and save for, like cars, major appliances, or vacation packages. Buying a specialty product, because it's a big investment, practically requires that consumers do some research comparing features, brands, vendors, payment plans, and so on. Consumers spend time and effort before making up their minds to buy. Make your product strategy match your specialty product by offering detailed information and mixing your "Four Ps" to highlight exclusivity, quality, and desirability.

Really!

How can you tell which category your product fits into? If your customers would be unlikely to drive very far to find it before settling for a substitute, your product fits the convenience category. If your customers need to make comparisons to choose the right products, you've got a shopping product on your hands. If your product is purchased only infrequently, and requires significant investment and research before buying, like a car or a home gym, it's a specialty product.

Businesses Buy Products, Too

Business-to-business products can also be broken down in the same categories. (Purchasing managers tend to shop for paper clips like convenience products, and for a new color photocopier like a specialty product.)

Mentor

No matter what type of product you sell, there should be lots of interaction between product strategy and other strategies as they're developed. Don't make firm decisions as you read this chapter—just jot a few notes, and speed on for a look at the other components of the marketing mix.

What all the products offered on the business side have in common is this: The need for them derives from the demand for something else. A picante-sauce manufacturer doesn't buy tomatoes because he wants a BLT for lunch. He buys tomatoes as a raw ingredient in the process of making sauce.

Purchases by businesses fall into one of these classifications:

- **Raw materials,** like pigments headed for the paint factory.
- **Component parts,** like valves destined for a water-heater manufacturer.

Pitfall

Hey you! With the service offering! Thought you could skip this chapter? Service organizations benefit from examining their offerings from a product perspective. Slow down and give this chapter a chance. You might learn something.

- **Process materials,** like the chemicals used to clean silk screens down at the screen printer's shop. (Process materials are necessary to the end product but don't actually become part of it.)
- **Manufacturing installations,** like the bottling line the picante sauce manufacturer must purchase and upgrade from time to time. (These are usually custom-designed and installed.)
- **Accessory equipment,** like photocopiers and computers, that assist the process of manufacturing but aren't custom-made.
- **Operating supplies,** which include items like pencils, copier paper, and floppy disks.
- **Services,** which can be broken down into distribution and consulting services.

And that covers most of what's going on in the marketplace.

Time for an Example Already! Charlee Bear Treats

Charlee Bear Farms markets a convenient, healthful, all-natural dog treat. It looks like an oyster cracker and can be carried in your pocket without crumbling.

The product's small size and low-calorie health aspects provide unique benefits for use as a training treat. "People love to give their dogs treats. This gives them a taste and that's all," said president Fritz Findley.

The introduction of Charlee Bear treats helped to create a new niche in pet-food stores and supermarkets—gourmet/health food for pets.

Mentor

Is the Charlee Bear treat a convenience, shopping, or specialty product? Because of the emphasis on the healthfulness of the product, I say this is a shopping product. It appeals to customers who make comparisons to choose the right products and will search out the best nutritional options for their pets.

One of Fritz's triumphs centers on his understanding of the importance of packaging. Charlee Bear Farms positions itself as a small company run by dog lovers, dedicated to enhancing the relationship between people and their dogs, with an open and honest attitude toward customers and the world.

Mentor

Charlee Bear Farm's *core product* appeals to dogs, who love the treats for their taste and satisfying crunch. The Charlee Bear *expanded product* includes its attributes that appeal to humans—the treat's tiny size, resistance to crumbling, price point, and brand image. Charlee Bear's *product concept* covers the company's product quality, packaging, distribution, openness to customer feedback, and so on.

How the product itself is packaged is a perfect example. Each unit—there are three sizes and three flavors—is packaged in clear plastic bags or canisters. That's of great benefit to the customer, who can see the crumbs (not many) on the bottom and the air (not much) on top. You don't see pet food giants being this open about their products.

Inside each clear package of Charlee Bear treats is a label that lists the ingredients (few and all-natural) and a newsletter that tries to start a two-way conversation. Charlee Bear encourages communication from the end users of the products. They even like to hear what the dogs have to say.

Where does Charlee Bear Farms' product line fit in the tapestry of commerce? The company offers what I would consider a shopping product, not because it projects a brand image that reflects well on me, but because the product has recognizable differences that are important to me and my dog. I will breeze past the dog-treat aisle at my grocery and drive over to the pet-supply store to pick up my Charlee Bears.

Your Goal: To Find Your Place

Sit back and think about all this for a minute: The truck bearing industrial coatings passing the photocopy-repairman on the highway as the mail-order packages are coming on the UPS truck and the sauce-bottling equipment upgrade is being installed. Makes your head swim, doesn't it?

And somewhere in all that you've got to find your niche, or your suite of niches. Where do you fit in the tapestry? Where you are and where your customers are affect how you design your product strategy.

In the following worksheet, find your place in the fabric of commercial activity. You should be able to locate your product or service somewhere on this chart. Circle it. Keep it in mind as you continue to learn about product strategies in this chapter.

If you're having trouble with this concept, practice on Charlee Bear. Circle the word *Shopping* at the bottom of the left leg. Charlee Bear sells a shopping product to consumers. Now, think about the suppliers who sell organizational offerings to Charlee Bear. Where would they fall on this chart? All over the right leg. The fellow who brings the wheat flour and liver extract is selling *raw materials*. The company that supplies the clear cylinders for packaging and the printer who brings the little newsletters to slip into the cylinders are providing *component parts.* And the ad gal who created the newsletter sells the consulting service of *marketing.*

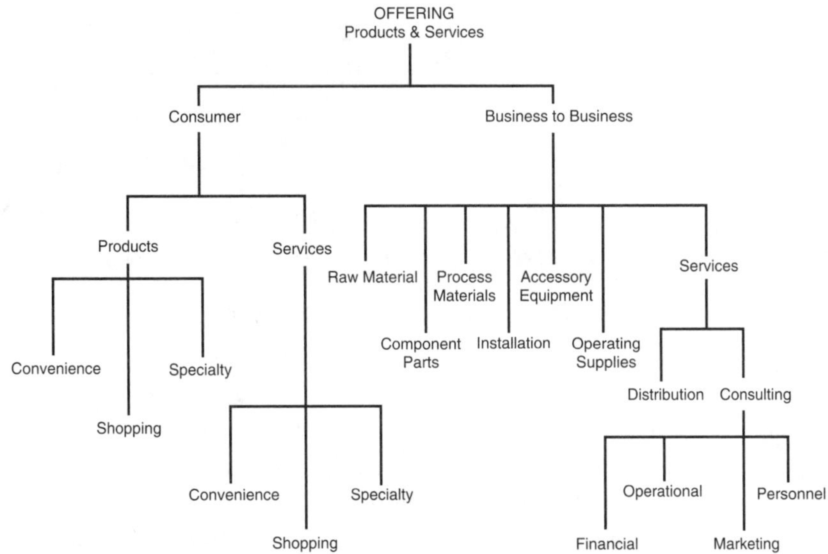

The Tapestry of Commerce. Where is your product or service offering on this chart? Circle it.

All are influenced by their place in the scheme of things. All have a core product, expanded product, and product concept. All of the companies involved in this scenario have product strategies in place. And so do you.

To Everything There Is a Season: The Product Life Cycle

The product life cycle is one of those gross over-simplifications that instructors use because you have to start somewhere and because a lot of mass-market products actually follow this pattern pretty closely, resulting in good teaching examples. The following figure shows a typical product life cycle. Do you know where in the cycle your offerings are?

A product begins as an original idea, a spark fanned by your understanding of customers. If your idea is good, your timing's right, and you've been good in a few past lives, your product will enter a growth phase. That's very nice, but others will notice your good fortune, and competitive products will soon intrude upon your happy scene.

Product life cycle.

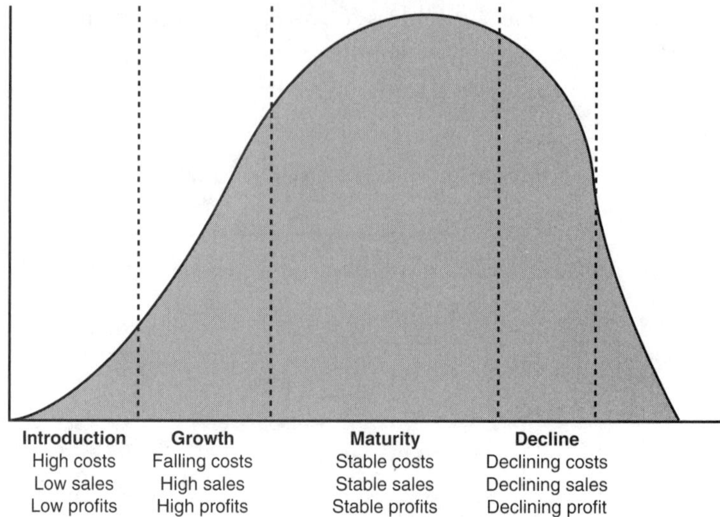

Now you enter a difficult time. Your attention is drawn away from your customers and focused on competitors instead. (Sound like adolescence?) The rivalry stimulates you to tinker with product strategy. You might respond with a focus on sub-segments, or add something "new and improved." This phase of a product's development, where you are challenged to hang on to what was good in the growth phase, can go on for decades if you manage it right. (Sound anything like maturity?)

Eventually most products will go into decline. You must choose one of several ways to put the product quietly to bed. You may decide to scale down but stay in production, catering to the remaining buyers for your product. Blacksmiths aren't as common as they once were, but most rural areas still support one or two. You may sell the product line to someone who values its assets. Or you might simply cease production in a timely fashion.

> **Pitfall**
>
> When is a decline not a decline? Not every drop in sales indicates the end of your product's life cycle. Sometimes poor sales are indications of other problems, like mix-ups in the distribution channels or activities of competitors. If a temporary downslide in sales occurs, treat it as a warning sign, not a death knell.

Your strategy as a company might involve being a market leader like Charlee Bear Farms, bringing new products on line early. Or you might prefer the more conservative "me-too" position, entering more mature markets, as A Life of Faith Dolls has. You can even make money on products that are in a declining phase, with the right price/value combination. Bob's Bottomless Boats still sells canoes, even though kayaks are currently more popular. What's important is this: You should have products spread over several phases of the curve, to avoid uneven peaks and valleys in your sales and profits.

Who Tries New Products?

Some people by nature will try every new product that comes along. Others take a more conservative approach. Marketers take these degrees of venturesomeness quite seriously. Here are the groups they've defined:

- **Innovators.** Innovators are likely to be young, but financially stable—able to take risks. They are typically well educated, have high confidence in their ability to think for themselves, and follow no one's lead.
- **Early adopters.** Early adopters are less free-wheeling than the innovators but are still more likely to lead than to follow. They are particularly important to the success of new products because they tend to popularize products through their acceptance. Once early adopters begin to buy your product, it's moved from birth to growth stage in the product life cycle.
- **Majority.** The majority shares certain psychographic factors: They tend to be conservative, more traditional, and less willing to take risks. They respond to social pressure and are concerned with the opinions of their peers.
- **Latecomers.** Latecomers are the last to take up the product. They tend to resist change and to cling hardest to tradition. Once they adopt your product, it's a wake-up call to you—it's time to take stock.
- **Nonadopters.** Nonadopters will never buy your product, and you need to know why. Their objections might just inspire your next new product idea.

CAUTION

Pitfall

Nonadopters will never buy your product, so you can ignore them, right? Wrong. It might interest you to know the reason they won't buy. Maybe a product that addresses that reason will be your next new innovation. People who never bought your chocolate pies because of the calories will become your best early adopters if you bring out a new low-cal version.

Characteristics of the various groups provide the basis for target marketing. Study how your current products have moved through the adoption and diffusion process, and you'll gain insight into how your new products should be marketed. (Say, does that give you an idea for a customer research project?)

Your New Product Development

If I'm doing my job right, you're getting the idea that developing a new product every now and then is a good thing. It keeps the bond between you and your customers evolving, which is a good thing in just about any relationship.

So what steps can your company take to ensure you have new products in the pipeline? Establish a *new products committee.* If your organization is a one-man show, you're just going to have to fill several chairs.

> **What?**
>
> In big companies, the heads of the various functional departments sit on the **new products committee.** That means there will be a marketing manager, a product manager, and an entrepreneurial venture manager, someone who can hold the new product development process to the company's overall vision. Even if it's just you filling all the chairs, make sure your new product ideas pass muster from all three perspectives.

Most companies that sell products make a new product development process part of their ongoing operations. This process is essentially a series of filters. The final products you bring to market will be the few that manage to pass successfully through each filter. I'll just list the steps (filters) here, and suggest you read more on this topic if your company relies heavily on bringing new products to market.

1. Brainstorm ideas
2. Screen ideas
3. Analysis
4. Development and testing
5. Marketing
6. Result: success

> **Really!**
>
> One of the ways to give old products new sales potential is to find new uses for the product. When Avon found that consumers believed Skin So Soft lotion repelled mosquitoes, it began marketing the lotion as a dual-action product. Arm & Hammer did the same thing when it began marketing baking soda as a refrigerator deodorant. Could your product find new life through new uses?

A successful product might come from anywhere; it might be a brand new concept, like VCRs and microwave ovens, or it might be a simple repositioning of an existing product, like Avon's Skin So Soft. In either case, most successful products share certain characteristics. There's something new about them that provides a relative advantage over anything previously available, and they are easy to try and easy to use.

The easier it is to try a new product, the more likelihood it has for success. It's not that you can't introduce a hard-to-try product, but you'll have to work harder. My favorite dog treat is an example of an easy-to-try product. Kayaks are an example of a hard-to-try one. (You have to get over the thought you might look silly figuring out how to even get into a kayak.) If the product is easily divided into small samples, like pizza tasting at the grocery store, it's much easier to launch.

Why Products Fail

Bad things happen to good people. Bad things happen to good products, too. Some products fail because of inherent weaknesses in their design—weaknesses someone should have caught well before the product launch. Others fail because of factors no planning could have revealed. The inventors of typesetting equipment were making better and better typesetters. It's not their fault that inexpensive personal computers and desktop-publishing software came along.

A product can fail because it doesn't solve real needs. You may build a better mousetrap, but if no one has mice, who cares? It might fail if it's the right product but it comes at the wrong time. Luxury products are particularly susceptible to timing problems. But one of the biggest factors in product failure has nothing to do with the product.

A weak company can kill a good product. If the company fails to support the product with internal planning or doesn't follow through with sufficient advertising or distribution, that product may fail.

> **Pitfall**
>
> Too much success can kill a product, too! If a company is unable to keep up with a successful product launch, ka-*boom!* Down it goes. Supply must meet demand or you're in trouble. Likewise order processing, customer service, and shipping can trip and fall under the strain of handling demand. Be ready for a best-case scenario—or it might turn into your worst nightmare.

What's a Poor Marketer to Do

No guts, no glory. It's just another way of talking about risk and reward. Are you feeling conservative? Know you should keep new products in the pipeline, but fear the costs and the energy expenditure? For you, I recommend the no-guts approach. Look at your current product line and try a line-extension strategy. Listen to your customers, improve a facet of a current product, and position it to excite new interest—if you can.

On the other hand, you may have a truly innovative product idea in mind—something the world has never seen before. The most successful new products are those that open up whole new frontiers. That they involve risk should come as no surprise. The greatest potential danger facing you is the competitors who will move in when they see what a good thing you've got. You may not survive long enough to recoup your development costs.

If you're in this position, a good offense is your best defense. Capture the potential market as thoroughly as possible with low pricing, aggressive promotion, and thorough distribution. You'll own the market before competitors can get their share.

Standing by Your Product

Associated with every product are intangibles that are as important to what the customer buys as the core product. Your brand image, return policies, delivery and installation services, post-sale support, and corporate ethics are all factors in the purchase decision.

The Buzz About Branding

There's nothing new under the sun, but the way people have been talking about branding, you'd think it was the next massive oil deposit waiting to be tapped. And in a way it is. Branding provides the push that propels products and services into consumers' hearts like Cupid's arrows. A brand is made up of a complex mix of components that together create an emotional feeling about your brand. By encouraging an emotional attachment with your brand, you can break through the clutter of products and advertising messages. Branding is such an important concept that we'll go into it in much greater depth. Just hang on until Chapter 16.

Support Every Sale

Marketing doesn't end when the goods are sold. Remember it costs a lot to get a new customer. The second sale to that customer costs much less to get. If you don't keep those new customers coming back, you're working harder than you have to. Your customer service after the sale has a lot to do with getting those subsequent, highly profitable sales.

A generous return policy will almost always work to your advantage. The occasional jerk may get away with murder (one florist I know complains about customers who don't water plants for three months and then ask to return the "defective" product), but the loyalty your generosity earns from good customers will pay off.

You might augment your return policy with a warranty. A warranty is a legally binding guarantee of the manufacturer's responsibility for the product after it is delivered to the customer. Knowing that a product comes with a warranty makes us human beings more comfortable buying it. It's insurance that says if this thing doesn't work, we can get our money back.

Effective marketers create customer satisfaction by using plain English to make their warranties easy to understand. Lands' End, the catalog company, simply says, "Guaranteed. Period."

Mentor

Customer service can give you a real competitive advantage when the products themselves have little to distinguish them. Your offer of free delivery, gift wrapping, or installation can be the point of difference that earns you the sale.

Product Ethics

Somewhere in your product strategy, take an ethical stand. Make sure that you pursue product safety, durability, and earth-friendliness. Don't paint your kiddy cars with lead paint. Engineer your product to have a decent life expectancy. Consumers are wary of planned obsolescence. In fashion accessories, a short life span is acceptable; in water heaters, it is not.

Produce and package the product with concern for the environment. There are many ways social responsibility comes into the product strategy. Ignore these concerns at your own risk.

How All This Adds Up to a Product Strategy

It takes different strategies to promote a product at different stages of its life cycle. Here are a few suggestions to get you started:

- **The introduction stage.** Typically at this stage, the whole product concept is new. You'll probably need to use promotions to create demand for the whole category of products, not just your offering. Use sales, samples, and other techniques that will encourage first-time trial. Focus on innovators and early adopters.
- **Growth.** Now positioning becomes really important because you're starting to need to differentiate yourself from the competition. Use creative advertising to build your brand image. Explore broader distribution strategies.

- **Maturity.** Reward loyalty—customer loyalty and especially dealer/retailer loyalty. You need champions on the front line who will keep consumers interested in your product.
- **Decline.** Stay alert to marketplace trends and take control where you can. With the right price/value combination, you can make money even on products that are in decline. Bundle your declining products so they ride piggyback on your stronger offerings.

There are a few strategies you can try before you call the liquidators or the bankruptcy court. Apply the "Three Rs": Rejuvenate your product by Repositioning and Relaunching it. If you can find new uses for your product, you've found a new life. Just think of all the new uses Arm & Hammer Baking Soda began marketing a few years ago. One century's baking ingredient is the next century's all-purpose deodorant.

> **Mentor**
>
> You could rejuvenate your product not by changing its makeup but by changing the feature being promoted. An amusement park might relaunch its product by selling the excitement of its rides to children, but the value of its all-day family admission ticket in its advertising to adults.

Okay, so how do you take all these musings and make a product strategy out of it? Let's remind ourselves what we're talking about here. Earlier I stated that "The purpose of marketing is to stimulate buying exchanges in which both buyer and seller profit in some way." What your product is, from its features to its warranty, must be designed to increase that buyer's sense of satisfaction with the purchase. Product strategy is one of the elements in your marketing mix.

The Least You Need to Know

- Find your product's niche in the tapestry of commerce.
- Keep in mind the issues affecting product strategy.
- Be aware of your product's life cycle; keep new products coming along or reinvigorate older ones.
- Support your product with branding, warranties, service, and ethical corporate behavior.
- Remember that a product strategy is part of your marketing mix.

Chapter 10

When Your Product Is a Service

In This Chapter

- How services are like products, and how they're different
- What services consumers and businesses buy
- How to make your service offering the best it can be
- Advice on developing new services
- Some thoughts for nonprofit service marketers

In earlier chapters, you met Kalika, an immigrant to this country who runs a juice cart on the campus near my home. From her cart she dispenses a variety of freshly squeezed juices, blended "smoothie" drinks.

Is she selling a product or a service? Both.

The clue to the service component of her business lies in the phrase "freshly squeezed." She brings you the product, peaches and raspberries, but she adds value by processing those raw materials into the form you like, a delectable juice drink.

Restaurants (and that's what Kalika's cart really is) make an excellent example of an offering halfway down the continuum from pure product to pure service. Restaurants provide a tangible product. But the services they provide, from food preparation to serving at table, add the value that distinguishes one restaurant from the next. At the far end of the spectrum are services that leave no trace, the intangible services like pumping out your septic system or defending you at trial.

Let's take a look at that continuum and what makes a service different from a product.

What Makes a Service Unique?

Pop Quiz.

Question: What's the First Law of Marketing?

Answer: People don't buy products; they buy solutions to problems. Looked at this way, there is no difference between a product and a service. Both are simply vehicles for delivering solutions.

But anybody can tell you a service is not the same as a product. When you buy a service, you don't get to take something home in a box. And that fact of life brings with it a host of issues for marketers.

Shades of Gray: How to Tell Products from Services

Services have characteristics that set them apart from products.

- **Products are tangible; services are intangible.** Buyers can't see, feel, smell, hear, or taste a service before they agree to buy it. When they purchase services they have to purchase a promise of satisfaction, and that requires a leap of faith that purchasing a product does not.

- **Services can't be separated from their providers.** This fact affects you in fundamental ways. Most services are delivered by people. To buy a service, you must come in contact with the one who provides it—you watch Kalika as she spins the blender to make your smoothie; you make small talk in the chair while the stylist cuts your hair. Naturally, you come to believe that that person brings something special to the process. A smoothie from another cart might taste a little different. A haircut by someone else might ruin the next month of your life.

- **Services are perishable.** Services provided by people can't be stored. Suppose you're a dentist, and you're expecting a patient at 10 A.M. When that patient blows you off, it's too late to sell 10 A.M. to someone else. When the plane takes off with empty seats, they can never be sold again. Your service is not like a product that will sit on the shelf waiting for a buyer.

There are several strategies for dealing with perishability. You might perfect your ability to forecast demand (booking appointments well in advance) or use tiered pricing strategies such as early-reservation discounts or a no-show charge.

Really!

The "Four Utilities"(See Chapter 4) can help you see what people really value about services. The Form utility has to do with the way the service is rendered. The Place concerns where the service takes place; a delivery service that picks up and delivers adds a lot of place utility. The Time utility comes from having the service available when the customer wants it. And the Possession utility involves pricing your service right and going out of your way to ensure customer satisfaction. If you know what customers value, you're more likely to market your services successfully.

The Marketing Mix for Services

How can you use the tools at your disposal, your product (actually your service), your place, your price, and your promotions to cope with the unique situation facing you as a marketer of services?

To deal with intangibility, use a product strategy. Try designing your offering to include satisfaction guarantees. You can plan your promotional strategy to make service seem tangible, too. Your promotions can feature testimonials and demonstrations—these give customers a chance to encounter the service before they purchase. Promotions help you to drum up demand.

The inseparability of service and provider is a tough riddle to solve. Some respond by attempting to make the service uniform, so that anyone can step into the role of service provider and deliver the same outcome. When Kalika needs help at her cart, she trains her helpers in the art of making smoothies "Kalika-style."

Others customize. If each offering is completely tailored to a customer's needs, the contribution of the individual providing the service has less impact on the service delivered. After all, the customers are defining the service they seek.

Pitfall

Price discounts are great for some businesses, but not for professional services! In some fields, consumers rely on price as an indication of quality. If you're in a consulting field, like law and accounting, for example, don't use promotions that offer discounts. When price is the main indicator of quality, price discounts send the wrong message.

Of course, if you do a terrific job of executing that service, you score a lot of points with each customer you serve. Either standardizing or customizing could be a potential strategy for marketing your services. But, right now, I want to ask you, who are you serving? Where will you set up camp in the landscape of service possibilities?

Exploring the Landscape of Service Providers

How you sell your services is, of course, dependent on who you are selling to. Advertisers use different styles and approaches depending on whether they are selling products or services to consumers or to businesses. Consumers can use a lot more emotional and psychological appeals than businesses. If you're selling services to business, you're going to have to be more direct and more practical. In both cases you're still selling solutions, but the benefits are different. Let's look at both.

Serving Consumers: When a Service Is Like a Product

Service retailers sell directly to end users. Kalika and your hair stylist are in retail. The person who pinstripes your Corvette (okay, Ford Taurus) is also in retail. Your plumber serves both consumers and businesses, and you can bet he sells different services in a different style to each. If a business person is buying for himself, he is just another consumer, although he could be a big one.

For retailers, big and small, it makes sense to understand the following categories, introduced in Chapter 9. Those categories apply to consumer services as easily as products: They are *convenience*, *shopping*, and *specialty*.

> **What?**
>
> Services, like products, can be divided into three types: **convenience** (an inexpensive recurring need), **shopping** (a service that requires evaluation before purchase), and **specialty** (rarely purchased, and usually expensive). A convenience service calls for a different marketing strategy than a shopping service or a specialty service.

What makes a service a convenience? Just like a convenience product, a convenience service is typically inexpensive, the need recurs on a regular basis, and you don't care much where you buy it. A car wash is a convenience service. So is a shoeshine.

Shopping services require more involvement than convenience services. As a shopper, you do care where you get them. You want to be able to compare price, style, and value. Hiring a maid service for monthly housecleaning qualifies as a shopping service. You care about finding a reputable firm; you want the job done well; you want to pay a fair price and not more. You would probably interview several potential firms before you chose one for this personal service.

Specialty services, like specialty products, are rarely purchased, are expensive, and require a high degree of consumer involvement. The person you hire to put a new roof on your house is offering a specialty service. The architect you hire for your new custom-built home is even more so.

Most home repair services begin as either a shopping or a specialty service. Once you choose a shopping service, like your maids or even your plumber, it can become a convenience service if you are satisfied with how the job was done. Plumbing problems may not happen every day, but they happen often enough to make a reliable plumber a convenience. Specialty services are too rare to move into the convenience category. Even if you are wildly happy with your roofer, you won't need that service again for, hopefully, 20 to 30 years.

Does one of these categories describe your business? Determining which one will directly affect how you assemble your marketing mix. Obviously, a car wash uses different strategies to price and promote than an architect.

Serving Retailers: When a Service Has a Feeder Function

Retailers need a very special kind of service. They need to get their merchandise selection from distributors. You may or may not want to become a distributor, but if you sell a service other than consulting—which I'll talk about after exploring distribution—you need to know what services a distributor can provide.

Pure distribution consists of breaking bulk, assembling lots, and creating assortments. You wouldn't believe how much actual service is coiled in these functions. Retailers could be product poor without the services of distributors, and consumers could be deprived of lots of variety.

I got my introduction to distribution working with a company that distributes imprintable sportswear (that's T-shirts and sweat pants) to the screen-printing and embroidery trades. I'll use them as an example.

First, the bulk-breaking function: This company buys truckloads of products from manufacturers. Semi loads from Fruit of the Loom and others show up every day and are emptied into a vast warehouse. From that stockpile, smaller quantities are picked to fill orders for cases of sweatshirts, dozens of T-shirts, and

> **Really!**
>
> Given that the distributor is actually buying the product he distributes from the manufacturer, it may surprise you to be told that the manufacturer is also buying a service from the distributor. How's that? Think of it this way. The distributor's service relieves the manufacturer of the headache of trucking the goods around the nation and relieves the retailer of spending time hunting merchandise.

even single units. To perform this function, the distributor takes ownership and assumes the risks, such as spoilage, storage cost, and prediction of demand. In return, he earns the right to charge retailers a higher price than he pays the manufacturers for the goods.

The second function is assembling lots. When the Green Bay Packers won Super Bowl XXXI, T-shirt printers all over the Midwest wanted green and gold active wear by the gross. Even the big retail chains got in on the action, placing orders for hundreds of thousands of Packer-imprinted green and gold shirts. My distributor rose to the challenge! He met the demand by working with manufacturers and other distributors from coast to coast.

> CAUTION
>
> **Pitfall**
>
> Distributors make it possible for their customers (often end users or retailers) to have products they want, when and where they want them. But distributors are middlemen. If they cease to provide a real economic value, they are soon squeezed out by the intense competition around them. Keeping everyone happy can be a challenge for a distributor.

The distributor's third function is creating assortments. Let's say it's early August. A screen printer has taken in orders this week for three cases of orange T's (assorted sizes) for a Halloween fun-run, 36 red and black windbreakers for the new high school football team, and 200 polo shirts for the employees of a restaurant chain. He faxes the distributor his order, and my guy pulls and ships the required merchandise from his warehouse full of goods.

That's breaking bulk, assembling lots, and creating assortments—distribution in a nutshell. The other services that businesses buy are lumped under the heading of "consulting."

Serving as a Consultant: When Service Wears a White Hat

Consultants don't always come to the rescue in the nick of time, but they are individuals or firms who offer expertise that a client needs now, but only for a specific project or for a limited time. If they needed these services on a continual basis, they'd create a staff position instead. But they don't, and so they hire consultants to deliver those services. Repair services fall in this category whether they sell to consumers or businesses.

Remember, we buy solutions to problems. Solutions are what consultants provide, and they provide them in four general areas: finances, operations, marketing, and personnel. A temporary help agency provides bodies to help a client cope while staff are on vacation. A human resources consultant helps the personnel department write a new manual. A graphic designer helps marketing make a new brochure. A consulting engineer helps reduce workplace injuries by redesigning the assembly line, thereby improving operations. An electrician repairs a faulty circuit breaker. An accountant helps find the bookkeeper who embezzles—and a lawyer helps prosecute him. These are all consultants providing services that help solve customers' problems.

Does one of these categories describe your business? Whether you are a retailer, distributor, or consultant will have an impact on your marketing activities. Retailers, for example, have to keep themselves in the public eye, using the media as often as they can afford. Since distributors are closely tied to the world of products, they can rely on a range of product-oriented marketing tools, such as catalogs, to make their activities profitable. Consultants walk a narrower line. What they sell comes by the hour in hours billed to the client. Marketing consulting services can't be done with a catalog! A much more customized marketing mix is needed.

So far I've been creating a map, helping you see where you fit into the landscape of service providers. Now it's time to start talking about directions. How do you start from where you are and get where you want to go? That's the next subject we'll take up.

Analyze Your Service Offering

Job one is to develop your service offering for maximum profit potential. To do this, you need to analyze your offering, examining it from the perspectives of both your existing and your potential clients.

Examine the Three Aspects of Service

Just as with products, every service has three aspects to it: its core value, the basic solution it offers; its expanded service, the added values that enhance the core value; and its service concept, the big picture surrounding that service's development, marketing, price point, style of delivery, and long-range place in the company's overall objectives.

You are going to want to ask yourself how well your service does in providing a core value to your clients, what you do for each client to enhance that value, and how completely you have planned to make your offering profitable.

Let's go down to Barney's Car Wash for an example. Barney has three or four of these establishments in my town, and I visit them because they have a core value that is important to me. I drive a vintage car, and it demands a brushless car wash to keep its fragile paint looking spiffy. Only Barney's offers the brushless wash, so I go to Barney's.

Once there, I choose from a variety of packages available. In the winter, I go for the extra polish coat and the anti-road salt under-carriage flush. In the summer, I skip those preventatives, but maybe I splurge on one of the detailing packages, like hand-polishing my chrome. Me and my baby like to look good on our Sunday drives. Barney has assembled these packages of extended services to enhance his core value, meet my varying needs, and tempt me into purchasing more than the core service.

Barney saw a niche in the car care market, a need for higher-quality cleaning than the coin-op and gas-station car washes were offering. He responded by assembling a variety of services that fit his concept of a premium car care provider. He tailors them to the needs of special clients, like corporate fleets and rental companies, as well as the various consumer niches like vintage cars and sport vehicles. (He even has a Sunday night mud-off special for weekend cowboys.) These offerings illustrate Barney's service concept.

Mentor

Manage the physical evidence of your service to your advantage. Give it form in a way that supports your brand. Create a "service identity plan" that isolates the something extra you provide to make your service unique. Then turn that into a promotional position. Barney's Car Wash could offer "the car lover's choice." Pros use every opportunity to give their service an identity that helps communicate what makes it special.

To achieve your greatest potential, analyze your service offering from each of these angles and make changes where necessary, focusing core services to meet defined needs, adding value with such things as timing, and monitoring the success of your service concept.

While you're at it, consider other aspects of your offering, such as the people who participate in delivering your service and the process of delivery. These, too, contribute to what your service is and how it sells.

Pay Attention to the Service Encounter: "Where Rubber Meets Road"

When the consumer interacts with the service provider, that's the *service encounter.* If you're in the rental car business, it's not enough that the car works when the driver gets in. The process of getting the car has to be satisfactory as well. If your customer had to wait too long or put up with an inexperienced clerk, you're failing at managing the service encounter.

There may be one or many encounters in the delivery of a service, depending on the nature of your business. In some businesses the service encounter makes up the entire delivery of the service, and in others there is much work done between encounters.

A barber giving a haircut is performing a one-encounter service, with no behind-the-scenes activity, unless you count sweeping up between customers. A graphic designer producing a brochure has several encounters with the client, and considerable work goes on behind the scenes between visits.

Failure in the service encounter can ruin a client relationship as easily as failing to deliver good service. If the barber tells off-color jokes, the customer may not return even if the cut was acceptable. If the designer is always late or disorganized, her firm will not get additional work from this client even if the creativity of the brochure was top-notch. Get the picture? You can't just deliver a good service; you have to deliver it well.

What?

Service encounter is a very important concept. It's the customer touch points on steroids. It refers to the quality of the interaction between the customer and the person providing the service.

"Yes Sir!" Are You Managing Your Customer Touch Points?

The quality of the contact between you as service provider and your customer gives you an opportunity to sharpen your competitive edge. If you're in a law firm, the personality of your receptionist is as much a part of your product as your senior partner's legal ability. What do you do about it?

For some, standardization is the answer. Standardizing services is possible if you run a car wash or juice cart, but nearly impossible if the service bought is, say, dentistry. Even so, you can instill in everyone who has contact with customers the manner you'd like them to project. A print shop or fast food restaurant trains customer service personnel to project a friendly demeanor. If you can, standardize elements of the service delivery process, so that new employees can be trained to deliver just like the old hands. Consistency improves customers' perception of service quality.

Another strategy for managing service quality is customization. In some circumstances, a service is truly individualized to each customer. A chartered plane flies to whatever destination the customer chooses. "Know your customer" is the guiding rule. Find out what they will perceive as service quality—then deliver it. If they want champagne instead of chardonnay in flight, get champagne.

The very nature of Anita Hecht's Life History Services requires customization. Each family she serves has a choice of avenues to explore and a choice of ways to present the results of those explorations. Anita has to be a master at quickly grasping what her customers want.

One thing to remember when we're talking about service quality: It's very much a matter of perception. You can believe you're delivering a high level of service quality and find out that your customers disagree. What you do about that is called "managing the gap."

If you have direct front-line contact with customers, you're probably in the know about what they expect. But if you're not, you may be suffering from a *negative gap*. You need fresh information: Return to Part 2 of this book for some clues on the customer's perspective, customer relationship marketing (CRM), and market research.

A local bank ran an ad campaign promoting its "whatever it takes" customer service attitude. While the ads aired around me, the same bank turned me down for a mortgage. "Whatever it takes?" Not in my opinion! I pulled my account and never looked back. That's another type of negative gap—a gap between promise and delivery.

But *gaps* can be *positive* as well. A young man celebrated his birthday by taking his mother to a fancy restaurant. He was tactfully asked for his I.D. when he ordered a bottle of wine. A bit disgruntled, he presented his driver's license and was served, but he overheard the waiter say "We'll have to do something about this." What was the problem? Nothing, as he discovered when complimentary desserts were brought after the meal. The waiter, noticing his birth date on the license, took the occasion to offer more service than expected. The young man and his mother were delighted and impressed. Will he go back there? You bet! Will he tell others how great that place is? You bet, again. Can you buy those kind of endorsements? No. But you can earn them, and that's one of the secrets to success in the service business.

What?

When customers have complaints about your service that you aren't aware of, or when you don't know exactly what they want, I call that a **negative gap.** If you surprise them with better service than they expect, that's a **positive gap.**

Look for the negative gaps that may be undercutting your efforts to deliver service quality—and fix them. Look for the opportunities to create positive gaps, and encourage your staff to exploit them.

Look for New Services You Can Supply

Whether you have a new idea for your existing business or your first idea that could lead to a new business, it pays to keep a look out to see if you can supply a service that others will pay for. Here are a couple places you can look.

A New Service for Existing Customers

The good news about service businesses: You have such close contact with customers that you're well prepared for brainstorming successful new service offerings. The seeds your customers plant with you will grow into your new profit centers, if you nurture them.

The thing you must be sure of, as you develop new services, is that they work for you—not just for your customers.

A boarding kennel in my town sent me an announcement of a new service: home visits, allowing your pet to stay at home while you're away. I thought that was odd, since what they previously sold, lodging for pets, involved physical resources amounting to a considerable investment. What was the reason for the new strategy? Why not build new kennels if they wanted more business?

> **Really!**
>
> Two trends—the changing ethnicity of American people and the aging of Baby Boomers—are fueling the development of new services and products. Trend forecasters are predicting extensive growth potential in five areas. They predict there will be increased demand for services related to education, health, finances, home, and leisure.

After talking with the owners, I understood. Not only does this allow them to serve more people without a capital investment, it brings them into a slightly different market as well. Cats are the typical recipients of the at-home service, while dogs are more likely to be kenneled than left at home unsupervised. (It's a litter-box thing.)

Their boarding business, having cornered as much of the kenneling market as they could expect, chose to add the home-visit service as a way to grow into a new market. So it works hand-in-hand (paw-in-paw?) with their current operations.

A Service to Fill an Unrecognized Need

Maybe you've been itching to sell your talent as a problem-solver, but you haven't defined which problem people need solved so much that they'll pay for your service. It gets vague in your mind and you end up thinking about needs that others are already filling. But that's not what you want. Let's think now … something new?

Irene and Michael Tobis, a couple of Ph.D.s, did some powerful thinking about what they'd observed and what they could offer, and they came up with a great idea: People need organization. Irene is a psychologist and Michael is a systems engineer. They created a consulting business called Ducks In A Row. They targeted entrepreneurs, professionals, collaborative teams, and busy people. They offered services to help individuals achieve their goals by developing skills, strategies, and tools to handle information, space, and time.

The Ducks' service could be delivered in your home, your office, your company—anywhere you need to get organized. But they don't just organize you; they aid your psyche. They help you overcome obstacles, develop strengths, and handle your organizational problems for yourself.

Next time you are poking around in the messy closet of your mind, remember the Ducks and figure out what you can offer that lots of people need.

Mentor

You could have a talent that others need. You never know what service would make life happier, easier, or more functional for people. So think about talents you have that can fill an unrecognized need people have. Dog-walking services had to start with someone who knew people were getting busier and could use relief from some of their daily chores. Hmmm? Wouldn't it be nice if you could be someone's eating service? Oh well, keep thinking.

Check Out Offering Online Services

Online service is primarily a new method for purchase and delivery of products, or a form of advertising through a home page, or an information provider. It also provides a tool for collaboration over long distances. Offering new services online is still a possibility—it's a competitive field, but who can stop you when you have your thinking cap on! I know a business that sells demographic reports via the World Wide Web. I know desktop publishers, transcriptionists, web designers, and researchers who provide their service and deliver the end results entirely through the web. You might have an idea that could lead to a website offering information-based services for a fee.

Mentor

Many online services, like those provided by web designers, transcriptionists, and researchers, work well as home-based businesses. Broadband Internet connections and the reliability of the PDF (Portable Document Format) have made it possible for workers separated by space to collaborate just as if they were working next door to each other in the "cube farm." If you're interested in a home business, check out online service offerings—and if you're skilled at a service that can be delivered over the web, check out your home office options!

Nonprofits Don't Market! (Yes, They Do.)

Most nonprofit organizations market services or intangibles like good health, so let's talk about them. They have different marketing objectives because success can't be measured by the same financial statements as a for-profit business uses. Instead, success is measured against general goals—like changes in attitude, behavior, and social norms—or measurable goals, like numbers of clients served, total funds raised and distributed, lower crime rates, fewer heart attacks, and higher school grades.

Most nonprofit organizations serve two different publics: the people who enable them to serve and the people they actually serve. Depending on your niche, you might call the first group donors, patrons, friends, or contributors. Their objective is to help your organization deliver services, rather than to receive those services personally (though they might be on the receiving end at least partially if the organization is a church, for example).

The other group, who actually receive services, might be called recipients, clients, constituents, patients, or members, depending on what you do. In a for-profit situation these people would be called customers. They are consumers of the services provided.

When you market to donors, you are actually fundraising. While fundraising uses many marketing tools, it is itself a separate activity with its own rules and principles of behavior. I suggest you get a specialty book on fundraising.

When you market to recipients, you are actually doing "social marketing," and that is the subject of the next chapter.

The Least You Need to Know

- Most offerings are neither purely product nor completely service in nature, but some combination of both.
- Services are intangible, perishable, and inseparable from the person providing the service.
- Analyze your offering to ensure you deliver a high quality of service and a pleasant service encounter.
- Look for new services you can supply by following demographic and technological shifts.
- Nonprofit organizations serve two audiences—donors and recipients—who are best served through target marketing.

Chapter 11

When Your Product Is a Cause

In This Chapter

- What social marketing is and who it serves
- The three stages of change and your chance of success
- The social marketing mix—the seven Ps
- How to plan a campaign
- Strategies for social marketing

(Hello. This is your author speaking. For this chapter I'm going to hand you over to my good friend Ray Olderman, a veteran advertising strategist and social marketer whose expertise in this area surpasses mine. I'll let him give you the inside dope on marketing good-for-you intangibles. Take it away, Ray.)

So you want to sell a cause. Or maybe you just got hired by an organization like the Red Cross or American Lung Association. Sometimes a cause is a one-time affair, and sometimes it's the business of an organization.

Nonprofits are usually cause sellers, selling to those referred to as recipients in Chapter 10. The end product is usually a behavior change, and we all know what a hard sell that is!

How are you going to get people to buy good behavior? There has to be a better way than sticking up some posters, sending out a press release, and waiting to hand out T-shirts to all the respondents. *Social marketing* is the better way. It got its inspiration from sociologist G. D. Wiebe in the 1950s, but really took off in the early 1970s. You can put it to use to promote your cause—your social or health issue.

Be aware, however, that informing people about how to take care of themselves or how to make changes for the good of society and the environment can be like getting a kid to take icky-tasting medicine. It doesn't go down easy. Social marketing offers a system for getting the word out about positive behavior changes.

What Is Social Marketing?

Social marketers want to influence awareness, attitudes, and social behaviors concerning very specific issues. Let's say you want to "sell" not smoking to preteens and teens. First, you'd have to confess to your friends that you're a social marketer. They'll look confused. Tell them you adapt specific commercial techniques of attraction and persuasion, and you use these techniques to get your audience's attention so you can sell them information and education instead of running shoes.

The goal of social marketing is to get carefully selected audiences to understand and accept new ideas, alter old ideas, and value their new awareness enough to change attitudes and take positive action.

Is Social Marketing Right for You?

Social marketing's systematic approach is designed especially for …

- Nonprofits.
- Government agencies.
- Community-based organizations.
- Private foundations.
- Social issue coalitions.
- Health issue coalitions.
- Environmental issue coalitions.
- Any group that wants to effect a social change.

What?

Social marketing is the planning and implementation of programs designed to bring about social change using techniques adapted from commercial marketing. These commercial techniques are the ones used to get people to buy a product or service.

Are You Right for Social Marketing?

It may be a variety of marketing, but social marketing doesn't offer the same benefits, rewards, and qualifications as does commercial marketing. As a social marketer, your benefits serve specific target audiences and the general society, while commercial marketers in the end benefit the companies they sell for. Commercial marketers are selling either tangible products and services or intangibles ones that have profitable outcomes, so it's all a matter of commerce to them. Commitment to the company or to the buyer is good but only goes so deep.

You, on the other hand—as an upstanding social marketer who befuddles friends with your idealism—have to sell concepts, ideas, and attitudes with no tangible profit attached. You have to put your heart in it. Entirely. You have to begin with a passion to inspire change, and follow through as if your personal fortunes depended on it. In social marketing, commitment is the necessary fuel for success.

> CAUTION
>
> **Pitfall**
>
> Investing your heart requires some kind of balanced sense of reality. Be grateful for small successes. Recognize that when you sell behavior change, it takes a long time before you can truly measure the impact of your efforts. The caution here is disillusionment. Avoid this pitfall by having no illusions about what you can achieve.

A Realistic Look at Success

To be successful as a social marketer, make believe you're someone like Darwin or Copernicus. Most of the people you want to address won't see the world the way you do. You have to sell them a new vision. It will take persistence and systematic planning.

You might not be able to start out suggesting a change in behavior. Your audience may not even know they have a problem that needs fixing. Changing attitudes and beliefs takes time. You're not selling laundry detergent. Attitudes and beliefs mean much more to people than their choice of a consumer product.

Be Aware of the Stages of Change

To be realistic and to plan your strategy, you should recognize the stages your audience will go through before they arrive at change:

1. They become aware of your message.
2. They understand what the message is saying.
3. They agree that the message is good and that people should listen to it.

4. They recognize they could benefit from the message.
5. They change their attitude.
6. Their new attitude leads them to take action and change their behavior.

This process influences the focus of your marketing efforts. You need to organize these efforts in three phases:

1. Raise awareness.
2. Change attitudes.
3. Encourage action.

You can see how these are really three different goals. Here's how it works. If your target audience is totally unaware of the issue you are promoting, you may need to simply provide information as a preliminary stage to raise awareness. Asking them to make a change when they don't know the issues is a waste of time.

If your audience knows the issues but doesn't connect them to their own attitudes, you may have to do a different kind of education campaign where you connect attitudes to the forces that create them and to their consequences. For example, in the national campaign that preceded the Census of 2000, the marketers targeted minorities and worked on attitudes that had led to resistance and nonparticipation. The campaign connected the census with real benefits to the communities they targeted. Then when it came time to change behavior (participate in the census), the target audience was much more willing to participate as individuals. The strategy worked.

If your audience is informed enough to be bored by any more information about issues and attitudes, it's time to push for a change in behavior. To know which one of these approaches you need to pursue, you have to know your audience.

Really!

Academic theorists disagree about the value of social marketing. The sticking point is whether social marketing as a strategy for interventions should target individuals or social structures. Some feel that putting the burden on individuals to change only excuses the relevant lawmakers and institutions from making a change. As a social marketer I add potential policy changes to my definition of what I should be doing, so I target the individual, the community, and social structures.

Research Your Audience

Knowing your audience is even more important for social marketing than for commercial marketing. You have to know their present attitudes, what *appeal* would attract their attention, and what *benefit* would persuade them to change.

Don't think you can go directly to the general public and start campaigning. Even if it's a big issue like drug abuse or breast cancer, you still need to know your audience's attitudes. How much do they know? What are their points of resistance?

I recently participated in a campaign to prevent the initiation of tobacco use among middle school and high school students. I did lots of reading of studies about how to appeal to this target group, what benefit would entice them away from the temptations to smoke.

The young are a volatile target. Nationally, they were courted with several different appeals: real-life stories about people suffering the effects of smoking, deglamorization of tobacco use by graphic images of its ill effects, the impact of smoking on younger siblings, humor about how dumb smoking is, the bad smell of smokers, and rebellion against the manipulation of young people's habits by the tobacco industry.

These appeals worked for brief periods, or they worked in one state but not another. The real-life stories of people dying or suffering from the effects of smoking were successful in Massachusetts, for a time. Highlighting manipulation by the tobacco industry scored big enough in Florida in the late 1990s to become the basic appeal for a national campaign.

My clients and I took all this information and began talking to groups of young people to find out which appeal would have an impact on them.

Really!

A quick way to get started researching is to first read the available information on how others have dealt with an audience similar to yours on the same cause you are advocating. Then, to learn about your specific audience, check with a state or local agency that can give you basic demographics. Next, interview some "key informants," or bring a group of them together to interview in a focus group.

Key informants are people who know the community or segment of the population you want to target. They are often community and church leaders, but they can also be "street" people. Their responses can usually be generalized to a larger but similar population. If you are doing an antismoking campaign targeting teens, get several groups of teens together to discuss smoking and nonsmoking. Choose different age, ethnic, and interest groups. And be sure to talk to the "at-risk outsiders."

Once you know your audience, you can begin to plan. Ultimately, you will want to arrive at a strategy, but first you need to set the context. You need to see the total marketing picture. We're going to take a look at how to plan and at some basic strategies, but first, start your planning by describing, in writing, your particular "social marketing mix."

Put Together the Social Marketing Mix

Recall that commercial marketing uses the "Four Ps plus one" to define the total marketing picture. Let me repeat them here so you can see how they compare to what they mean in social marketing.

- **Product.** The individual item to be marketed.
- **Price.** The cost of obtaining the product.
- **Place.** The distribution plan.
- **Promotion.** All the advertising, public relations, and promotional efforts a company employs to get an audience to buy a product.
- **People.** This is the P your author added to the traditional mix. I cover this later under the heading "partnership."

How to Adapt the Commercial Mix to Social Marketing

- **Product.** Your product is an intangible; it's a specific change in awareness, attitude, and behavior. It's a good idea to include the *unique value* of the change you are trying to sell when you define your specific "product."
- **Price.** Redefine the meaning of "costs," and address them as barriers you need to overcome. In commercial marketing, the benefits to the consumer must clearly outweigh the cost of a product or service. In social marketing, the costs are primarily psychological. They are the costs of changing attitudes and behavior. In some cases, there are also financial costs. For example, if you are selling energy efficiency, people need to invest before they see any savings benefit.
- **Place.** Social marketers seldom have a product that needs distributing. So I'm using the term

> **What?**
>
> In social marketing, the **unique value** of the cause you're selling is usually a virtuous outcome, like better health. When you define your cause's unique value, be sure to make the benefit it offers as appealing as possible. Female teens responded to the nonsmoking message that males like to kiss girls who don't smoke. To teens, that had more value than the value of health benefits.

differently from its use in commercial marketing as described in Chapter 13. Distribution for social marketers means message distribution—how they will get their message out, deliver their brochures, and use the media.

For your social marketing campaign, put an effective message distribution plan together early in your planning process. Here are some questions to ask: Are you doing ads and brochures to get the word out? Posters and radio commercials? What media channels can you afford? Do you need people to literally hand out your materials? Look for partners to help you get the message seen and heard. If you do press releases, call the places where you send them. Talk with someone about an angle you can use to help the press justify making space for your information.

- **Promotion.** Create a brief media plan detailing the audience you have chosen to target, the phase they are in (do they need raised awareness? Are they ready for a direct appeal to attitude change? Are they already receptive to a call for changed behavior?), and the most effective uses of advertising, promotions, and public information to achieve your goals.

- **Partnership.** Think of people not just as your audience, but as a group of partnerships. A single organization may not be able to make a dent in solving complex social issues. Team up with other organizations, partners, and agencies to stretch your resources. Partners help in many ways besides supplying funds and volunteers. They are particularly necessary when it comes to distributing your information. Remember, that's a delivery problem. Where do you put your brochures and posters? You have to put these bedrocks of public information and education somewhere your target audience will see them and pay attention to them.

  It can be easier than you think to enlist help in spreading the word about a good cause. You can't lose by asking. In a Wisconsin state campaign to inform working mothers about child care options, we wanted to get out the word about a phone number mothers could call to get more information. With quick messages, posters work. So, among other things, we enlisted video stores to display the posters. You can be sure that mothers with children who need child care visit video stores. The video stores were very willing to help.

Really!

You can get more mileage from a TV or radio spot than you might think … and you can keep it from airing at that deadly 4 A.M. time slot. If you have enough of a budget to do a small TV or radio buy, ask your local stations if they can "leverage" the buy. Leverage means they give you two or three extra time slots for each one you buy. The advantage—besides getting extra time on air—is that buying helps you negotiate a more prime time spot for your information.

Now Add Two More "Ps" to the Mix

When you're selling causes, you usually have to substitute creative thinking for the budget you need but won't get. That's where these two Ps come in: policy and politics.

- **Policy.** Changed behavior may not last if a community or cultural environment is not supportive. You may need to organize campaigns around seeking policy changes to help achieve your goals. For example, if you are trying to counter tobacco use, you may need to campaign for changes in tax policy, pricing, compliance checks, or drug classification. Some large organizations like the American Cancer Society may even hire professional lobbyists.
- **Politics.** You can be sure the issues involved in a social campaign are complex and often controversial. You may need some political diplomacy to gain support from partners, like-minded organizations, other stakeholders, allies, and policy makers. I don't mean just being polite or smiling a lot. That might help, but you also need to be informed about the people you negotiate with, their values and areas of influence. Know your issues, too, and learn how to be pleasantly persuasive.

Planning Is Also a Virtue

Yes, social marketers write marketing plans. They are similar to commercial marketing plans, like those we'll talk about when we get to Part 6. Here are the elements:

What?

I bet you are wondering how good works can have any **competition.** Actually, any bid for the audience's attention is competition. But, if pressed to a definition, I would say that your main competitors for raised awareness, attitude, and behavior change are lethargy and habit. Rumors also compete. Bad information—about diet or medication, for example—can compete with your information and persuasion.

- **Element 1: Situation analysis.** This includes examining cultural and social influences, finding out about individual differences, defining and identifying target audiences, segmenting and positioning, looking at the *competition*, and getting buy-in from your internal organization—personnel and operational assignments.
- **Element 2: Objectives.** This is where you need to determine if your target audience needs to raise their awareness, change their attitudes, or take action to change their behavior. In all cases, be sure you make it as easy as possible for your audience to respond. Be sharply persuasive about the issues if you are raising awareness. Help people recognize the destructiveness of

attitudes they have inherited without examination. Show consequences of those attitudes. For behavior change, give your audience both a goal and a way to achieve it.

- **Element 3: Determination of funding.** This, of course, is the key element of your planning. Know exactly how much you can spend. Get a price sheet for media components from a social marketing or advertising agency so you can see the standard costs for what you need or what you can afford.

- **Element 4: Strategies and tactics.** These include advertising and public relations, partnership building, events and community activities, and timetables. (More on this coming up.)

- **Element 5: Coordination of efforts.** You need to create a task outline to know everything that needs to be done to achieve your objectives. Include all campaign partners and internal participants in creating your task list. That way, there is less chance of tasks falling between the cracks.

Mentor

In social marketing, the Internet is useful for communicating with partners, for sending out updates on information, and even for making some initial contacts. A website can be extraordinarily helpful. You can communicate much more information about your issue, make it interesting, and extend your impact with less budget. You can also make it a place to join a movement.

- **Element 6: Measurement of effectiveness.** Plan from the beginning whether you will use surveys or some statistical measurement for evaluating your campaign. Be aware that pinning down results can be difficult. You can find out how many people saw your materials. Recall of those materials indicates some level of impact. But even statistical evidence can be a little blurred. When we targeted middle school students in the antismoking campaign, statistics revealed a sharp drop in first-year high school student smoking. That was a goal of the campaign, but other unknowns could have influenced the actual numbers. So, do your best to get specific reactions through surveys or focus groups.

- **Element 7: Follow-up actions.** Evaluation may reveal that your audience doesn't understand or even notice your message. Making campaign changes after it starts is one kind of follow-up. Another is to plan a follow-up advertising component. Send a reminder postcard. Take out an ad asking people to take action. Or, for low budgets, see what your partners can do to remind their constituents about the importance of the issues.

Strategies for Social Marketing

Now you are ready for the meatiest challenge of social marketing. (Unless, of course, you are a vegetarian. Then, let me say you are ready for the most organic challenge of social marketing.) In any case, you have to create your marketing mix strategy. This part of your planning devises your strategy for how to address a specific audience and persuade them to change their awareness, attitudes, or behavior.

Here are some sample scenarios.

Strategy 1: When the costs are small compared to the benefits. Information on new treatments, for example, costs little in the way of a change to the target audience's behavior. If they have the condition addressed, new treatment is of high interest. This strategy is the closest to commercial efforts. In all cases, even the tougher ones, look for a way to communicate the benefits of the change in awareness, attitudes, or behavior. Make sure you let the audience know how easy it is to adopt the change. The treatment, for example, is easily available.

Mentor

Always test market any concepts, ideas, or advertising efforts before releasing them. Hold several focus group meetings with members of your target audience and get their opinions. You'll be surprised how little you can predict. We tested a TV spot aimed at teens to prevent smoking initiation, offered by the Centers for Disease Control. It showed a deep winter scene and panned over to a young boy, shivering outside having a smoke. We thought it perfect for Wisconsin. But our focus group of target audience members rejected it as "unrealistic" because the shivering kid in the TV spot didn't have a coat on!

Strategy 2: When there are no direct benefits for the individual. Use your research to find what would make the change attractive and convenient for the audience. For example, installing renewable energy equipment is too costly to have anything but an intangible benefit. Research may tell you the size of your potential audience. Interviews may reveal that your audience might take on the expense for their children and future generations. You would use that to appeal when you promote change.

Strategy 3: When the costs for social change outweigh the obvious benefits. To many people, the psychological cost of quitting smoking is more immediate than the benefits of good health or even survival. So how do you get them to sacrifice their psychological comfort for a smoke-free future?

There are two possibilities. You can use the research on your target audience, as in Strategy 2, and find a more appealing benefit. Some smokers respond, for example, to the reminder that smoking may cut them off from enjoying their children or grandchildren. This warning makes many smokers willing to pay the costs necessary to quit.

The second possibility is to aim the campaign at a small portion of the target audience—to segment, in other words. Social marketers frequently isolate a group of early adopters and appeal to them first. Segmentation is always a good idea, but choosing the early adopters as your target isn't always the best way to segment. It can work with energy conservation, for example, but a lot depends on the cause you are selling. Segmenting your smokers, for example, into preteens, teens, adults, and older adults can be more effective than recruiting some early adopters, who may be seen simply as "goody-goodies" rather than someone to emulate.

The segmentation strategy works best when you can take the next step and get a small committed audience to use their leverage in their community. Then you can persist until your audience gets big enough to make each individual change add up to the improvement you passionately seek.

For one segment of the antismoking campaign, I conducted focus groups with six different groups of African-American teens in Milwaukee, Wisconsin. By the time I was finished, I was convinced that with a big enough budget, focus groups themselves would be a great approach to spreading the word. By the time I got to the fifth group, the teens were repeating ideas expressed by the earlier groups. The word had gotten around.

Really!

Studies consistently show that peer-to-peer education is always more effective than hearing messages from a distant authority, an anonymous voice, an actor, or even a celebrity. Kids respond better to what other kids tell them. Smokers respond better to other smokers. It isn't the whole answer, but it is an important piece of the puzzle.

This phenomenon reminded me of one of the latest trends in marketing—"buzz marketing," where individuals actually sell to each other by recommending specific products or services. It's something like the old "word of mouth." The teens were very taken with the idea that they were being manipulated by tobacco companies, through heightened addictive ingredients in cigarettes and a whole number of truly questionable tactics. The word spread that it was cool to reject manipulation by "The Man."

(Hello, this is your author again. Let's give Ray a big hand for sharing his insights and experience. And let me know if you'd like to talk to him about your social marketing situation. Now get out there and get to work bringing about social change!)

The Least You Need to Know

- Social marketing uses the techniques of commercial marketing to "sell" behavior change.
- Campaigns to raise awareness or change attitudes may have to precede a campaign to change behavior.
- Knowing your audience and using them to help spread the message is crucial to social marketing.
- The social marketing mix adds Policy and Politics to the Four Ps plus the one added by your author and redefines them all.
- Effective social marketing begins with a marketing plan.

Chapter 12

Pricing Your Offerings

In This Chapter

- Setting your initial price
- How to calculate costs and demand
- Setting a pricing strategy
- How changing price changes everything else
- How to price professional services

A friend of mine went into a store to buy a futon. He and his spouse spent time examining the styles of folding frames, choosing the mattress, and selecting the custom covering. A sales clerk helpfully presented the range of options. The couple's selections came to nearly $500. The clerk wrote up the order and ended by mentioning a $28 finishing charge and a $40 delivery fee. My friend, according to witnesses, boiled and then blew. To be nickeled and dimed for surcharges equaling more than 10 percent of the original purchase didn't sit right with him. The futon store lost the sale, not over the final price, but over a pricing strategy that failed to meet this customer's needs.

What's wrong with charging an additional fee for additional value delivered? Nothing—it's all in the presentation. Nobody likes surprises when it comes to money. More customers would be delighted if the futon seller's pricing strategy could have offered the total sticker price with discounts for services waived. Also, the owner could have empowered an employee to negotiate the price with customers. That might have saved the sale.

The lesson is simple. Consider your pricing strategy when you set your initial price, and review it as experience shows you what works and what doesn't. Now, let's take a look at how you can do that.

Setting Your Initial Price

In Chapter 3, I introduced Price as one of the "Four Ps," and I defined it as the consideration (usually money) that is exchanged for the product or service offered. It's our most quantifiable way of measuring the value customers place on an offering.

In your planning, be sure to take into account the other marketing variables—the other three Ps of promotion, place, and product. Many businesses tend to treat price as a function of operations, a simple arithmetic problem that calculates the cost to make a product, and then tacks on a percentage for profit. But how far-sighted is that?

Successful marketing is about seeing things from your customer's perspective. What a customer thinks about your price is much more important than what it costs you to make a product or how much profit you would like to earn. When my friend balked at the costs added to the price of his futon, he was feeling a loss of trust.

If the price asked doesn't "feel right" in relation to the value delivered, customers are not going to buy. You would expect this to be most true in markets that are price-sensitive, but in fact, customer surveys show that even in markets considered less price-sensitive, like luxury goods and industrial components, the "feel" of the price is a critical factor.

Value is the essence of your pricing strategy. According to the "Customer Value Pyramid," a model I introduced in Chapter 4, a customer's perception of value is tied to three things: product quality, service quality, and a reasonable price.

Really!

In many ways, we can think of price in terms of value. People are willing to pay a price that matches the value to them of a product or service. How do you make sure your offerings will be considered valuable to customers? Think again about the Four Utilities. Focus on making improvements in those areas, and you'll increase the value of your offerings to customers. That allows you to charge a price you and your customers will consider reasonable.

Any element of your offering's makeup—from its quality of manufacture to its styling to its convenience to its quality of service delivery to how it fills needs—will contribute to a perception of value that tells a potential customer the price is right.

Determine Demand

What it costs you to make a product defines the bottom floor of your pricing strategy. How badly customers want it defines the ceiling. In between these two lies the supply and demand equation. Let's look at demand here and talk about costs a little later.

If you've ever listened to a seven-year-old plead for the latest toy before Christmas and then schlepped to six or seven stores only to find that toy sold out, you know more than you want to about supply and demand. Kid's gotta have it—you gotta find it. If your kid's a good manipulator, price will be much less important to you than availability of that toy.

In a typical demand situation, there is an inverse relationship between price and demand: The lower the price, the higher the quantity of units the market will buy. The higher the price, the fewer the units sold. Not all situations are typical, though. Given the psychological relationship of price to quality, a higher price might sell more units because they are perceived as more valuable. Plus, there is the "prestige" factor—the halo of desirability an expensive (and well-marketed) product wears.

What we perceive to be valuable changes depending on how badly we want the item in question. Its value is never higher to us than at the moment we are about to buy it—our desire burning at its peak—and never so low as when we've just purchased it. Having gotten the thing we sought, we have no need for another, and might not buy it even if it were suddenly offered at 50 percent off. (Remember Maslow's Hierarchy of Needs from Chapter 1? A need satisfied frees us to move on to satisfying other or higher needs.) Pricing has more to do with behavioral science than it does with math.

Know Your Costs

Establishing the exact price for your product or service depends a lot on knowing what it costs you to make it.

Pitfall

Don't collude with your competitors to set prices. This is known as restraint of trade or price-fixing and is illegal. It is against the law to sit down with your competitors to decide how much you're going to charge customers.

"Markup" Is Not a Dirty Word

If you're in wholesale or retail, the equation is fairly simple. (I talk about how to price services a little later.) Note the cost of the product to you, and then determine the markup—the multiplier you will use to establish your selling price.

The difference between your selling price and the item's cost to you is called the margin. This is the amount you need to charge based on your overhead and profit goals. Once you have that adequately defined, the rest is easy. The difficult stage is the testing and adjusting you must do to make sure the markup covers your expenses and desired profit.

Pricing and Your Financial Projections

You're going to write a marketing plan, aren't you? Aren't you? The financial projections you prepare for that plan will be one of the most important management tools you will have. You will prepare a break-even analysis that describes the point at which your company's costs and its revenues are equal, the point where profit is nil but so is loss. We call that situation a wash.

You'd rather make a profit than come out a wash. You definitely want to avoid being taken to the cleaner's. So prepare a break-even analysis. Do this by projecting fixed and variable costs. Set aside your targeted profit for now. This establishes the price you must charge per unit to break even. This is not your final price; rather it is your "don't go below" price. If phrases like "prepare a break-even analysis" cause your palms to sweat, I suggest you find some information on financial management for small businesses; *The Complete Idiot's Guide to Business Management* might be a good place to start.

In the beginning, the analysis will help you choose a first-price strategy. As time goes by, you'll compare demand and real performance to projections, and adjust price strategy accordingly. It is important to refigure the break-even point whenever your operation changes. Added staff means higher overhead. A new investment in capital equipment will mean the same, but may be offset by increased production capacity, giving you greater efficiencies of scale.

Wherever your break-even point falls, it can be improved by controlling costs. If you sell something for a dollar and you can change the cost of making it from 50¢ to 49¢, you've just made a penny. Once you've established the customer's perfect price point, controlling costs is your next best chance for a pay increase.

Now Put Cost and Demand Together

Once you've calculated your break-even point, you must project demand for the product. No easy task, but presumably your market research has given you some feel for how many units you can sell at what price.

No doubt you'll see a relationship between projected price and demand for your offering. As the price goes up, demand will probably decrease. But maybe selling fewer units at higher prices is just fine by you. Your problem is to determine what relationship of price to demand works best, given your company's overall objectives.

Work Out Your Pricing Strategy

What you do about pricing your offering also depends on your objectives. A pricing strategy can help you ...

- Increase sales.
- Increase profit.
- Offset competitors' actions.

One Price or Many: How the Pricing Structure Sets the Pace

Do you charge the same price to everybody who comes along? Seems like a simple question at first. Let's say you own a dress shop and you've ordered a too-big supply of daisy-print dresses. You hang them out front, mark a price (say $37.50) on them, and that's that, come one come all, $37.50. But if Ms. Smith, a good customer, comes along and says, "I'll buy it if you'll take $30," what would you say? Your goal is to get the dress off your hands; $30 is a lot more than nothing. If you say yes, you have just crossed over to the land of variable pricing.

Variable pricing is the accepted norm in many parts of the world, but not so here. In America we tend to expect marketers to practice a one-price policy, on the assumption that it is the fair and democratic thing to do. Should a millionaire pay more for a gallon of milk than a college student pays? I won't try to tackle the ethics issues here. I'll settle for giving you the pros and cons of one-price versus variable-price strategies and let you decide.

A one-price strategy is easy to administer. You don't have to train your salespeople to haggle with each customer. Your record-keeping will be simpler, making cost projections easier. On the other hand, you may be missing sales you would make if your strategy allowed for a little give and take. It may be to your advantage to give Ms. Smith the daisy-print dress for $30, pleasing a customer and getting some doggy merchandise off your hands at the same time. A rigid price structure can be unfriendly to customers, as the futon story at the start of this chapter illustrated.

On the other hand, variable pricing opens up a veritable can of worms. It takes management time to teach each employee how to negotiate and considerable knowledge about break-even points on each product to inform the employee how low he or she can go. If that futon sales clerk had been empowered to waive the surcharges in the face of a disgruntled customer, she could have saved the sale. But she would have needed more training and more understanding of the whole price and profit objectives of her employer. Maybe the futon store couldn't afford to hire an employee capable of practicing a variable-price strategy.

Let the norms of your industry tell you which policy makes more sense for you. Be aware that many situations call for a little give and take—and don't be afraid to borrow from the variable pricing approach even if a one-price strategy is your general rule.

Discounting Without Giving Away the Store

The price you ask is a starting point. Whether you use variable pricing or not, it's common to adjust your price with various discount strategies. Sometimes those strategies are part of short-term sales promotions, strategies designed to offer customers added incentives to purchase.

When is a discount not a sales promotion? When it fits other goals of management. (We'll talk more about sales promotions in Chapter 15.) Sometimes a discount is offered as a reward for prompt payment, a strategy to improve cash flow. Sometimes it's offered to members of the trade—a carpenter charging less to contractors than to the general public to encourage repeat jobs, for instance. And sometimes, as in the case of our daisy-print dresses, a close-out price is offered, just to get the bad goods to go away.

Discounting prices, for whatever reason, is very likely to be a part of your pricing strategy.

Keep Your Eye on the Competition

Pricing strategies are also a way to respond to competition. "Fare wars" in the airline industry in the '80s and '90s forced some carriers to cut their fares below costs, creating industry-wide havoc. That's an example of pricing to hurt competition, a strategy that works in the consumers' favor, if not the industry's. It takes big companies with deep pockets to survive an extended price war.

In most situations, one company is the price leader and others follow its lead. They set prices a little above or below the leader to indicate their own position in relation to the Customer Value Pyramid—a little more expensive and worth it, or a little lower and still a great value. But the leader defines the general range of price acceptable to consumers.

What the Cutthroats Know

In highly competitive situations, the successful marketer becomes an expert at tactics. One tactic is to consider your prices in terms of the whole product line, rather than looking at each product as if it existed in its own vacuum. Here are a few examples of product-line strategies that might get you thinking.

Captive pricing means pricing an initial purchase low if it requires a stream of additional purchases, where the profits can be made. Selling a computer printer cheaply makes sense if you're also in the printer cartridge business—particularly inkjet cartridges for home-use printers. The price of the inkjet printer is low, given the R&D that went into it. The real money is in the billions of inkjet cartridges that are needed to keep the printer running.

Bundling is another useful pricing strategy. If you've shopped for a car and haggled over an options package, that was bundling. The key feature of a bundle is that the items sold together are priced lower than they would be if purchased separately.

This strategy is often used to solve inventory problems. Remember your problem with too many daisy-print dresses? A canny merchant might offer one daisy-print dress with every purchase of a more-desirable fashion, "enhancing" the offering by bundling a slow-seller with a popular item.

To attract bargain hunters, generate excitement, and create store traffic, you might try using loss leaders—pricing one or two items so low they may even be sold at a loss. Loss leaders give marketers an opportunity to use other strategies, from personal selling to in-store promotions, to get customers to buy other full-price products while they're in the store. You've probably heard of "bait and switch," the less savory version of a loss leader. If a merchant advertises an item simply to generate store traffic with no intention of selling, that's bait and switch. He'll probably be hearing from the Federal Trade Commission before long.

What?

Learn these common terms and become a cutthroat yourself. **Captive pricing** means offering a low initial price on articles that promise a stream of additional purchases to feed the original item, like ink cartridges for printers. **Bundling** means creating a package of features that cost less sold together than they would cost separately.

A Psychological Price to Pay

Status is one of the things we pay for when we make purchases. Fur coats or luxury cars are commonly called status symbols because their ownership projects an image that says, "I have status." For many products, a high price is one indication of the prestige its purchase will convey.

What?

Reference pricing is a handy marketing tool to know about. That's when several versions of a product in a range of prices are displayed together, causing the moderately priced one to look like a great bargain.

But that's not the only way psychology comes into play with pricing. Let me tell you about *reference pricing*. Retailers may carry several versions of a product, displayed together, with price points ranging from moderate to high. They're counting on you to perceive the moderately priced item as more desirable by comparison. You could walk into a camera store hoping to spend about $100 for a simple entry-level camera. If what you see on display ranges from $140 to $300, the $140 camera is going to seem like an excellent value. The extra $40 is fairly easy to pry out of your pocket using this strategy.

If your pricing is high, marketers call that *skimming*. If it leans low, that's called *penetration pricing*. Set your price toward the high end and you'll skim off the cream of the market, those willing to pay whatever it takes to get what you've got. This works where demand is steady, the product is unique, or where volume selling is not easy to achieve. On the other hand, a low price allows you to penetrate the market much further.

What?

Skimming is going for the high end of the market, the few who are able to pay top dollar. **Penetration pricing**, on the other hand, is going for as much market share as you can as fast as you can by setting your price low.

If your goal is to get a large market share as quickly as possible, if you can achieve economies of scale (profit from high volume), and if you need to discourage competitive knock-offs by getting in and out of the market rapidly, set your price low and try a penetration strategy.

In short, pricing strategy involves a lot of delicate decisions as you look for the right point between what it costs to make an item and what the traffic will bear.

Price Strategies: Change Your Price and Change the Game

Assuming you're in business today, you have a current pricing strategy. Does it need to change? Should the direction be up or down?

You may be contemplating raising a price in hopes of increasing profits, or lowering it in hopes of increasing sales. You may just be wondering whether the price you're charging reflects a sensible pricing strategy. Let me give you some ways to think about price changes.

Revisit Demand: No Umbrellas When the Sun Is Shining

Some product categories are sensitive to price changes; others, less so. This is called the *elasticity of demand.*

Demand is highly elastic when a small price decrease brings about a large increase in sales, or a small price increase causes a large decrease in sales. Demand is inelastic when a price change has little effect on sales. If a big price drop only sells a few more units, you've got inelastic demand. Where does your offering fit on the continuum?

To figure that, ask yourself whether substitutes exist, whether the product is a necessity or a luxury, and whether the price is significantly high.

What?

Think of **elasticity of demand** this way: Demand is a rubber band. If a price decrease causes the band to stretch, demand for that product is elastic. If price changes don't move the rubber band, it's inelastic.

The more alternatives or substitutes available, the more likely people are to pass rather than spend when you increase the price. In this situation, demand is very elastic. If fancy running shoes become a little too expensive, some customers will just buy cheap sneakers instead.

If a product is a necessity, it will exhibit inelastic demand. The customers need it, and they'll pay the price required to get it.

Outside influences can make a product a necessity. The owner of a beach cottage tells me that just before a hurricane, the price of particle board at the local hardware store jumps from $20 to over $100 a sheet, and he and his neighbors line up to buy it.

The higher the price of a purchase, the more likely it is to show elastic demand. Cars, vacations, and luxuries are price-elastic, even if they rank high in necessity, as cars do for most of us. We'll make do with our old wheels rather than pay a price that seems exorbitant.

So what do you do about elasticity of demand? You don't try to sell umbrellas when the sun is shining. If the demand's not there, the profits won't be either. If your product experiences highly elastic demand, choose your pricing strategy with this in mind: Profiteering is definitely out, and cost control is in.

If your offering is at the inelastic end of the scale, you have more freedom to set your prices for higher profit.

Really!

When you raise or lower your price, don't ignore the effect of elasticity of demand. Whether the product is a necessity or a luxury, whether substitutes are available, and whether the price is itself significantly high, all influence the elasticity of demand for a product or service.

When demand is highly elastic, a small price decrease will stimulate a large jump in sales. If price is inelastic, however, price changes will have little effect on sales—even if the price change is a big drop downward. Understanding the degree of elasticity of demand for your particular offering will help you know whether and by how much you can play with your prices.

What a Price Change Can and Can't Fix

A price change can increase sales, increase profits, increase the competitiveness of your offering, or increase the perceived value of your offering. Or it can do all of these things. It can also decrease all of these things, so be careful!

- **A price change can fix mistakes.** A price change (good news!) can fix a poor management decision. Let's look again at your dress shop and your overly optimistic projection of demand for daisy-print sundresses. Some people would stick their heads in the sand and refuse to admit the mistake. Others might be afraid to put the dresses out on a sale rack, for fear customers will now perceive them as a discount house.

  Still, those dresses aren't getting any more stylish or more desirable sitting in your warehouse. Better to get them moving with a price markdown if that will get customers to buy. Turn over the merchandise and get what you can from the investment, including a lesson from your mistake.

- **A price change can give a promotion its kick.** Lots of promotional strategies involve a reduced-price offer. Coupons, rebates, and "buy one/get one free" bundles are just a few examples.

  Some managers are afraid to use price discounts in their promotions, for fear of training customers to wait for discounts before they shop. It's a real concern, and one we'll talk more about in Chapter 15. You should be wary of too many price promotions, but don't ignore this important way to get customers in the door. Since price is such a critical component of value, it's a key tool in creating excitement about your offering.

That's what reducing a price can do for you. Now, what about a price increase?

- **A price increase can anger current customers.** Raising prices is a thing to be handled delicately, to avoid angering your customers. I got a letter from my computer consultant—the guy who keeps my hardware talking to my software and vice versa—announcing that his new rate would be $100 an hour. He was charging $25 when I first started using him, and I never really thought about how his prices were edging up over the years. I was shocked when I saw the new rate. My first thought was, "That's the last time I call him." While that's probably not true, I am going to be vulnerable if another consultant contacts me offering services at a lower rate. A long-term relationship is in jeopardy because of an unsubtle approach to a price increase.

  Any price increase must communicate the logic behind it. My guy's letter didn't indicate that he had increased overhead costs, or additional training that adds value for me, or anything else that gives me a justification for the increase. Bad move.

> **Mentor**
>
> Price changes, either up or down, have an impact on your customers' perceptions. Don't use price as a way to react to sudden supply shortages or excessive demand. Your customers are too likely to feel jerked around, and they won't forget it.

Remember, a customer's perception of a reasonable price is more important than what you want to charge. It doesn't matter that you think your product is worth more if customers don't agree.

Think About Price Changes and Business Growth

The objective of most companies is to grow, and increased sales can obviously lead to that growth. A price reduction is one way to increase sales, but be careful before you set off down this path. You have to be able to produce more units so that efficiencies of scale kick in—that way you'll make up the difference and grow through greater volume and reduced production costs. But this might not happen, and you may wind up losing money even though sales are growing.

> **Pitfall**
>
> Not every increase in sales leads to an increase in profit. If you cut prices to stimulate more sales, you can go so low you lose money on every sale. It's easy for overtime wages or rush delivery charges to eat away your profits from those extra sales during busy seasons.

Another strategy to achieve growth is to pursue increased profits rather than increased sales. How much increase is enough? Guide your profit strategy using the Return on Investment (ROI) equation (the ratio of profit to invested capital). Target a certain percentage of your investment as your profit goal, and then control the costs of production and marketing to achieve that goal.

> **Pitfall**
>
> There is a danger that accompanies newfound success. If you achieve a high level of profit, competitors are likely to notice. The potential for profit will bring other hunters into your neck of the woods.

To put a price increase in place takes thoughtful action. You're changing not only your price but your whole Customer Value Pyramid. The new price must still be perceived as a good value for the quality of product and service offered. You have to convince the marketplace of the merits of the new offering. You may need to adjust promotions to project a more prestigious image, adjust delivery to offer a more convenient place, or adjust product or service to include more benefits.

Pricing for Professional Services

Because services are for the most part intangible, they are more difficult to price than products. Consumers of services tend to use price as an indication of quality. This is especially true with consulting services, like law and accounting. When buyers are at risk if they hire a bad service—the way hiring a bad lawyer or a dishonest accountant is a risk—price is even more critical in establishing credibility. If you're selling services, pricing strategy is one of your best tools for building confidence in the quality of your service.

Quoting a Fee: Hourly Rates and the Proposed Job

So how do you decide how much to charge? At the root of that question is your hourly rate. To determine what you should charge per hour, I recommend you start with costs. Estimate overhead costs for one year. Now estimate how much time will be billable in that year—30, 50, or 80 percent? Figure in how much support staff you'll have around to help keep you billable and how much time you'll spend on marketing and other nonbillable tasks.

Let's say you plan on being 50 percent billable, which works out to 1,040 hours per year (figuring 40 hours per week). Multiply the rate you'd like to charge (take my computer guy's $100 an hour) and you'll come up with $104,000 dollars in billings per year. For the second half of the equation, estimate your overhead, rent, any expenses like accounting fees, office support, or office supplies, and so on, and come up with a yearly sum. Since my computer guy works out of his home, I don't think his overhead can be more than $5,000 or $10,000 per year. Subtract the overhead, and you have your net annual income.

Adjust the hourly rate (or find ways to cut overhead) until you find a match between an income that suits your lifestyle and a rate that suits customers. You can see the computer guru is favoring lifestyle over a rate that suits me.

So now you've established an hourly rate. To quote a fee, take the proposed job, break it into steps, and estimate the hours needed to perform each task. Add 'em up, multiply by the rate, add some more for out-of-pocket expenses, and voilà—your proposed fee.

Get the Fee You Want

Now, how are you going to get your prospect to agree to that fee?

If the formula I just described made you go "Yoiks! They'll never pay that," you have two options. Have you defined the client's need properly? Think about the proposed job. What exactly are the outcomes the client is seeking? Could you break it into different steps and come up with a lower estimate of hours? That may be your best strategy.

What?

It's worth discussing the value of your work to your client in terms of profits generated. Help your client see that your work doesn't just cost; it also pays. If you don't raise the issue, you don't stand to gain anything. If you do, a contract including bonuses for performance may be your reward.

You may need to turn down some projects that simply don't allow you to charge the fee you need. There's no point in selling hours for $30 when it costs you $40 to open the door, unless it meets other goals of yours like aiding a charity or gaining an entree into new markets.

Consider whom you're bidding against. Some firms soliciting proposals will let you know who else is on the list—others prefer to keep that card close to their chests. If you get a clue that you're bidding against high-priced competitors, you might raise your estimate accordingly.

It would be nice to be paid for the value of your contribution to the client, rather than by the hour. After all, if I design a package for you that helps your product achieve international fame, is my contribution to your success worth some recompense? Should a logo seen around the world cost more than a logo for a local bakery? It takes the same time to develop either, theoretically, but the value to the customer is quite different.

Chapter 26 is devoted to the topic of selling professional services. You'll find more there about the process of presenting and persuading a client to pay your fee.

You're surely groaning, "It's all too much," just as I am now, and contemplating going to walk your dog. Go—but take with you one last thought. Whatever price you choose, test it by setting it a little higher. Why underestimate what the market will bear? You'll never know what you've lost unless you test. Your reward will come in your paycheck.

The Least You Need to Know

- When setting your price, you should take into account the Customer Value Pyramid, costs, and elasticity of demand. The environment around you constantly changes, and your pricing strategy should be changing to match.
- Changing price changes everything else. Your pricing strategy is as important as the other three Ps: Promotion, Place, and Product.
- The secret key to success in everything you do is in controlling the costs of doing it. Knowing your break-even point and what to do with it is one of the most important management tasks you'll ever undertake.
- Professional services, because of their intangible nature, are often judged by a relationship of price to quality. Not charging enough can hurt you more than charging too much.

Chapter 13

Channels of Distribution: How Products Get to Customers

In This Chapter

- Who's who in the distribution channel
- Developing distribution channels and managing physical distribution
- Getting your product to market: cost control versus customer satisfaction
- Using distribution, transportation, and warehousing strategies to contain costs and please customers

If you're in business, you've got a distribution function. There's no way around that. From Kalika driving her juice cart down to the college campus to Bob's Bottomless Boats accepting another shipment from Chris-Craft, there's a whole lot of distribution going on. Unfortunately, distribution can be a big pain. Goods get lost or broken. Customers get the wrong shipments and get upset. Wholesalers go behind your back and sell direct to your customers.

How do you manage a function that by its very nature leaves you so vulnerable? Verrrrrry carefully. Let's do a little problem analysis. There are two halves to the problem of distribution: the "who" and the "how."

We're going to look at the players in the distribution game first, examining both the channel sellers and the physical product deliverers. Then we'll examine how the distribution process works, and finally some potential strategies for making distribution decisions. The goal is to arm you with the knowledge you need to improve your distribution function. But first, let's take a look at the big picture.

Distribution's Place in the Scheme of Things

Remember the "Four Ps" plus the one I added? (How could you forget them?) Distribution is all about the concept of Place. The basic question asked by the marketing term "place" is "How do I get what I sell to the buyers?" It's really a question of distribution, but the term got its start from the place (the pushcart, the store, the shop) where a seller or "maker" exchanged with a buyer. It starts out simple, but as a business comes into being, the distribution or movement of goods and services from the maker/producer to the buyer gets more complicated.

Let's immerse ourselves in the "Place" issue by taking a dip in the river that marketers call the *channel of distribution*. Like most rivers, this one doesn't flow straight from its source to the sea—it wanders in all directions, reflecting the landscape around it.

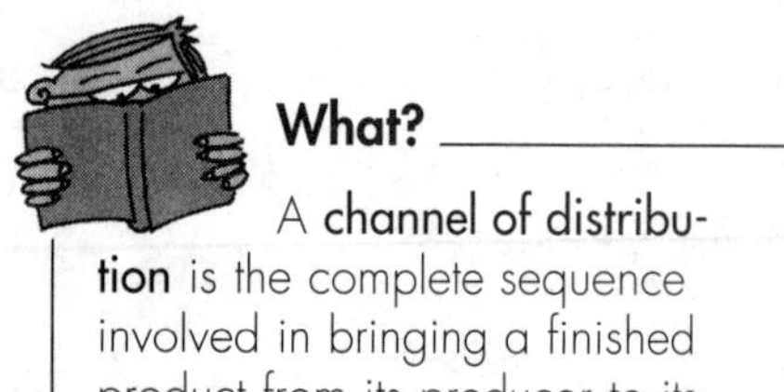

What?

A **channel of distribution** is the complete sequence involved in bringing a finished product from its producer to its ultimate consumer.

Distribution channels are made up of a sequence of transactions between business partners: manufacturers, wholesalers, retailers, and all kinds of agents and dealers' representatives in between.

A short channel might flow like a spring on a mountain-side plunging into a lake, with no intermediaries—just one straight rush from producer to end user. A longer channel might involve many twists, turns, and side branches. And that's about as far as I'll follow this river analogy.

In almost all cases, you won't be able to get the offering you produce directly into your buyer's hands in a timely and convenient way. You'd have to be running all over the place, or getting your customers to come to you, which isn't always convenient.

You need to distribute your offering through a strategically chosen channel. Your distribution channel will add the time and place utilities to your offering. They'll reduce the distance between buyer and seller, making your offering available at more times and in more places. When a product is located near the people who want it and is available at a time convenient to these folks, they are happier. That's why when you need a gallon of milk, you don't go to the farm or even to the dairy. You hit the convenience store down the street. Now, let's look at the potential players in the distribution channel.

Who's Who in Your Channel

Kalika, with her juice cart, handles distribution when she sells a freshly made banana-kiwi smoothie to her end user. In her distribution channel, one person assumes the roles of manufacturer, distributor, and retailer.

Not all producers can distribute their products so easily. Most have to choose one or more of the available distribution channels. Dozens of intermediaries can be involved in the movement of goods from producers to end users. Call them wholesalers, distributors, retailers, agents, and middlemen—they're the people who provide various services to help keep products and services flowing to buyers. It's a good idea to keep your channel short. So let's see if you can distribute in one step—through a retailer.

How the Retailer Works

Your first stop in looking for a distributor could be a retailer. If you can get a retail distributor who you deal with directly, you'll shorten the channel and reduce the number of possible glitches and costs. If Kalika decided to spend her time creating and bottling her smoothies, she might look for a retailer to sell them for her. Most retailers are not producers of the goods they sell. Most concentrate on core retailing functions, such as choosing a market niche and selecting the mix of products and services that niche will buy. If you're looking for a retailer as your distributor, your first step is to search out retailers whose mix of products and services would accommodate your offering.

The word "retail" can cover every kind of store, from a shop specializing in light bulbs to a giant warehouse store with something for everyone. Picture these two on a continuum from high markup, high service, to low markup and low service. Along the way, you would find wholesale clubs, discounters, department stores, and many others.

Each retailer, no matter where he or she falls on the continuum, is faced with the challenge of creating the right merchandise assortment. How does a retailer decide what to carry? The process begins, of course, when she chooses the location and market niche she'll serve.

Really!

What a retailer decides to carry in her store is called her "merchandise assortment," and it's the difference between success and failure for many merchants—as important as "location, location, location." Successful stores have buyers who show a talent for merchandise assortment that borders on genius.

It wouldn't hurt to interview buyers for stores whose assortments impress you. You can also make a point of bringing some evidence to retailers that your offering is something their customers would like to see you carry!

To create her merchandise selection and keep it lively as the seasons go by, a florist friend of mine follows suggestions from channel members upstream—distributors, wholesalers, and manufacturers. She reads trade magazines. She follows the local newspapers, talks to customers, and visits stores in other cities. She sniffs out trends wherever the clues can be found. She never visits another city without stopping in at local flower shops, browsing the selection, chatting with the merchants, and studying their display techniques. She—like many other retailers—is very willing to hear proposals for new offerings. So, if you're just getting your feet wet, try talking to some relevant retailers.

Of course, location is important to the retailer, and important to you when you're looking to hook up with a retailer. Location merits a chapter to itself. That'll be the next chapter. So stay tuned.

What the Distributors/Wholesalers Do

Retailers don't just wait for merchandise to show up. My florist friend assembles her eclectic merchandise from a number of sources. She's a channel-of-distribution case study. Picture her near the end of the stream, turning around and looking back up to see sources for merchandise she can sell. She is now in the role of a customer. She pursues every possible source, from mainline distributors to growing her own.

Intermediary distributors are essential for makers, manufacturers, small entrepreneurs like my friend, and all her peers up and down our Main Streets and shopping malls. As you'll see, distributors as intermediaries assume the risks and tackle the chores of distribution. Channel members upstream and down—like you, the manufacturer, or the retailer—would have to take on those functions. In such a world, only the large would survive.

To a great extent, distributors expedite the purchasing function, making ease of possession a reality. They'll take a quantity of your offering—a bulk lot—and break it into smaller lots, or assemble large lots from small ones. Then, they deliver your offering to the retailer, sorted into the desired quantities and varieties, and the retailer "delivers" it to the end user. Because the distributor does this sorting and delivering function, my florist friend can plan and order the quantity and variety she needs.

Distributors also finance customer purchases over 30, 60, and even 90 days, providing credit services more flexible than a bank's. Further, they provide the all-important function of taking risks, assuming the responsibility for problems such as spoilage, storage, and uncertain demand. They are responsible for the physical safety of their products, accepting the risk of fire or damage in transit or loss in any other way.

Finally, distributors play a big role in facilitating the flow of information between manufacturer and retailer. In return for all this, the distributor earns the right to charge his customers a higher price than he paid the manufacturers for the goods—and you'll complain if he's making more than a few pennies on the dollar. Rough life, isn't it?

Bring in the Specialists: Using Agents and Independent Reps

Okay, let's say Kalika has bottled her smoothies. Her demand is steady, and she turns her cart over to a trained employee. Then she contracts to provide a specific quantity to Natalie, an alternative beverage sales rep from a nearby city. Natalie begins selling smoothies in her "territory." She sells other drinks as well as Kalika's, but she is now a fixture in Kalika's distribution channel. She's not on staff. She either buys Kalika's offerings outright or works on percentages.

Agents frequently operate on commission; the manufacturer has no obligation to pay the agent if the product doesn't sell. That's an advantage over hiring a staff person to sell for you. Agents also typically cover large geographic territories, stretching your reach to places where thin demand wouldn't justify having your own sales force.

Now, the question you want to ask is, "How do you know when you need a sales agent or rep?" After all, you could do without a sales rep and still sell in other territories than the one you live in. I know a shoe dealer who designs her own children's shoes, has them manufactured in Spain, imports the finished products, and then gets in her car and travels the country selling that year's models. She's a pro at the process. Of course, if you want to expand to another city and don't want to travel as part of your business, an agent would be a good idea.

Mentor

A good rule of thumb for making the decision about sales agents is this: The less you know, the more you need to work with those who do. That's one of the most important pieces of advice I can give you, and it's particularly true when it comes to working with agents. Agents know the territory. Think of them as guides you share profits with. They bring insider knowledge, a familiarity with who wants what and who can provide it. They know who's tried what and whether it did or didn't work.

Some go-betweens receive their remuneration from the buyer in the deal; others are paid by the seller. You should "follow the money," as the saying goes. Make sure you have a general understanding of how your agent or rep is being rewarded for her trouble before you get in too deep. A good agent makes deals that are good for all parties. Don't be afraid to lean on your agent for help.

The bottom line: When you know nothing, you hire people for their expertise. When you've learned what you can from them, you can decide whether to assume the job yourself.

Physical Distribution: The Wheel Dimension

Okay, so Kalika is now selling her offering in several geographical territories. Her new company, "Smoothies for the People," has to send 20 cases of orange-kumquat-banana smoothies to one place, 40 cases of carrot-peach-guava smoothies to another … and so on. Selling is no longer the issue. Now, Kalika faces physical distribution concerns—what shippers, warehouses, and packaging are needed for her cases to make the trip to the purchaser on time, in good repair, and at reasonable cost.

Physical distribution introduces a lot of opportunities—and some of the deepest pitfalls you'll encounter. You will always be balancing the desire to keep costs down against the desire to give your customers the best possible service. Sacrifice one and you'll lose your customers—sacrifice the other and you'll lose your shirt! Excel at either, and you will find your reward in your improved bottom line.

Physical Distribution Issues

You'll have to do more than consider what packaging, warehouses, and shippers are needed to get your offering on the road and into the right hands. Who sees to it that it arrives safely on time and at a reasonable cost? That's the job of physical distribution.

The goal of physical distribution is to minimize cost while assuring that your delivery mechanism provides maximum customer value and service. Unfortunately, these are often contradictory goals. A customer would like you to drop everything to drive over, deliver and, perhaps, install the new Jacuzzi. But instant service would add an unacceptable cost, since you'd need to have workers standing by around the clock. So you and the customer arrive at a mutually beneficial compromise. The Jacuzzi comes next Tuesday, and the customer pays what he perceives to be a fair price for installation.

Mentor

Place (distribution) is the slowest to change of the original Four Ps. You can change prices overnight, and your product and its promotion usually can be changed in a few months. But building a solid distribution channel can take years.

Since the challenge is to minimize cost while delivering maximum customer service, planning and coordination are essential. Make sure these ingredients are in your distribution planning mix:

- Authority and responsibilities are clearly defined and clearly assigned.
- There is a structure for communication between each functional area that touches distribution: marketing, operations, finance, and personnel.
- Each channel member has access to the information he needs to do his job; each member's input is listened to; each receives feedback on how well he is performing and how he can improve.
- A distribution manager is in charge, and this position is filled by a person with strong leadership ability.

Cutting Costs

Cost is the main reason you care about physical distribution. If you can reduce cost in this area, you can claim a serious competitive advantage. A few pennies saved on freight, packaging, or storage go straight to your bottom line.

Customers care about getting their goods; they don't care about how. That's your business. So if you can reduce costs through a change in operations, and that change is invisible to the customer (or perceived as a benefit), you're doing the right thing.

How do costs add up in the distribution channel? There are handling costs at each step, transportation from manufacturer to wholesaler/distributor, wholesaler/distributor to retailer, and retailer to buyer (if delivery or installation is required).

There are costs associated with storage at each step as well, real-estate costs for warehousing, insurance costs, and less obvious costs for products lost to damage or obsolescence.

How can you cut those costs? Advanced technology is the first place to look. Computers reduce errors and save labor costs associated with order processing, inventory management, and billing. Other cost-reduction strategies result from changes in warehouse location, increased automation, and use of lower-cost freight carriers (land instead of air, for example).

Shipping Out! Transportation Decisions

Now we'll talk about the actual movement of your offerings from one place to another. Your decisions will involve what routes products take to market, who carries them there, and how much this process costs you. Let's look closer at each of the components of the transportation question.

Using Shippers

Most of us will use shippers of various sorts to meet our physical distribution needs. In many instances, distribution will involve a mix of shipping modes. A truck may ride piggyback on a railroad car. A package may be transferred from package service (taxi) to air freight (Federal Express) and back on its way from producer to end user. For information businesses, distribution has become increasingly electronic. When online data transfer became reliable enough, products like stock photos and type fonts began traveling by modem rather than CD-ROM.

> **Mentor**
>
> Changes in energy costs often affect shipping decisions. A temporary spike in gas costs may cause surcharges from over-the-road haulers as they struggle to protect their profit margins.

Each mode has its advantages and disadvantages; each has its part to play in the balancing act between customer service and cost control. If they needed it yesterday, the customer will pay for air freight. If they need it next year, water transport will probably do.

Paying the Fare

The main factor affecting which shipper you choose will be cost. What is the lowest possible expense that will meet your customer's need for timeliness? The main factor affecting the cost of the various options is that carrier's energy cost. It obviously costs more to fuel an airplane than to keep a freighter floating in the right direction. Keep an eye on energy costs and let increases be your clue to reexamine your transportation strategies.

What If You Need a Warehouse?

Goods often have to be housed for the time between their production and their consumption by the end user. Bulk lots are often broken down in the warehousing phase of distribution. For you to buy a stuffed bunny at the toy store, a toy distributor buys a pallet of bunnies from the factory, a chain buyer takes a case of 12 dozen bunnies, and each of his stores gets a bag of a dozen and breaks that open to sell me one.

At any of those stops along the way, that bunny was vulnerable to damage by fire, water, theft, or accident. If you need to consider warehousing as part of your distribution strategy, here are some things to think about.

Inventory Control

How many stuffed bunnies is enough? That's the fundamental question of inventory control. The ideal level of inventory is the one that keeps your costs low and at the same time provides the service customers want. (There's that balancing act again.)

Your only hope of answering the question of "how many" is to make accurate *sales forecasts*. If you were able to sell 144,000 bunnies last year, your projections will start with 144,000 bunnies for this year. You can adjust that by any factors you see affecting you.

What?

A **sales forecast** is a projection of future demand expressed in terms of dollars and units sold. The Consumer Expenditure Survey (described in Chapter 6) is useful for projecting demand in dollars for many products and services.

Materials Handling

Boxes of bunnies have to hop off the trucks from the manufacturer, on to and off of the storage shelves, through the picking and packing process, and back out the door. That process is called materials handling. People and machines are necessary to unload, identify, package, and reload the goods. Check to see if the warehouse your distributor uses has automated systems. Automation can reduce risk and cut costs.

Order Processing

Closely related to materials handling is the processing of orders that goes along with it. For each quantity of bunnies shipped, there's also a bunny order form, a choreography of picking from the shelves and packing for delivery, and with that an invoice.

Packaging for Shipping

Packaging for shipping is of vital importance. Your product must be protected during both storage and transportation. Packaging has to be strong enough for stacking and secure enough to prevent mildew, dirt, or insect invasions. Packaging can also improve order-processing accuracy if you use color-coding or other labeling to allow boxes to proclaim their contents.

Warehouse Cost Control

Each of the issues of warehousing—inventory control, materials handling, order processing, and packaging—represent opportunities to increase or reduce costs, depending on the balancing act you perform between customer service and cost control. Technology is an excellent tool to reduce those costs. Another way is to stock no more units than necessary.

Just-in-Time (JIT) Delivery

Just-in-time delivery is an excellent choice for cost control. It involves having the raw materials and parts arrive just in time for assembly, and then feeding the finished product into the distribution channel just in time for final purchase. Money is saved all along the channel. *JIT* attempts to reduce shortages or surpluses anywhere along the way. As well as controlling costs, it helps avoid disappointing customers. Dell Computer uses this strategy, and look where it's gotten them.

What?

Just-in-time (JIT) delivery means reducing problems of warehousing by having materials and products arrive just in time for use. In this way, the cost to store them and the potential for damage while in storage is reduced or eliminated.

Clearly, you need to make some strategic decisions about warehousing as well as decisions about distributors, retailers, and other actors in your channel of distribution. I've worked with distributors who found that having one central warehouse worked best, and others who deployed dozens of warehouses across the country and swore by that system. What works best for you depends on your strategic objectives.

Distribution Strategies

The key to your physical distribution strategy is understanding customers. (I know I sound like a broken record.) If you know their priorities and your own, you can perform the right balancing act between cost control and service.

Of course, you'll want to choose a channel of distribution that will work to your satisfaction. Two factors influence your choice of distribution channel: your marketing mix (the influence of the other Ps on this P) and the environment, the sea you swim in.

Your strategies regarding price, the characteristics you've designed into your product, and the degree and nature of the promotions you've committed to will all influence your distribution strategy. If you're committed to being the low-cost leader, you can't afford a long channel with lots of markups to pay along the way. You'll have to look at direct marketing and other cost-efficient ways of getting the product from producer to consumer.

What characteristics does the market display? What is the projected number of customers, where are they located, what is the average size of their purchase? If the buyers are few but large, that lends itself to a short channel. If the market is made up of many small customers, more complex channels are likely to develop.

What intermediaries are available to your market? In some geographic areas, there may not be an intermediary suitable to your needs. That's why Sears and Roebuck started a catalog operation all those years ago—the frontier stores were too few and far between.

How Many Outlets?

One, two, three, or many? Distribution can range from exclusive, where only one outlet in an area is allowed to sell a product, to intensive, where that product is placed as widely as possible. To determine what approach is right for you, consider the nature of the purchase. Is this offering a convenience, shopping, or specialty product or service?

As noted in Chapter 9, a convenience product is typically inexpensive, the need for it recurs frequently, and purchasers would rather settle for another brand than go out of their way to find the original. This situation calls for an intensive distribution strategy to get your product placed wherever the consumer might look for it.

If you sell a convenience product, distribution is the key to a healthy business. Anything you can do to make your product available in more places, at more times of day, will increase your sales.

Mentor

Well-established relationships are the key to successful channels of distribution. Unless you're in a completely unworkable mess, stick with what you're doing now, and look for ways to make it better.

Really!

The World Wide Web combined with the convenience of electronic data transfer presents a technological advantage for products that can be distributed electronically. These include numerical- or text-based products like data or white papers, and electronic graphics products like type fonts and stock photos.

Specialty products are the seldom-purchased items that require a significant investment. These typically require a more aggressive degree of sales and often some after-market service. An exclusive distribution strategy gives only one retailer in an area the option to sell a product and protects him from direct price competition. That motivates the retailer to provide the sales and support effort this product needs.

In between these two extremes is selling the "shopping product," which calls for a selective distribution strategy. A shopping product requires more involvement on the consumers' part than convenience products. These items have recognizable product differences, and often where they're purchased has an impact on their desirability. Makeup purchased at Marshall Field's makes the wearer feel different than makeup from Wal-Mart, although the difference may not be perceivable to a casual observer. A selective distribution strategy limits the number of outlets where your product is available. This protects the cachet of your product or service and gives you more control over marketing strategy.

Remember, the strategy you choose has to mesh with the rest of your marketing mix. Convenience items need maximum distribution. Shopping items that project a prestige image must arrive looking prestigious, not bashed-about or shop-worn. A specialty product that took months to sell had better not be delayed too long in delivery, or buyer's remorse may set in.

Push and Pull Strategies

There are really three strategies here, since you can opt for push, pull, or a combination of both.

In a push strategy, the manufacturer concentrates on wooing channel members and then using them to push products to the consumer. Wooing channel members means offering incentives that encourage middlemen to carry the goods. Your goal is to get those channel members fired up about moving your product. If that takes offering a Caribbean cruise, do it.

A push strategy fits when the product is in the mature phase of its life cycle. Essentially, you're recruiting your distribution channel members to help you stimulate consumer demand. This is easier than using a pull strategy, especially when the product lacks "new and improved" features to generate consumer excitement.

In a pull strategy, the manufacturer concentrates on reaching and persuading potential consumers, stimulating demand. These consumers go to the middlemen in the channel and demand the product, in essence pulling it down the channel.

When a new product creates a new product niche, sometimes a pull strategy is the only option you have. Distribution channel members have no motivation to take risks on untried products. Why would they? Creating consumer demand is the fastest way to show them you've got a viable product offering.

Mentor

While customer focus is critical, so is company focus. Keep your company's strategic goals in mind as you develop distribution strategies. There's no point in serving customers if you aren't serving yourself as well.

In a combination strategy, the manufacturer tries a little of both. Warning: This takes money! You will need to design promotions and devote marketing energy to each segment, and that means spending more money.

The most important rule of thumb you can follow in distribution is to maintain your customer focus. If you pick a target market and then orchestrate the channel members and physical distribution strategies to serve that market's needs, you'll stick to the right track.

A Life of Faith Dolls provides a tidy example of using push, pull, and combination strategies. The doll line was launched using a pull strategy. The company mailed catalogs to several thousand families who had registered at the website promoting the Elsie Dinsmore books. That mailing brought a 14 percent response—extremely good for direct mail. Next, the company developed attractive in-store display units that presented the entire line of dolls, books, and accessories, and displayed the line at a major Christian booksellers' convention. Robin and her team used the success of the earlier direct mail shot to demonstrate demand to the Christian retailers. The retailers responded positively, and a whopping 17 stores signed up to carry the dolls—three times the number A Life of Faith hoped to gain from that show. The catalogs pull consumers toward the product, while the in-store display units push product toward the consumer.

Next, A Life of Faith moved into a combination strategy, using the catalog in areas where Christian booksellers are scarce, but using retailer promotions in areas where the dolls are available in stores.

Select Your Channel Members

So you've decided which strategy fits your situation. Perhaps it involves your channel members or a change in your channel lineup. How will you go about choosing your business partners?

This checklist will help. Ask yourself, does this organization …

- Have the right people in place in management?
- Display the right attitude of cooperation?
- Carry other lines that are compatible with yours?
- Have the talents and skills to advertise and promote the product?
- Have a strong financial track record?
- Have the necessary services available to its customers?
- Have a good reputation in the industry?

You can't really decide if this player is right for your team until you know what your strategy is for the game. A pull strategy requires different characteristics in the channel than a push strategy does.

The Least You Need to Know

- A channel of distribution is an interdependent system of manufacturer, wholesaler, distributor, and retailer.
- Distributors provide services, such as flexible financing, risk taking, and assuming the tasks of physical distribution, earning them the right to charge a markup on the products they carry.
- Physical distribution is about balancing desire to minimize cost with desire to deliver maximum customer service.
- Successful physical distribution involves getting your product to market—deciding what routes your products will take, who will carry them, and how much this will cost—and making sure this strategy meshes with the rest of your marketing mix.
- Understanding transportation and warehousing operations will help you discover ways to contain costs throughout the distribution process.

Chapter 14

Location, Location, Location

In This Chapter

- Evaluate a shopping mall versus a "Main Street" location
- Consider your needs and those of your customers in choosing your workspace
- Look at contemporary alternatives, like home-based business and shared-service environments
- Examine steps and criteria to help you choose a business location
- Understand the pros and cons of locating in "virtual reality"

What location is right for you? Let me just hop on a plane and fly over for a visit. We'll have a look around your city. While we're driving around, I'll ask you about the kind of business you do and the kind of customer you target. The right location depends on your answers. If you're an avant-garde architect, we might look at a warehouse loft on the daring side of the tracks. If you're starting a dress shop targeting middle-aged women, we'll spin past a renovated strip mall instead.

The location you choose can make or break your business. Saddling yourself with a location that's too expensive can rob your bottom line. But a cheap space in the wrong place is an even worse mistake. How do you make a good decision about your location? Very carefully, I hope. Luckily, you're not alone; others have faced this question before you. In this chapter, I'll show you some tools others have developed for location decisions and some useful alternatives to consider.

Retailers Know: It's "Location, Location, Location"

If I came to your city and did what I just described, I'd be acting informally as your business location consultant. The real professionals in this area use formulas and checklists to study the merits of a potential location. Its assets and liabilities will be weighed in the balance. If you're about to launch a major new enterprise, you may want to invest in a consultant's help with choosing your location.

> **Mentor**
>
> Choosing your location is as important—or more so—than choosing the merchandise assortment you'll offer. Both are questions of customer focus. You have to be where customers will go, with an offering customers will buy.

> **Mentor**
>
> As you look for complementary businesses, keep an eye out for a restaurant and a bank. The proximity of either—and better yet, both—is good for your business because they draw lots of traffic.

A bad decision will cost you more than a consultant's fees. A specialist will help you develop specific guidelines for your situation, including proximity to population densities, the demographic makeup of the area in relation to your target customer base, analysis of local traffic patterns, and more. Later in this chapter, you'll find a similar checklist for evaluating potential sites.

The most important question when it comes to location is not really where, but who with? You must find a location that puts you in the company of other businesses that are complementary to yours—not competitors, and not completely unrelated either. One area might feature a cluster of service businesses, like a dry cleaner, a package shipper, and a copy shop. Another might lean toward youthful clothes, with a shoe store, a retro-fashion shop, and a hip boutique all in a row.

As you think about location, consider the nature of your offering. In earlier chapters (Chapters 9 and 13, but who's counting), I used the labels *convenience*, *shopping*, and *specialty* to categorize products and services. For convenience products, finding precisely the right location is critical. You can be where the traffic count is right and the population demographics perfect, and yet still have a loser location—for a reason as simple as requiring a left turn to enter your parking lot.

Consumers of shopping products have different priorities. These shoppers will prefer making a purchase from a well-known retailer over discounters, and will pay more for the cachet of a name like Marshall Field's, even if the same product is available elsewhere for less. In this situation, location must support the overall tone the retailer wants to project. Why do some malls have dozens of similar dress shops? Because dresses are a shopping product.

The third category, specialty products, covers the seldom-purchased items that typically require a substantial investment. The boats over at Bob's Bottomless Boats are specialty products. The location of Bob's is driven not by proximity to customers but by proximity to water. When it's time to look for boats, people will drive to where the boats are. Being able to test-drive in the water and look at a huge selection are more important to consumers than convenience.

Really!

Sometimes locating near a competitor can be a winning strategy. A manufacturer and retailer of all-natural ice cream products in San Francisco set up shop in the early 1970s by choosing locations near Baskin Robbins outlets. Baskin Robbins had done all the location research. The all-natural ice cream producer figured his product was different enough to not be a direct competitor but similar enough to piggyback. It worked.

Old Versus New: Malls and Downtown Districts

Where you'd like to work and where customers would like to shop are two different questions. In service businesses, and especially those that serve other businesses rather than the consuming public, location is practically a non-issue. You could be faxing from the moon and it wouldn't change your client's perception of you. A little later in this chapter we'll pick up the discussion of location and the service business. For now, let's talk retail. Retailers (unless you're a big-box superstore, in which case I wonder why you're reading this book) have basically two choices when it comes to location: a shopping mall or a traditional business district.

Shopping malls come in three sizes: neighborhood, community, and regional. A neighborhood mall is likely to be a strip mall, a design featuring a string of stores separated from the road by a parking lot. Most of the products sold in strip malls are convenience products. A community mall is larger and usually features an anchor store, a large well-known store that attracts high traffic. The smaller stores attracted to that mall will target the same market segments the anchor store draws. Most shopping products feel at home in this atmosphere, surrounded by complementary and even competing products. Regional malls are the largest, featuring as many as 200 stores. They draw from a large geographic area and feature a mix of convenience, shopping, and specialty products. You'll find a whole world-within-a-world under the roof here.

Then there's downtown. Downtowns are an important option for all types of businesses to consider. Until a few decades ago, these were the shopping centers of America. Many of us still prefer their urban characteristics to the bland Nowheresville of most malls.

City governments, with the assistance of federal programs like the National Trust for Historic Preservation's Main Street Program, are reversing the suburban shopping trend. Borrowing concepts like covered walkways and convenient parking from their young competitors, many older business districts are finding exciting new life. Minneapolis, Seattle, Boston, and Chicago have all tried and succeeded at downtown revitalization.

Really!

Older downtown streets are becoming a protected species. The federal Main Street Program helps to fund beautification projects, marketing programs, and redevelopment. Other government mechanisms, like business improvement districts (BIDs) and tax-incremental-financing (TIF) districts are giving businesses in older areas a helping hand.

If you're looking at a downtown location, ask your real estate agent or potential landlord whether any of these programs are in place.

How can you make a downtown location work for you? One key is to find a spot on the verge of redevelopment. Restaurants and artists' studios are often the first to pioneer a new area. The cachet of their success encourages other businesses to join them. Old warehouses, former mansions, and recycled civic buildings have all been successfully converted into downtown "malls." They will never match malls amenity for amenity, but they offer a viable alternative.

Pitfall

A frequent complaint about older business districts is that the stores' hours vary considerably. There's nothing stopping the merchants from forming an association and negotiating common hours, joint promotions, and other mall-like amenities. If you are looking at a "Main Street" location, ask your potential neighbors about this.

Whichever you choose, shopping mall or downtown district, certain basic criteria must be met. First on the list are comfort and safety. You need climate control, cleanliness, social order, and aesthetics.

Malls offer certain advantages because of their centralized management. If you feel strongly about joint promotions, administrative support, and good landlord/tenant relations, including your right to have a say in who replaces old tenants in neighboring storefronts, a mall location is the right choice. Those amenities come at a price, however. Your least-expensive option will be the undiscovered gem in an up-and-coming part of town where overhead is lower. Your tradeoff will be the lack of a central managing body.

You're the One Who Has to Work There

Let's say we've finished driving around town and we've found several locations that might work for you. We've even met some real estate agents and walked through some properties. Let's go get a steak and talk about your work life. I want to uncover the little things that you'll overlook in your first blush of infatuation with this exciting architectural feature or that fabulous traffic count.

We don't stop being people when we get to work. Entrepreneurs are especially prone to long hours. The ideal is a workplace that has all the comforts of home.

There are human needs the workplace has to satisfy. The obvious ones, like parking reasonably nearby and a safe way to get to and from your car, you'll think of. But what about a good place to wash up your coffee cups and microwave your lunch? How many bathrooms are on each floor, and are they laid out in a way that works? How's the janitorial service? More and more office buildings are paying attention to the "social life" of buildings, including break rooms and cafeterias, workout facilities, or at least showers on-premises. These will make a big difference to you when you work those 14-hour days.

What about views? Nature? A place to walk over a lunch hour? In my opinion, a business location can and should provide a spiritual lift to its occupants. Don't underestimate the impact of your space on your life.

How is the space you're looking at laid out? Do your business's daily operations get done by teams or by individuals? The answer affects whether an open floor plan or a suite of offices will suit you better. Don't think you can plop a group of people accustomed to one style into the other without making some waves.

And lastly, is the location near a source of potential employees, and is it accessible to them by means other than a car? If your employees can live simply, you reduce their overhead, and indirectly yours.

But Your Customers Are the Ones Who Have to Shop There

About the time we've finished our steaks and ordered chocolate pie and coffee, our conversation will turn from your perspective as a potential inhabitant to the other perspective: that of the potential customer.

Every store that opens for business projects an atmosphere. Remember the hardware store your father took you to as a child? The bins of bolts and nails, the toy aisle, the strange gewgaws for sale around the cash register? That store projected an image just as surely as a hair salon. But it's the hair salon that takes a marketing approach to doing it.

Atmosphere is what brings customers to a store and keeps them enjoying the experience when they come in. A good retail location offers you potential to control the exterior and interior displays and store layout. Your efforts can increase store traffic, encourage shoppers to stay longer in the store, and stimulate them to make purchases on impulse.

Consider all five senses when you think about atmosphere. Use color and light to please the eye, music, textures, and scents to involve the other senses. A harshly industrial setting might be the right atmosphere for one clothing store. A country cottage à la Ralph Lauren might suit another. All senses come into play in perceiving atmosphere.

Really!

For years background music has been used in stores to create atmosphere. Now retailers are appealing to other senses as well.

Many retailers have found that the right scent increases shoppers' inclination to buy. For example, a furniture store uses apple and spice scents to help shoppers feel more at home. It costs next to nothing, I'm told, and it has been shown to produce measurable results. Large department stores frequently put their cosmetics and perfumes department near the front entrance of the store to increase their sensual appeal.

The exterior of a building sends clues about the businesses inside. In malls, the signage and exterior graphics are often tightly controlled. In a free-standing location, on the other hand, you can build your hot-dog stand in the shape of a giant bun if you so desire. It pays to coordinate exterior with interior, and to coordinate both with the brand identity you want to project.

To sum up customers' perception of your place of business: It should feel comfortable and safe, allow for a pleasant shopping experience, and exceed expectations in a way that will be memorable. That's the "breakthrough" that marketers strive to achieve in everything from merchandising to advertising.

Location Concerns for Service Businesses

Let's focus on the service business for a moment. I don't mean retail services like dry cleaning. I'm talking about the accountants, graphic artists, nonprofit organizations, and others of the hundreds of types of businesses that deliver a service offering to other businesses and individuals.

If you need to meet with clients and can afford space in a standard office building, use the criteria for making a choice described later in this chapter. If your service requires that you visit with clients rather than have them come to you, or if you are not yet financially prepared for the cost of a standard office, you might try one of the following alternatives.

There's No Place Like Home (The Home-Based Business)

The business of home businesses is booming. More and more people are trying this alternative. Why do we want to work at home? After all, it's still work.

Some home-workers are entrepreneurs who see the wisdom of keeping their overhead low. Others are employees who have negotiated telecommuting as a perk. Employers have found that, contrary to their initial fears, allowing employees to go home to work has paid off in a number of ways. Some workers are more productive away from the distractions of the office. Others need flexibility to manage their child care needs. A company can gain benefits from allowing the home-work option, including retaining valuable employees and deferring expansion moves. Modems, e-mail, faxes, and all that have made telecommuting a healthy, practical, normal way to work.

There are dozens of books and magazines out there addressing the realities of home-based business. The idea has never appealed to me—I like to use my home for relaxing and my office for work. I have worked from home and I couldn't keep one from invading the other. But for some people, working at home is a practical solution to a number of problems.

Really!

One type of business has always been based at home: the family farm. An exciting trend in farming has been the increased professionalism of the farm office, with computerized production records, accounting, payroll, and marketing functions.

Another fast-growing trend at home is the day-care enterprise. Many women with young children find this a satisfying way to combine professional and personal goals. Other options for working from home include arts and crafts production; dispatch operations for maintenance services like lawn care, snow shoveling, and janitorial work; and more. Look up and down the street where you live; are there businesses under your nose?

There are a few things to think about before you get started wiring the basement for a new office:

- Do local zoning codes allow home-based business?
- Will your business cause neighborhood traffic and parking problems?
- Do you have the discipline to maintain a regular work schedule?
- Do your family and friends understand your endeavor well enough to take you seriously and not interrupt your work day?

If the answer is yes, you're 90 percent ready to work at home. One more concern: How will you combat the isolation? Service clubs like Rotary or Lions, meetings with your clients and vendors, even volunteer work can be important social outlets to replace the 'round-the-water-cooler life of an office. Social sports—such as tennis, squash, soccer, softball leagues, and so on—also are effective replacements for the water cooler (plus great ways to get exercise *and* meet potential new clients).

Mentor

A home business can be big business if you do business on the World Wide Web. For example, A Life of Faith Dolls runs a sizable operation out of two home offices in two different states. At its start-up, A Life of Faith Dolls' warehousing and fulfillment (shipping of orders) operations are managed by Robin Woods Sumner out of her Texas country home. "It's our plan to find out what it takes. Then we'll hire or start a fulfillment company when the volume is there," said Robin, who is currently sharing her home with her design workshop and considerable inventory.

An online business run out of the home offers convenience to customers combined with the comfort of working from home. And the low overhead doesn't hurt either party.

Shared Services Office Space

Another trend in recent years has been toward shared services under one roof, sometimes in simple rental arrangements and in other cases in *business incubators*.

An incubator provides both space and services for start-up businesses. Some are privately run for profit; others receive assistance from local community economic development bodies. The value of incubators as a tool for generating jobs and recycling abandoned industrial buildings is widely recognized. An incubator, as its name implies, helps businesses grow and then forces them to leave the nest. Rent is often staged from well below market rate in the first year to near-market rates in the third or fifth year, after which the business is presumed to be viable and sent out to compete in the "real world."

> **What?**
>
> A **business incubator** is real estate with a mission. Incubators provide space and services to start-up businesses, often at well below market rate. Economic development groups will subsidize incubators to create jobs, stimulate growth, and revitalize certain geographic areas. The key feature of an incubator is that successful tenants must eventually graduate into the "real world."

Both incubator and shared-services real estate provide an assortment of amenities ranging from access to photocopiers and conference rooms to shared receptionists, bookkeepers, and even experienced business consultants.

Finding office space for a one-man band can be very difficult. It's easy to rent 5,000 square feet but difficult to rent 500. It pays to be creative in your search. If your community doesn't have shared-service office environments, look for an informal arrangement. A business complementary to yours with excess space might be delighted to rent you a spare office and allow you access to its office equipment. Approach the business with a focus on the benefits to its operation and see where it gets you.

It's Your Turn: Get Started Finding Your Location

The site selection process should begin way before the driving-around-town stage. When it comes to locating your business, only you, in your unique situation, can tell when a particular location is appropriate for you. So for the time being, while you face the location question, you have to become an expert in an area unrelated to your usual business activities. Even if you hire a specialist, you're going to need to understand the many ways that location impacts your business and what you're willing to trade to get what you want.

First Step: Conduct an Asset Survey

Start by making a checklist of assets your potential location should have. It certainly must be accessible for you and your employees. Ask yourself how far you're willing to commute to work before you begin looking across town. It may be less important to be accessible to clients if you serve them by mail order or by visiting their offices. If they come to see you, check out your potential location through their eyes. It wouldn't hurt to ask a good customer to come with you on a location-scouting trip.

How many square feet of office space do you need? If rent per square foot is not too high, look for about 200 square feet per employee for desk and computer-type work. The layout of the space will cause you to adjust that up or down. Are there common work areas, conference rooms, private offices where you'll need them?

Don't forget to think about storage, either. Why do offices never have enough closets? Think about where the cleaning supplies, old files, and office-supply stockpile will go. To save money, many businesses use off-site storage for old-but-necessary files. How much sense does it make to rent quality office space and then dedicate it to storage?

After surveying both your needs and those of your clients, prepare a wish list for your potential space. Sort it into must-haves, would-be-nice features, and fantasies. Then match each proposed location against the list.

Really!

Office space rents are typically quoted in terms of cost per square foot per year. To compute the monthly rent on a 1,000-square-foot office priced at $15/sq. ft., multiply $15 by 1,000 for cost per year, and then divide by 12 (months). The answer, $1,250, is the monthly check you'll write to your landlord. Ask whether the quote is "triple net," a real estate brokers' term meaning that janitorial services, utilities, and routine maintenance are included as part of your rent payment.

Information Resources

Seek out information on business relocation. The library isn't much help here: Your professional contacts and the community resources available to you will be more helpful. Contact the nearest office of the Small Business Administration (SBA) and ask for help. Find out whether there is a Small Business Development Center in your community.

These SBA/university partnerships offer a tremendous amount of free consulting and other services to small business. If there is a college campus in your town, contact the business professors and ask questions. You may find MBA students busily compiling the statistics on population density, traffic, and other trends and patterns you'd like to be aware of.

Start asking everyone you know in business about their location/relocation experiences. Talk to brokers, but remember, just as when you're buying or selling a home, a commercial real estate broker is not a neutral party. Check in with the Chamber of Commerce.

I've moved my business twice. The first time, I fell in love with a space much too big for my needs and laid out in a beautiful but thoroughly impractical way. That bad decision nearly put me out of business. When I finally found my way out of that lease I moved again.

This time I shopped smarter. I grounded my thinking in reality; I engaged a specialist to negotiate on my behalf rather than taking on the broker on my own. As a result I found a new "home" that was not just comfortable but led to new business contacts and more efficient work habits. And then I sold my business to another tenant of the building, with whom I had successfully collaborated on many projects. How's that for a happy ending?

I'm telling you from personal experience. Location can make or break your business!

Five Steps to Location Decisions

There aren't really five steps that will take you from "where?" to "there!" But I can offer you some criteria that will help you select a site.

- How strong is the local market? Consider demographics, competition, and market trends.
- Is the site visible and accessible to suppliers and customers? Are the traffic flow and the available parking space adequate?
- What are the costs, first for acquisition (purchase or renovation) and then for ongoing operations (rent, utilities, and taxes)?
- Is the right labor pool available? (Particularly important if you need seasonal help or are looking at a remote location.)
- How's the community? Is the neighborhood filled with complementary stores, and is it safe and well-maintained? Are the neighbors amenable to your locating there? (Don't plan on putting a chemical plant in a residential district without opposition.)
- Would you be in compliance with local zoning codes if you chose this location?
- Does this site meet your needs for proximity to population densities, and does the demographic makeup of the area match your target customer base?
- Does the site offer sufficient operational advantages? (Consider both cost and physical layout.)

If you're the analytical type, you can make yourself a score sheet and rank each location from 1 to 10 on each question.

Mentor

It's very common to negotiate for some upfront "freebies" when a long-term lease is at stake. Ask for a few months' free rent to offset moving costs. Ask for the landlord to cover any remodeling needed—costs referred to as "build-outs" in the real estate business.

Now I'll try to come up with five steps, as promised.

1. Do your asset survey. Define the perfect space for you.
2. Consult your information resources. Become as educated on the "space" question as you can.
3. Start driving around, talking to brokers, and letting it be known that you're looking. You'll soon assemble your slate of candidates.
4. Interview. Rank each location based on the preceding criteria.
5. Begin negotiating for the spaces that would meet your needs. Be sure each candidate knows that you have other options under consideration. Maybe you can get a bidding war going.

Really!

Watch out for rent increases spelled out in the lease! It's not uncommon to see some serious rises in the later years of the lease term. Don't just look at a figure of "3 percent" or "6 percent" and say "that doesn't sound like much." Do the math and work out what your rent will be in each year of the lease. If you're stretching to meet the first year's rent, don't assume your success in the intervening period will cover the demands of the past year's rent increase. None of us can predict the future.

The Least You Need to Know

- Retailers need to evaluate the pros and cons of a shopping mall versus a "Main Street" location. For service businesses, replace "shopping mall" with "office building."
- Both you and your customers have to like the place—consider your needs as well as those of your customers.
- Consider alternatives, like home-based business, shared-service environments, and incubators before you make a final decision.
- Take a disciplined approach, using asset surveys and decision criteria, to make a business-smart decision. Whatever you do, don't "trust your gut" when it comes to location.

Chapter 15

Sales Promotion

In This Chapter

- What a sales promotion is and why businesses use them
- How to balance the three possible objectives of a sales promotion
- How to understand a sales promotion by looking at its components
- How to develop a sales promotion from start to finish

Ever since Chapter 3, when I introduced the Four Ps (plus the fifth P—people), I've been using the word "promotions" as a big catch-all. Depending on the context, when I said "promotions," I could have been referring to advertising, selling, or the use of incentives to stimulate short-term sales. Advertising and selling are big topics. They are the major components of the P for promotion, and I'll deal with them in Parts 4 and 5. For now, let's turn our attention to a small P: the specific techniques used to promote short-term sales. It's time to introduce sales promotions.

In some professions, like psychology or accounting, gimmicky promotions would seem tacky or even unprofessional. That doesn't mean a quiet loyalty-reward program won't work to your advantage. But this chapter is probably less relevant to the professional service provider than to the wholesale or retail business. Many of these use sales promotions almost all the time.

What Are Sales Promotions? Promotions That Generate Sales

Sales promotions are special short-term strategies you come up with to give your customers incentives to buy. When you offer coupons for an oil change, advertise two-for-one dry-cleaning, or offer a loyalty reward like a frequent-buyer card, you're using a sales promotion.

The good news about sales promotions is that they produce results quickly. The bad news is that the impact doesn't last. When the promotion ends, its effect usually tapers off rapidly. However, sometimes a very well-designed sales promotion can have long-term effects. The proper sequence of sales promotions can cause new behaviors to be tried and perhaps even to become habit. In that case, a well-planned sales promotion can be an excellent way to introduce a new product and get people to learn about it.

What, When, and How Much Off: Sales Promotion Strategies That Work

Sales promotions can be directed at consumers, wholesalers, or retailers. The ones that come to your mind when I say "sales promotions" are probably consumer promotions, the coupons that come in the mail, rebates on packages at the store, or the free gift with your new checking account. But not all sales promotions are pitched to the end user. Many occur up the distribution channel, in the form of free products, discounts for volume purchases, point of purchase materials, co-op advertising, and contests for dealers.

What?

A **sales promotion** is an activity intended to stimulate purchases over a specific time period, by offering an incentive in addition to the inherent features of the product or service for sale.

Who Uses Promotions and Why

Half the world is using promotions as part of a pull strategy, encouraging consumers to buy. These promotions pull products through the distribution channel in response to new demand, which wouldn't be there without the promotional incentive. The other half is using a push strategy, encouraging distributors to sell. This strategy pushes products along the channel by giving dealers incentives to sell specific products or brands.

Why do you care? What can a sales promotion accomplish for you? Here's how to know when is it time to pull out this particular bag of tricks.

- **You need a quick fix.** Maybe a competitor is stealing market share and you need to counter his move. Grab the spotlight with a special event or contest.
- **Customers aren't trying a new product.** Maybe you should try a money-off incentive to reduce financial risk.
- **You are a manufacturer and you want to encourage retailers to push your product.** Offer a system of discounts that are tied to volume sales.
- **You want to increase recall of your advertising.** You want learning to take place, so take a lesson from the behaviorists: Offer a reward to customers who mention they saw the ad.
- **You need a way to measure your advertising's effectiveness.** Promotional devices like coupons give you a way to track and evaluate your responses.

Mentor

Loyal customers are the key to growth and profitability, providing a base upon which your business can grow. Remember, it costs less to hold a customer than to find a new one. As you plan promotions, think about how to attract and hold customers, not just how to get a one-time sales shot in the arm.

Three Promotional Objectives

You can use a promotion to accomplish lots of things, but whatever your goal, the action you take is going to achieve one of three things: Your promotion is going to encourage trial, build awareness, or reward loyalty. Any of these will increase sales, at least temporarily. A careful balance of all three is going to lead prospects along the course from nonuser to loyal user. Maintain a balanced promotional program, and you'll keep the sales flowing.

Sales promotions are very good at leveraging your other advertising and sales efforts. Each tool helps the others to work better. Sometimes a sales promotion is the tiebreaker you need when competition is tight. (If two banks offer free checking but one is throwing in a toaster, which would you choose?) That's a good thing, but it shouldn't happen by accident. Make sure your sales promotion strategies are carefully integrated with the other parts of your marketing strategy.

Sales promotions require considerable planning. The logistics of timing, duration, and message must be worked out, and, of course, these must be coordinated with the rest of your advertising plans. Can you get the promotional gizmos distributed throughout the territory in time? Will you run your specials back-to-back, or alternate with periods of no promotional activity? How does that plan fit with your media schedule? Is your sales staff trained and ready to follow up on the new leads a consumer contest will generate? When you set your promotional objectives, don't underestimate the management of time and effort required to do the job well.

Promotions Defined: A Look at the Components

Every promotional program is shaped by three components: the *incentive*, the means of delivering it (coupons, contests, etc.), and a media strategy for informing your buyers about the promotion. Your choices add up to a promotional strategy. How you make those choices is up to you—let your creativity or your budget be your inspiration. You'll decide what to offer, how to offer it, and how much it will cost you. Breaking promotions into these components helps you come up with fresh ideas time after time.

What?

An **incentive** is something that satisfies a particular desire or motivation. Behavioral scientists use incentives to teach lab rats new mazes; advertisers use incentives to teach desired behaviors to their prospective customers; large distributors or manufacturers offer incentives to sales reps to encourage competition for the highest sale figures.

Motivate with Incentives

Incentives are the value that will be offered in the promotion. What might motivate a person to behave the way you'd like? Marketers offer any of the following, alone and in combinations:

- Saving money
- A chance to try your offering for free
- A gift
- An experience

What?

Delivery method in this context means how you get word of your sales promotion into the hands (and eyes and ears) of the customers it's intended for. At its most complicated, the delivery method packages the promotion as part of a larger set of activities, like a contest or special event. At its most simple, the delivery method is a sale price offered at the cash register.

Consider Methods for Incentive Delivery

The *delivery method* is how you package that incentive. Here are some methods that will get your incentive in front of your intended audience:

- A sale-price label
- A coupon
- A multiple-purchase discount (buy 10, get 1 free)

- A product sample
- A premium (from small gizmos to expensive gifts)
- A contest
- A special event

Be Sure to Have a Promotional Media Strategy

Where are the members of your intended audience getting their news and views? Where are they making their purchase decisions? Place your message where they're most apt to be persuaded by it. Here are some potential media at your disposal:

- Advertising (print and/or broadcast)
- On package
- Point of sale
- Direct mail
- Newspaper insert
- In person

> **Mentor**
>
> When the price or the profit margin is low on the item you're trying to sell, make your incentive require a purchase (or several). When the price point is high, you can offer a discount even on the first purchase. And when the goal is to get people to try something for the first time, you may have to give it away for free.

Once you've made a choice for each component, you know what you're doing. But for how long will you do it? What's the timing of your promotion going to be? First there's the duration question: How long will the offer be in effect? But then the timing question gets stickier.

Timing can be immediate or delayed. An immediate promotion gives the reward right away and with no commitment. Picture yourself accepting the frozen yogurt sample in the grocery aisle.

Delayed timing, on the other hand, requires that the prospect make some move toward adopting the desired behavior. Picture yourself buying 10 café lattes in order to get that eleventh cup free. By the time you get your incentive, the coffeehouse has got you needing a daily latte fix.

Know the Three Promotional Objectives

A little earlier in this chapter, I stated that a promotion is going to do one of three things: encourage trial, build awareness, or reward loyalty. Designing your promotional activities to include a little of each will lead prospects along the course from non-user to loyal customer. Let's take a closer look.

> **Pitfall**
>
> Giving away free samples is more expensive than offering a coupon. Control those costs by deciding just how much to give away. Giving too much free product will drive up your promotional cost. Give your bottom line careful thought before you hand out product samples.

Step Right Up: Promotions to Encourage That First Sale

People who've never tried certain products might just do so with the right incentive. For some, that means a free sample—a taste of frozen yogurt at the grocery or a miniature cereal box in the mailbox. Others might need a money-off incentive to remove some of the financial risk of trying something new. Coupons are the typical delivery method for money-off incentives.

Take Two, They're On Sale: Ways to Grow Little Fish into Big 'Uns

It's not hard to get someone to try something once. But how do you turn that into a loyal habit? The answer is called building awareness. You can't let them forget how good it was when they tried it, whatever it was—a product or behavior. You've got to generate enthusiasm that makes them want to do it again and again.

Contests and special events are great ways to get those incremental sales. They can be designed to support your advertising themes and positioning strategies. A brewery sponsors an Oktoberfest event and builds awareness of its seasonal brews. Bob's Bottomless Boats rewards its highest-grossing sales associates with a scuba-diving weekend in Cancun. Both generate excitement, and that leads to the desired behavior: in the first case, purchasing the beer; in the second, increasing the sales effort.

> **Mentor**
>
> If you're pursuing the push strategy, try a contest. Sales competitions and achievement rewards are an effective way to motivate dealers and salespeople. Good salespeople are naturally very competitive, and they will work very hard to win.

Loyalty Pays Off

Some marketers are leery of loyalty rewards. After all, why would you take customers who are paying full price for something and offer it to them for less?

On the surface that's logical, but I encourage you to look deeper. Your competitors may be dangling promotional incentives to lure your customers away from you. You can't afford to assume they're loyal to you as a matter of course. Show them occasionally that you appreciate their business.

A special event or tasteful gift can be a nice way to recognize loyal patrons. And many businesses offer rewards for cumulative purchases. Once upon a time it was savings stamps, redeemable for merchandise; today it's multiple-purchase rewards like coffee cards and frequent-flyer miles.

Promotional Pricing: A Controversy

Lowering prices for a short time is one of your best tools for creating urgency to buy. But once you lower your prices, what have you done? Some people feel every discount you offer teaches your customers to wait for a sale before they buy. Make sure your promotional messages communicate that lower prices are for a limited time only. Then make sure you have some time periods where no promotions are in effect. Otherwise, your offering will be pegged as a discount product, something of lesser value commanding a lower price.

Price Adjustments: How to Use Consumer Discount Pricing

A sales price can do two things. It can allow consumers to purchase more for less, and it can allow you to dispose of merchandise you want to get rid of. When your goal is the latter, try a bundling strategy. Offer two products for the price of one, if that will get them to move, or include the less-desirable product free with something that has more "legs." Upscale retailers commonly use this strategy at the holidays, bundling makeup, perfume, or, for some reason, stuffed animals, with other purchases. Many types of businesses—not just department stores—use bundling strategies effectively.

Really!

If you do have a big promotion, don't be surprised if the period immediately following it shows lower than normal sales. Some of the sales you get are the result of moving ahead sales you would have gotten a few weeks later anyway. This can especially be the case for products that consumers can stockpile during a sale, such as soft drinks, as opposed to fresh produce.

Just as a sponge can absorb so much water and no more, in many cases a market can absorb only so much product before it becomes saturated. No amount of promotional fireworks can encourage people to buy what they do not want or need.

When your goal is allowing consumers to purchase more for less, offer a sale price as an incentive. But be wary: Don't get caught in the crossfire of a price war. If you drop prices, your competitors may retaliate with more of the same. Before you know it, everybody's selling at or near cost. Consumers are delirious and able to stock up. Next thing you know, demand is down, profits are down, and there's no quick fix in sight.

Price Adjustment: How to Use Discount Pricing for Retailers

If you are a wholesaler or a retailer who deals with large-scale wholesalers, you might look at an incentive plan that provides a lower price for volume sales. Oscar Mayer foods, for example, has offered a fairly elaborate system of price levels that depend on how much product a retailer moves. Buy a certain amount of sliced ham, and get one price; buy more, and get a better price. Oscar Mayer put considerable effort into this system, using detailed brochure booklets to explain the promotion.

Adjusting prices to correlate with volume sales is a great incentive offer for wholesalers, and can increase the profit margin for retailers who can push volume by creating promotions of their own.

Summary: It's Time to Develop Your Promotion

Absolutely the number-one place to start is deciding what you want the promotion to accomplish. Choose specific objectives and set measurable performance goals. You must be able to tell if your promotions are successful, so decide what your definition of success is going to be.

Bob's Bottomless Boats might state a goal like this: "Motivate sales associates to increase power boat sales by 10 percent between June and August," or "Use a special event to build retail traffic before the boating season begins."

The University Credit Union frequently offers promotions tied to the seasons—in early spring, it offers a special promotional rate on home equity loans because spring is home repair season. In early fall, it offers a special promotional gift for new checking accounts to woo students beginning a new school year.

Choosing the Offer

When you choose the components of your promotion, what constraints influence those decisions? On the one hand lies the greater context of your marketing strategies—positioning and advertising themes. On the other hand (and it's a tight fist) lies the return on investment projected for the promotion.

Every sales promotion has costs associated with it, including something as obvious as the foregone revenue created by a price-off incentive. More elaborate promotions entail costs for production and delivery of the message, plus the incentive itself. What if sales don't increase as projected? You're up a creek wishing Bob were around to sell you a paddle.

Using promotions successfully means learning to project your costs and then project your revenue. You find the right offer to make by taking a guess and then analyzing its break-even costs at some projected volume of sales. And how do you arrive at those projections? There are no easy answers, but let's try.

> CAUTION
>
> **Pitfall**
>
> Every promotion has a cost associated with it. It may be only the revenue passed up in making the offer, but the cost can be substantial if there's media or direct mail to buy to advertise the promotion.

Projecting Response

A number of factors can affect response. Does your offering lend itself to promotions? Is the purchase cost large or small? My best advice to you is to seek out your trusty advisors, your banker, trade association, and the sales reps for the media where you might advertise the promotion. Solicit their help in projecting your response rates.

Take a "guesstimate" of how many responses the promotion will bring, and how many of those responses result in sales, to arrive at your best guess for the sales volume you'll generate. Subtract your promotional costs, and you'll have your promotion's contribution to your bottom line.

That's the revenue side of the equation. Now, let's figure out the costs. And while we're at it, let's take a look at the logistics, too. It doesn't matter if a thing is affordable if it's not doable.

Bringing It All Together: Plans, Schedules, and Budgets

I'll bet you're thinking, "I wonder if Bob's Bottomless Boats has a sales promotion planned?" You bet—and it's going to require detailed planning and estimating to pull it off. Use Bob's outline to describe your own promotional plans.

- **Promotional goal.** This year Bob wants to see an increase in store traffic in the early months of the year. He's decided to throw a February Beach Party.
- **Incentive.** Bob will offer a festive experience, product samples (chances to test-drive certain boats on his indoor lagoon), gifts, and money to be saved on new boat purchases.

- **Delivery method.** The Beach Party event will deliver the festivities, with a live radio broadcast, contests, and lots of premiums to add to the fun.
- **Promotional media strategy.** Bob's wants to get the whole family excited about spending summer on the water, so the mass media get his orders: some cable TV, some radio, and the Sunday newspaper. A direct-mail piece goes to a hot-prospect list and the press.
- **Timing.** Bob's promotion will only last one day. And he's not going to make his prospects buy something to get the incentive. He'll give them a fun time along with some gifts and prizes, offer them a chance to save some money if they feel like buying, and sit back and count the results.
- **Schedule.** Once he's decided on the Beach Party plan, what does Bob have to do to pull it off? For one thing, develop and place the ads so the word gets out. The mail piece: Ditto. Simultaneously, Bob's got to take care of every detail, from getting the floating key chains imprinted with his logo to arranging the catering to personally inviting local celebrities. The work's not over until the results have been analyzed and the lessons learned for next time around.

  So you make yourself a big wall chart or a clipboard and a detailed to-do list. Then do the work until all the details are taken care of.

- **Budget.** What goes with a schedule like peanut butter goes with milk? A budget. Bob had to do a break-even analysis before he even agreed to the Beach Party plan.

  What information will you need to prepare a budget with an eye on results? You'll need the fixed and variable costs that go into your plan. The fixed costs will be your media budget, plus the cost of the incidentals—the food, premiums, and so on that you'll pay for no matter how many people respond. The variable costs will be whatever the incentive costs per respondent, the dollars foregone due to discounted prices, the labor in redeeming coupons, or whatever you can predict that mounts incrementally as response mounts. But not every response equals a sale. Depending on what you consider success, you may want to estimate a *conversion rate* as well as a *response rate.*

What?

Two scores matter in a sales promotion like Bob's: **response rate** and **conversion rate**. The response rate measures how many people are drawn by the promotional message to participate in the promotion. The conversion rate measures how many people are persuaded by the promotional incentive to actually make a purchase. Your response rate gives you leads—but your conversion rate gives you sales.

All this estimating and projecting is leading up to one thing: calculating the potential payback from this sales promotion. Bob's going to have to take a guess at the dollar amount of the average sale his event will generate and multiply that by his estimated conversion rate to come up with an estimate of the total revenue he can expect. Then he'll subtract the fixed costs and the variable costs, and voilà—his promotion's ultimate profitability.

The Least You Need to Know

- Sales promotions are short-term strategies that give customers incentives to buy. To work, they have to be coordinated with all the other parts of your marketing plan.
- Decide what goals you expect to achieve and how you will know whether you measure up.
- Figure out what incentive you'll offer, your delivery method, and your promotional media strategy.
- Decide whether you'll use the promotion to encourage trial by new customers, to build awareness among occasional customers, or to reward the loyalty of your current customers.
- Plan what you'll choose to offer and then estimate how many will respond and how you'll manage the promotion for profitable results.

Part 4 Getting the Word Out: Advertising and Publicity

Sooner or later, most marketing leads to advertising. That road can take you into the land of advertising agencies and consultants, where creative types and super-salesmen will plan your advertising strategy, develop creative ideas, produce and place the executions, and send you the bill every month. Or you can turn the other way and go your own road, trying each of those tasks yourself.

If you're the kind who always has to be the driver, this section is your map. Our route will begin in the land of branding, positioning, and creative message development. Then we'll cross the heartland of media strategies, including ways to evaluate your various options such as print, direct mail, and broadcast advertising. We'll swing onto the information superhighway for a short cruise through advertising on the web and then drop in on the publicity hounds. With luck, you'll arrive in time for dinner at the smorgasbord of guerilla tactics for stubborn situations.

All packed? Let's go!

Chapter 16

The Art of Branding: Developing Your Positioning Strategy

In This Chapter

- How branding helps differentiate your offering from competitors'
- How to build brand equity and put it to work
- Positioning strategies and how competition affects them

One summer not too long ago, the new-product folks at Coleman (the camping equipment company) cooked up a strange idea: Let's create a gas grill for the (gasp!) backyard. Coleman had a successful brand built over its 100-year history, but the company had never produced a product that wasn't camping gear.

The product development team researched what, exactly, the Coleman identity meant in consumers' perception. And they found? That Coleman products are perceived as reliable, durable, and above all—*green*.

So how to bring this heritage into a new product category? By leveraging the "Coleman green" brand. At the end of its development process, the company produced not the most advanced grill on the market, but one that had the company's signature hefty feel and green paint job. This is branding in action. By building on long-established elements of the company's brand, Coleman has ensured that, when you see this grill in a store, you know instantly, "That's a Coleman."

A brand is to a company what a personality is to an individual. When you were a teenager discovering yourself, you expressed that self by how you dressed, spoke, and behaved. You projected an image and, if you behaved consistently, soon others accepted that image as "you." You were using branding, sometimes literally projecting affiliation with a brand by wearing logo-splashed apparel.

Now that adolescence is safely in your past, you can use branding in more sophisticated ways. Branding means imbuing your product with a memorable image. It tells your customers you stand behind your product: You want it associated with you, and you with it. Branding reassures your customers that "this is my kind of product" as they match up their image of themselves with the image you're offering. Most companies benefit from branding, and the sooner you start building your branding strategy, the better.

Branding will drive your strategic use of positioning—and in turn, positioning will guide your development of a creative approach, which you'll then use to develop specific advertising messages. But that's jumping way too far ahead—all the way into the next chapter. Let's start at the beginning. Let's figure out what a brand is and what a branding strategy can do for you.

Branding: What It Is (and Isn't)

At the core of a brand lies the question: "With our [product or service], how do we make our customers feel?" Making customers feel good about your product or service is the key to breaking through the cluttered marketplace of products and messages. Branding helps customers build loyalty to your company and its offerings. A strong brand, consistently communicated, creates a relationship between a company and a consumer that grows in value over time.

> **Mentor**
>
> Even if you sell only one product, as Charlee Bear does, branding is still important. When you introduce the next product you'll be able to give it a push with your current brand's good reputation as Coleman did.

A brand is much more than just a trademark or slogan. A brand is made up of a complex mix of components. These can include the following:

- Logo or symbol
- Name
- Slogans and taglines
- Musical signature or "jingle"
- Color scheme
- Packaging designs
- Staff phone demeanor
- Uniform or dress code

Each of these components contributes to the feeling that is your brand, but none by itself creates a brand. The brand is the result of consumers' accumulated experiences with and perceptions about your company, its people, and its products.

Really!

Branding works for services as well as for products. Branding can be created around ingredients or around whole companies and even geographic regions. Examples? Think about the "I (Heart) New York" logo, originally designed to promote tourism. Think about California marketing boards' campaigns for raisins ("Heard it through the grapevine") and milk ("Got Milk?"). The power of branding turned these farm commodities into cultural icons. Consider the ingredient-branding strategy in BASF's long-running slogan "We don't make a lot of the products you buy. We make a lot of the products you buy better." These examples prove that a branding strategy works for a wide range of offerings.

Why Branding Works: A Little Cognitive Science

You began to develop your understanding of consumers' minds in Chapter 4, where we discussed the "P" that stands for "People." Let's turn our attention to their minds again.

One of the ways the human mind handles the barrage of advertising it receives is to pick something to believe and then hold that notion until forced to change. Snap judgments become permanent beliefs, since it is uncomfortable and difficult to change convictions once formed. The mind tends to filter out new information that doesn't support already-held beliefs. This attribute of the mind explains why branding is an effective strategy.

Branding works because it gives the mind something to hang on to. Several aspects of cognitive behavior explain why branding has become a key component of marketing strategy:

- **Looking for "good enough."** In the search for products and services to fulfill their desires or solve their problems, people are looking for "good enough." In an uncertain world, we value consistency over quality, predictability over risk. Most of us are satisfied if we avoid making a bad choice. The brand purveys a promise of reliability.
- **The Halo Effect.** The mind works by associations. For example, we tend to believe attractive people are smarter than less attractive ones, even though we know that one trait has nothing to do with the other. Our minds associate many positive traits with each other. Through "halo effect" a product and company become associated with positive attributes conveyed by the brand's advertising.
- **Anchoring.** The mind doesn't simply form impressions; it becomes anchored in them. Our first snap judgments are apt to become our enduring beliefs. The brand communicates directly at the "feelings" level, and thus is easily anchored as a core belief.

When All Products Are "Good Enough," Branding Makes the Difference

Once upon a time, products had real differences. For example, the first running shoes on the market were a remarkable improvement over the old sneaker. A vast array of features, from heel stabilizers to shock absorbers, made it clear why a consumer might choose the new shoes over the old. It was easy to create advertising that persuaded people to buy the new shoes, just by explaining their benefits.

Mentor

There was a time when products had real differences. Today, just about everything is good enough. Cheap junk seldom makes it to market, and when it does, it won't survive long in competition with better alternatives. When everything is good enough, what's a marketer to do? Turn to a branding strategy to make your offering stand out from the crowd.

But soon the market was crowded with parity products. Before long, running shoes from different manufacturers all met the consumers' baseline needs for comfort, style, and function. Now how do you persuade consumers they need your brand above others? By selling the emotional bond that purchase creates. By choosing Nikes the consumer projects a "Just do it" attitude. Adidas projects a more "hip" image, whereas New Balance proclaims that its wearer is more interested in quality than fashion. By choosing Keds over more high-tech shoes, a customer displays a different attitude, cheeky or just cheap. Branding lifts a simple offering into the realm of feeling and self-expression.

In a world of product parity, it's crucial that you leverage consumer emotions in your favor.

Consider University Credit Union's situation. All financial services are pretty much the same; if you peek behind the fancy lobbies and the glossy racks of brochures, you find all the players are competing to sell you access to *their* money (loans) or storage of *your* money (deposits). To stand out from the crowd, University Credit Union exploits two angles: the fact that it is cooperative-owned, and the natural loyalty people feel toward their alma mater. A branding strategy that emphasizes the slight price advantage of credit unions and the warm fuzzy feeling of allegiance to the old school helps UCU rise above "product parity."

CAUTION

Pitfall

Branding and product development need to be closely tied at all levels in your company, from long-range strategy to day-to-day operations. Keep thinking about your products as you develop your understanding of branding. And if deep and significant thoughts about your products aren't coming to mind as you read this chapter, please review Chapter 9.

Help potential buyers see that your offering is "good enough" by showing how your offering is similar to other offerings. Then help potential buyers see that "this is better" by communicating the differences only you can claim. A Life of Faith Dolls first establishes that its products are similar to American Girls Dolls, and then communicates its dolls are different and better, through the focus on religious faith. Bob's Bottomless Boats establishes parity and difference through its claim to have "bottomless inventory." It promises you'll find at Bob's every product you might find in competitors' stores—and more.

Really!

A breakthrough product can end the stalemate, but any advantage so gained is likely to be temporary. Inventor Harry Miller brought to market a shoe with a real product difference. Inchworms are children's shoes that grow with your child, adjusting up to two shoe sizes with the press of a button. An accordion-like plastic molding in the middle of the shoe allows for expansion. When competitors copy his technology, as they no doubt will, Mr. Miller will need to rely on branding to maintain his point of difference. Watch for this story to play out in shoe stores near you.

Building Brand Equity

Marketing activity builds a brand's equity, if done well. You invest advertising dollars to build awareness and to form positive associations in the minds of your targeted audience. These are banked over time and converted to profits when brand-loyal consumers purchase your offering. Coleman had banked enough good feelings over its 100 years to enter a new product category with ease.

> **Mentor**
>
> Keep in mind—even if your business model is business-to-business, the person who cuts a purchase order for your product is just that—a person. Look for what stirs feelings and connections in the hearts and minds of these individuals. Build your brand identity around that.

Every marketing activity your strategy calls for should be carefully chosen to support your brand. Your advertising campaigns, sales promotions, special events, and team or event sponsorships must reinforce the brand.

Managing the Brand

Branding is not an activity you can accomplish overnight or purchase ready-made from a consultant or advertising agency. A successful brand is built over time from the hundreds of little things you do right.

> **Really!**
>
> The brand is, at its heart, a promise. It warrants that the product or service carrying that brand will live up to its name. The value of that brand rises or falls with the integrity of the people behind it. The ultimate authority for managing the brand lies with the highest officers in the company. The "principles of the principals" make or break a brand.

When most people speak of branding, they are referring to its external components—the elements consumers experience directly, like your advertising jingles and the logos painted on the company fleet. But there are internal components to branding, and these must be managed as well. Internal branding reflects the efforts you aim at people inside the company, so that they can help you project a consistent image for the brand. In order to fully benefit from the power of branding, it is important to take a 360-degree view of branding in your company.

Successful brand managers learn how to turn every customer touch point into a "moment of truth" that reinforces positive aspects of the brand. Bob's Bottomless Boats hires passionate paddlers to work the kayak kiosk because he wants every customer touch point to build the "Bob's" brand.

Mentor

Does your offering need a brand name? Yes! People need labels to help them identify things. Brand names provide labels for individual offerings and for product/service lines. Consider the handy taxonomy of "Stouffer's Lean Cuisine Thai-Style Chicken Entrée." It communicates a brand, a product line, and a specific product. The name you choose should project your brand image, identify the function of your product, and lend itself to memorable advertising.

Measuring the Brand

Over the life of your brand, you will need to measure its performance. You can study how your marketing initiatives are creating or shifting brand awareness using techniques like focus groups, quantitative surveys, comparison of sales volumes, and internal review of customer accounts.

To measure a brand, you want to answer the following questions:

- Is the desired audience aware of you?
- What attributes do they associate with you?

Before you deploy a branding strategy, use research to probe perceptions regarding your company and its offerings. Based on that knowledge, you can build a brand that plays to your strengths.

Then, simply ask these questions again over time to measure change. As you implement your branding strategy, you repeat the research process to track changes. You'll learn more about the weaknesses or strengths in your branding strategy. Adjust your advertising and other marketing strategies to counter the weaknesses or leverage the strengths revealed by research. Review Chapter 6 on market research if you need to get motivated!

Putting Branding to Work

Putting branding to work for you is not difficult—in fact, because of the way human minds work, it will happen whether or not you are controlling the process. To use branding strategically, integrate branding into every aspect of your business, from top-level corporate strategy to the last detail of packaging and display. Your branding strategy will make you stand out from the crowd.

Branding is closely tied to the next concept we're going to talk about: positioning. Branding and positioning go together like graham crackers and a glass of milk. Positioning helps the brand go down.

Positioning occurs as the brand takes shape in the audience's hearts and minds. Positioning connects your overall brand strategy to your specific advertising campaigns and sales promotions.

CAUTION

Pitfall

Cognitive behavior is shaping how your audience perceives your brand whether or not you are aware of it. Even if you are not consciously pursuing a branding strategy, prospective customers are still associating positive or negative traits with your company and anchoring on those first judgments. If your company is a new entrant in the market, be very careful! Like the new kid at school, others' snap judgments made on first impressions are going to follow you for a very long time.

Coming to Mind: Positioning

If I walked up to you in a mall and asked you to name the top three local shoe stores, the one you mention first has *top-of-mind awareness* with you. If I ask you why you rank it tops, you'll probably be able to tell me: because of its large selection, cutting-edge styles, or low prices. What you're describing is that store's positioning, and the fact that you know it is a reflection of its positioning strategy. You can bet the store has spent good marketing money to deliver that positioning message to you.

In Chapter 7, I talked about segmenting markets and targeting those most likely to buy from you. What I didn't talk about then is how you bring that targeting to life. That's what *positioning* is about. Positioning gives your offering a unique place, or position, in the minds of your prospective customers.

What?

Top-of-mind awareness is one of those fun marketing phrases. It means that a particular product, business, or service comes first in the mind of a customer—ahead of the competition.

There's a fundamental law of physics that says no two objects can occupy the same space at the same time. That law is true in marketing as well. In consumer perception, no two shoe stores can have the lowest prices, or the best selection, or whatever. One store leads the competition in any dimension you care to measure.

It's Better to Be First Than Best

The easiest way into a person's top-of-mind awareness is to be first. In the mind, second is not a unique position—it's merely the start of "the rest of the pack." The mind can remember some levels beyond "first" and "other," but divisions quickly become fuzzy among the also-rans.

Because of the "anchoring" tendency, being first is better, even if being first is not logically important. Developing your positioning strategy is the art of choosing and communicating a dimension in which you can make a compelling claim to be first—and therefore, in the marvelously illogical mind, best.

Choosing a position usually means finding a "hole" in the marketplace that you can fill. That position takes into account not only your company's strengths but competitors' weaknesses as well. Think about those cognitive behaviors we discussed—the "Halo Effect" and "Anchoring." We remember "firsts" and, given the right encouragement, associate positive traits with them. As you work out your positioning strategy, consider—where do you come in "first"?

What?

Positioning is the way you present your product or service that helps you stand out from the competition. It's about how you want your customers to remember you. It's been said that "positioning is the art of sacrifice." Positioning requires focusing on only one or two dimensions of competition in which you can claim to be "first and best."

Mentor

Experience proves that we remember firsts but not also-rans. Who was the first person to fly across the Atlantic Ocean? Who was the first woman appointed to the Supreme Court? Charles Lindbergh and Sandra Day O'Connor, respectively. Now try to name the seconds in these categories. (And if you figure it out, let me know, because I can't.) The lesson for marketers: It's easier to gain a "first" position by opening new territory than it is to knock somebody out of an already-established category.

Dimensions of Competition

Each *dimension of competition* is an area where you might be able to drop anchor and claim your "first." In deciding whether to shop with you or the competition, what influences customers the most? Certain dimensions are going to be more important than others to any given market segment. Some customers care more about price, still others might care about selection, others about convenience. And that's just a few of the many dimensions that come into play.

Here's a partial list:

- Image (style/fashion)
- Innovation

- Geographic location
- Customer service
- Performance (the form/function utility)
- Selection
- Distribution (time/place and ease-of-possession utilities)
- Convenience
- Price

Pitfall

Don't forget: You care about your potential customers' perceptions, not your own. It doesn't matter how you think you rate on these various dimensions of competition. It matters what they think. If you can't get into the minds of your customers, it's time for research … and a return visit to Chapter 6.

What?

Dimensions of competition are areas in which you can claim a memorable point of difference, some aspect in which you are *first* or *better* than similar offerings.

In most situations, no more than two *dimensions of competition* are duking it out in prospective customers' minds. This is because Western philosophy, with its bias toward dichotomy, has groomed modern consumers to process either/or decisions. As a result of that influence we prefer decisions that are presented to us that way.

I bet you can name the beer that used the slogan "Tastes great. Less filling." That slogan is a classic demonstration of two dimensions of competition. The marketers addressed two concerns of a niche market of beer drinkers. Dieters who didn't want to give up drinking beer couldn't find a low-calorie beer that tasted good. By convincing that target group that this particular light beer tasted better, marketers solved a consumer problem and increased the brand's sales.

What's your position in the marketplace now? Don't tell me you don't have one. We all do, from the day we open our doors. What do customers think about your business? On what dimension would they rank you "first?"

Sample Positioning Strategies (Including One That Will Work for You)

Here are a few popular positioning strategies now playing in a marketplace near you. As you read these examples, you might recognize yourself in one or more situations.

But how do you translate this into relevant advice for your situation? Let's try. Follow along as Bob's Bottomless Boats tries on each for size.

1. **Product's superior attributes.** Positioning on superior product attributes is an obvious choice if your product has features (benefits) that show innovation or are a breakthrough in some way. Because Bob sells basically the same boats as his competitors, this strategy doesn't hold much promise for the business as a whole. For introducing a superior new kayak to its target market, however, this strategy may be right on the money.

> CAUTION
>
> **Pitfall**
>
> Be wary if the unique quality of your product or service is easy to duplicate! When a laundry detergent entered the market in a disposable paper carton, it positioned itself on a superior attribute. But other detergents rushed to duplicate that feature, and the first entrant lost the advantage fairly quickly.

2. **Price/quality/value equation.** Consumers tend to let price be an indicator of quality. In most cases it is true that what you pay a little more for comes with benefits that make it worth the price. Value is whether those benefits are important to you. Because of his depth of inventory and his buying clout, Bob is able to offer an excellent value on lower-priced but still reasonable-quality watercraft. Here he has an advantage he can claim and live up to.

> CAUTION
>
> **Pitfall**
>
> Many political campaigns feature particularly nasty against-the-competitor positioning. Avoid playing dirty if you choose this approach! You might be voted right off the shelves for poor sportsmanship.

3. **Against a competitor.** "We're Number Two. We try harder." You knew that was Avis talking, didn't you? Even though that campaign hasn't run in years, it still stands as one of the best examples of against-the-competitor positioning. Because people remember firsts, this strategy leverages others' investment in their position and exploits it in your favor. This strategy is usually chosen by a late-entrant competitor who wants to overtake the number-one player. Market leaders usually refuse to acknowledge that other competitors even exist. Bob is the "Hertz" of the boating market, so this strategy doesn't hold water for him.
4. **Specific uses.** One good way to encourage people to remember your product is to give them clues about when and where to use it. The plethora of nutrition products for athletes, such as Power Bars and Gatorade, are examples of otherwise ordinary food products positioned for specific uses.

Bob's market is broad, covering everyone from kayakers to pontoon boat purchasers, so this approach is a sloppy fit at best. This approach would work better if Bob could target specific uses, like paddle sports, exclusively.

5. **Response to customers' needs.** Find a problem that your competitors' product has failed to address, and engineer a solution to it. Now let the world know, and presto! You have a successful "response to customers' needs" strategy. Bob's Bottomless Boats is basically a distributor of products, so innovation and responsiveness are not subject to his control the way they should be to choose this positioning strategy. Again, this might work in relation to a new product launch, like the new Kaya Canoe Bob's brother has designed.

6. **Product users**. If the "80/20" rule of thumb holds true, it's likely that 80 percent of your business comes from the 20 percent who are your best customers. What are these people like? Dramatize their loyalty to your offering, and you will attract others like them. The most obvious example of "product user" positioning is the celebrity endorser. From "I liked it so much I bought the company," to "Choosy mothers choose Jif," we've seen pitchmen and -women encourage us to affiliate with certain products just because they've set the example. This works, especially in categories that are essentially commodities, with little real difference between one product offering and another.

   I like this positioning for Bob's Bottomless Boats. I can see a bottomless supply of humorous TV spots with fishermen, kayakers, and water skiers demonstrating the fun life a Bob's boat bestows. If local celebrities like the football coach or the mayor have boats from Bob's, we've got a great local product user opportunity.

   So Bob's positioning strategy is looking like either the price/value leader or some variation on product users. How he chooses to express those strategies will result in a catchy tagline and a creative advertising strategy, I hope. How do you select a positioning strategy for your offering? Start as I did here, with Bob's Bottomless Boats. Just think about your situation, and try the different possibilities on for size.

There are more than six possible positioning strategies, of course. How will you discover the other variations and permutations of positioning? Read up on it. A good book is *Differentiate or Die: Survival in Our Era of Killer Competition*, by Jack Trout. Check Appendix C for other book recommendations.

Remember, positioning demands sacrifice. You can't be all things to all people; choosing one of these positioning strategies will help you choose what to be and whom to be that to.

In short: Target your market. Develop a brand personality to please them. Choose a positioning strategy and work it to communicate your brand in a clear and focused way. That's all there is to it!

Use this worksheet to jot down some thoughts about you and your toughest competitor's branding and positioning strategies.

My Branding and Positioning Notes

Brand Components

Describe how (or if) you/your competitor are currently using each component to communicate brand identity.

Strategy	Me	My Toughest Competitor
Logo or symbol	______	______
Name	______	______
Slogans and taglines	______	______
Musical signature or "jingle"	______	______
Color scheme	______	______
Packaging designs	______	______
Staff phone demeanor	______	______
Uniform or dress code	______	______

continues

My Branding and Positioning Notes (continued)

Dimensions of Competition

Describe what you/your competitor are currently offering in regards to each dimension of competition. Indicate which ***two*** are ***most important*** to your target audience.

Strategy	Me	My Toughest Competitor
Image (style/fashion)	______ ______	______ ______
Innovation	______	______
Geographic location	______ ______ ______	______ ______ ______
Customer service	______ ______ ______	______ ______ ______
Performance (the form/ function utility)	______ ______ ______	______ ______ ______
Selection	______ ______ ______	______ ______ ______
Distribution (time/place and ease-of-possession utilities)	______ ______ ______ ______	______ ______ ______ ______
Convenience	______ ______ ______	______ ______ ______
Price	______ ______ ______	______ ______ ______

Audition These Sample Strategies

Jot down a few notes as you consider how each strategy might apply in your situation. Are any of these strategies being used by your competitor?

Strategy	Me	My Toughest Competitor
Product's superior attributes	________	________
Price/quality/ value equation	________	________
Against a competitor	________	________
Specific uses	________	________
Response to customers' needs	________	________
Product users	________	________

You'll find this completed worksheet helpful in combination with next chapter's worksheet on positioning. Pull these notes out when you start creating your advertising messages or when you reach Part 6 of this book, when we tackle strategic planning for marketing.

The Least You Need to Know

- Brands help differentiate your offering from competitors' by leveraging the way the mind works.
- A brand's value builds over time; brand equity must be managed and measured like any other business asset.

- Positioning requires knowledge of the dimensions of competition that are top concerns to your target market, such as price or styling.
- To find your position, try different strategies, starting with the samples listed in this chapter.

Chapter 17

Use Your Positioning Strategy to Craft Your Ad Message

In This Chapter

- Turning features into benefits
- Finding your creative concept
- Copy approaches for crafting successful ads
- How to test and improve your ads over time

"Where's the beef?"

"I liked it so much, I bought the company."

"When it absolutely, positively has to be there overnight."

Do these phrases ring a bell? Can you name the companies who produced them? If so, you're already a good student of advertising. It's time to connect your advertising abilities to the marketing skills you've learned.

You know your product and its market. So what do you want to tell your prospective customers, and how do you want to "dress up" your message? There's actually a pretty well-defined path that will take you from questions of message and creative concept to finished ads.

To start at the beginning, the first question to ask is: What's your ad going to say? You could just put a picture of your product (or the finished results of your service) under a headline that says "Buy This." But would it work? Would it help you meet marketing objectives? I don't think so. Let's find something for your ads to talk about.

Presto Change-o! Turn Features into Benefits

Before a purchase is likely to happen, a magical act of transformation must take place: *Features* must be turned into *benefits*. A feature is anything you have designed into the product or service. A benefit is what the customer gets out of it. A feature may be useful, but it is not of compelling interest in and of itself. A benefit is a solution to a problem, a fulfillment of a desire. A feature of a credit card is its size: 2⅛" × 3⅜". The benefit that feature delivers is the convenience of fitting in your wallet. Coleman turned "green" from a feature to a benefit. Coleman made green synonymous with durability and value, and by doing so turned "green" into a product benefit—a symbol of the promise made by the Coleman brand.

What?

A **feature** is something intrinsic to your product. A **benefit** is what that feature does for the buyer. Benefits explain how features solve problems.

It's time to get to know your offerings—and the offerings of your competitors—from this perspective. What is it that you want to know? What features does each offering make available, and what benefits do those features deliver.

Mentor

Benefits can be tangible or intangible, especially when the product is really a service. Having trouble turning features into benefits? Remember the First Law of Marketing: People don't buy products; they buy solutions to problems. What is your offering's problem-solving benefits? What features are responsible for that benefit?

Ducks-In-A-Row Efficiency consultants can perform a workspace-decluttering session in about two hours. The benefit of this session is improved productivity for the desk's owner. Features of the service that produce this benefit include a lesson in efficient task processing techniques and deployment of specific tools for organization, like an upright file holder for active files and a "tickler" organizer.

What's Your Creative Concept?

Advertising needs a creative concept. Creative concepts are the creative expression of an idea, the openings that lets you slip a new thought in where a previously held one provides a hook to hang it on.

Creativity is essential, but a creative concept that doesn't attract the right prospect or sell the offering's most important benefit is wasted. A seemingly good concept makes bad advertising if it appeals to the wrong market segment or doesn't promise a meaningful benefit.

Mentor

Every advertiser, no matter what medium, must develop a creative concept and come up with a Big Idea for the ad message. We'll cover how to do that in this chapter.

The Advertising Strategy

An ad strategy sums up who (target market), what (product or service benefit), and why (the rationale supporting the benefit). An ad strategy defines the message each ad should communicate and opens the door for creativity, but keeps the ideas produced tied to the right brand identity and positioning strategy.

That ad strategy is the result of needs identified and decisions made earlier in the marketing sequence. We can use everything in this book up 'til now to help create an ad strategy. The marketing mix of product, price, place, promotion, and people (customers and competitors) will all help you figure out what your advertising strategy should be. The ad strategy defines who you want to reach, what benefits you want to offer them, and what results you expect from your ad. It gives writers and artists the information they (or you, if you're doing the writing and the graphic design) need. The strategy issues a challenge to creativity: Find a way to get this thought across to these people.

Mentor

What's the truth about truth in advertising? When we say, "Dramatize the benefit," we don't mean, "Stretch the truth until it breaks." Advertising has an obligation to be truthful—not just a moral obligation, but a legal one as well—just ask the Federal Trade Commission. My advice: Avoid making claims that would mislead a reasonable reader or viewer.

What should the ad message be? How will it help you meet previously determined marketing objectives? Science (research) gives insight into attributes, benefits, and target marketing. Art (the products of verbal, visual, and musical creativity) works the magic of changing that dry data into compelling advertising. An ad message must include both.

An ad message is a *compelling presentation of an idea to a target audience*. That idea might be that a particular beer is less caloric, a particular public figure would make a good president, or puppies and kittens need homes. In any case, that compelling presentation consists of two parts: *information* and *persuasion*. Sometimes one is minimized to allow the other full scope. A perfume ad, for instance, might be all persuasion, via a romantic visual image, with only the logo for information. An ad for home exercise equipment would be more likely to feature information, using photos of users, diagrams of the equipment, and benefit statements.

What?

Two elements must find a balance in the presentation of an ad message: **information** and **persuasion**. The former tells you what the product is, while the latter makes you want it.

"This is your brain. This is your brain on drugs." Remember that image? It's a classic example of advertising by persuasion. If you're not persuaded by that searing egg that drugs are not good, you have no imagination. For more information-based examples, turn your attention to the pharmaceutical advertising you see. "Just two Advils equals a whole day's relief," is a slogan backed up by facts and figures about measurable pain relief.

A compelling presentation stops the consumer and holds attention. Whether that is achieved through persuasion or information, through words or pictures, is up to you in response to your unique situation.

Use Your Positioning Strategy

An important reason I presented positioning in the previous chapter was to prepare you for this moment. *Your positioning strategy gives your advertising both message content and style*. Your advertising will evolve over time; campaign themes will come and go. Still, your ads should retain a personality that reflects your underlying positioning strategy. This is the key to building brand equity over time.

Ads sell by dramatizing a benefit. The creative approach is our term for what dramatic angle you choose. Sometimes that involves dramatizing a problem and then offering a solution. Sometimes it means dramatizing the characters who've already found the answer and inviting prospects to join them. You can tell a story, use a testimonial, or exaggerate to dramatize a benefit. Many angles work equally well.

Your positioning strategy tells you which direction to start in. Let the key benefit identified by your positioning show the way.

Image vs. Response Advertising: Deciding the Call to Action

Ad messages can be divided into two general categories, depending on the *take-away* of the ad. What is the one thought you want your readers to remember when they've spent a few moments with your ad? That's the take-away—the benefit they can anticipate from purchasing your offering or changing their beliefs in response to your message.

Image advertisements communicate a feeling about your company. Image ads don't ask for more than a gradual shift in perception. Their take-away is pretty fuzzy compared to response advertising. Response ads convey specific news and call for a specific action, like "Vote this Tuesday" or "Have your credit card handy and call today." The goal of response advertising is a swift and measurable response. Their take-away is a call to action—inciting a direct action on the reader's part.

What?

Every good ad has a **take-away**—a thought the reader or viewer will remember. If the ad is aimed at generating a specific behavioral change, the take-away will include a call to action. That's an explicit request like "Save the whales by calling the number on your screen."

Image advertising is often used in conjunction with other marketing efforts. It is aimed at long-term results, not immediate response. Image advertising builds brand equity. If a company has received negative publicity or has outgrown its previous image, it may need to do some image advertising. Companies looking for stock investors run image ads.

For most of us, response advertising makes more sense. If you've got a small budget and you need to see results, don't be subtle—ask for what you want. Include a promotional offer if you like (Chapter 15 may have given you some ideas already) in order to motivate a response.

Crafting the Ad Message

Ads sell by dramatizing a benefit. There, I said the "b" word again. Someone responds to a particular ad because that ad makes the benefit vividly real to them, and that creates desire. You can create that drama in a number of ways, which we'll talk more about in just a moment.

The ad strategy, with its definition of "who" and "what," provides focus for the ad message. You must know whom you want to talk to and what you want to tell them, before you sit down to write.

The *Big Idea* is the other half of the equation. It's the "hook" that brings your chosen benefit to life in a unique and memorable way. You must have that before you can get up again.

What?

Ad concepts, messages, creative approaches: How are they different? Let's take an example from a local bank. If I decide all the ads will feature the bank's president in silly situations, that's a **concept**. If I say let's put him in a magician's costume pulling rabbits out of a hat, that's a **creative approach** expressing the concept. And when that idea leads me to a headline that says "Your savings multiply like magic," I've got an **ad message**.

The Big Idea

Big ideas start in the fertile ground of ad strategy. They grow from there in crazy and creative directions.

When it's time to have the Big Idea, the best way to begin is to put yourself in the shoes of a prospective customer. Review the needs this product will satisfy. Feel the emotions of those needs. Imagine you're selling a car—now imagine you're its prospective buyer. As a customer, you might be buying freedom, status, or safety.

Mentor

You might not be a "creative person." Many people, even good communicators, don't have what it takes to create breakthrough ideas or even to write good advertising copy. Why should you be good at every aspect your business calls for? Not everyone changes his own oil, either. This may be the right time to hire outside experts.

Now begin projecting dramatic scenes that depict those emotions. To show "freedom" for a car might mean driving it into a painting or up a wall. Status might mean smoothly panning over the leather interior while a narrator purrs, or depicting the owner receiving stares of awe when he shows his co-workers his new car. Safety might mean showing the little ones sleeping snugly as Dad drives on through ice and snow. Peel back the curtain that separates our inner dreams from our outer actions—that's where big ideas come from.

Whether you're the creator or just the judge, you must sift the good ideas from the bad. One advertising wag said, "You can tell it's a Big Idea if it leads to a sigh and 'why didn't I think of that?'" Here are a few additional tests for Big Ideas:

- Is it in keeping with the advertising strategy?
- Does it dramatize the key benefit recommended by your positioning strategy?
- Does it have substance? Is the claim believable and exciting?
- Is it easy to understand? Can you summarize it in a few words?

- Does this idea project the right personality according to your brand identity? (If it's down-home funny and you want to be sophisticated, throw it back. Audrey Hepburn never appeared in overalls.)
- Is it unique? It can pass all of the above, be a great idea in its own right, but be useless to you, simply because a competitor got there first.

Really!

Where do ideas come from? Advertising professionals have some methods to help them get started. Here's how they work: First, make a fact sheet. List all the facts and then rewrite the list from memory, just to get your thoughts percolating. Next, brainstorm a large quantity of ideas without stopping to criticize or evaluate them.

If frustration stops you from being productive, take a break. A change of activity allows the right brain to go to work on what the left brain has taken in. The result, sooner or later, will be a volume of ideas on paper, and a reasonable number of them will be usable—maybe even brilliant.

Copy Approaches: How to Write Ads

It probably won't surprise you to hear that advertising copy is one of the most formulaic types of creative writing around. Like sonnets or haiku, there is a precise structure that must be followed if the copy is going to have the desired effect.

That structure is called the AIDA formula, and we're not talking opera. "AIDA" stands for:

- Get *Attention*
- Arouse *Interest*
- Create *Desire*
- Motivate *Action*

However you tell your story, whatever copy approach you choose, your ad must move through this formula without losing readers to boredom or confusion.

A copywriter's first step, usually, is to draft a *headline*. The headline's job is to get attention. If it can't do that, it doesn't belong on the page. But a good headline does more. It identifies the proper market segment and tells them, "Hey, this concerns you." Once a headline has accomplished these jobs, it should move on to promise a benefit or solution to a problem. A good headline does all this in a few words.

Mentor

In this chapter, you'll find my advice is geared toward writing print ads. This is because more marketers use print advertising than use broadcast (radio or TV) advertising. Working in those media is more like writing a mini-movie. (Even lowly radio ads create adventure sagas in the "theater of the mind.") I suggest you start with a print ad before trying your hand at the more demanding forms. The advice in this chapter applies to all kinds of writing—it's just easier to show you writing for print.

"Gotcha!" There's a headline that might get attention, but it does nothing more. "'Gotcha!' Farmers Exclaim." selects a market segment, and farmer-readers might be interested enough to explore further, but it's not great advertising. "'Gotcha!' Farmers Tell Bugs with One Application of Miracle Insect Spray" delivers all the components of a good headline. It gets attention, segments the reader, and promises a benefit.

What?

The **headline** of an ad is the attention-getter. Bold statements in big type, usually at the top of the layout, are headlines. The text that follows is the **body copy**. Not every ad has body copy, and not everybody reads the body copy if it's there. A good headline stands on its own.

But the headline is just the first component of an ad. What about the *body copy*, the 50 to 500 or so words that complete the AIDA formula? How can you guarantee your copy brings the reader through interest to desire and finally action? The copy approach you choose is one method.

The copy should be a logical extension of the headline. If your headline sounds like it's spoken by a specific person, you might want to put the copy into the mouth of a spokesperson or character, like Maytag's "Lonely Repairman." Here are some examples of copy approaches:

- **Testimonials**. A believable "expert" delivers the pitch, lending his credibility to the claims. "I liked it so much, I bought the company" was Victor Kiam's long-running testimonial ad for Remington shavers. "Bo knows" was a popular series of ads in which that multi-talented athlete showed he knew the best shoes for a variety of sports.
- **Demonstrations**. An example dramatizes the claim. This could be a straightforward comparison or a humorous spoof. You could even demonstrate the problem your product solves, rather than the solution. An ad for "Nexium," a cure for acid-reflux disease, shows an arid landscape magically transforming into a fertile paradise. I may be tired of seeing that ad but you better believe they've burned into my mind their demonstration of the sensation before and after taking their "little purple pill!"

- **Storytelling.** Ever since the birth of advertising, people have enjoyed storytelling copy. A case history or testimonial can sometimes be presented in this dramatic style. The Saturn campaigns of the early '90s featured many great storylines, often couched as letters from loyal customers. One of my favorites was the schoolteacher who found a note from the assembly line workers in her new car's glove compartment. Volkswagen's commercials tell stories, too, but in a more elliptical, cinematic way. Watching for storytelling commercials is a lot of fun.
- **"X" Reasons why.** This approach, and its sister, the Q and A described next, are the easiest copy approaches to use. Simply rank your benefits in order of priority, give each a number and make it a subhead. Now write an explanation of the rationale for each. Give your copy a little opening and closing pizzazz and you're home free.
- **Question and answer.** Instead of numbering your benefit subheads, phrase each as a question. Answer them and—voilá—you have ad copy! For radio or TV, try scripting the questions and answers as a conversation between two people.
- **Humor.** Dangerous stuff, humor, in inexperienced hands. If you're a funny person, try puns, exaggerations, and incongruity to give your key benefit a funny twist. But be sure you show your work to someone who will give you honest criticism before you place those ads. Humor that makes fun of the target prospect or shows poor taste can easily backfire.

Leaf through a couple of current magazines and you'll quickly find examples of each of these styles of copywriting. Which approach you choose depends on your creativity, positioning strategy, and the ad strategy you've chosen.

CAUTION

Pitfall

Creativity is not enough. There are some great ads out there, engaging, humorous, and memorable, except for one major problem: Afterward, people don't remember which brand the ad was promoting. Such ads are creative successes and marketing failures.

Mentor

Copywriters find it very helpful to read their drafts out loud. You'll quickly spot the awkward phrases this way. Ad copy should read the way people talk. Don't be too concerned about good grammar, but one thing your English teacher told you holds true: Avoid passive language! Change all sleepy verbs into active ones.

Really!

No matter which copy approach you try—and you should try several—make your copy move in a spiral.

Perhaps you've heard the advice about teaching: Tell them what you're going to tell them; tell them; then tell them what you told them. In advertising copywriting we do that, too. The opening of an ad should deliver the main benefit because you never know when you're going to lose your reader. The middle of the copy is where you tell them, unfolding the pitch in all its glory. And in your closing paragraph, restate the benefit, and give your call to action. Skimmers, browsers, and deep thinkers will follow you anywhere if you just follow this advice.

Ad copy can dwell on rational arguments or stimulate emotions—there's no surefire formula that works best. Follow your instincts, and study what you see around you. When your ad copy is done, give it this test:

- Does the opening target a niche segment of readers?
- Does the first benefit statement come in the headline or first sentence of copy?
- Does the copy back up that promise with a believable rationale?
- Is your product or service mentioned by name at least three times?
- Does the copy close with a compelling call to action?

If you have trouble answering any of these with a resounding "yes," your copy isn't done. It's time to edit again.

The following is a sample of ad copy for Bob's Bottomless Boats.

Does this copy stand the test?

What?

A **tagline** is a "mini headline" that rides in your advertising near your logo. Its purpose is to make a quick impression. A tagline should be a cleverly phrased summation of your brand.

The headline doesn't segment the reader much, but then, the market for Bob's is very broad. "Men and women ages 18–dead" pretty much sums up Bob's demographic. The photo does more to segment the readers by showing an exciting boating activity. If this turns you off, you're no boater.

The first benefit comes right in the opening with the promise of more fun. The rationale for that claim comes from the hard-working staff and the breadth of inventory at their command. If these people can't fit a boat to your lifestyle, who possibly could?

Bob's Bottomless Boats

Ad promoting full product line (no co-op)

Lake City Herald Tribune

2 column by 10" ad, spot color

Headline: Some People Are Never In When You Call

Visual: Sailors on sailboat

(other ads in series change visuals to depict white-water kayaking, fishing, etc. Same head.)

Copy: That's because they're out—having the time of their lives.

At Bob's Bottomless Boats we believe that balancing work and play is the secret to happiness. We work hard to help people like you enjoy your play. Whether your idea of fun means kayaks or canoes, pontoons or power boats. Whatever your style, it's waiting for you at Bob's Bottomless Boats. We can't make work go away—but we can make the hours you play more fun.

Subhead: **Get Your Feet Wet.**

New to boating? Come get a feel for the water. If it floats, we rent it by the hour, day, or week. Take a few lessons. Talk to some old hands.

Or are you already a boater? Thinking of trading up? Try out the latest models and options.

When you're ready to invest in the boat of your dreams, you'll find a variety of styles and prices to suit you at Bob's Bottomless Boats.

Subhead: **Jump In.**

Come join the fun. Life's too short not to spend it on the water!

Logo: [insert Bob's logo]

Tagline: With an inventory just like our name!

Closing: 2080 Riverfront Parkway, Dial 229-BOAT

The copy spirals down through the same two benefits, breadth and knowledge, first speaking to nonboaters and then preaching to the converted. The call to action ties neatly back to the opening benefit—more fun. And it couldn't be more direct.

Under the logo at the bottom, you'll see a *tagline*—a catchy phrase designed to communicate the positioning strategy (and the overall brand) in a memorable way. (Perhaps the best tagline ever introduced was by Federal Express—"When it absolutely, positively has to be there overnight!"

Producing Your Ads

After writing your ad copy, you'll need a skilled technician or creative artist to produce the final ad that gets delivered to the media outlet where it will appear. The requirements for each medium are quite specific. For now I'll just mention this reality and point you toward the more detailed discussions of production you'll find in the upcoming chapters on print, broadcast, direct mail, and online advertising.

Testing Your Ads

So now you know how to come up with a concept for your ad, how to write copy, and how to prepare the actual artwork for printing. Are you finished with your print ads? Hardly. Unless you test the effectiveness of your ads and use what you learn to create more effective ads in the future, you're not maximizing your investment in print advertising.

The Madison Avenue ad agencies do some pretty refined research on the ads they create for clients. This is partly done when the ads are still in the idea stage. Alternative mockups will be shown to a focus group, for example, and their reactions used to refine or discard certain ideas.

Once an ad appears in print, its effectiveness can be measured if you include a means of tracking response to that ad. If there's a coupon in your ad, put a code on it that will tell you where and when this ad appeared. For telephone responses, you can arrange a special phone number, or just use your ad copy to say something like "Ask for Betty when you call." The result: a tally of which ads are pulling the most responses.

Compare your successful ads with your less-successful ones to figure out what elements are getting results. Is it a change in the offer, the creative approach, or the timing of appearance? Use what you learn to tailor your ads for increased effectiveness.

Crafting My Ad Message

1. **Features into benefits.** List several features and the benefits they deliver. Focus on benefits that relate to the dimensions of competition that are most important to your target audience. Do this for *both* your offerings and your competitors'.

   ____

   ____

   ____

2. **Describe your creative concept.** What is your ad strategy? Sum up *who* (target market), *what* (product or service benefit), and *why* (the rationale supporting the benefit).

   ___

   ___

   ___

   Your positioning strategy guides your creative approach. What is the key benefit identified by your positioning?

   ___

   ___

   ___

   Choose image or response advertising. What will be your take-away/call to action?

   ___

   ___

   ___

3. **Choose your copy approach.** Which of the approaches presented in this chapter holds promise for your ad message?

   ___

   ___

   ___

You'll find this completed worksheet helpful when you build your marketing plan.

The Least You Need to Know

- Consider features and translate them to benefits that solve problems or fill desires of your target audience.
- To find your creative concept, review your positioning strategy and decide on your call to action.

- Adopt a tried-and-true copy approach to make crafting your ad copy easier.
- Test and improve your ads over time by including codes that let you track the performance of various ads.

Chapter 18

When and Where to Advertise

In This Chapter

- Create your personal media plan, tailored to your goals and audience
- Find the right timing strategy to stretch your ad dollars
- Meet a sales rep and learn how to get him to toe your line

As an advertising consultant, I tend to meet people when they have advertising needs. It always begins with a phone call. About half the time, somebody launches into a tale that reveals poor media planning, and almost all the time, that story ends with the same question. "Can you help me get out of this mess?" There was the dentist who bid $200 at a charity auction and got an advertising "hole" in a local magazine but didn't know what to do with it. There was the cleaning service that bought a radio station's package to get a booth at a business expo but didn't know how to fill the 30-second spots that came bundled with the booth. Take note. These people weren't using their noggins when it comes to when and where to advertise. But more about them later.

How much should you spend on advertising? When, where, and how should that investment be deployed? If you only have a few thousand dollars to spend, or if your offering is extremely specialized, the mass-market media are not an option. Maybe you should forget paid media and go with other marketing techniques instead. How are you going to know? And what method will you use to make your decisions?

The lion's share of your advertising dollar will likely go to the media: the newspapers, television stations, billboards, and so on that carry your message to the marketplace. That's an investment you'll want to manage, just as you would your stock portfolio. Are your investments earning a good return? Are your ads getting the right word to the right people? You need a media strategy to help you answer these questions.

What Is a Media Strategy?

Your *media strategy* is an action plan, a personalized set of decisions about how you'll use advertising to get a message to your market.

A media strategy consists of three components:

- A goal statement
- A media calendar
- A budget

A *goal statement* might sound something like this: "Advertising will reach and persuade young moms that Dyno-Bite cereal is nutritious and delicious." There are two messages in that goal: who the audience is (young moms) and what the benefit promise should be (twin benefits of nutrition and taste appeal). To create your goal statement, you'll need to know who you want to reach with your advertising and what you want to tell them. That knowledge comes from the customer imagination and positioning of your brand covered in earlier chapters of this book.

To make that goal statement more precise, state it in measurable terms. A measurable goal statement would be: "Advertising will achieve an 80-percent awareness of Dyno-Bite cereal among mothers age 18 to 35 in the greater metro area within three months. Those moms will retain the impression that Dyno-Bite is nutritious and delicious." With a goal statement like that, you could do pre- and post-testing in the marketplace to quantify the return on your advertising investment. The more precise your goal, the better able you will be to tell whether you've reached it.

The *media calendar* outlines when and where you'll place each ad. The final calendar is the result of comparing different scenarios and discarding some ideas in favor of others. To define "when" means you have to develop a timing strategy; to define "where" means choosing among competing outlets for your advertising. An example of a media calendar is shown later in this chapter.

A *budget* details whatever costs are associated with each component of the plan. The sum of these three components—the goal, the calendar, and the budget—equals a media strategy.

The media strategy, if you put it in writing, is a great tool. It helps you manage your advertising activity without dropping the ball in this intensely deadline-driven field. And over time, the written plan creates a diary of your advertising activity. That helps you learn from past mistakes and create ever-more-efficient strategies as time goes by.

Really!

Test the effectiveness of every component of your media strategy—the content of your creative messages, the style of your ad layouts or broadcast productions, and the choices of when and where they run. Compare your successful ads with ones that performed poorly. What elements made the difference? Occasionally perform surveys to measure whether your ads are getting their messages across. Which of your strategic efforts worked the best? Why? The only way you can improve your advertising plan's effectiveness and efficiency is through discovering what works.

How do you get from no plan at all to a time-tested media strategy? It's not that hard. It just takes three things: a willingness to do some math, the cunning to turn the media's salespeople into your media buying assistants, and the follow-through to measure response so you can learn and improve your media strategy over time.

Your Media Plan: What It Is

To make your media plan, you have to come up with a calendar listing each media outlet where ads will be placed. That calendar might include newspapers, magazines, radio, TV, direct mail, or outdoor boards … or more creative alternatives, like sandwich boards on a clown or a flyover by a blimp. You will negotiate a contract with each outlet, confirm the final schedules, and see that the right artwork or recordings make it to the right outlets on time.

As you carry out your media plan, you'll find that worksheets will come in handy. I do all my media planning work using variations on two spreadsheets. The first is the media calendar. This example shows Bob's Bottomless Boats' media calendar for two quarters.

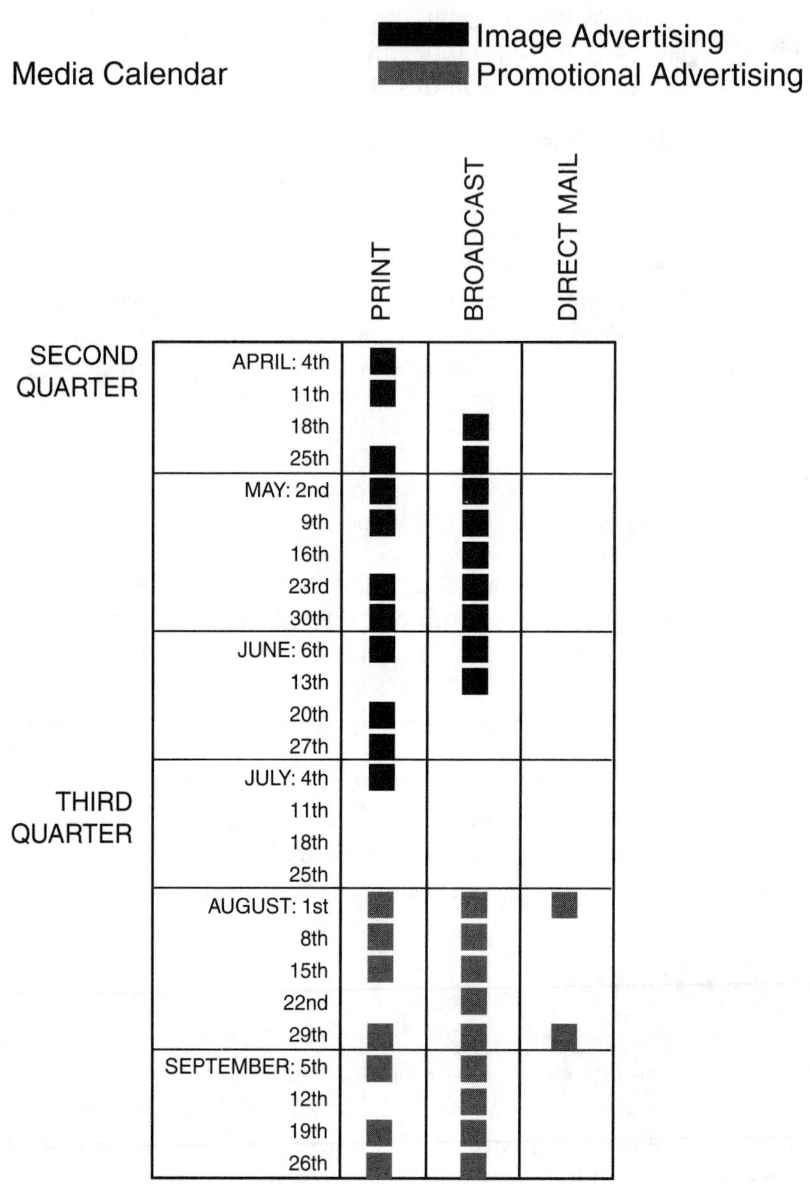

Bob's Bottomless Boats' media calendar for second and third quarter by type of outlet.

The second worksheet I rely on is the media budget. This example shows Bob's Bottomless Boats' media budget for two quarters.

Media Budget

		PRINT	BROADCAST	DIRECT MAIL	TOTAL FOR MONTH:
SECOND QUARTER	APRIL: 4th	$2000			
	11th	2000			
	18th		$2400		
	25th	2000	2400		$10,800
	MAY: 2nd	2000	2400		
	9th	2000	2400		
	16th		2400		
	23rd	2000	2400		
	30th	2000	2400		20,000
	JUNE: 6th	2000	2400		
	13th		2400		
	20th	2000			
	27th	2000			10,800
THIRD QUARTER	JULY: 4th	2000			
	11th				
	18th				
	25th				2,000
	AUGUST: 1st	2000	2400	$12,000	
	8th	2000	2400		
	15th	2000	2400		
	22nd		2400		
	29th	2000	2400	4000	28,800
	SEPTEMBER: 5th	2000	2400		
	12th	2000	2400		
	19th		2400		
	26th	2000	2400		15,600
	TOTAL BUDGET:	$36,000	$43,200	$16,000	$88,000

Bob's Bottomless Boats' media budget for second and third quarter.

Note that these worksheets don't give you all the information you need—nowhere do they show what size/length of ads are scheduled, or what the costs per ad might be.

Supporting notes will fill out the picture, recording your assumptions about prices and schedules to be negotiated.

A successful media plan meets these standards:

- It delivers the message to the right audience.
- It maximizes reach (the total number of people in your target audience who are exposed to your ad at least once) or frequency (the average number of times a member of your target audience is exposed to your ad) while minimizing costs.
- It's effective; that is, it achieves the stated goal.
- It's efficient; that is, it achieves all the above at the lowest cost possible.

To begin creating your media plan, list all the media that might be available in your marketplace. The following table lists most of those that you are likely to find in any metro market or industrial sector.

Print	**Collateral**
Consumer magazines	Direct mail
Trade journals	Point of purchase
Business press	Outdoor boards
Newspapers	Transit
Yellow pages	Out-of-home
Industrial directories	**Online advertising**
Broadcast	Website
Radio	Online ads (banners, skyscrapers, islands, etc.)
Cable/Satellite TV	E-mail
Broadcast TV	

If your market is North America, you'd better look for a niche or subset to sell to, or get ready to buy the back page of *People* magazine. You'll need either a huge budget or a plan for targeting a segment of your market that's easy to reach through affordable media. (Take a look at in-flight magazines, for example.)

Really!

Media can mean print, broadcast, direct mail, or none of the above. Some of the more unusual media include out-of-home media (billboards, ads on buses, and other ads you see outside) and imprintable novelties like coffee mugs, key chains in funny shapes, travel bags, and more.

If your market is local, listing the available media will be fairly simple. But be careful not to name just the media that reach *you*. It's not important what you read and hear—what matters is what media reaches your prospective customers.

Mentor

Are you trying to figure out which media outlets reach customers like the ones you have now? Time to reach for the old customer survey again. It's a great way to find out.

One of the best sources on media in your market is the SRDS book series, which lists all the things you need to know, like rates, circulation, deadlines, and phone numbers. Separate editions are published covering trade journals, consumers by region, the Hispanic market, and so on. Find these online at www.srds.com or ask at your library's reference desk.

Really!

There's a good place you can go if you are a beginner at media planning and want to know more. Start following "The Advertising Show." It's a radio show that does for local advertisers what Click and Clack do for cars. The audience is a mix of business owners, entrepreneurs, advertising professionals, and no doubt a few armchair advertising enthusiasts. The nationally syndicated program airs live on Saturdays. You can catch it in broadcast or Internet form. The website is worth a visit, too: www.theadvertisingshow.com. You'll find useful information there, assembled by the show's two gregarious hosts—Ray Schilens and Brad Forsythe. Check the website to find out if "The Advertising Show" is aired in your locale.

Tools of the Trade: Rate Kits, Circulation, and CPM

There has to be some way to put your various options on an equal footing. After all, you don't care whether an ad costs $1,000; you care whether at $1,000 the ad is a good buy. Media planners use a comparison that calculates CPM, or Cost Per Thousand ("M" being the Roman numeral for "thousand"). This calculation puts rate and circulation options into relative terms. Its purpose is to add meaning to the cost of an ad in a particular magazine, TV program, or newspaper. The CPM calculation facilitates comparison.

This calculation is most meaningful when you compare the same ad size in similar media outlets, as shown in the following CPM comparison for a half-page black-and-white ad in several similar magazines, prepared for a financial-services consultant.

1. Media Outlet:	City Biz (regional business magazine)	Consulting Profess (professional journal)	Our Business (statewide business magazine)
2. Rate in Effect:	1996	1996	Oct 1995 + 7%
3. Frequency:	12x	12x	12x
4. Space/Length:	1/2 page b/w	1/2 page b/w	1/2 page b/w
5. Monthly Cost:	$1,050	$600	$1,140
6. Circulation in 1000s:	12	23	41
7. CPM (Cost Per 1000)	$87.50	$26.09	$27.80
8. Index	100%	30%	32%

CPM comparison: same category magazines. (All monthly, glossy, standard-size magazines.)

Set up a spreadsheet like this. Save a blank copy of it as your template. Then, start trying your own media scenarios.

Lines 1 through 4 are simply spaces to record whatever information you used to arrive at the rate figure in line 5, which is what rate card you were looking at and what size and frequency you were considering. It's easy to lose track if you're running multiple scenarios, so I always keep this information in the spreadsheet along with the actual calculations.

Line 5 is the rate for the advertising space or time being described. In this case, Line 5 is the rate expressed in monthly cost. It could instead be expressed as a cost per week, or per year—it doesn't matter, so long as it's comparable across the board.

Line 6 is the circulation in 1,000s—a count you'll get from each media rep. Line 7 is the product of the rate in Line 5 divided by the circulation in Line 6.

It's not as confusing as it sounds—just study the figure for a minute. This simple calculation helps you bring options into a comparative relationship.

The eighth line, "Index," shows you which is the most cost-efficient option. In this example, *Consulting Professional* comes out ahead by a slight margin over *Our Business.*

The index is the key that helps you see your best option at a glance, but many people find it confusing at first. It's simpler than it sounds: The index is a way of ranking each ad's cost per thousand relative to the other ads. You select one vehicle (it doesn't really matter which), and assign it the rank of "100." Then you divide the other rates into that one and express the result as a percent. For example, *Consulting Professional's* $26.09 divided by *City Biz's* $87.50 equals .298, which I've rounded up to 30 percent. *Our Business's* $37.80 divided by *City Biz's* $87.50 equals .432, or 43 percent. This tells you that *Consulting Professional* is a slightly more efficient buy than *Our Business,* and much more efficient than *City Biz.*

Pitfall

Beware of automatically buying the outlet with the lowest CPM. First check the fit of its audience to your prospective customer profile. Unless those thousands of readers are really members of your target audience, you will end up paying to expose your ads to lots of people who would never buy your product.

Are you ready to try a CPM analysis? Start with print—it's easier. You'll need two numbers to make this calculation work for you: the rate for the ad space under consideration, and the number of copies circulated, expressed in thousands. To get this information you simply call each publication, and before you know it the skies will have opened and it will be raining advertising media sales representatives, also known as "media reps" or "ad reps."

Really!

CPM analysis can be applied to online advertising—in fact, the cost for online ads is often phrased as a CPM. The formula of ad sizes and circulation numbers works with online advertising just as for other media. Ad sizes on websites have settled into a half dozen or so standards, with descriptive names like banner, skyscraper, and island. Media planners use the number of people who visit the website in a set period of time (usually monthly) for the circulation figure. If you are considering advertising on a website, contact the site for size and rate information. Get audience demographics as well, and usage statistics, such as the length of time the typical user stays on the site. Look for more on this topic in Chapter 22.

Your goal is to get a rate card and an estimate of the circulation or audience for each magazine, radio station, website, or whatever you're considering. But to get it you'll find yourself sitting through sales pitch after sales pitch, hearing a new language of reach, frequency, audience, share, and more.

Meet the Media (Reps)

Media reps will call on you until they drive you crazy. They have a hundred persuasive reasons why you should choose their product, and a hundred more special deals that, if you act now, will save you hundreds of dollars. They're well-prepared representatives of a system designed to sell advertising—but that system doesn't always have your best interest at heart.

The trouble is, salespeople for the media are trained to sell media, not trained to sell whatever you sell. They have great ideas for you on using promotions, or how package deals can stretch your dollars. What they don't have is an understanding of your business and where your marketing should take you. They all make a living hounding you to part with your ad dollar, which is a good reason to have serious second thoughts about taking media advice from them.

This is where the cleaning service I mentioned at the beginning of this chapter went off track, opting for a package that sounded good but entailed hidden costs to create ads to fill radio spots they hadn't particularly wanted. Don't let a good salesman talk you into a bad decision!

Really!

Media planning has been one of the most carefully guarded secrets of the advertising agencies. And yet it's where most of their entry-level managerial employees start out. What does that tell you? It's so easy even a kid can do it. Just keep these thoughts in mind: First, learn to do CPM calculations with ease. Then you can show hard numbers to back up your hunches, which can be very useful whenever big investments are at stake. Second, make a hard choice. Will your plan emphasize reach or frequency? (When in doubt, opt for frequency over reach.) And third, remember the importance of dominating one medium before you expand into others.

Successfully Negotiating with Media Reps

Take the lead with your media reps. Put them to work for you. You need specific information from them. We've touched on the basics—rates and circulation—but there's more to come. To get the information you need and keep the sales hype to a minimum, practice thinking of your media reps as your assistants. Have them bring you the information you need to make your decisions. Do your decision-making yourself, using our CPM calculation to evaluate your different options.

Once you've made your decisions, use your media assistants to help you negotiate the final contract rates and schedules with each outlet you've chosen and to expedite your buys by taking care of paperwork and the follow-through details. When you need someone to pick up the artwork or deliver the tapes around town, call your media rep.

A Vocabulary Lesson

Here are some of the terms you'll hear when you meet with the sales reps. Understand these terms, and you won't have to rely on your rep's interpretation of the facts.

- **Media vehicles and outlets.** Use these terms interchangeably to mean one specific instance of a particular medium. "Print" is a medium; *The New York Times* is a print vehicle or media outlet.
- **CPM or cost per thousand.** CPM represents the cost of reaching 1,000 people over a set schedule of ads.
- **Audience/circulation.** With radio and TV they call it audience; with print they call it circulation. Either way, it's the people exposed to your message. (In online advertising you'll encounter CPM and also other measures, but more about that in Chapter 22.)
- **Reach and frequency.** Reach is the total number of people who see or hear an ad at least once during a set time period. Frequency is the average number of times those people are seeing or hearing the same ad.
- **Flighting.** A flight refers to running a bunch of ads in a short time, like a flight of ducks.

CAUTION

Pitfall

Be wary of inflated circulation figures! Magazines will try to convince you that their circulation is higher than it really is by claiming "pass-along readership," suggesting each copy of their magazine gets read by several people besides the one on the address label. Maybe so, but how do you quantify such a claim? Stick to numbers that have been verified by third-party monitoring organizations.

Evaluating Your Media Alternatives

You must find the most similar profile between your target market and the media vehicles available. But with a wide field of media outlets to choose from, how do you find the right combination to reach your goal? You've got your CPM calculations, for starters. The CPM ranking gives you a cost comparison between alternatives. But each media outlet is fundamentally different. The morning paper has different readers from the afternoon paper. The audience for one radio station is very different from another station. Broadcast media are inherently different from print media. So you'll need to make qualitative as well as quantitative comparisons.

Quantitative Rankings Help You Measure ...

Whether we're talking about radio or television or direct mail or newspapers, the basic unit of measurement is CPM, the cost per thousand people reached. Print media uses circulation as the basis for comparison. For radio and television, audience ratings help you measure how many people are listening or watching, while for direct mail, your circulation is simply the number of names you mail to. For billboards, traffic counts are the equivalent. Each media outlet has its own measure.

Mentor

Sometimes a media plan involves choosing between several roughly equal alternatives. A great idea for silly sound effects might tip you to decide for radio. Or a chance to create a compelling visual might send you in the direction of print. The most effective ads marry great creativity with great exposure through the right media buys.

CPM calculations can help you compare alternatives within a category, like one radio station or another, or they can help you compare across categories. But don't forget that each medium is inherently different. CPM scores alone can't dictate where your advertising goes.

Compare apples and oranges, and your CPM comparison will be about as useful as fruit salad. For best results, use rates for ads of the same size (or with broadcast media, the same time length) and the same frequency. Only when you base your comparisons on roughly equal "products" will your results help you make sound decisions.

... And Qualitative Rankings Help You Evaluate

Your media assistants, the reps from each outlet you're considering, should help you here. Ask them for demographic information about the audience they reach. How closely does it match your target audience? Will there be wasted circulation? How's the aesthetic appeal of the medium? Good editorial content, well-respected, good production values? Are your competitors advertising there? Does your positioning strategy suggest you should be there, too, competing head-to-head, or that you should look elsewhere for a medium you can claim and dominate on your own?

Good media planners give considerable thought to the qualitative aspects of each outlet.

Timing Is Everything

If you bought 30 radio commercials in one week, and over the course of that week 30,000 people tuned in to the station at the various times your commercials were on the air, you would have achieved a *reach* of 30,000. But chances are, each of those people heard the commercial just once (at best). What are the odds they noticed it, comprehended your message, and developed a desire for the product you're selling? Not good. That's why advertising pros recommend *frequency* goals as well. Let's say you increase your schedule to 60 commercials a week. The same 30,000 people tune in as they did before. But now there's twice the chance that those people will hear your commercial more than once.

Mentor

You should run any radio commercial a minimum of three times a week to have any hope of being remembered at all. A number more like 60 or 70 times a week works far better. Don't piddle your money away on a schedule that's too weak to assert itself.

Finding the Right Balance of Reach and Frequency

The goal of advertising is to teach your audience a new behavior—something that persuades them to take an action or change a belief. It's obvious that you must reach as many of them as possible.

But reach is not enough. Repetition is the key to learning, and so you must advertise with some degree of frequency. And frequency brings with it the question of timing.

Once learning has taken place, forgetting begins. That makes continued repetitions of an ad message necessary. Longer flights of advertising keep the audience from losing its ability to recall your message. The rule of thumb is that an audience should hear your ad at the very least three to five times, to remember and act appropriately.

If you're trying to change behavior for good, it's important to keep your message out there in front of the market. Keep this in mind when you choose your timing strategy.

At the beginning of this chapter, I mentioned a dentist who purchased advertising space in a charity auction. The problem with that? The dentist lacked an understanding of timing strategy. He had no plan or budget for repetition to build frequency in his advertising. That one ad alone is worse than worthless—not only does it fail to achieve any useful purpose, but it also draws money away from better uses.

Choose Your Timing Strategy

If you can't afford to be advertising everywhere, every day of the year (and who can?), you're going to have to look for effective alternatives. How do you get the biggest bang for your buck? That's where timing strategies come in. Look back to your marketing goals and objectives. Are you introducing a new product, or are you trying to reinvigorate an existing brand? Are there seasonal influences on your sales? Respond to these challenges by scheduling your ads in flights.

Here are a few of the timing strategies that media planners use. Each "on" period is called a flight. Each "off" period is called a hiatus. Remember that when your ads stop appearing, forgetting begins. Flighting is a way to return your audience to learning mode, while stretching your ad budget through the use of "off" (no expenditure) periods.

- **Continuous flighting**. A great little pasta restaurant runs an ad in the dining guide of the local newsweekly every week of the year. That's a *continuous* timing strategy.
- **Startup flighting.** A brewery brings out a special summer beer. It schedules an eight-week flight of radio commercials around the Fourth of July to get sales rolling. End of summer: end of commercials. That's *strategic start-up flighting*.
- **Front-loading.** If that brewery had run extra commercials at the start of its flight, to kick it off big, we'd call that *front-loading*. It's a great way to get people talking about your commercial and get that extra word-of-mouth advertising. Definitely a strategy for retail business to consider.
- **Pulse flighting.** To save money, that brewery might adopt a *pulse flighting* strategy. Instead of running in a continuous pattern, ads would be on and off again on a regular basis. Just as it takes time for people to notice your ad, it takes them time to notice when you've stopped advertising. You can take advantage of this delay to give your budget a break.
- **Seasonal push.** Just about every business has peaks and valleys throughout the year. There are two ways you can respond to them. You can look to push the high points higher, going with the natural flow of things, or you can try to raise

the valley floors. If you choose the timing of your flight by the seasons of your business, your advertising shows a *seasonal push.*

The following diagram shows some examples of flighting schedules. Come up with your own variations on the strategies shown here.

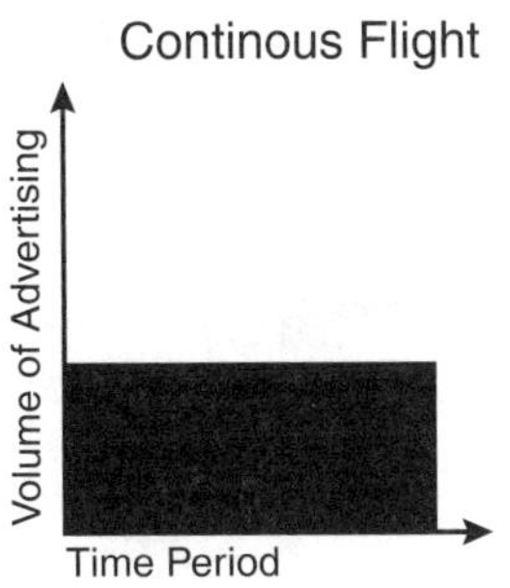

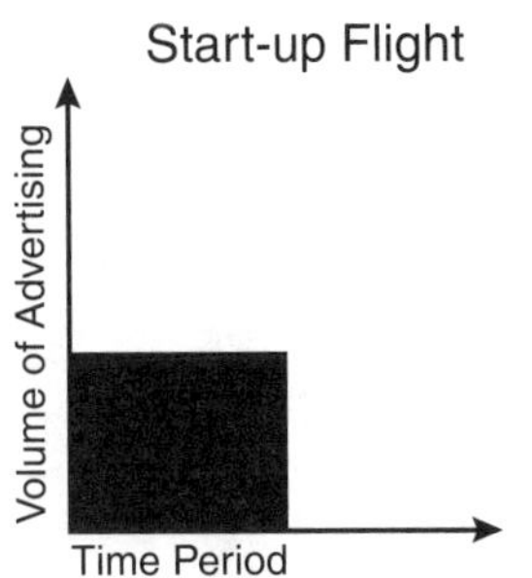

Timing strategies.

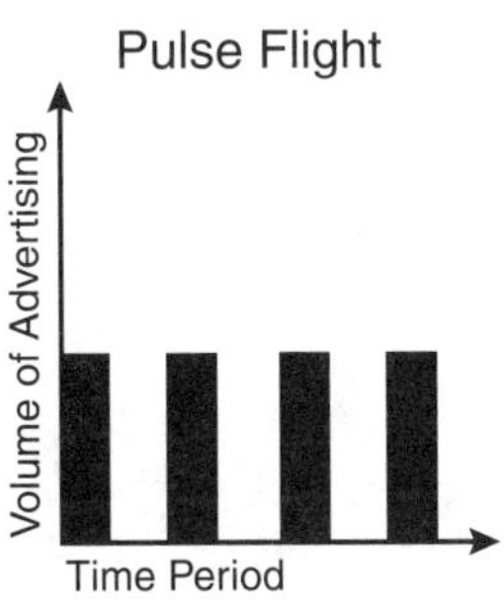

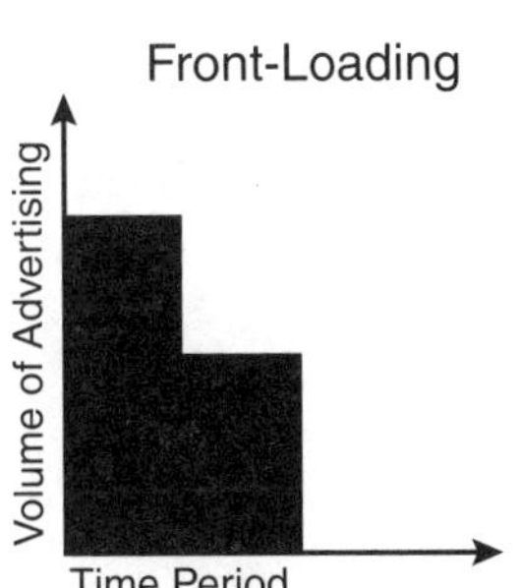

When I do a media plan for a client, I make a lot of alternative scenarios, comparing different schedules and the rate structures they bring into play. I haven't found a better way to do this than with pencil on graph paper; sometimes computers just mire you down in the detail of things. I'll use my computer to work out a good CPM comparison, and then sit down with a calculator and a cup of coffee. In about a pot and a half I can usually find a sensible approach for my client to try.

And that brings us to negotiating the cost for the ads you've decided to run.

Mentor

If you're not sure why you'd choose one strategy over another, you need focus! A snappy promotional plan will help you make decisions about media strategy. A promotion gives you an exciting message to deliver and specific ways to measure response. That's a great way to explore which media work best for you.

Getting the Most for Your Money

None of us has money to burn. The most important thing you can do to ensure you get the most for your money is to match the target to the budget. If you've targeted young moms, as Dyno-Bite has, and you discover you can't afford to reach all the young moms in America, then redefine the target. Try "young moms in Michigan." Now your target is a much more affordable size. Still too expensive? Try "young moms in Battle Creek."

Really!

Print and broadcast media are inherently different in a way that illustrates the law of supply and demand. The "inventory" of ad space in a newspaper or magazine is flexible. If the sales reps move a lot of inventory, the publisher adds pages to the whole. Likewise, he can shrink the page count if ad sales are weak.

On the other hand, broadcast media (radio and TV) have a limited amount of inventory to sell. After all, there are only so many commercial minutes in a 24-hour day.

So who's more willing to negotiate? The broadcast rep. Any unsold time will air anyway, but will be filled with PSAs (public service announcements) and station promotions.

A Good Deal Is Good for All Parties

Remember, your media reps are just trying to earn a living, too. Your sales rep works on commission. If he offers you 75 spots for $2,500, and you respond saying you'll only pay $2,200, what have you done? You've cut his take-home pay by 12 percent. There's a better way to negotiate the deal.

"Is that the best you can do?"

That's your opening line. "I was thinking more like 100 spots for that price," you continue. Now you've got something to work with. You haven't cut his pay, just asked for more value for the money. He goes back to his boss and puts his sales skills to work. But this time he's working for you. And since a bird in hand is worth several in the bush, the boss will likely agree. Everybody winds up happy. (You could also try asking for free production of your ad, to get more for your money!)

Explore Co-Op

Are you in a retail business? Then look for co-op support. That means a cooperative advertising program—rebates and contributions from suppliers to help people like you move more of their products.

Watch the newspaper for a few days (the consumer electronics category is a good one to follow) and ask yourself: Did a local advertiser pay for this ad, or did a national company back up the local store ? A clue to watch for: logos of national brands. You'll quickly spot the advertisers whose media strategy relies on co-op support.

Finding co-op programs available to you may require a little detective work. Start by asking your ad reps and your suppliers what they know. And if you don't find a preexisting program that works for you, do it yourself. Approach a supplier with a suggestion like "How about I run a sales event featuring your product? Would you kick in a couple hundred bucks to cover advertising to promote the sale?" Propose a win-win situation, and I predict you'll create a cooperative co-op partner.

Collecting your money from a co-op program can be hard work. The rules are often complex, and you'll probably need a *tear-sheet*, but don't let that stop you. The money you'll save is worth working for.

Pitfall

There is a downside to co-op. Co-op programs put restrictions on your advertising. It might be rules about how the product is shown, or how big the manufacturer's logo is next to yours, or whether you plan to feature competing products in the ad as well. It's up to you to decide whether the money you're offered is worth the compromises they ask you to make.

What?

A **tear-sheet** is literally that: a page torn from a newspaper or magazine. It's indisputable proof of when and where an ad ran. The newspaper or magazine you advertise in will mail you several tear-sheets along with the bill for the space. You will forward one of these to your co-op partner to apply for your rebate.

Your Media Budget

You'll have two sources of expense in your media budget: production expenses and your bills for space or air time.

The question that's really bugging you is, "How much should I be spending on advertising?" And, of course, there's no way I can answer that. If you only have a few thousand dollars to spend, don't think that traditional mass-market media like newspapers or television are going to work for you. Radio stations appeal to more of a niche audience, and that might offer a reasonable alternative for you. If your budget's tight, stick to this rule: Be a big fish in a small pond, even if that pond is so small it's a puddle. Dominate one medium before you add others to your schedule.

The only way to make spending this much money feel good is to measure the results it buys you. Over time, your media strategy will become a money machine.

Use these worksheets to record your media calendar and media budget, quarter by quarter. Keep the plan sketched in for at least two quarters out, or you'll lose out on the benefits of time for negotiations. As each flight of advertising is completed, note any performance measures and observations. Over time you'll find this collection of completed worksheets very helpful in budgeting, planning, and learning from experience.

Media Calendar

		PRINT	BROADCAST	DIRECT MAIL
SECOND QUARTER	APRIL: Week 1 2 3 4			
	MAY: Week 1 2 3 4 5			
	JUNE: Week 1 2 3 4			
THIRD QUARTER	JULY: Week 1 2 3 4			
	AUGUST: Week 1 2 3 4 5			
	SEPTEMBER: Week 1 2 3 4			

Media Budget

		PRINT	BROADCAST	DIRECT MAIL	TOTAL FOR MONTH
SECOND QUARTER	APRIL: Week 1 2 3 4				
	MAY: Week 1 2 3 4 5				
	JUNE: Week 1 2 3 4				
THIRD QUARTER	JULY: Week 1 2 3 4				
	AUGUST: Week 1 2 3 4 5				
	SEPTEMBER: Week 1 2 3 4				

TOTAL BUDGET:

The Least You Need to Know

- Your media plan consists of a calendar, a budget, and a statement of goals that describes the audience you want to reach and the change in belief or behavior you'd like to induce in them, in quantifiable terms.
- The right timing strategy maximizes your investment by placing your ads often enough to make learning take place, and over a long-enough time period to delay forgetting that message until after the desired result has been achieved.

- You'll get the most for your money when you learn what motivates your sales reps. Remember, a good deal is good for all parties.
- Test and measure your advertising to improve the efficiency and effectiveness of your media strategy over time.

Chapter 19

All You Need to Know About Advertising in Print

In This Chapter

- The three kinds of magazines and their advantages and disadvantages
- How newspapers deliver more than news
- How directories, print collateral, and outdoor advertising fit in the picture

Let's embark on a whirlwind tour of a new country—the world of print media. We'll visit five locales on our tour: magazines, newspapers, directories, direct mail pieces, and the big outdoors. As we visit each print media location, I'll describe the lay of the land. I'll explain the advantages and disadvantages of each and bring up any media-planning concerns you should be aware of—particulars of reach and frequency, timing, cost, and production. Got your bags packed? Let's go.

What's Right and What's Wrong with Print

The thing about print is that it's there. It's a physical, tangible product. Print is the only advertising medium you can study. The printed page is an object you can examine as much as you like.

> **Pitfall**
>
> Don't make your media decisions too rationally. Maybe all the logical reasons point toward print, but you still aren't sure it's right. What's your creative side telling you? A great creative idea that dictates broadcast media is all the reason you need to silence the arguments in favor of print.

Leaf through this morning's newspaper and concentrate on the ads. How many do you see that present information "catalog-style"? I'm certain you'll find at least one ad for consumer electronics and one for furniture that describes specific products by listing the features and stating a selling price. These advertisers are demonstrating the ease of comparison made possible by print. Many consumers use the print media to preshop for the products they want, arriving at a short list of stores to visit after comparing competing products via print advertising (much like they use the World Wide Web).

Is print for you? You can't tell until you've considered all the other media, but here's a checklist to help you decide.

Print is the logical choice if …

- Your product or service needs detailed information to be understood.
- The desire for your offering is more rational than emotional. (Caribbean cruises are sold through TV; office furniture is sold through print.)
- You have a limited budget. Print space and production charges are low compared to television.

Magazines Are the Cream of the Crop

Magazines offer the highest-quality printing and the longest shelf life—important assets when you want your advertising to attract studied attention. Depending on the specific type of magazine, you can find vehicles that are capable of reaching a highly targeted or a broad mass market.

Magazines come in many descriptions. There are mass-market "glossies" such as *People* or *Time*. Then there are mass-circulation publications that target specific demographic types, such as *Seventeen*, *Modern Maturity*, or *Black Entrepreneur*. Magazines also target audiences on the basis of shared interest, whether that's a regional lifestyle (magazines like *Atlanta* or *Chicago*), or a hobby (*Model Airplane* or *Quilter*). Business publications exist in a parallel universe, where audiences can be targeted by vertical markets (*Paper Trade Journal* or *Graphic Arts Monthly*), by job function (*Business Marketing*), or by region (*Corporate Report Wisconsin*).

A bewildering array? Not at all, because only a few out of the multitudes are relevant to you. When you evaluate magazine advertising, look for the publications that deliver readers most closely matching the profile you've targeted. The media kits for each should give you the information you need.

Magazines offer a very specific audience compared to a mass medium like television. While TV attracts everyone in the family to gather around the glowing screen, sharing not only the programs but also the commercials in between, only the targeted reader is likely to pick up a magazine. Little Stevie isn't likely to pick up Mom's *Quilter* or get a chance at Dad's *Playboy* either.

What are the advantages of magazine advertising? Let's talk reach and frequency. Because magazines target specific audiences, they deliver specific reach opportunities. They're not a mass medium; they're a precise medium. If your "reach" goal is precise, the right magazine may give you 90 percent of your desired audience.

Frequency is slow to build with magazines but can be achieved if you appear in consecutive issues. Consecutively appearing ads give you a good opportunity to build image for your company. You can project a personality and develop a message, teaching your audience over time. Another advantage with magazines is prestige. If your ad appears in a highly renowned magazine, such as *Fortune*, the prestige conveyed by the magazine's format and editorial content provides a flattering "halo" for your ad.

Disadvantages of magazine advertising? Cost and a relatively nonnegotiable atmosphere when it comes to the ad contract. The cost of a magazine ad is at the high end for print media. What that buys you is a high production value—glossy paper, nice reproduction of photos, and clean printing. Just compare an ad in a newspaper with one in a magazine and you'll know what I mean.

Rates for ads are priced by size, frequency, and number of colors used. The rates are published on a rate card, and there's usually not much chance to negotiate price. If the magazine sells more than the usual number of ads one month, they just add more pages to the issue. If ad sales are down, so is the page count. The "more value for the money" approach to negotiation still applies here (see Chapter 18 on media planning). It's easier to ask for—and

Mentor

Because magazines are slow-acting vehicles, tailor your ad's message accordingly. Magazines are better used for image advertising or communicating detailed information than for announcing sales or other timely messages.

get—the twelve-time rate for your six-time schedule than to get the publication to give you 20 percent off the rate card.

Consumer Magazines: The "Glossies"

In consumer magazines, you'll see advertisers with names like Toyota and Microsoft. Could there be a place in that world for your business? Surprisingly, yes. Many mass-circulation publications have as many as 500 different regional editions. A car dealer in suburban Chicago can advertise in *Sports Illustrated*, buying space in just the copies distributed in his market area.

Mentor

Ads don't have to be big—ads have to be *read*. Targeting the right audience in your media buy is more important than developing big exciting ad layouts.

If you sell a product with a specific niche, small ads in specialty magazines are worth looking into. A client of mine who markets books on tape places tiny one-inch ads in magazines like *The Atlantic* that appeal to people who love books and reading. Other ads promoting specific products are placed where they'll find interested readers. A product titled "War and Peace in the Nuclear Age" pulls well when advertised in *Military Enthusiast*.

Business Magazines: The "Trade Rags"

Business magazines target readers by industry, job function, and region. The regional journals are important if you sell business-to-business and there's a well-established vehicle in your area. I've been disappointed by too many of these regional publications, however, finding them attractive in their production value but marginal when it comes to actually being read. Larger metro areas have the best business publications. If you're in the sticks, look for other ways to promote yourself to your neighbors.

Journals that serve specific industries are animals of another stripe. Industry-specific trade journals are often called *vertical market publications* because they contain editorials and advertising that address everyone in an industry from product manufacturers through distributors to retailers of those products. Take for example *Impressions*, the journal of the imprintable active-wear industry. (That's "T-shirt screen-printing" to you who like things simple.) *Impressions* features news from the knitting mills, articles about improvements in inks and printing techniques, and advice for managing a screen-printing business or a retail store. There are technical articles on how to print with unusual techniques, and interviews with industry leaders and consultants. Everyone from production worker to marketing director can find something of interest in the magazine. (Is that why there's a stack in the bathroom at most of those print shops?)

If a vertical market can be compared to a small town, then its trade journal is its newspaper. Do you want your product or service to be news in town? Advertise in the appropriate journal and aim your public relations efforts in that direction, too.

What?

Vertical market publications are magazines that address readers across the job spectrum of a specific industry, from the production worker to the CEO.

There's one thing to beware of, however: In a vertical market, not everyone in the pond is *your* customer. While your ad will reach your channel members, there may be some waste as well. Let's take a different example. *Graphic Arts Monthly* is read both by graphic designers and printers. If you're selling desktop publishing equipment, your target audience matches the entire readership of the magazine. If you're selling ink, however, your target audience matches only half that audience. Graphic designers don't buy or specify individual brands of ink. Your ad is wasted on them.

The media kit for a trade publication should tell the breakdown of readers by job type. This shows you how well their readers match your target. If half the audience is wasted, cut their circulation in half when you plug that number into your CPM Calculations.

Myths of Magazine Advertising: Pass-Along Readership and Shelf-Life

One of the main advantages of magazines is their long life. They are kept and revisited several times as the reader works his or her way through the articles and features. My rule of thumb: The better the editorial content, the more shelf life you can expect from a publication. If you're considering advertising in a particular vehicle, get more than one issue from your sales rep and really study the editorial content. If you know some subscribers, do a little informal research. Ask how long they keep the magazine and how often they look at an issue once it's arrived.

Many magazines tout their pass-along readership. Those regional business magazines I mentioned before are famous for this. "We're in all the lobbies in town," they'll say. "Dozens of people will be exposed to your ad beyond the subscriber on the mailing label."

Aside from in-flight magazines, which by their nature have high pass-along readership, I tend to discount these claims. Yes, many browsers may be exposed to your ad, but what do we know about them? Nothing. There's no way we can know whether those additional readers fit your target profile or not. So I say you have to discount their existence when you consider circulation figures. Their value to you is more myth than reality.

Newspapers Struggle to Keep Up

Each medium has a task it does best. For newspapers, that task has always been to deliver news. People turn to their papers not just to read about the events of the day but to catch the latest advertising as well. Your news about what's in stock, what it costs, and what sales or promotions may be in effect belongs in the newspaper.

> CAUTION
>
> **Pitfall**
>
> People are spending less time with newspapers every year. The birth of television initiated newsprint's decline, and the Internet, with its power to deliver news as it happens, is trying to finish the job. Pay careful attention to who's advertising in your local newspaper before you jump in. If there's no one advertising to people like the ones you want to reach, that's a bad sign.

Most advertisers in newspapers are retailers, and fairly large ones at that. Newspapers deliver an audience that is broad demographically but narrow geographically. In most communities, newspapers reach from 60 to 80 percent of the households in the market—wealthy families and poor, students and senior citizens, and all the other denizens as well. The good news is that higher-income households are more likely to subscribe to newspapers, boosting that market penetration figure as high as 90 percent among people with potential to purchase products and services.

Fish Wrappers and Fire Starters: Disadvantages of Newspaper Advertising

The most frustrating aspect of newspapers as an advertising medium is their short shelf life. You've probably heard the saying "Today's news, tomorrow's fish wrapper." If people don't notice your ad the first time they read the paper, it's not likely you'll get a second shot. Research shows that people are spending less time with newspapers than they used to even a few years ago.

Cost is also an issue. Newspaper advertising space may be less expensive than broadcast time, and print production costs are certainly lower than broadcast, but that doesn't mean newspaper advertising is a blue-light special. It takes a big budget to achieve frequency over time, and yet, given the cluttered environment, you've got to go in with some size as well as some frequency in order to be seen at all.

And while we're talking about disadvantages, here's my pet peeve: the poor printing quality of most newspapers. The paper is terrible, and the ink tends to print light in some copies, dark and smeary in others. Your ad design had better be simple and legible, or it could be undermined by bad reproduction. Technology has improved newspaper printing a lot but great art it's not (yet).

Advantages of Newspaper Advertising

On the "pro" side of the balance: Newspapers work fast. Today you can decide to have a sale and your ad can be in tomorrow's paper. Ad production is simple and usually free if performed by the paper's art department.

Newspapers are a crowded venue, with hundreds of ads competing for the readers' attention, but by their nature, you can counter that by having your ad placed in an appropriate section. Bob's Bottomless Boats likes to advertise in the Sports section; a craft store, on the other hand, would go in the Lifestyle section (what used to be called "the Ladies' Page").

This ability to reach a broad market and then select by interest within that market is definitely an advantage. For many products that require a joint decision (both husband and wife have to approve of the expenditure before they head down to Bob's Bottomless Boats, for example), the newspaper is definitely a smart place to be.

But the real advantages in newsprint may not be found in your local daily paper. Take a look at the alternatives out there! Many communities have free "shoppers" that consist of ads and classified listings. These work extremely well for many types of products. College towns usually have daily or weekly college papers. Many cities, especially college towns, have alternative newsweeklies, or music and entertainment guides, that deliver a hip audience with money to spend. I really like alternative newsweeklies' ability to achieve both reach and frequency for small-budget advertisers.

Really!

Your community may have an alternative newsweekly. These papers grew out of the counter-culture decades ago to their current position of respectability. They deliver an educated, affluent 20- to 40-something demographic. These have some of the positive attributes of magazines, including a longer shelf life. Many carry entertainment listings that increase the number of times their pages are opened—and the number of times your ad may be seen. I think they're the great undiscovered bargain in media buying.

Is there an alternative newsweekly in your market? Take a look at the media kit and who's advertising in their pages. These alternatives to the daily paper appeal to a broader demographic than the students you might think of as their audience.

Directories Reach People Who Are Ready to Buy

Directories are compilations of listings, organized to help people find specific businesses by looking in general classifications. You'll find directories organized by geography (your city's Yellow Pages) or by industry (*Thomas Register* and similar books). Don't discount directory advertising's importance in your media plan. They serve a function, and you'd be worse off without them. You will probably want to include them in your media plan.

There are two big problems with directories. The first is the commitment they represent—the ad you place today will be out there at least a year, and sometimes several years. Directory advertising is the most long-range of the print media. You can't pull out later if you've contracted for a big ad and find it isn't pulling its weight. If you move or change a phone number, there's no way to correct your directory ad.

The second disadvantage is that they may well be a dying breed. Search engines on the Internet fill the same function and (in the user's perception anyway) turn up more current information than a printed directory might.

Still, when you need a plumber in a hurry, you may be more likely to reach for the Yellow Pages than for the Internet.

Yellow Pages Are Useful Geographical Directories

With the deregulation of the phone industry, many competing local directories have sprung up. There are some scams around, too—companies that use sneaky "look-alike" tactics to make you think you've purchased the "true" local Yellow Pages but that really don't offer its distribution or exposure. Read the fine print and ask for samples of any directory before you sign a contract.

You may be tempted to cover your bases by advertising in all of them. That will not be cost-effective. Beware the hard-sell approach of your sales rep. It makes more sense to look for new business than to pay high directory advertising bills while you wait for new business to look for you. Faced with competition from online search engines and community portal websites, the printed directories are dropping from a "must" to a "maybe" in your media plan.

Mentor

The Internet with its search engines are giving printed directories a run for their money. I haven't talked to a directory salesman recently, but the very fact that they haven't been clamoring at my door is a sign of significantly reduced activity in their field! Local retail businesses still maintain a lively presence in Yellow Pages directories, but few other business types find it the necessity it once was.

Business Directories Are Helpful Tools

Industrial directories are a standard tool in business-to-business marketing. There are national books like *Thomas Register*, and regional and local directories published by trade associations and chambers of commerce. These can be very important if your market includes industrial buyers. Here you don't have to be quite so wary of scams, and you won't be pursued by such aggressive sales reps. Check with your trade association to find out whether there are industrial directories appropriate for you. Join your chamber of commerce to be included in its listings. The rule of thumb for business directories is this: If your competitors are there, you'd better be, too. Look for ones with companion websites, so you catch solution-seekers no matter which medium they prefer for their searches.

Print Collateral

There's a whole other category of print media that doesn't rely on subscribers or newsstands to reach its audience. This category goes by the unlikely name of *print collateral.* This umbrella covers direct mail and point of purchase displays. All these vehicles have in common is that a printer has to put some ink on paper in the process of creating them.

Print collateral can be converted to cost-per-thousand (CPM) figures for comparison with other media options. You look at the circulation by estimating the audience who will be exposed to the message, and you come up with the advertising rate by estimating the production and distribution costs.

Unlike print advertising, print collateral isn't locked into the rectangles of ads in pages or fractions of pages. Collateral offers some of the most exciting opportunities to be creative with the format and message of your advertising.

What?

Print collateral is a term advertising agencies came up with to describe all the elements that are collateral to, or tangentially related to, their core business of preparing advertising for television, radio, magazines, and newspapers. The term covers direct mail and point of purchase displays, and some people use it when referring to outdoor media like billboards and bus ads. It's a convenient catchall.

Use Direct Mail to Sell to Market Niches

Direct mail is unique. To understand just how it's unique, you have to understand the essential difference between advertising and selling. Advertising reaches people you don't know. It causes some of those people to turn themselves in to you as prospects. Then, obviously, selling begins. Selling is about turning people from prospects into buyers.

Direct mail is best used for selling—not advertising. It can be quite expensive in terms of CPM, and if some of that cost is for wasted reach, that's bad. Postage, printing, and paper costs have all been spiraling upward, making this once-cheap vehicle too expensive for any but well-qualified prospect lists. To reach those hot leads you must either ante up for a targeted mailing list or devote resources to building your own house list.

Mentor

To determine CPM for a direct-mail piece, use the number of names on the mailing list in place of the circulation figure you would use for other media. In place of the rate you will want to add up your postage and mailing list cost, plus your production cost (from creative design through printing).

A whole industry exists around creating and maintaining mailing lists. Most communities have a local or regional list service, plus local contacts for national companies. Look in your Yellow Pages under "mailing lists" to see what your local market offers, or hop online and conduct your search.

Should you try direct mail? If you asked me that question, I'd counter with a question. How good is your list? If you're confident you're reaching buyers, go for it. But first visit Chapter 20, where you'll find much more detailed information on direct mail marketing.

Point-of-Purchase

Point-of-Purchase, or *POP* as everybody in the marketing biz calls it, refers to the gimmicks and displays you see in retail stores. These are merchandising aids provided by manufacturers or distributors to help push product through the distribution channel. Occasionally, retailers, too, create POP to help products sell. But typically it's the manufacturer who foots the bill for these gizmos.

In your mind, take a walk through your local grocery store. Look around. In the meat department you find little coupons and recipes clipped to the coolers. In the dairy section you find banners with slogans and logos dangling from the ceiling. In the aisles you find floor decals and cardboard assemblies that promote products in creative ways. Sometimes inflatable characters and products accompany the displays. All of these are POP.

What?

The term **Point-of-Purchase**, or **POP** for short, covers all the different kinds of retail displays that promote products to consumers. These can include countertop brochure racks, wall banners, and crazy things dangling from the ceiling or standing in the aisles. POP requires constant innovation to stay effective.

Are these relevant for you? If you're in manufacturing or distribution, maybe yes. The various forms of POP are promotional tools, useful for waking up sleepy product sales. But be warned: It's hard to keep POP cost-effective if you're not a major national merchandiser. Print runs are too short, and fabrication too unique, to achieve any economies of scale.

As you can imagine, it costs something to have an inflatable blue bunny designed and manufactured with your logo on his chest. If you're a small-scale manufacturer who needs some POP to add punch to a push strategy, don't give up, but do think in terms of printed pieces like banners, flyers, and shelf-strips. If it can be done with ink on a square piece of paper, you can afford it. If it requires an irregular shape or a manufacturing genius, give it up.

Outdoor and Transit Advertising: Eyesores or Entertainment?

Outdoor advertising has been around since Pompeii and has contributed some great art to the world. Many of the works of Toulouse-Lautrec, Manet, and Mucha, among others, were commissioned for outdoor advertising. Today this term has expanded to include transit advertising and mall and airport kiosks, as well as the traditional roadside billboard. And some of these are still beautiful works of art.

Outdoor media have a lot of advantages. They build frequency rapidly because people tend to move in the same patterns every day. The same people pass your ad dozens of times each month. Outdoor advertising reaches a geographically targeted market inexpensively. Advertising rates are based on traffic counts by location, and discounts are offered for long-term contracts. Outdoor advertising can be easy and inexpensive to produce.

The main quirk—I can't really call it a disadvantage—of outdoor advertising is its limitations in terms of message. If it doesn't work in five to seven words, you can't say it on a billboard. If your name is Hibernia Financial Institution, don't even think of advertising out-of-doors. Outdoor is the right medium for simple slogans and funny one-liners. Humor in outdoor advertising does a service to the community, in my opinion.

Novelty Techniques Keep Billboards Booming

New technology is having an impact on billboard advertising. Special printing effects, irregularly shaped extensions, three-dimensional props, and inflatable add-ons have appeared on the scene. These make new creative opportunities possible. Here's an example: When our local phone company changed its name, it used outdoor boards to communicate the message. First boards went up with the original name. Then each billboard got a ladder with a workman on it, painting out the old and replacing it with the new name. Over the next few weeks, these life-like dummies were moved slowly along the sign face until the transformation was complete. The company received numerous phone calls, including some concerned about the "employees" working nights and weekends.

Transit: The "Other Outdoor" Is Growing

Any fleet that moves may offer advertising opportunities. Taxis have simple signs mounted on their roofs or trunks. Buses have placards mounted on their sides, mini-billboards that roam the city. By their nature, these offer high frequency with geographically targeted reach. New technology is having an impact here a well. Whole buses can now be "shrink-wrapped," turning them into rolling novelties.

Transit advertising is branching out beyond signs in or on buses and taxis. Public transit locations, like airports, train stations, and even shopping malls, are offering new signage and display options. Benches, wall-posters, and free-standing kiosks are just the start. These reach business travelers well, so keep your eye out for developments in this area.

Ethics and Outdoor Advertising

I happen to like outdoor advertising. I think it's one of the more entertaining features of the civilized landscape. I agree billboards don't belong in the national forest, or even the countryside, but there's not much motivation to put them there, either. Outdoor advertising goes where people go and where they'll be passing at a slow enough speed to comprehend a quick message. That's why public waiting areas attract displays. That's why commuter routes feature numerous billboards. High-speed highways do not.

Still, some locations are inappropriate—residential neighborhoods, farmland, and scenes of natural beauty. Don't support their presence by purchasing those locations, and express your opinion that they should be removed, if you feel so inclined. Vendors of billboard space respond to economic pressure just like the rest of us.

Mentor

The most "eco-friendly" outdoor option for you to use is the bus ad. Bus systems are good. They reduce our reliance on individual autos for transportation. City-operated transit systems earn money from the advertising, reducing their reliance on fares and subsidies. They're good for our cities and for our environment. You can say "yes" to transit advertising with a squeaky-clean conscience.

Layout and Production

So you've got a media plan that calls for print. You've chosen one of the media types discussed in this chapter. Now you just need to get through a process called layout and production.

The process starts with a sketch depicting the arrangement of art and copy elements on the page. The initial sketch can be very tight or very rough, what we call thumbnails. These get shown to all of the people who have a say in it—your spouse, for instance, or your marketing director. The layout is a blueprint showing the people who make the ad where to put the parts.

Many parts might be called for by the layout. Elements may come from photographers, writers, illustrators, or logo artists—any or all of the above. Most ads you see around you were created by teams of professionals with talents, experience, and tools not available to the average person. You may want to hire their expertise. This is one of the most widely visible forms of your marketing, and like location, it is not a place to screw up.

But meanwhile, let's say you're closely involved in your advertising production, whether that means do-it-yourselfing or supervising others. You need some knowledge of the necessary sequence of tasks.

Designing Your Print Ad

You sit down to design an ad. What goes where? Studies have shown that most readers in our culture tend to start in the upper left, and then follow a Z-curve down the page, coming to rest at the bottom right. That's why virtually every ad has its logo at the bottom, and most to the right of center.

Whether the layout is formal or informal, there ought to be some sense of order to the page. The elements need to relate in proportion to each other in a way that makes sense, giving the ad a focal point without inviting boredom. Your attitude or personality will dictate the degree of funk or formality you adopt. What's appropriate for a rock band won't work for the symphony.

Using Photos and Illustrations

Most ads contain a picture of something or someone. Why? Those pictures, whether they're photos or illustrations, serve three purposes. They must …

- Attract attention (remember AIDA!).
- Convey the main benefit.
- Provoke an emotional response.

The really great ads feature pictures that tie in cleverly with the headline. Think of examples you've seen, all the way back to the famous Volkswagen ad of the '60s that showed a tiny car under the headline "Think Small."

Mentor

Start keeping a collection of ads you like, along with notes as to what stirred you—the copy, pictures, or layout. Nothing helps so much as tangible examples when it's time to convey your concepts to other people.

Photos convey reality in ways that illustrations never can. At the same time, however, illustrations can evoke emotions and stir imagination in a way that is difficult for photos to match. Follow your hunches about style. Keep in mind that photos can require props, sets, models, and a studio full of technicians. If your ideas lean toward the grand scale, find an illustrator. It's cheaper to draw five luxury cars speeding through misty mountains than it is to get that photo!

Pitfall

Illustration can be less expensive than photographs, but be wary of amateurish efforts. Stick to simple or humorous ideas. Ask others' opinions about your artwork; your own aesthetic taste may not be your best guide here.

Regardless of technique, what should the picture show? You have options. You can show the *product alone*—informative, but not too exciting. You can show the *product in use*—preferably with people. The more your reader can relate to an ad, the more interest it will hold. People are always more curious about other people than they are about things. You can *show the benefit* of using the product; you can show the *problem of not using* the product; or you can *dramatize the feature* of the product that delivers the benefit.

This all sounds pretty abstract until you start looking around you. Leaf through the next *People* or *Vanity Fair* or whatever you read, and classify the subject of the pictures in the ads. Which approach do they use? How do they serve the three purposes of arousing attention, demonstrating the benefit, and evoking emotion?

Using—Not Abusing—Typography

Typography is the way you use sizes and weights and type styles to give additional meaning to the words of copy you've written.

Type projects style in subtler ways than pictures. Type can be whimsical or solid, thrashingly antiestablishment or conservative as a navy blue suit. Type is like clothes for words. You need to discover what style your words should wear. Just as you collected ads with pleasing layout and pictures, collect samples of type that you like.

Really!

Anyone who's ever poked around in a page layout program has gotten exposed to the terminology of type faces and weights, serif and sans-serif fonts, justification and spacing, and more. If you'd like to learn more about typography, there's an excellent little book called *Stop Stealing Sheep* by Erik Spiekermann and E. M. Ginger. Read about type's influence on mood, legibility, and so on, or skip the extra-curricular assignments and just fire up your software and experiment.

Putting the Ad Together

This whole process has been about getting to that mysterious thing the printers call camera-ready art. Only it isn't that, or not what that term used to mean. Today, camera-ready art is most likely to be a computer file, created in page layout software like Quark X-Press or Adobe's PageMaker or InDesign.

Elements flow toward the electronic page from several directions: the photographer, illustrator, writer, and bits and pieces clipped from previous ads, like logos and addresses. A layout artist brings the copy and art together in a page layout program and gets the final file in the right format for the publication or printer.

Following are the thumbnail and the finished ad for a Bob's Bottomless Boats magazine ad. Do you recognize the ad copy from the example in Chapter 17?

To summarize, producing an ad means designing a layout, creating the photos or illustrations, and then bringing the final artwork together electronically. That final "artwork" (really a computer file) must meet the precise specifications of the various publications where it will appear. Don't try producing your ad yourself unless you have relevant experience in the graphic arts.

To find the appropriate technical assistance for this task, you have options. One good—and inexpensive—route is to ask the media vehicle where your ad will appear if they will produce the ad for you. If, on the other hand, you would like more creative attention paid to your ad concept (or if you want to be more closely involved in the process), you will want to work with a local resource. Ask among your business associates for referrals, or check the local directory for advertising agencies or graphic designers. You'll pay more … and learn more, too.

A thumbnail for Bob's ad and the finished artwork.

The Least You Need to Know

- If your competitors are using a print vehicle, you should be, too—or at least looking at their strategy and asking why it works for them.
- Don't spread yourself too thin. If your budget is tight, pick one medium, or even one vehicle, and dominate that.
- Magazines target specific audiences. Try to choose one that will deliver your message to your target market, but don't expect overnight results.
- Newspapers are a good choice for limited-time sales and promotions. With a short (two to three week) flight you can run enough ads to build the frequency you need to be effective, and then pull the plug before you've spent a fortune.
- With direct mail and point-of-purchase displays, success depends on your ability to control costs while reaching the right audience.
- Outdoor advertising offers some exciting opportunities to reach a broad demographic group in a tight geographic area.

Chapter 20

Direct Mail: A Controlled First Step Toward Friends You Haven't Met

In This Chapter

- How direct mail and direct marketing work
- The types of direct mail pieces and the functions they perform
- The "three Ms" of direct mail
- The importance of mailing to your house list
- Creating a mail piece that's efficient and effective

Let's take a look at what came in my mailbox yesterday. Of course, there were the usual bills, and along with those, I found a postcard from Kai Miaka, a postcard from University Credit Union, and one letter from my health care provider. I used to find letters from my mother and envelopes of snapshots of my nieces and nephews, but now those come by e-mail.

What the mail carrier brings me these days is pretty much limited to mail pieces from businesses. There's less mail from them than there used to be, too. Does that mean direct mail is dying as a form of business promotion?

Hardly.

The Beauty of Direct Mail

Direct mail isn't dead—it's a solid promotional technique that's still paying off for many. The reason I see less of it is because users of direct mail are targeting their efforts with more precision. Most of the mail I see is meant for *me*—based on a trail of my past purchase behavior and my demographic data and lifestyle preferences on record somewhere "out there" and available to marketers for a price. "Junk mail" is on the wane, as marketers gain skill at targeting messages to their recipients.

Mentor

Some days I sound like an itinerate preacher, traveling the country delivering my sermon on target marketing. In Part 2 of this book, I pounded that pulpit pretty thoroughly. If you're not a believer yet, maybe the benefits of a targeting approach applied to direct mail will save you.

In my mailbox, there is no catalog from A Life of Faith Dolls because I don't fit their target niche. I'm not a young girl or related to one. I'm not a devotee of the faith the company advocates, and I don't home-school any children. More likely prospects than me are benefiting from A Life of Faith's direct mail dollars.

And that's the beauty of direct mail. It's a perfect medium for reaching the right people and leaving the rest alone. And in case you haven't figured it out yet, I believe in that very strongly. It's not nice to bother people. It's very nice to help people find solutions to their problems. The best way to be nice is to practice target marketing.

Pitfall

I still get lots of "junk mail" from one source: financial service providers. Dozens of credit card offers and home equity loan pitches still land in my mailbox and those of my neighbors. I guess financial service marketers believe that just about everybody could use access to a little more money, so they continue to use last century's mass marketing techniques. I think that's just plain stupid. It's painful to watch money minders waste their marketing dollars in this way! Let them be your example how *not* to use direct mail.

Why Direct Mail Is Alive and Well

Businesses spend something like $36 billion dollars a year on direct mail—more than they spend on print and broadcast advertising combined. It doesn't matter what you're selling; dollar for dollar, no promotional technique provides a better return on investment than direct mail.

A complete direct mail strategy begins with targeting a market niche and ends with response analysis. Between those mile markers lies a fertile landscape.

Once a market niche has been defined, a marketer develops a mail piece—anything from a simple postcard to an envelope stuffed with letters, flyers, response cards, and flattened freebies. That piece goes out to a sample of the mail list, responses get tracked, and components of the piece get tweaked if the response rate wasn't good enough. Maybe the list criteria get tweaked if changing the piece doesn't goose up the response rates enough. After two or three rounds (or more!) of this kind of testing, the perfect piece mails to the perfect list and again, responses are tracked. The company executing this direct mail strategy calculates the *cost of acquisition* as prospects become customers. By managing the costs of the campaign to keep that cost of acquisition in proper relation to the sales it generates, the direct mail strategy works its magic.

What?

Divide your total cost of a mailing by the number of new customers that come from that mailing—the result will be the **cost of acquisition** for those customers. Use this number to calculate another important number: the amount each customer must spend before you break even on that mailing. If your mailing cost $5,000 and results in five new customers, each must spend at least $1,000 before your mailing breaks even.

Direct mail is alive and well as a marketing strategy because with a little math you can determine cost of acquisition and return on investment. No other advertising avenue offers such precision of measurement. Direct mail is a great medium for control freaks and marketing managers who like measurable results.

Who Uses It?

Who uses direct mail? Businesses that need a steady stream of new leads; businesses that get requests for information; businesses that make direct marketing their sales strategy; businesses that just want to stay in contact with their customers. All use direct mail.

Just about anybody can use this technique profitably. A consultant I know keeps a few dozen prestamped postcards—the kind with pictures of local attractions—with him wherever he goes. When he has a spare moment, he pulls out his business card file and starts dropping lines to his contacts. Every few months, Kai Miaka mails his fans a postcard jammed with listings of his upcoming gigs. Those are pretty simple direct mail programs … but they do the job.

What Does Direct Mail Do?

Every direct mail piece in my mailbox, both at home and at work, is designed to do one of three things. Its goal may be to …

- **Generate a new lead.** Lead generators are the direct mail equivalent of advertising. They come unsolicited to my mailbox and hope to get me interested in something. They ask me to take some action, the net result of which will be to land my name on a company's prospect list for follow-up.
- **Fulfill an inquiry.** Inquiry fulfillment pieces show up in my mailbox after I've shown interest, usually by requesting more information as a result of an earlier exposure to some kind of advertising. More and more inquiry fulfillment pieces are being delivered electronically since the PDF format did what it promised—created a portable document format. But most companies still maintain printed inventories of literature for use in responding to inquiries.
- **Request a purchase.** Purchase request pieces are the bread and butter of the direct mail biz. An order request piece asks its recipient to do one thing: Buy now. It might offer a special price discount, explain the product's availability for a special limited time period, or mention benefits I'm likely to consider important. Purchase request pieces gamble the whole budget on one shot. There are no customer touch points in this game. The mail piece has to take a recipient all the way from "It's a beautiful day here by the mailbox" to "I want this product, and I want it now!" Marketers who use this technique lay their groundwork, testing the message and the mail list until the result is as highly distilled and as predictable in its effect as a shot of moonshine.

CAUTION

Pitfall

Don't leap blindly into direct mail. Lead times are long and production budgets are steep. Direct mail works best when you use it to match compelling promotional offers with a well-targeted list, and then test and improve each element of the mail piece.

Is "Direct Marketing" the Same as "Direct Mail"? Not Exactly.

What?

Direct marketing is a strategy that seeks direct action from the recipient and focuses on measurable results. Whether directed at consumers or business buyers, it involves sophisticated database management. The key to direct marketing success is to reach the right people at the right moment with the right offer. Easier said than done!

Purchase request pieces are the backbone of a whole industry, called *direct marketing*, that mines this technique for profit. Direct marketers are the businesses that bypass distribution channels to do commerce directly with the purchaser with little or no person-to-person contact.

What Defines Direct Marketing

There are a couple of requirements for marketing activity using the mail to qualify as "direct marketing." Direct marketing focuses on getting the customer to take action—not on warming him up to your brand, not on giving him information so he can contemplate how your offering might benefit him. Direct marketing is at its core all about stimulating direct action, and the sooner, the better.

The other requirement of direct marketing? It focuses on measurable results. Even a small test mailing generates information that makes the next mailing more effective. It's generating and using information to continually tune the direct marketing machine for better results.

Mentor

All marketing should be measured, no doubt! But measuring results is the hallmark of direct marketing. Start small to minimize your risk, and start measuring. Learn and grow from there.

There's a requirement you might be assuming, since I've brought up "direct marketing" in a chapter on "direct mail." No—using the post office is not essential to direct marketing. In fact, direct marketers have been running to the web like settlers in a land rush, using e-mail and online advertising come-ons with great success. You'll see direct marketers' ads in magazines and other traditional advertising venues as well. Direct marketing is a strategy that works wherever persuasive words can work their magic.

Direct Response Packages

My very favorite kind of direct marketing is the direct response package, for the same reason I love classic cars, I guess. Direct marketing engines have been chugging away using the direct response package for half a century. Over that time, they've developed a formula that runs as smooth as the Slant 6 in my '65 Valiant. The formula calls for …

- **An outbound envelope.** The package starts here, with a *lift line* printed above the space where the recipient's address will appear. Use personalized printing, rather than mailing labels, if at all possible.
- **A cover letter.** How I could go on! And cover letters do. "The letter sells, the brochure tells," say the experts. Make the letter a direct conversation between you and the reader. Write in the first person and address your recipient by first name (a technique called *personalization*). Compose the text as you would ad copy, using the AIDA formula. Don't worry about long copy; some cover letters stretch to four pages when the subject is complicated!
- **Brochures, lift notes, or premium sheets.** Whatever you call them, these printed pieces take up where the letter leaves off. Use photos and full-color printing to make these add-ins demand attention. Brochures deliver the information too detailed or technical to fit in the cover letter. Lift notes catch those about to bail with headlines like "Read this only if you have decided *not* to order." Lift notes attempt to set a hook in those fish too wily to bite on the letter or the brochure. Premium sheets emphasize the discount or guarantee or whatever gives the offer a price advantage or ease-of-possession benefit. (You can test different offers by using different premium sheets.)
- **An order piece.** Every direct response package *must* contain a way to respond to the offer. This might be a reply card or a business reply envelope. This piece is the "closer" that moves in to get the order after the other pieces have done their work.

> **What?**
>
> A **lift line** is a catchy promise printed near the recipient's name, in hopes of drawing attention. Lift lines have been responsible for measurable increases in response. They're a key part of the formula for successful direct response packages.

Leave out one of these components, and your response rate will drop. Try to roll them into fewer pieces (for example, by printing the letter as the first page of the brochure), and your response rate will drop. Do not tinker with this engine. (Look in your mailbox—I bet you'll find a credit card solicitation or a magazine subscription offer that follows this formula precisely.)

There was a time when, concerned for the environment and all that, I urged clients toward condensed versions of this package. Didn't work. Response stank. To save the planet, *please target your mailing list*—don't mess with the magic formula for the direct response package. (You can insist your printer use recycled paper and note that on the printed piece; that should make you feel better.)

I have great respect for Bob Bly, author of *The Complete Idiot's Guide to Direct Marketing* so I will leave deeper discussion of direct marketing to him and suggest that if what you've read here interests you, go get his book. That book is written, in his words, "to give you the information, tools, resources and strategies you need to make direct marketing work for your business." After reading it, he promises you will have the bumps and curves smoothed out of your path to direct mail success. So drop a bookmark here and go get that book if you're salivating for the income a direct response package can bring you.

What?

There's a marketing technique that your house list makes possible, and it's making waves as a means to increase response in a flat economy. This technique goes by several names: variable printing, personalization, or the oxymoronic mass customization. Technology that allows a database to drive a printing press makes it possible for you to print thousands of pieces, each customized to an individual recipient. Fields in the database are specified to drive the content of certain fields within the mail piece. These can be either image or word elements, or both. One mail piece can go to my husband with "Dear Jim" in the salutation line and feature a photo of a left-leaning male baby boomer; the next in the series can go to my elderly neighbor with "Dear Margaret" and a photo of an elderly Republican-looking female. While this technique requires some additional attention in the planning phases, the production costs can be near that of mass printing and the response rates are typically much higher.

Brochures, Postcards, Catalogs—Mailers of All Kinds

Let's back up and talk about the other kinds of printed literature that arrive through the mail. These are the lead generators and inquiry fulfillment pieces that hope to spark recipients' interest and fan it into a flame of desire. Brochures, postcards, tech-spec sheets, catalogs, price lists … items like these keep dozens of commercial printers busy. Let's take a quick look at those different types of mail pieces.

Mentor

Marketing language is, unfortunately, unscientific. What one person calls a brochure, another calls a flyer or even a flier … or a sell sheet or a … you get the picture. In my humble opinion, "brochures" talk about your company, whereas "sell sheets" and the other possibilities talk about the *products* offered by your company. Sell sheets are the "what" and brochures are the "who" in this conversation.

Mail Pieces: What Are Your Options?

A *brochure* is like a salesperson for your company. When someone says "Send me your brochure," she is probably saying "Present to me who you are, what you're about, why I should do business with you—but please don't send a salesman over." Brochures can be hard-sell or soft-sell, but they should always answer the "who, what, why" of your offering. Also, they should be designed to harmonize with your corporate image and brand identity. Brochures and corporate websites perform similar functions; a website designed to answer these questions rather than to perform e-commerce is called "brochureware."

Mentor

Every printed piece you create has the potential to be a PDF document. It's a simple step for your designer or printer to save all your documents in PDF format. Include a place on your website for visitors to find and download PDF files. This will save you postage and printing costs in fulfilling inquiries. However, ask visitors to leave some form of contact information, such as an e-mail address, or you will lose the ability to track and follow-up on these glimmers of interest!

Sell sheets and *tech-spec (technical specification) documents* are the printed pieces that help make a sale by providing answers to questions about product functionality. If I'm considering buying a piece of software, I need answers to what it will do for me and what hardware requirements it will demand. I will visit a website for PDFs or call the company and say "Send me some literature on your software." Be prepared for these inquiries—have documents prepared and ready to go in both PDF and printed formats.

A *catalog* is a bound booklet or folded piece offering products (typically in the same category, like office equipment or toys) for the same use (business or play) to the same audience (office managers or little girls). The catalog is the technique to use when you want to offer multiple products through a single promotion. Catalogs can work as lead generators or as inquiry fulfillment pieces; they will always function as purchase request pieces. Some consumers love the convenience of catalogs, especially people who live in rural areas. The arrival of safe e-commerce transactions and the increases in printing and postage costs have caused many catalogers to migrate to the World Wide Web. You've probably noticed you're receiving fewer catalogs in the mail now than you did in the past. Printed catalogs still work well; for products where precise colors are essential, full-color printed pieces still work better than websites that rely on your monitor to tell you what color "shell pink" is. The Color Marketing Institute is working on a system of numbered color swatches to help catalog houses and their shoppers communicate about color, but this system will take time to gain wide acceptance.

Postcards are the last type of mail piece we'll talk about. Postcards can be used as lead generators designed to reach out and get inquiries, or to keep in touch with customers between other touch points. Postcards must be no larger than 4.25" × 6" to mail at the post office's post card rate, but many people pay the premium postage and use larger post cards. Either way, the beauty of postcards lies in their immediacy. No envelope stands between the recipient and your message. Postcards can be folded pieces (these must be sealed for mailing) which gives you a whopping four "pages" to carry your persuasive images and text.

Take a look in your mailbox—I bet you'll see some postcards there. (And I'll bet at least one will be from a financial institution.) Another variation on direct mail, the stand-alone flyer (no envelope) that pitches a product, service, or cause, has for the most part been supplanted by postcards due to the card format's advantages (lower postal and printing costs, plus heavier paper that is in better shape when it arrives.)

Really!

Postcard decks are bundles of postcards packaged together, often with catchy names like "Val-pack" or "DollarWise," and are directed to consumers or business buyers. These contain cards from many different advertisers; you buy a card in the deck as you would buy print advertising space. Card decks can be an excellent advertising medium. Some are published by direct marketing companies; others are published by magazine publishers and mailed to their subscriber lists. You can find out about them by contacting SRDS at 847-375-5000 or www.srds.com, or by looking for the SRDS books at your library. Services that are purchased repeatedly, like oil changes and dry cleaning, work well when advertised in these decks. (Hint: Include a coupon offering a modest discount.)

Who's Using Mail Pieces?

The musician Kai Miaka makes strategic use of several types of mailers. He uses postcards to drive his fans to his website, where they can pick up information about upcoming concerts and buy the CDs and T-shirts he offers. He also prints a tiny catalog as an oversize postcard; its postage-stamp-sized photos are designed to send the recipient to the web to see larger, full-color pictures of the merchandise. Kai prints a brochure describing his solo and band performances, with lots of pictures and testimonials. This he mails to band bookers associated with colleges. The copy and art are carefully chosen to convey his popularity with the college crowd.

A Life of Faith Dolls prints and distributes a beautiful little catalog. There are two reasons why this company might choose to continue investing in printed pieces: The rich detail and color schemes associated with the dolls and their products benefit from high-quality reproduction, and a fair portion of the target audience is not crazy for the Internet. A print catalog and a companion website allows A Life of Faith to approach each segment of its audience in the way that segment prefers to be approached.

Anita Hecht answers requests for information about her Life History Service by sending out a simple folder containing a brochure, articles, demo video, and a personal note.

University Credit Union uses postcards a great deal, targeting non-members with messages about the benefits of credit unions and targeting its own members with messages personalized on the basis of each member's current product usage and likely needs.

And what about Bob's Bottomless Boats? He uses direct mail—but only when manufacturers supply co-op dollars to help fund the mail shot. You'll get a postcard promoting Old Towne canoes when Bob's made a promotional deal with Old Towne.

Targeting, Testing, and Managing the Mailing Lists

Direct mail programs can be designed to fit any budget. For a small business, direct mail can be much less expensive, and more effective, than print or broadcast advertising. However, most small businesses don't use direct mail as effectively as larger businesses. What can the little guys learn from the big ones to improve results and put this powerhouse strategy to work for them? Work the "three Ms" of direct mail: the target Market, the Message, and the Mail list.

The market is (you guessed it) the people who fall within an identifiable market segment, a niche worth targeting because those people have proven or seem highly likely to have a desire for your offering and a willingness to purchase it.

The mail list is the list of actual people who will receive the mailing. The better this list matches the target market, the better your response rate will be.

The message is the creative approach, expressed in words and images, that leads a recipient down the AIDA path toward purchase. The message may well include special offers and promotions.

To get good results, you must get these three Ms singing three-part harmony.

Targeting: Everything You Need to Know You Can Learn from Your Customers

Direct mail is a gold mine if you dig where the gold is. A targeted mailing list is your map to the mother lode.

When you rent a list, your goal is to pick the geographic and demographic characteristics that are most likely to respond to your offer. Of course, you'll start by studying your customer records to find common characteristics. Then you'll hand that information to the list broker and tell him to "send in the clones."

The lists available may be compiled simply from directory-type information or (and this is preferable) from people who have bought or responded to direct marketing in the past. If you sell a weight loss product, wouldn't you be interested in a list compiled of people who have responded to a weight loss infomercial? You'll pay more—but that's what targeting is all about. You invest in reaching the *right* people.

Mailing list companies compile lists of individuals, households, and businesses, and then provide selections by a variety of criteria—for a cost. How many criteria you want affects that cost. For instance, a list of all households in a 5-digit zip code with a licensed driver and children in school would be a list qualified by three criteria. In this example, the data compiled from postal, transportation, and purchase records must be sorted to arrive at your desired list. If you added criteria like "earning $50,000+ and registered to vote," the number of data sorts is increased. As a result, the number of names on your list would go down and the cost of your list would go up.

Quite possibly, that cost would be an investment well worth making. After all, you're buying improved targeting of your list. A basic list, sorted by three or so criteria, will cost at a minimum of $200 to $300 plus a cost of perhaps $70 to $100 for every thousand names. Add more sort criteria, and that cost spirals up as the

CAUTION

Pitfall

There's an operational price of admission to the direct mail game: You must have the internal systems in place to manage a mailing list. Even if you're renting your initial lists, you'll want to capture and track the people who respond, and use that list for future mailings. If you can't manage a house list, fuggedaboutit.

focus narrows. How focused do you want to get? My advice: The more specialized your offering, the more important a well-targeted list becomes for your direct mail success.

Finally, don't overlook the gold buried in your own house list. This list is the most powerful of all because it contains people who already like you and are doing business with you.

Testing Is the Key to Success

Tracking response is easy with direct mail. That makes it easy to close the loop—to gather information about results generated. Testing specific components of the mail program by monitoring results is the key to getting those three Ms in sync. First, you can do focus groups and customer surveys to make sure you have targeted the right market. Then, once you've developed a message targeted to that audience, you can test elements of that message to make sure each is doing its job. Change headlines, change pictures, change the amount of the discount offer—each element of that piece deserves a good tweaking to make sure it's working its hardest. Finally, test the mail list. Sample every "nth" name and send a few hundred pieces out. This random selection of names will accurately reflect the response rate you'll get if you mail this piece to the whole crowd.

So there you are, printing a few hundred, mailing, tracking response, tweaking the message and printing a few hundred more, tracking response … the process takes time, but it's like sharpening a knife. At the end of the process, you'll have a well-honed tool that produces exactly the results you expect it to.

Mentor

Please! Commit to maintaining your house list! Mail to your customers about four or six times a year. It's a great way to nurture customer relationships. Use personalized printing and target small subsets of the list with messages related to items they've bought previously, or news of new offerings. Make sure you request (and pay for) return mail service to keep your house list up to date.

Managing Your Mailing Lists

Behind every successful direct mail program is a well-managed database of customer and prospect names. You may be renting lists for your initial mailings, but every individual who responds becomes a legitimate prospect of *yours*. Add them to your house list and start compiling information on their demographics, lifestyle attributes, and purchase behavior. You can also match against voter records, hunting and fishing license registrations … a variety of state-collected data exists that might fill in the details regarding your customers' lifestyles.

Maintaining your house list is critical if you want to move those prospects from "kinda interested" to long-term loyal customers. Fail to do so and you've just walked away from money on the table. Return to Part 2 of this book and do not pass Go if you have somehow missed my message that gathering and using information on the people who make it onto your house list is crucial.

"But how would I find out their lifestyle attributes?" you ask. It's possible to take your list and match it against data compiled by market research vendors. To find them, enter the magic words "Microvision" or "Prizm" in your search engine. (These are proprietary lifestyle segmentation schemes developed by national research firms.) Give yourself half an hour to scan the websites you turn up; you'll have a good idea of the options and costs for augmenting your house list with data from these vendors when you're done. If this helps you separate your "gold standard" clients from the riff-raff (and find more like the former), I say it's worth the investment.

Creating Your Next Direct Mail Piece

Creating a mail piece is no different from creating a print advertisement, except that you will be seeing that piece through the printing process. To get started, consult Chapters 16 and 17 to get your brand strategy and your creative approach in gear. Then you can move on to production. At this stage, you will need to take into account the demands of printing presses and compliance with postal regulations about direct mail. Your printer should be able to guide you toward formats that are compatible with regulations and economical to print. You can also contact the post office; ask to speak to a Direct Mail Specialist. These individuals work with graphic designers and printers to make sure printed pieces conform to postal standards. These specialists can give you templates and helpful publications if you're the do-it-yourself type.

Are you sitting on the fence, not sure direct mail is right for you? Look at it this way. Are you using sales promotions? Offering coupons or other limited-term sales incentives? Use direct mail to get the word out. Leverage your sales promotion by using a deadline to create urgency. "Respond by 5 P.M. Friday and mention this postcard to receive your discount." See how it works?

Direct mail allows you to target prime customers and communicate with them effectively and efficiently. Manage the three Ms—the market, the message, and the mail list—and you can take your results to the bank.

The Least You Need to Know

- Direct mail and direct marketing work by using printed pieces to connect with prospects and customers.
- Direct response packages, brochures, catalogs, and postcards each have their place; one of these formats might work well for you.
- The "three Ms" of direct mail are the target Market, the Message, and the Mail list.
- Start compiling information on the demographics, lifestyle attributes, and purchase behavior of individuals on your house list.
- Creating a mail piece that's efficient and effective requires the same steps as creating print ads, with the addition of working with the printer and post office to comply with formats and plan for production efficiency.

Chapter 21

All About Broadcast Advertising: Radio and TV

In This Chapter

- Why the broadcast media deserve a closer look
- How radio uses the power of imagination
- What goes into producing a radio commercial
- Why cable TV shouldn't be treated the same as broadcast network programs
- How to supervise production of a TV commercial

Maybe you remember hearing this on the radio a few years back? "All right, watch this. Okay people, now when I give you the cue, I want the 700-foot mountain of whipped cream to roll into Lake Michigan, which has been drained and filled with hot chocolate. Then the Royal Canadian Air Force will fly overhead pulling a ten-ton maraschino cherry, which will be dropped into the whipped cream to the cheering of 25,000 extras. All right, cue the mountain."

And you probably remember the sound effects that followed: the bulldozers, airplanes, and cheering crowd. This was a radio commercial created by the Radio Advertising Bureau to convince advertisers to use radio commercials. It neatly demonstrates what's unique about radio as a medium. Even if you don't remember this commercial, you can still see (or at least imagine hearing) how it might get your attention.

Although television and radio are lumped together in the term "broadcast media," the only thing the two really have in common is that they both take place in time rather than space. Radio is much less expensive than television, both in terms of production cost and airtime. TV, on the other hand, adds a dimension that radio is lacking.

Radio: The Power of Imagination

Anyone who has ever listened to Garrison Keillor talk about Lake Wobegon on *A Prairie Home Companion* knows about the power of radio. Radio sets the listeners' imagination loose to create images that are more dramatic, and more personally significant, than could ever be created by a camera crew. Even a team of computer animators can't come up with the unique enhancements the mind's eye creates—and the mind's eye doesn't cost a thing. That's what radio offers.

Who Should Use Radio?

Radio is an excellent "beginner medium." It is fairly inexpensive compared to other media; production is simple, and prices can be negotiated to your advantage.

Radio stations sell commercial time, but what they are really selling is access to markets. Each station has its unique format. Some offer music; others talk. The music stations span the possibilities, from Top 40 to country-western to classical music, and every variation in between. Talk stations vary in their political leanings and types of programming as well.

Mentor

One of the special advantages of radio is its loyalty factor. People tend to be loyal listeners of two or three stations, and they tend to extend their loyalty to the advertisers on those stations. If you sell an offering to the same customers repeatedly—like dry cleaning or car washes—radio is effective at encouraging repeat sales.

Each station uses its format to distinguish itself from others in the same listening area. The format dictates what audience the station attracts. As you can imagine, a different group listens to Top 40 hits than listens to country-western music. Is there a station in your market offering a format that fits your target market? Radio is a low-cost way to reach a narrowly defined target audience with precision.

Whether radio is right for you depends on what you want to accomplish. Radio advertising is very effective at increasing customer traffic. You can pull people right off the highway and out of their cars if your message offers the right benefit.

Start paying attention to who is advertising on the stations you listen to. You'll hear lots of local retailers on the air. Business-to-business products and services also take to the airwaves. As I've said before, people don't stop being people when they get to work. Buyers of office copiers and business printing listen to the radio just as buyers of refrigerators and new cars do.

Really!

Weighing the merits of broadcast? Consider this … Frequency is critical in broadcast because your message is on the air only a few seconds and then it's gone. Without frequent repetition, your ad doesn't have much of a chance to claim the audience's attention. I see and hear advertisers using creative ways to grab attention, but creative gimmicks don't mean you can get away with running an ad once. Broadcast media are inherently different from print media, and the need for frequency is one of the key differences.

From a creative perspective, the broadcast media are quite different as well. Creating for broadcast means using a palette of sights and sounds to stimulate emotions and offer entertainment. You create mini-movies, taking people through attention to interest into desire—and then get 'em to act.

When and Where to Advertise on the Radio

When and where depend on two things: what you can afford, and where the audience you want to reach is. Radio—and TV, too—is sold on the basis of the length of the spot you want to run, the number of times your ad will air, and the time of day, or day-part, in which it will run. A radio station will sell between 18 and 24 minutes of commercials every hour in increments, also called *spots*, of fifteen (:15), thirty (:30), and sixty (:60) seconds. Ask the station how many commercials per hour it averages; 24 is definitely too many. Your spot will get lost amid that audio clutter.

Day-parts are the broad divisions that match shifts in listener audience. Rates vary dramatically depending on the day-part you buy. The same station may charge $75–90 for an A.M. drive time :30 commercial spot and $10 for the same :30 during the evening, and may give it away for free in the late-night segment.

What?

Commercial **spots** are referred to by their length in seconds, expressed in digital time. Broadcast commercials can be :60s, :30s, :15s, and (in television) :10s.

The day-parts are usually described as follows:

- A.M. drive time (6 A.M. to 10 A.M.)
- Midday (10 A.M. to 3 P.M.)
- P.M. drive time (3 P.M. to 7 P.M.)
- Evening (from 7 P.M. to midnight)
- Late night (from midnight to 6 A.M.)

Each day-part has its own characteristics of listenership. Because people are creatures of habit, the audience for each day-part is predictable and can be described by demographics and lifestyle attributes. Radio station ad sales people can give you a detailed profile of the demographics and size of their station's listening audience for each day-part. Look at that profile by age, gender, lifestyle, and other factors. If there's a good fit to your target market, consider radio for your ads.

Really!

Radio in the workplace is powerful. Bosses may not like the employees tying up the phones entering contests and making requests, but the fact that people do proves that many people at work consider the radio their friend and companion.

If you're in a "shift town" (one where factories employ workers on second and third shifts), radio can be a very important component of your media budget.

The law of supply and demand dictates that the selling of radio time involves negotiation. To get rid of those late-night spots, your sales rep will bundle them with some attractive A.M. drive spots and try to get you to see them as extra value, not extra baggage. Packages aren't a bad thing. Most people I know buy a package deal for a certain number of spots, with a guarantee that so many will run during each day part. These plans give the station some latitude in deciding when your ad will run, as long as they hit the right total in the right day-parts. This is to their advantage and will get you the best average cost per spot.

Whether that's the most cost-efficient way for you to buy depends on how well the station's overall audience demographics match your target market. Two situations would steer you away from this kind of package. First, if you have a very small budget, remember that it's important to reach break-through frequency—no matter how small a market you break through to. I'd recommend you buy one commercial a day at a specific time and incur the surcharge for specifying a time slot, rather than spread the same budget too thin buying a wide rotation for slightly more spots. The second reason is if you sell to a very tightly defined niche market. A package will dilute the audience too much for your purposes. If your audience is CEOs and entrepreneurs, buy the early drive time, maybe even a 5:55 A.M. slot. If you're trying to reach avid sci-fi fans, try the late-night spots on an alternative rock station. You get the drift—look for your audience's peak listening time, and then buy that and only that.

Sponsorships are the most expensive option in radio. Sponsoring means having your commercial air as the station goes into a program segment like news, sports, or weather. These spots are more valuable than most because of the increased audience attention to these features. Announcers will often say something like, "Stay tuned for the sports reports, brought to you by Big Bill's Sports Pub" as they segue into the feature, giving you even more value.

Sponsoring specific programs associates you with the subject matter, a useful image-building tool. If you want to broaden recognition of your veterinary practice, run your ads during the pet-care call-in show.

> **Mentor**
>
> Radio stations offer lots of other package deals, including live remote broadcasts, special events, games and contests, and giveaways. They all feature positive ways to associate advertisers with the station. If you want to do a special promotion (see Chapter 15), be sure to consider radio as one medium for getting the word out.

Choosing the Right Station for Your Advertising

So let's say you've defined a pool of several potential radio stations that offer an audience matching what you want to sell with demographic groups that are likely to buy. How do you choose which station gets your final order?

Radio sales reps are some of the most aggressive in the media business. The statistics they bring you are often based on unreliable survey techniques. So ignore them for now.

Survey your customers. Start asking what stations they listen to and at what time of day. Ask where they are when they're listening—at work, in the car? Getting a fix on what your best customers are doing is the best way to find more like them.

Making Radio Work

The wonderful thing about radio, as I mentioned earlier, is the way it lets people use their imagination. The person who uses his mind *imagining* what you've described is *interacting* with your commercial. That degree of involvement leads to greater recall, just as taking notes helps you remember what a speaker has said.

But to work like that, radio has to be heard. That's hard to achieve, because the radio tends to be on in the background of our lives. When someone picks up a magazine, he or she generally means to read it—not so with radio. The commercial you create has to reach out from the background and get the listener into a more active state. The tools you have to do this with are voices, sound effects, and music.

Copy Approaches for Radio

The first rule of effective radio advertising is this: Create a visual image that stimulates your listeners' imagination. With that as a starting point, the copy approach you take from there is limited only by *your* imagination. Use one announcer or several; employ dialogue to dramatize a situation; use music to give your spot a signature feel. You can even create a custom jingle for your business that you'll use again and again.

In deciding which approach to use, be guided by the positioning strategy you've chosen. Remember, everything you do has to project that positioning as consistently as possible. If you're going for a high-quality, high-value position, try writing a dialogue between two snooty voices. (Sometimes British accents are used to convey an upper-class image.) Or use sound effects that convey quality—the precise hum of a well-tuned engine or an orchestra playing the graduation anthem "Pomp and Circumstance."

Mentor

Use mnemonic devices like jingles and songs to help your audience learn. Why did your parents teach you to sing your A-B-Cs? Because that's the way the brain learns.

What Goes On in a Radio Production?

What do you need to know about radio production to create your first commercial spot? Let's take a closer look at radio ads.

A radio ad typically combines three elements: voices, music, and sound effects. Any or all might be called for in the script. A sound engineer brings these elements together as the spot is produced. You will need to choose "actors" for the voices and perhaps hire someone like Kai Miaka to compose a jingle. Or you could pick music and sound effects from a stock CD.

No matter how you go about producing a radio spot, it's going to cost you some money. Your least expensive option is to choose a radio station for your production partner. In fact, if you negotiate well, you could get the cost of production "for free"—rolled in with your package price.

More expensive are the independent production studios, which you'll find under "audio production" in the Yellow Pages. Your most costly route is to pay an ad agency to produce the spot.

Your invoice for producing a spot will show the total of costs in two categories: studio time and materials required. Studio time is billed at an hourly rate, ranging from $50 to $100+ per hour, depending on your market. The materials bill will include people (voice talent), fees for music you use, and the cost of tape used in producing and distributing the spot.

Pitfall

Many radio stations offer production at very low cost. One problem with this: The people who do the voice work are the same people who are hosts or DJs on that station. If you choose to have a station produce your commercial, make sure the voice talent is not the same person who will be working on-air at the time your commercial airs. You want to break through the regular programming, not fade into its stream of sounds.

Television: It Walks! It Talks! It Makes Products Fly Off Your Shelves!

When the television set entered the cave, humankind was changed for all time. TV combines the elements of persuasion to reach us in ways no other medium can. It's the only advertising that comes into our homes and engages us with emotional appeal. If you don't believe TV advertising is powerful, pay attention to the restaurant advertising you see just before the dinner hour.

Television is made up of *broadcast* and *cable* options. Broadcast television stations are usually affiliated with national companies like ABC, CBS, NBC, and Fox, which deliver broad audience demographics—Mom, Dad, Grampa, and the kids gathered around the set watching programs together. These stations allot a percentage of their commercial spots to national advertisers, and the balance goes to each local market. Most viewers don't catch the difference, and when they see your ad on broadcast television, they think you're a big-time player.

What?

Broadcast television has been around since the '50s. The signals originate from local broadcasting towers and travel out in expanding circles. **Cable** television offers the alternative of receiving signals through a wire that carries many more channels, both basic and premium services. Satellite TV service offers an alternative to cable and delivers the same type of programming.

Cable stations have brought local advertisers an excellent way to buy television spots at affordable cost that reach highly targeted audiences, almost like radio.

Cable programming is quite different from broadcast programming. While the broadcast stations seek to be a truly mass medium, cable channels differentiate themselves by appealing to special interests. You'll find ESPN for sports fans, CNN for news, BET for Black Americans, A&E and the History Channel for the culturally inclined, and MTV and Nickelodeon for the young and younger crowds.

Really!

Cable channels attract specific audiences in much the same way radio stations do: by targeting a market with specific programming. Both radio stations and cable TV channels resemble magazines, in that they also target specific audiences. For example, Lifetime and Oxygen are geared for women the same way *Cosmopolitan*, *Working Woman*, and *Ms.* are. By its nature, print zeroes in on a narrower market than television or radio.

If you're looking for a broad demographic, look at broadcast stations. If you're looking for a narrow demographic, look at cable. If you're looking for a very narrow demographic, drop TV from your schedule and go back to radio, print, or direct mail.

Who Should Use Television

Television is the most expensive advertising medium available, but don't assume it's out of your reach. You can produce a spot for as little as $700 to $1,000, if your ideas aren't too grandiose. You can buy an effective flight of a few dozen commercials for $5,000 to $7,000, if you choose your placements carefully. Will that be enough to accomplish the job? That depends on the job you want done.

Some advertisers use TV for image advertising, using its visual power to build recognition of a company or a brand name. The same commercials might appear over a long schedule, giving time for the message to gradually build and build.

Other advertisers use TV for response advertising, designing special incentives to purchase and promoting them with television's proven emotional impact.

For example, a restaurant that specializes in home-style meals might not ordinarily advertise on television. But in the weeks leading up to Mother's Day, the restaurant wants to mount a special promotion. It employs the visual appeal of TV in a commercial spot that pans over delicious food and the comfortable dining room. An announcer describes the menu in succulent terms and explains a "Mom eats free" special. Because the schedule is brief—just a few weeks—and the spot perennial, this advertising is cost-effective for a small restaurant.

The greatest strength of TV advertising is the way it intrudes into the home. With televisions in 98 percent of households and those sets turned on over seven hours every day, you've got access to a huge number of people if you advertise on TV. That is both its strength and its weakness: broad reach and little market segmentation.

Pitfall

TV and radio time is complicated to buy—and too expensive to buy poorly! Discounts are available to qualified media buyers that you may not be able to get on your own. Rather than negotiating your own deals, try working through a media service. Look in your Yellow Pages under Advertising Agencies or Media to find your media-buying partner.

TV time is complicated to buy. Rates change each time a new ratings book comes out. Bargains become available when other advertisers change their plans. Discounts are given to advertisers willing to accept preemptable spots, allowing the station to sell that time slot to a higher bidder if one comes along. Because of these complications, it is to your advantage to work through an advertising agency's media buyer or a freelance media broker to negotiate your TV buy.

When and Where to Advertise on Television

The time of year and the time of day have an effect on the cost of each commercial spot, because demand fluctuates throughout the year. The first quarter (January, February, and March) are the slowest months in TV sales. If your offering has no seasonal cycle, plan your TV campaign for that first quarter to get the best cost efficiencies.

In the second quarter (April, May, and June), the demand increases. Seasonal events, from Easter through Mother's Day to the Fourth of July, give retailers excuses for special promotions, and they flock to television to spread the word.

In the third quarter (July, August, and September), things slow down again, as people are busy outside and away from their TV sets. The pace only picks up in late September when the new network shows premiere.

Mentor

Look closely at cable before you make your decisions. In most situations, I think cable TV delivers a better value for your dollar than the broadcast stations do. Rates are more negotiable and audiences more narrowly defined, and that adds up to a better buy.

In the fourth quarter (October, November, and December), retailers' holiday promotions fill up the schedule quickly. You have to plan ahead, booking your time as early as May, if you want good time slots in the fourth quarter.

Like radio, TV time is divided into day-parts, and the rates vary depending on when you want your spot to air.

Cost per spot (TV spots come in :10, :15, :30, and :60 second increments) starts out fairly high in the morning, levels off during the day, peaks in prime time, and then plummets in the late-night segment. Look for the day-part where an appealing viewership crosses paths with an affordable time slot. That's where you should be.

Radio and TV commercials, when done well, are fun to hear or watch. They entertain and they sell. They can be funny and memorable (think Super Bowl ads). That's the power of the broadcast media. But if you want to use television to your advantage, you need to know something about how to produce TV ads.

What Length Should Your TV Commercial Be?

The only thing television and radio have in common is that they both take place in time rather than space. How *much* time? That all depends on what you want to get across. Remember that you are a teacher with a lesson you want your students to learn.

Back in the bad old days, all commercials were 60 seconds long. Then 30-second spots were introduced, making broadcast advertising affordable to more and smaller businesses. Then the pie was sliced again to make 15-second spots available, and even 10-second spots are now available.

Really!

One reason shorter commercials have appeared is to make broadcast advertising available to more and smaller businesses. But another reason exists, and it's not exactly flattering to us—the audience.

The shortened length of commercials reflects the shrinking attention span of audiences. A commercial has to entertain immediately, or else the channel will be changed. People sometimes call this the "MTV Effect." Younger audiences demand lots of action, including fast cuts, hyperactive camera moves, and upbeat music, all crammed into 15- or 30-second commercials.

Sixty seconds is a very long time. You can have quite a conversation with your customers in 60 seconds—and rack up quite a media bill, too. Radio advertisers still use :60s, but they're very rare on television. About the only times you see them used are around elections, by politicians, and on late-night TV, selling steak knives and home fitness equipment. TV advertisers looking for an in-depth conversation with the audience have migrated to the infomercial format.

In this format, the advertiser buys a full half-hour time slot on an inexpensive channel instead of a brief commercial on an expensive (widely viewed) channel. Some cable channels, such as the Home Shopping Network, feature only infomercials.

A 30-second spot gives you room for 60 to 120 words or so, with which you will establish a context, deliver a benefit message, and make your call to action. Repeat that a few times and your audience will, you hope, begin to learn the lesson you're teaching. The shorter commercials, :15s and :10s, are useful as "refresher courses" to remind the audience of the lesson they've recently mastered.

So the right length for you is probably a :30, followed later in the schedule by some :15s to pound home the message. A vast generalization, of course, but when I've asked a rhetorical question, it's only polite that I should answer it.

TV Production: Getting the Picture

Television is the one medium that brings you sight, sound, and motion. It's not just your print ad given sound or your radio ad given a picture. It's a rare opportunity to use multiple stimuli to create desire.

TV's greatest strength is also its greatest weakness. It's a grueling task to get the visual and audio elements exactly right. When seen next to national advertisers with huge budgets, any flaws in your production are thrust into stark contrast. Weak production leaves a bad impression of your company. That's a bad use of your ad budget!

How do you get a TV commercial to come out right? The process begins with storyboarding.

> **Mentor**
>
> If you're going to produce a TV commercial, study up first. Ask your TV station or production house for trade journals that show examples of effective ads. Or check at the library for periodicals such as *Advertising Age* or *Adweek*. It will help you a great deal to learn more about what makes a successful TV ad.

Storyboards: Writing for TV

A writer of television spots creates instructions for both audio and video production. She writes a script and then fleshes that out into a *storyboard*, which shows a row of framed images depicting the main scenes of the spot. Next to the pictures goes a description of the action occurring in each frame, and the script for the audio track, sound effects, music, and narration. Actors will be hired, sets designed, and scenes directed based on the storyboard.

What?

A **storyboard** is like a comic book. Sequential panels depict the action. Accompanying text cues the audio track. The drawings can be quite rough, as long as they get the story across. The storyboard functions as a blueprint for everyone involved to follow.

The script and its storyboard establish the copy approach. Like radio, TV spots can use one announcer or several, show a demonstration, dramatize a situation, depict a slice of life, employ a song and dance routine, or use animation or special effects to get a point across.

The great majority of commercials are straightforward announcements or demonstrations. Use your imagination to get away from the norm, or at least look at them from a new angle. Be sure your script meets the AIDA test!

Where to Get Your TV Spot Produced

Three types of organizations have the skills and facilities to produce a TV spot:

- TV stations
- Independent video production studios
- Advertising agencies

You will need to choose one of these to be your production partner. Which should you call first? That depends on your budget and your degree of confidence in your skills as a movie producer. The TV stations are the least expensive choice, but they won't be able to offer much in the way of creative services. Be sure to tour the facilities and view samples of their work to get an idea of their abilities before you start to imagine what your ad will be.

Independent producers are specialists and often bring more creative talent to the table as well. You'll pay more for their services, but the higher value you'll receive will probably be worth it.

Ad agencies are the most expensive option, and the value they bring to the production is at the strategic level. If you're not comfortable with your take on marketing strategy, the ad message, positioning, and so on, you need the expertise you'll receive from an agency partner.

Which tool for the job? I have two rules of thumb that apply (I can do that because I have two thumbs). One, if you don't know what you're doing, hire someone who does. Airtime is too expensive to waste on amateur productions. Two, good work seldom comes from bad process. Hire people you feel comfortable working with, even if you have to pay more to get them.

Once you've chosen your partner, what happens next? Production. Or more specifically, pre-production, production, and post-production.

Pre-production covers planning the shoot, including coming up with the script and storyboard, whether you do that yourself or hire creative people to help you. Before the commercial can be shot, lots of decisions must be made. For one thing, you have to get estimates to see whether you can afford it. Once that's decided, you can get on to casting the actors, readying the props and costumes, deciding on a set or a location for filming, and so on.

Production covers filming or videotaping the scenes and recording the soundtrack. You may choose film for its richer, softer, more movie-like aesthetic look, or you may choose the more inexpensive and versatile production medium of digital video. Either way, you'll need to do many takes of each scene. Every frame of the storyboard gets its turn. On the set will be a producer, a director, cast members, costume and prop people, lighting designers, sound engineers, and maybe others.

What?

A TV commercial comes together in three phases. In **pre-production,** the shoot is planned via a script and storyboard. In **production,** the scenes are shot and the soundtrack is recorded. In **post-production,** the visual images and audio track are combined to create the final commercial.

What's your role in the middle of all this? Mostly to stay out of the way—and to approve when you feel that each element of the commercial has been adequately shot. I hope you've been clever enough to work closely with your producer before this stage, so he already knows what you have in your mind's eye. This is *not* the time to say, "Let's shoot it both ways."

Post-production involves mixing the twin streams—visual images and audio track—to create the final commercial. There's also a last step of duplicating and distributing the completed spot.

After filming the shots, the producer pieces together a visual sequence from the best takes of each scene. A soundtrack is synchronized to the images, and any special effects like dissolves, type superimposed over scenes, or animation get added. You may be sitting at the producer's elbow as this takes place, or approving rough and then final cuts. When you sign off, the duplication takes place and the task of television production is done.

The Least You Need to Know

- The broadcast media work through repetition—your spot must air many times before the audience will recall the message you wanted them to learn.
- Radio uses the power of imagination in a way TV can't because the listener who has to imagine what you're describing is interacting with you, which leads to quicker learning.
- Radio uses voices, sound effects, and music to break out of the background. Use the power of these elements to create a memorable visual image in the mind's eye of the listener.
- Because cable TV, like radio, targets specific interest groups, it can deliver the visual power of TV advertising at a cost close to radio.
- TV offers a rare opportunity to use all the available stimuli—sight, sound, and motion—to motivate behavioral change.

Chapter 22

Advertising and the Internet

In This Chapter

- How to tell whether your business belongs online
- Planning your website's function(s)
- Marketing your website
- Managing your e-subscriber list

I went through a crash course in online advertising not so long ago. A client wanted me to goose the traffic to its web store up a notch. With my trusty legal pad in hand, I stumbled online, searching for a good ad venue or two. I found myself in a confusing arena. People were speaking a language of search engine optimization, banner ads, sponsorships, affiliate programs, and the like. An alphabet soup of abbreviations like CPC, CTR, and PPC spilled onto my screen.

I sifted through it all … and came up with a few concrete ideas I could afford to do right away, and some other ideas for future consideration as the budget becomes available. I worked on my metatags. I placed small ads in a few online newsletters. I added a little elbow grease and started an e-newsletter of my own. Over time, my efforts brought results. The site's registered user list grew and the sales volume crept up.

This experience doesn't make me an expert at online advertising, but it gave me a little perspective on the questions that arise when someone like me—or like you—considers the Internet's impact on his or her business.

When It Comes to Marketing, Every Business Belongs Online

It makes no difference whatsoever whether your business model is e-commerce or traditional. You are going to include some form of web presence, including online marketing, in your plans. Every local pizza joint and florist has a website. At some point in your marketing, you are going to face this question: If the web is how people like to do business with me, what will my website be, and how will people find it?

> **Pitfall**
>
> Creating a website and failing to promote it is like opening a grocery at the end of a dead-end street. You can't survive on the few people who'll stumble in. "If we build it, they will come" isn't going to work for your online presence. Submit your site description to search engines. Exchange links or banner ads with other businesses. And start collecting visitors' e-mail addresses right away.

A business that exists strictly online will, of course, deploy a sophisticated online advertising strategy. But even a simple pizza delivery service—as tied to the physical realities of production and delivery as you can get—needs a website because consumers have grown accustomed to finding local restaurants' menus available online. For that reason alone, the pizza store owner finds it prudent to maintain a website.

Offline Businesses Use Websites to Communicate with Customers Online

For similar reasons, my florist friend finds it convenient to post some pictures of plants and floral arrangements online. Her site includes a simple shopping cart for purchasing, but most customers prefer to phone in or stop by to place their orders. They enjoy talking directly to a floral designer to customize their arrangements. For this florist, a website serves a simple function of reference pricing that makes the one-to-one encounter more pleasant for all parties. On the website, several versions of floral gifts for local delivery are displayed, with price points ranging from moderate to high. Customers "preshop" at the website to get a sense of prices and options and then come to the store or call with clear ideas about what they want and how much they will spend.

Really!

Who's going online? Worldwide, the total passed 600 million in late 2002, according to www.nua.ie, "the world's leading resource for Internet trends and statistics." Of those, 182 million are in the United States and Canada. When are they going online? A lot of them hit the web while at work—37 percent of the working population has Internet access at the office. Of these workers, roughly 70 percent have graduated college, and about half of them earn more than $75,000 a year.

The average Internet user is about 40 years old, is as likely to be female as male, and has more than one child at home. Over 70 percent of the U.S. population has gone online in the past month. Canada is not far behind at 62 percent. These numbers I bring you from research by the Gartner Group and Ipsos-Reid, quoted on that www.nua.ie site, dated year-end 2002. These stats have been rising and no doubt will have risen further by the time you read this—go online and see what the numbers are up to today!

Keep Your Online Presence Consistent with Your Brand Identity

Your online marketing, like all your other marketing activity, should be consistent with your company's brand identity. You've invested time and money to position your brand—now is no time to drop the ball. The tone of voice and the style of dress you choose for your website and other online elements, like banner ads or an e-newsletter, must be carefully chosen to support your positioning strategy for your brand. A successful brand is built over time from hundreds of contacts that create positive associations. The impressions you make on the web feed into that brand experience.

Building a brand for a web-based business is somewhat different from branding for an offline business. In traditional advertising, brands are built with strong visual and sound elements—with dramatic images, catchy slogans, and jingles. Not so the web. The very tools that get brand messages across in the real world become drawbacks online. That dramatic image or catchy jingle will be slow to download. Visitors who enjoy your entertaining ads in traditional media will become frustrated and impatient if you serve them the same content online.

A web-based brand is concerned with helping people do things. The emphasis is on function, speed, and service. Each time a visitor succeeds in carrying out a task, your brand is enhanced. Each time the visitor is frustrated, the brand suffers.

Mentor

Use the following tools to build your brand on your website by helping people do the things they came for:

- Deliver current, well-written content. Provide a search process that works the way visitors think.
- Offer a classification and navigation scheme that makes sense even to first-time visitors.
- Make your purchase process simple.

Deploy occasional exit surveys (a pop-up window works well) to see how well you are using these tools to build your brand on your website. Make improvements where you discover the need.

Your Website: What Is Its Function?

Most websites I encounter are functioning in one of three ways. They are generally acting as landing pages, brochures, or stores. It's possible to serve more than one of these functions, of course, but it helps to consider each to be sure you're meeting the needs of all visitors who might look for you online. Define a clear purpose for each page you hang out on that giant clothesline, and you'll maximize the return on your effort invested.

What?

A **landing page** is a web page designed for visitors who click through from another online source or a website address printed elsewhere. It is engineered to address every information need to encourage visitors to follow through on a call to action. At the very least, it entices the visitor to spend some time exploring the website and experiencing your brand.

Landing Pages Bridge the Gap

The *landing page* is a concept anyone advertising in the traditional media can use to give that ad campaign an online boost. A landing page is a specific web page intended for prospects who click through from another online source or go online following a website address found somewhere. A landing page provides the next step following a glimmer of interest. It's the gateway to a site that might contain dozens or hundreds of pages, depending on the site's purpose.

The landing page is an environment designed to address every member of the "purchase committee" with persuasive messages. It should be designed to show or repeat elements from the advertising that brought the visitor to this site—but only if those elements load quickly! The landing page supplements the AIDA formula in the advertising. It answers questions; it touches on the four utilities to explore qualities of the product or service being advertised. Form and function, place, time, and ease of possession can all be explored in the limitless space of the Internet.

The ad did the job of attracting the attention of the prospect; now the landing page works to bring that prospect to the point of entering into a sales transaction. A landing page is the web-based advertising technique to use for anyone who sells a single product or is using the web to promote direct response. (Tip: If that's your goal, study what the direct marketing folks know. Successful online advertisers are adapting the techniques of the direct marketing model.)

Mentor

Use landing pages to maximize the impact of your traditional (offline) advertising. Each landing page should be a gateway that ties in with the ad campaign it relates to and repeats any offers made in the advertising. From this page, a visitor should be able to find answers to common questions or objections. Above all, the landing page must ask for the sale. Everything about the landing page should work to enhance desire, remove objections, and build trust in your company and your offering.

Online Brochures Meet a Wide Range of Information Needs

Not every website is a landing page, of course. For every company hanging out its shingle, there is (or ought to be) a website. The once-ubiquitous request to "Send me your brochure" has been replaced by "What's your website address?" Every business interested in communicating a trustworthy public image needs a web presence that displays its brand identity and meets the information needs of visitors.

A basic "brochureware" website should include the following elements:

- A brief outline or mission statement on the home page.
- A description of customers or industries served (including case studies if possible).
- A description of work processes and results.
- An overview of the product or service lines offered.
- Background on the company, including contact information.

- Resources for various interests, such as a FAQ (frequently asked questions) page for beginners, an index of articles for members of the press, links to related sites, and so on.

Any landing page will, of course, link to that advertiser's online brochure website.

The main advantage of "brochureware" websites is the increased level of customer service they deliver. Visitors can access your online brochure whenever and wherever they get the urge. Each user interacts with the site to choose just the information he or she came to find among the potentially vast resources you make available (and maybe picks up some new information about you during the visit).

Burned by decades of high-pressure sales contacts, many people appreciate the opportunity to find out a bit about your company without starting up a conversation in person. This is an advantage that cuts both ways: The prospects your people talk to will be better informed. Some people, for whom your offering has no relevance, will have simply weeded themselves out. Net result: less wasted time for everybody.

Pitfall

Some companies seem to go out of their way to keep website visitors from contacting them by phone or in person. They hide their addresses and phone numbers deep down in the website, in a misguided effort to "keep productivity high" by keeping call center staff from having to answer questions for which answers have been provided on the website! Don't count on visitors to your site being motivated to serve themselves. Some individuals are "people people" and, once they've formed a positive impression of your company by visiting your site, will want to take the next step and talk to a representative in person. This is a good thing! Encourage contact by making phone numbers easy to find.

Online Stores Provide Convenience

If it's at all relevant as a means of sales processing for you, consider adding an online commerce component in addition to your landing pages or brochure websites.

The web offers the ability to distribute a customized catalog complete with electronic order taking, without printing and postage costs. That's opening doors to some unusual businesses. For example, musicians like Kai Miaka are using websites that invite you to hear their music, order their CDs, and engage in discussion with your fellow fans.

Setting up an e-commerce website isn't difficult; the single most important factor is selecting the web-hosting service you will use. You don't really need special software to handle credit card purchases. You can plug in shopping cart e-commerce programs or employ a system like PayPal (www.paypal.com). You can find reviews of ordering programs (shopping carts) online by entering the phrase "shopping carts" in a search engine. Or try visiting www.wilsonweb.com/wct and looking for the e-book *The Shopping Cart Report* produced by "Dr. E-Biz" Ralph Wilson. I find Dr. Wilson's advice thoroughly practical and easy to follow.

An online store requires compelling product display and copy writing. It should incorporate promotional marketing techniques like volume discounts and bundling. It should leverage every aspect of design from a pleasing color scheme to an intuitive user interface to make doing business at the site a satisfying experience. Every barrier to completing the sale must be reduced or minimized, from publishing a privacy statement to providing a clear guarantee and return policy. Check out A Life of Faith Dolls at www.alifeoffaith.com and American Girls at www.americangirl.com. See how these examples stack up. Consider copy, color, ease of use, and friendliness of guarantees and other policies. (I'd give you my opinion, but there's too much potential for the sites to change by the time you read this. So check out what they're doing today and form your own opinion.)

Really!

Which is better, starting your new online store in an existing web mall or paying for your own unique location? The idea of an online "mall" is kind of a myth. What it really represents is inclusion in a search directory system used by an established base of shoppers. The more shoppers in the system, the better that online "mall" will perform for you. I know a number of people with thriving home businesses based around sales on eBay—text books, collectible swords, and belly dance costumes provide just a few examples of the possibilities. My friends are letting eBay provide the search system that effectively distributes word of their product lines. They concentrate on fulfilling the orders, not on marketing the store.

You could start your own online store, post your offerings on an existing web mall, or do both. A web mall is a site that aggregates different sellers into one consistent presentation to visitors with one check-out procedure (a little like multiple antique dealers doing business together in an antiques mall.) The website eBay is one of the most popular web malls online. Amazon has become a web mall too, since it began presenting used books from other sellers on its website. It makes sense to launch your presence at an online mall at the same time you are building up the traffic to your own unique site.

This is no place for an in-depth discussion of online retailing. I'll simply say—if your competitors sell it online, if your customers look for it online, then where should you be? That's right.

Pitfall

It's great that you can update a website daily, but who's going to do all that updating? If your goals are ambitious, your website is going to require frequent programming maintenance to add new information, delete outdated material, and harvest the data generated about visitors and page views. If one of your reasons for moving online is to reduce costs, don't ignore the maintenance cost when you compare a website to other strategies!

Mentor

Any page might turn out to be a landing page, so prepare your content with that possibility in mind. How could a person stumble through a "backdoor" onto your site? Indexing is done by robots, which go by the content of the page, not your concept of where it fits in your overall navigation. Absolutely any page on your site, therefore, will eventually get indexed and start turning up in search results. So make every page welcoming!

Whatever the Function, Content Management Matters

Whatever your approach to online advertising—landing page, brochureware, or online store—content is the most important element of that online presence. Most visitors don't come for your dancing hamsters, vibrating banner ads, or other entertaining clutter. You're lucky if they stay to find what they came for—many web visitors only allow a new site two seconds to prove its value before surfing on.

When it comes to slow-to-load graphics and other components, if it doesn't deliver what visitors came for, it doesn't belong online. Make the function of the site clear right from the get-go. Keep your messages current and correct. Use navigation that's easy to figure out. Provide several ways to contact you. And for crying out loud, test the load time for your brilliant web designs! Many of your visitors will have broadband high-speed Internet access, but by no means all. No one likes waiting in lines in the physical world, and waiting for graphics to download online feels even more pointless.

The Internet may provide a cost-effective way to do business, but not if your site is so frustrating to use it drives away customers. Make sure it's easy to use, and while you're at it, recheck how your site reflects on your overall brand identity. Is it enhancing your brand image?

Manage the content of your website as you would any other key customer touch point. The whole idea is to be of service and form a lasting positive impression.

Marketing Your Website

How can you have confidence that, if you build it, they will come? By taking a proactive approach to marketing your website. I'll give you several strategies. Please use at least one, and what the heck, why not plan to use them all? As I explain them, you'll see how they dovetail to make up a sturdy and comprehensive online marketing plan. The following actions are your building blocks:

- Advertise on other sites.
- Get indexed by search engines.
- Join affiliate and pay-for-performance programs.
- Offer visitors something of value in exchange for a little information about them.
- Use e-mail to keep in touch, but always respect your visitors' privacy.
- Go fishing—participate in online conversations and mailing lists related to your business or area of expertise.

Some of these website marketing techniques are pretty obvious; others deserve a closer look.

Advertise on Other Websites

Websites need traffic just like "bricks and mortar" storefronts do. It only makes sense that you would advertise online if your customers go online. And so a media buying model (a.k.a. advertising) came into being.

The first wave of online ad sales took the model that already worked in the offline world. The websites began selling ad space using the system of time/space units and audience numbers that worked for traditional media.

Websites monitored their traffic and sold advertisers access to that audience in units based on fractions of the browser "page." Most advertising was quoted and discussed in terms of CPM, the cost-per-thousand figure I described in Chapter 18.

But more online advertisers are moving toward a new model, preferring to pay only for advertising that produces measurable results. Payments that used to be considered a "kickback" have come out from under the table. This new model uses tools like affiliate programs and pay-for-performance deals. Online merchants and media sites now deal in alliances that refer visitors back and forth and share in the revenue that traffic brings.

Pay-for-performance deals represent a pricing model in which the advertiser only pays when site visitors perform a desired action, such as signing up to receive more information or filling out a preference survey. Media buyers are quick to ask for this type of ad pricing, since it typically produces better qualified leads and stretches ad dollars further. A pay-for-performance deal helps the advertiser build a relationship with prospects—and building relationships is very good for the bottom line.

Affiliate programs are mutually beneficial arrangements that drive traffic in exchange for referral fees. An affiliate program distributes your message much more widely than you could manage on your own. Affiliate programs are based around commissions or referral fees. Increasingly, those fees are being paid directly to individuals, rather than to companies. These programs are more like the "tell-a-friend" promotions we've seen retailers use for years, where one individual gets rewarded for introducing someone else to a new product.

Pitfall

An alphabet soup of abbreviations like CPC, CTR, and PPC get served up when online advertising is discussed. When you encounter these, don't be thrown off by the jargon. "CPC" stands for "cost per click"; "CTR" means "click through rate"; "PPC" is short for "Pay per click." CPC, CTR, and PPC can be measured precisely using website traffic logs. Each represents an attempt to transfer the risk inherent in purchasing online advertising from the advertiser to the website that hosts the ad. I'm not convinced that these metrics offer a lot more value to you, the advertiser, since costs go up in proportion to the sureness of the "sure thing" they promise. Watch out for inflated performance claims when you negotiate your online advertising buy.

Hop online and visit a few media sites like www.FastCompany.com or www.Inc.com. Study their advertiser information (especially rates) and check out the advertisers themselves. Visit some of the business resource sites listed in Appendix C and read up on the latest thinking in online advertising, because whatever I write today will change tomorrow. A few hours might disappear while you pursue this study, but you'll be much closer to negotiating your next online media buy when you've invested that time.

Mentor

Do you sell a product or service that other new/small businesses might purchase, like business planning or website design? Check out the business resource websites listed in Appendix C. These sites attract lots of traffic fitting a very specific profile that includes growing businesses. Advertising on these sites, or in their related e-newsletters, might be right for you.

A couple general observations on online advertising: This medium reaches both business and consumer audiences alike and reaches over 70 percent of the population. It combines some of the features of a specialized media channel with some of the features of the broad mass media. Like radio and TV, dayparts matter online. People surf at work, often over their lunch hour. Some of that surfing is for business needs and some for personal purposes. Both types of purchasing tend to rise after 8 A.M., peak between noon and 1 P.M., and taper to a trickle for the rest of the night.

Also like radio and TV, online advertising prices are affected by the timing of the ad's appearance. You can buy as little as an hour or two, deploying your ad in just the right place at just the right time. University Credit Union might sponsor a stock ticker over the lunch hour on the local news-and-weather website and catch lunchtime surfers looking in on their finances.

Advertising on websites is not your only option, nor should it necessarily be your first choice. Advertising response rates on the web are no better than other media, and may be trending toward even worse.

You can purchase ads in the opt-in newsletters that many websites publish. These are very effective and more affordable for smaller businesses than ads on the websites themselves. Too, these newsletter ads are generally simple two- or three-line listings, so there's no need for fancy graphic design. Put your effort into highly crafted sell copy and encourage readers to click through to a matching landing page you've created.

CAUTION

Pitfall

Online advertising is not a cure-all to reach Internet users. The Internet's origin among collaborative scientists made advertising an unwelcome intrusion in the Internet's early years. Once it became established, it became as easy to ignore as advertising in other media. A better strategy for businesses with limited budgets is to invest human capital instead. Participate in online conversations and e-mail lists related to your business and share your expertise. Include your web address in your signature.

Submit Your Website to Search Engines

For the most part, people use the Internet like a giant library. Search engines are the reference librarians. With their pet indexing robots, these saints of cyberspace sift through the billions of web pages out there, deducing their topics, depth, and timeliness of information, and placing them in classification schemes so that you can type "Iberian dance bands" or "potty training tips" in the search box and receive thousands of (possibly) relevant links to more information.

The big trick for anyone preparing a website for indexing is to write descriptions and keywords so clear and differentiating that even a robot can classify what you offer and match you up with people entering those search terms. This trick, termed *search engine optimization*, keeps getting more complex as more search engine companies like

What?

Search engine optimization is a strategy for getting traffic referred from search engines. This has become a highly specialized task and it's evolving at the speed of light. You can hire a specialist to do your optimization, which means (at a minimum) preparing the keywords and descriptions, and then submitting your website to the dozens of search engines out there.

Google and Yahoo evolve their indexing schemes and pay-for-position programs. Optimization used to be fairly easy but has grown to require new knowledge every month as the "bleeding edge" moves forward.

I'm inclined to think your need for optimal optimization depends on your geographic sales territory. If you're a start-up business intending to sell to all North America and beyond, by all means invest in optimization so you get in front of that big wide world right from the start. Money that used to be budgeted for advertising in print directories might wisely be redirected to pay for professional search engine optimization for your website.

When you pay for placement near the top of the list of search results from a search engine, that's called positioning. Some charge on a pay-per-click (PPC) basis; others charge periodic fees or sell the top 10 or 20 ranked positions to the highest bidders. This can get very expensive for a small business; unless you are dealing in a broad consumer marketplace, I recommend you focus your dollars on other kinds of advertising rather than get into a high-stakes bidding war for search engine positions.

E-Newsletters: Create Your Own!

Maybe it's my bias as a writer—I love e-mail newsletters. I subscribe to a dozen or so, relying on some to keep up with professional developments, others to help me hone skills. Some I subscribe to just because I find them entertaining.

If I can publish an e-newsletter, so can you. Your e-newsletter is an excellent way to get prospects and to keep those contacts current. Use your newsletter to touch them with specific useful information and at the same time maintain awareness of your brand identity.

Newsletters are one of the best ways to build a business on the Internet. It doesn't happen overnight, but work this technique slow and steady, and you'll reap the benefits. Combine it with participating in other forums and newsletters, and you're on your way.

Use your newsletter to form a community in which you lead, or to present quality information readers can't easily find elsewhere. Mix your valuable information with promotion for your products or services. Provide news, analysis, commentary, how-to, answer questions, offer opinion polls—I could go on. But don't go on too long—2000 words is about the maximum an e-newsletter should contain.

I publish a newsletter for Third Wave Research's "Market Research Tools." I compose each issue of short introductions or overviews of stories, with links to greater depth. This gives my readers a quick browse. Those who click through to the more in-depth stories provide me with a measurable click-through rate (CTR) that tell me which stories were interesting enough to draw readers deeper in. Using that information I tailor future issues' content to better match my audience's interests.

Mentor

Get your readers to write your newsletter. In other words, make it a forum for discussion. Prime the pump a bit, and soon your readers will ask questions, offer opinions, and generally fill your newsletter as full as you let them. Nothing like a good customer testimonial to make your newsletter a "voice of the people" instrument that casts you in a positive light.

Two questions come up frequently when e-newsletters are the topic of discussion.

Should you charge a subscription fee for your e-newsletter? Some do, some don't. The more valuable your content, the more likely readers will consider it worth paying for. Test price points (including *free*) as you would with any offering.

Every e-mail newsletter requires some content devoted to taking care of business—how to unsubscribe, correspond with the editor, and so on. Don't leave out these necessities.

For the rest of your e-newsletter education, I'll turn you over to an online resource I've found most helpful, dear old "Dr. E-Biz" mentioned earlier. Web marketing consultant Ralph Wilson has years of experience with small and very-small businesses (as well as larger ones and also an intriguing specialization in churches). I have been delighted with his advice and his approach. Visit www.wilsonweb.com and tell the doctor I sent you.

Using E-Mail in Online Advertising

E-mail marketing can be an effective and inexpensive companion to your other advertising. Achieving that effectiveness and economy requires a delicate touch, however. I have strong opinions about e-mail's place in the online advertising plan, and I have some concerns for businesses that ignore the subtleties. It's too hard to meet my basic measure of value in marketing tactics: Does this technique allow you to reach the right people and leave the rest alone?

People have been getting direct mail for generations, and most don't have a problem with that. Interesting offers get glanced at, and the rejects go in the waste basket without a second thought. Unsolicited e-mails are another thing entirely. These waste time and, even worse, carry a negative charge. Opt for mailing too often to a list too poorly qualified for interest in your message and guess what? You've just become a spammer.

If direct marketing by e-mail didn't work, there wouldn't be spammers or legitimate users of e-mail marketing, either. In my opinion, you are better off to focus your e-mail marketing not on generating new leads, but on communicating with prospects you've found via other means. E-mail's real strength is its immediacy as a communication medium. Use e-mail to develop your precious one-to-one relationship with each prospect, and you use its power to your best advantage, without harming your brand or reputation.

Really!

I get many requests from would-be e-mail marketers who think that, by renting the right mailing list and sending an e-mail "burst," they will drive traffic to their site at a fraction of the cost of direct mail. If only that were true. The harm you do your brand if you misfire has a far higher cost that must be factored in.

Remember the "three Ms" of direct mail: the target Market, the Message, and the Mail list. That third "M" is where direct mail strategy breaks down when you try to move lead-generating mail programs online. Someday there may be rentable e-mail lists that are as accurate and well qualified as the mailing address lists on the market today. But there are practical reasons why such a list is hard to assemble. Too many of the e-mail lists being marketed as "highly qualified opt-in lists" are just a recipe for spam, in my opinion.

Building and Managing Your Own E-Subscriber List

The real key to e-mail marketing is to build your own e-mail list, and then use it to …

- Discover customer needs.
- Communicate your offering's benefits.
- Respond to requests for information.
- Ask for referrals from satisfied customers.

How do you build your own e-mail list? By using the advertising techniques discussed in this chapter, of course!

You advertise on other sites and newsletters, and you offer visitors something of value in exchange for their e-mail addresses. You network by participating in mailing lists and newsgroups, contributing your expertise and always including your website and e-mail address in your signature. You produce an e-newsletter and offer subscriptions. You promote your website and its offerings in all your offline advertising, printing that information on brochures, business cards, and every other piece of literature you distribute.

> **Pitfall**
>
> Protect the privacy of your e-mail list members or kiss your *ss goodbye! All customers must be reassured that you will never sell or trade their e-mail contact information or use it internally for purposes other than those specified in your privacy policy. Put a link to your privacy policy at the bottom of every e-mail you send to your list, and post it on your website as well.

You build an e-mail list, and then you manage it. You track opt-in/opt-out status to honor discrete levels of permission. Here your database is the key. If you're using e-mail communication as part of your customer relationship management approach, you'll want to track who has received what message and when. Please! Make maintaining your customer database a priority, right down to keeping records of each e-mail advertising burst and every auto-responder sent!

E-mail is at the heart a personal communication medium. Your every message will appear to be a personal note from you directly to the recipient, so keep your style and tone in sync with that appearance. If you want to avoid the commitment of that level of personalization, don't use e-mail messages for marketing.

Develop an e-newsletter instead. It arrives in the same place, with similar immediacy to the recipient and similar cost efficiencies for you. The perception of personal communication is lessened, however—and so the expectation that your message *be* personal is reduced. Newsletters deliver a feeling of community that does your brand more good than a personalized e-mail's feeble personal contact.

In case you can't tell by now, I'm a big fan of e-newsletters and more than a little dubious of the advantages of marketing with e-mail messages.

Almost every business belongs online, and an online marketing strategy goes with the territory. For the new or small business, with few dollars to spend and maximum need for effectiveness in the advertising program, purchasing ads on websites is not what I'd recommend. Rather, I'd suggest you invest your dollars in developing a good professional site and then invest your time in networking and participating on the web in ways that encourage people to follow you back to your website—and to hear your pitch. At the risk of sounding like a broken record, know your audience, and use one-to-one techniques to keep a conversation going with each niche or segment. A good database of subscriber information is (you guessed it) a must.

In other words, build your Internet presence on good content, good data, and your personal touch online.

Mentor

Autoresponders or "triggered e-mail" is a great technique to apply to your e-mail marketing. Set up a series of messages, sequenced to go out automatically. Just as you can set your e-mail to respond with "I'm on vacation" when you're out of town, you can set specific messages to go out when specific events take place. When a visitor registers with an e-mail address to download a "white paper," let that trigger a follow-up e-mail asking "Would you like to discuss that white paper with its author?" If someone makes a purchase from your online store, follow up in a few days with a satisfaction survey or a cross-selling offer.

The Least You Need to Know

- Regardless of whether your business model is e-commerce or traditional, you need some form of a web presence and an online marketing plan.
- Websites can function as landing pages, brochures, or online stores; expect different areas of your website to serve these different functions.
- Market your website using a blend of advertising, search engine optimization, and one-to-one marketing techniques.
- Create an e-newsletter to communicate with interested prospects but avoid using e-mail lists for lead generation.

Chapter 23

Be a Publicity Hound

In This Chapter

- How to tell a publicity opportunity when it arises, and how to make one if it doesn't occur on its own
- How to use publicity activity that has nothing to do with news media—your community involvement
- How to make your own professional press kit
- How to be an effective assistant to your media contacts

You know how movie stars always end up being interviewed in the press or on the talk shows just when they have a movie coming out? That's not a coincidence. They have press agents at work getting them out in the public eye. It gets attention for the movie, TV show, book, or whatever. Now you may not be able to afford a press agent, but you can use some of their techniques to get your name in the local news in a way that brings some positive notoriety to your business.

For some businesses, like Anita Hecht's Life History Service, sustained effort at positive publicity is the main marketing activity.

It's not hard to be a publicity hound, if you have dogged determination.

Publicity? It Couldn't Hurt and It Might Help

There are two different things people can mean when they recommend you go after some publicity. The first is that you should encourage the media to write or air news about you. The second is that you should get yourself known in the community by other means. They might mean networking, doing charitable work, or hosting special events. Publicity is anything you do that keeps your name (or your business's name) coming up in conversation.

There's another reason having a handle on publicity is important to you. Sometimes bad things happen to good people. When bad things happen to you, the press will come calling. You need to have a disaster plan already in mind, or at least have a clue how to get the media to tell your side of the story.

What?

Publicity involves the actions you take—not including your paid advertising—to let others know something about you and your business.

By the way, people often use "publicity" and "public relations" as if they mean the same thing. They almost do, but not quite. *Publicity* is just one part of the larger activity of public relations, which includes a broader scope of communications activities, like customer relations and quality control.

How to Sniff Out Your Best Publicity Opportunities

It's possible to get publicity through a number of avenues, including the following:

- Word of mouth
- Communications to employees
- Special events
- Charity sponsorship
- Relationships with the news media

The last one comes to mind the most often when we think about publicity, but it can be the hardest and least-controllable way to get your message out. Take some time to consider other avenues before you decide you are finished with this subject. Some obvious ones can be productive. A garage owner located near a university campus became a public radio sponsor. His business was thanked every day at drive time. He calls it one of his best publicity investments.

Publicity's Place in Your Marketing

Everything you plan to do with your advertising and marketing has its publicity impact. The reverse is also true: Your publicity efforts have an impact on the success of your marketing. Let's say you're planning an advertising campaign that features an innovative technique, such as the telephone company billboards I mentioned in Chapter 18. When the company changed its name, lifelike "worker" mannequins appeared in front of billboards, painting over the old logotype with the new one. The company received numerous phone calls, including some from people concerned that the "employees" were working such long hours. The company saw the publicity potential in that and called the local media. The result was *good ink*—positive mentions of the company both in the print media and on local radio and television.

What?

Good ink is what you're looking for with publicity. It's an insider's term meaning that you or your company got into the news and the stories were positive.

The moral of the story: Whatever you are doing, publicity can amplify its effect. A corporate name change, a new product line, an innovative management decision—any and all can present opportunities for the media to look your way.

Don't think for a minute that publicity is a dance in which you lead. You can offer stories to the press, but you can't control the content or the timing of the coverage you receive. The wrong reaction can lead to long-lasting damage. Play publicity like a contact sport. Keep an offensive and a defensive strategy in mind.

If you are a solo home business, getting publicity is even more difficult. You might find it more useful to start an e-mail newsletter (where you are your own news outlet) or to use postcards to make the announcements and offers that keep your name in front of clients and prospects. But, if you find the right opportunity, the right story angle, you might still get yourself noticed by the press, especially if you can claim expertise in an area that is newsworthy.

If you have trouble picturing yourself pursuing publicity on your own, take note of Anita Hecht's approach. She invested her energy in helping the Association of Personal Historians (APH) become established. One of the main functions of this professional organization is to help members market their services. Publicity is a key marketing tool for all APH's 300-plus members. APH provides members with tools for generating publicity on a local level and also pays for a publicity agent to work at placing stories in national media. The group's marketing committee has created template press releases and suggests occasions for publicity like "May Is Personal History Month" so that members can time their efforts to build on each others' work.

Finding Opportunities and Story Angles

If you want to see stories about you in the press, send them the news you want to see. How do you do that effectively? By understanding the gatekeepers of the news—editors who make decisions about what stories will run and why.

First, understand their job. Each idea that crosses their desks has to pass this test: "Is this of interest or service to my audience (readers, viewers, or listeners)?" If the answer is yes and your idea is presented with a strong *story angle*, you're on your way.

What's a story angle? It's the approach you choose that sells the editor on the merits of your story. Here are some tried-and-true story angles:

- **News announcements.** Information or events of potential interest to the public are opportunities for a news announcement. Introducing a new product, changing location, breaking ground on a new building, or sponsoring a workshop are all worthy of an announcement. Profit growth, with a dose of optimism about the economy, can get an editor's attention. Even the routine happenings in your business are worth a shot. Personnel promotions and new hires deserve a news announcement. If someone receives advanced training, a professional certification, or an award, send an announcement. These may not be high-priority news, but editors usually have a bit of space in the business section reserved for these morsels. Be sure to try trade journals as well as local newspapers.

> CAUTION
>
> **Pitfall**
>
> Good reporters will try to present a balanced view. Chances are, they will fill out their stories by interviewing another authority who might not agree with your statements. Prepare ahead of time what you will say if you are challenged. A good response begins with something like, "I'm glad you asked that."

- **Features.** A feature story explores a subject that informs or interests the public but is less tied to a point in time. Ask yourself: What do you know well, that the public would find interesting? The beauty of this type of publicity is the positive light it shines on you, the expert informant.

  For example, a dry cleaner I know followed this advice. When a national story came in about the ecological perils of dry-cleaning processes, he was able to give the press a local spin by describing the measures his business had already taken to offset those dangers. The story ran as a local good news piece, rather than the usual hair-raising report of dangers. Our man came across as a proactive businessman who makes his community's safety a priority.

Features can be fillers, too—light news items that might appear as the last segment of a news broadcast. When a feature has no timeliness to it, publicity people will refer to it as an "evergreen."

- **Opinion.** Wherever a controversy exists, the media will be interested in communicating the opposing sides' points of view. Build a leadership image for yourself in your community by letting the media know where you stand on issues on which you have authoritative views. Write a letter to the editor, or explain your point of view and submit it as a story idea. Even if members of the public disagree with your position, you have established yourself as a person willing to take a stand and speak your mind.

  I'm not advocating you take extremist positions on controversial issues. Use this test: Is my position fair to all concerned and based in solid facts? Is my desire to express it coming not from my own ego but from a desire to help my fellow citizens? If you can answer yes, you can expect positive outcomes from expressing your opinions.

> **Mentor**
>
> If you want to provide a story idea for a local, state, or regional trade magazine, ask the editors for their editorial calendar. This will tell you what topics each issue will cover for a one-year period. Find a category that fits your business and tailor your story idea to fit the magazine's calendar.

Create a list of the media you want to target, and then create publicity releases using your different story angles. You'll quickly learn what sorts of stories the different editors are looking for. Feed them newsworthy material on a regular basis, and you'll soon build solid relationships. Before you know it, they'll be turning to you for the local angle, even on national stories that touch your area of expertise.

> **Really!**
>
> A story can be presented in one of two ways. You can send a news release informing the outlet of an item to write about, or you can actually write the story and submit it, leaving it to the editor to go with the piece as is or to rewrite it. Which you choose depends partly on your skill as a writer but also on the story angle and the type of media you're approaching. For example, daily newspapers prefer to write their own news, whereas the overworked staff at a trade journal will appreciate your writing assistance.

Working with the Media: What Do They Want?

Reporters and editors for the news media are some of the most hard-working, idealistic people you'll meet. They want to get the story right, and they have to get it on time. What they want—deep inside—is help! When you write a press release, tailor it to the exact needs of each specific contact. A feature editor will want a more chatty story than the general news desk; a business writer will want facts and figures; a lifestyle editor will want to hear the stories behind the numbers. So the most helpful thing you can do is to bring them the news they want, packaged in the style they need.

Here are some other tips to help you help them do their jobs:

- **Be a good assistant.** If you don't know the facts, offer to find out and follow up. Always keep your word. If you tell a reporter that a story is exclusive, don't break that promise by discussing the story with other journalists.

What?

A **sound bite** is a nugget of newsworthiness, a morsel of meaning, chopped out of the context of an interview and served up like a news canapé. Short attention spans and quick-cut visual styles have made the media more and more reliant on sound bite reporting.

- **Be quotable.** When a reporter calls, package your answers in concise *sound bites*. Start with the important items and keep your statements simple and direct. Here's a suggestion from the pros—restate the question in your answer. That makes it even easier to edit for concise reportage.
- **Use colorful descriptions.** Don't say, "We have five million cubic feet of storage in our new facility." Instead say, "All the water in Lake Watoosie wouldn't fill our storage facility." Colorful comparisons are more entertaining than straight statistics.
- **Be available whenever you're needed.** When a reporter calls, chances are she's on a deadline. Drop whatever you're doing to take her call.

Using Special Events to Get Publicity

"There's just no news," you say. "Nothing good has happened, and nothing bad either." My advice to you is to make an event that makes news.

You can create a newsworthy event by sponsoring a seminar, inviting a celebrity to appear on your behalf, or hosting an open house or plant tour. Your possibilities are only limited by your creativity. A planned event gives you a timely opportunity for a news announcement. Work hard at getting reporters and photographers to come to the event. Show them a good time, and you're likely to see a positive write-up afterward. For several years, Ducks In A Row hosted an "office holiday party" for the self-employed; the event was colorful and original enough to attract positive mentions in the business press.

I hope bells are ringing in your head right now about tying special events to sales promotions. In Chapter 15, I recommended that you use special events or contests to grab the spotlight. To your friends in the media, the invitation, the event, and the results (new sales goals met, contest winners, and so on) all constitute news. It may not make the paper if there's a fire at the wiener factory on the same day, but it's just the kind of filler that most editors need on a regular basis.

What to Do When Bad Things Happen

Some people are only happy when it rains, and some editors love bad stories best of all. Still others follow the maxim, "If it bleeds, it leads." The media won't limit themselves to reporting only good news. If you have adverse news, you can lay as low as you like, but the reporters may still come calling. How do you cope?

The most important strategy is to plan ahead. Just as you practice fire drills with your children (you do, don't you?), your business needs "publicity fire drills" as well. The place to start is with your press kit, which I'll describe a little later in this chapter. Keep up to date, and store copies of it at home as well. Decide who on your staff should and shouldn't talk to the media, and keep them briefed on the message you want to communicate. Follow this advice for best results:

- **Be honest at all times.** You don't need to tell all you know, but never tell a lie.
- **Do not repeat a reporter's incorrect statement,** as in "Are you saying I stole the money?" You might unwittingly give a sound bite that places you in a negative light. You never know how your comments will be edited.
- **Never try to kill a story.** You're more likely to increase interest in the news, or worse yet, you'll draw attention to your desire to withhold information.

The University Credit Union (UCU) had to handle one of those bad things that happen through almost no fault of their own. It's a classic case of a tough decision. Here's what happened. After the popular polar bear in the local zoo died, UCU arranged to have two polar cubs shipped to the zoo from Alaska. The cubs needed a home, so the cost of the donation was low. To get some publicity for the donation, UCU decided to hold a "name the cubs" contest. The cubs already had names, but UCU had been told they were just paperwork names. Unfortunately, news reporters from Alaska released a different story, which led locals to believe the cubs had been named by children in Alaska, so they flooded the papers and UCU with letters of protest.

The truth of the matter was that the names actually were given by the news writers themselves. But the UCU, with help from consultants, decided the truth would sound like an after-the-fact fiction. So UCU decided not to tell a lie, but also not to tell all. They admitted a mistake and enlisted their members to make suggestions on how to handle the contest already launched. In the end, popular opinion called for keeping the cubs' original names and donating the promised prize money to the local children's museum. The result was positive for UCU. Townspeople congratulated them on their openness to collaboration. Admitting a mistake (which they did make by not double-checking the original story) and sitting on the whole truth got UCU better publicity than the contest would have. The moral: Once again, even with publicity, you have to know your audience.

Community Involvement: Effective Marketing on Half a Shoestring

There's a side to publicity that has nothing to do with news releases and making friends with the media. It is about getting yourself known in the community. It's a solid publicity strategy, and a lot of successful people take a very planned approach to it. They network (and not in that boring business-card-shuffle way), participate in charitable activities, serve on boards, and coach little league. All are activities that keep their names (and hopefully their businesses' names) in circulation.

> **Mentor**
>
> Don't be afraid to mix business with pleasure. First, I'd suggest you balance your community involvement between business-related professional groups and the community service activities that interest you. When you've chosen what you'll participate in, give yourself fully and don't hide who you are. Talk about your business and let people see your enthusiasm.

Many professional service providers find advertising, and even publicity activities, too self-promotional for comfort. Some, like lawyers and doctors, are so recently arrived in the world of marketing that community involvement is the only avenue they feel comfortable pursuing. If you fit that description, I suggest you be sure to read Chapter 26. In that chapter, I talk about ways to quietly promote a community image for yourself, through techniques like public speaking, writing and placing articles, volunteer work, and more.

Selling Your Story Using a Press Kit

Whether you go looking for news or news comes looking for you, it helps to be prepared. That's where your press kit comes in. A press kit can be as simple as a set of stapled press releases, or it can be an elaborate folder with glossy photos and company literature included. It can be a generic description of your company and your products, or it can be dedicated to a specific topic, like your new product or a special event.

A press kit might include any or all of these components:

- Press release
- Photos
- Fact sheets about the company and its offering
- Personnel statements with credentials, education, and achievements
- Video or audio press releases
- Company literature (annual reports, brochures, and so on)

A Press Release for Every Occasion

The press release, or news release, is the meat of the press kit. It's the story presented in a way the editor can run as written, or use as the basis for her own report. You don't know which way she'll go, so you write it as follows, to cover all your bases.

The generally accepted format for a press release is …

NEWS RELEASE

Contact:

Bob Waterman
Bob's Bottomless Boats
3800 Riverview Parkway
123-456-7890 ext. 1

For Immediate Release

Headline: WHAT IS A KAYA CANOE? ASK AT BOB'S BOTTOMLESS BOATS Bob's Bottomless Boats on Riverview Parkway has launched the flagship of a new product line, a lightweight hybrid combining the sporty maneuverability of a kayak with the more comfortable ergonomics of a canoe.

Bob's Bottomless Boats has developed the new design with the help of experts in sports medicine from University Hospital. The forward-thinking kaya canoe positions the knees, hips, and spine for maximum comfort and power in motion. "Our goal is to ease the discomfort a body feels when it tries to participate in a demanding sport," said the boat's designer, Bill Waterman.

The new boat is a lightweight one-person craft with a unique new seat. The boat combines the comfort of canoeing with the mobility only kayaks have delivered. Because of their stability, kaya canoes are excellent for bird watching, fishing, and nature photography. Weighing in at about 35 pounds, the boats are easy to maneuver both in and out of the water.

By introducing a boat that's affordable, comfortable, and fun, Bob's Bottomless Boats once again demonstrates its leadership in all things boating in the Lake City region.

-30-

Contact:

Bob Waterman
Bob's Bottomless Boats
3800 Riverview Parkway
123-456-7890 ext. 1

CAUTION

Pitfall

Editors edit. More often than not, they will modify your release. At a minimum, they will shorten it, but they may also leave out critical statements so that the meaning of the release is changed somewhat. Editors on tight deadlines might get confused by what you have included in a release. Concise writing on your part is critical.

Every press release should begin with a header section, with the word "NEWS" first, followed by a release date or "for immediate release." Give your contact information, even if the release is on your company letterhead.

Next comes the body of your release. Start with a headline that demonstrates your most newsworthy element. Go on to a lead paragraph that gets attention and then tells your story. The whole story must be summarized in this lead paragraph. If the editor doesn't cut the story down to this, the average reader probably will. Writing the lead is the most difficult part of the press release.

Everything following the lead paragraph expands on what was introduced. Use quotes to keep the copy personal. Use subheads if they help you introduce points.

If your release is several pages long, write "more" at the foot of each page. Start each subsequent page with a two- or three-word *slug* for your story followed by the page number.

To close the press release, use the notation -30- to indicate the story's end. (This is a long-standing tradition with newsroom editors and typesetters.)

List any enclosures or available materials, like photos or videotapes. Repeat your contact information from the header section.

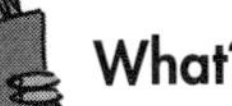

What?

Slug is one of those charming terms left over from the hot-lead days in the newsroom. The slug is a topic word or three at the top of manuscript to identify the story, author, draft version, page, and more.

Photographs: Worth a Thousand Words

If at all possible, include a photo with your press release. Have high-quality professional pictures taken that go with your story. Good photos can serve many purposes beyond publicity. Your effort here can cross over to brochures, advertisements, and other applications. One day spent shooting pictures around your business can provide resource material for the future. When you include photos with your press kit, always attach a caption.

Managing PR: Your Action Plan

Publicity activity takes a commitment. You have to exert energy consistently over time if you're going to see results. You must make time and a place for it in your work activities so you can stay on task.

Develop a calendar outlining the upcoming year's activity. This is the most important aspect of your publicity plan—it's what connects thought to action. Be sure to note when newsworthy events will take place, when advance work should begin, when follow-up is due, and when to begin future planning activities.

Your calendar should include a newsworthy event for each quarter of the year. It could be a personnel change, an anniversary, a special event, or a professional recognition. It's up to you to find the appropriate stories for your situation.

Plan your publicity strategy by defining the message to be communicated. Double-check that this message is consistent with the positioning and advertising messages you've developed. Then develop an implementation strategy to get that message out. Keep track of the media contacts who will help you do this.

Success Is in the Follow-Through

So you plan your activity, develop your messages, send out your releases, and wait for the stories to appear. What to do if nobody bites? Don't panic. Most stories you see about businesses—unless there's skullduggery afoot—are the result of months of follow-through by someone to get that story placed.

> **Mentor**
>
> The most important PR activity you can undertake is to get to know your local reporters by their beats, their styles, and their bosses. Take notes on who writes what about whom. Over time, your dossier will grow until you develop a sixth sense for whom to call with what type of story. Then tailor your communications to each individual's needs. Your efforts will pay off in good ink.

Most publicity work is done on the phone and supported by e-mail, faxes, and the mail. You send out your press releases and press kits. You develop story angles and pitch them to your media contacts. If you're lucky, eventually they bite, and your phone rings. (Most interviews are done over the phone; the deadlines are too tight for reporters to go running around.) If you've done your homework, you're ready with the facts at your fingertips. Handle the phone call with aplomb, and the story that appears will be accurate and flattering. Congratulations! You've mastered another angle of the marketing job.

The Least You Need to Know

- Use publicity to amplify whatever you're doing in your business. Your expansions, personnel changes, and innovative management solutions all present opportunities for good publicity.
- Whatever you propose must have news value. Ask yourself, "Is this of interest or service to this medium's audience (readers, viewers, or listeners)?" If so, pursue the story. If not, look harder for a newsworthy angle.
- When you start feeling like "nothing ever happens around here," stir up some excitement with a special event. Your sales contest, seminar, or visit from an industry leader constitutes news, if nothing better comes along.
- Community involvement, such as public speaking, writing and placing articles, and volunteerism, helps keep your name in front of your audience.
- Develop a professional-looking press kit, with press releases, background information, and photographs. Make yourself easy to report on, and you'll see your name in the news more often.
- Be a good assistant to your media contacts. Be available, prepared, and quotable. Follow through when you say you will.

Chapter 24

A Smorgasbord of Stubborn Situations (and What to Do About Them)

In This Chapter

- How "small town USA" fights against the "category killers"
- How to reach a young or disaffected audience
- Using friends and relatives for research and more
- Five niches for the new millennium that might just make you rich

This chapter presents a smorgasbord of comments and observations aimed at those situations that stubbornly resist the usual marketing techniques. I'll get up on my soapbox and preach a bit, but I'll slip you a guerilla technique or two as well.

Small Town USA: Up Against Category Killers?

Your business can survive, even prosper, right in the shadow of a retail giant. The trick is not being underfoot when the giant takes a step. You can work your position as "the little guy" to your advantage, and even leverage the big guy's steps so he carries you forward with his actions.

You probably know what I'm talking about when I say *category killers*—those big-box retailers that open stores the size of a football field or two, out on the edge of town. They go where the land costs are low, and then throw up a building that's little more than a pole barn. In go the floor-to-ceiling racks, and on them go the big boxes full of … whatever. Electronics. Home improvement supplies. Household goods. Groceries. Even a genteel profession like bookselling meets the giant when a category-killer bookstore, like a Borders or a Barnes and Noble, comes to town.

> **What?**
>
> A **category killer** is a retail operation that has deep pockets and uses those financial resources to make a value proposition that's hard to beat. The big retailer may scrimp on product quality or service quality, but not necessarily. Simply by wielding its huge buying power, a giant can cut costs and operate more profitably on a lower margin. It takes cunning to outmaneuver a giant, but it can be done.

With a cry of "stack it deep and sell it cheap," the giants have trampled over what was left of small-town retailing, already wobbly from years of shoppers' defections to the malls and commercial strips. They're called "category killers" because that's what they do: Pick a retail sector and drive all competition off the field. But I don't need to tell you this—it's old news.

What's news is that smaller retailers have fought back by working their small business advantage, and they've made significant headway in shifting shopping behavior in their favor. Not every shopper wants to hike around a block-long store and search the ghostly aisles for a sales clerk if she can't find what she came for. In fact, most of us would really rather do business with a personable neighbor with whom we feel a connection. We're looking for more sense of meaning and connection in our lives, and that's why magazines like *Real Simple* and *Living Simply* have appeared. Just ask Martha Stewart if you don't believe me.

It's the perception of *value* that drives customers past your store and out to the category killer's big-box store. So you work your advantages to shift that value proposition in your favor. Here are three ways to do that.

#1 Small Business Advantage: Size

You're small, and small is beautiful. You can learn and adapt quickly. You can devote yourselves to your customers with true personal service, not a facsimile made possible by a customer database and a call center.

Study the pricing, merchandising, and customer retention strategies of the big guys. If they're using loyalty rewards, you set up a loyalty program. If they're displaying products grouped by usage rather than category, you find your own creative way to display your products.

> **Mentor**
>
> As a small independent business, your store is a retail environment you can control and shape to your advantage. Think of your selling floor as a theater, and use the elements of stage design to heighten its drama. Use lighting and props effectively, and "block the action" so that traffic flows as it should.

Look at your operations; where might you eliminate waste from your operation? Do it. This is combat. Your business needs to run lean, mean, and ready to fight. And above all, devote yourself to your customers. When they feel their presence truly makes your day, you've added value to the transaction that no big-box retailer can match.

In *Up Against the Wal-Marts*, authors Don Taylor and Jeanne Smalling Archer put it so well I can't say it better. "Run every decision you make through a filter that asks, 'How will this help our customers?' or 'Will this make us more efficient and productive?'"

#2 Small Business Advantage: People

Small businesses can afford to treat people like people, a luxury that big-box retailers can't afford. Think about how shopping at a European fruit market differs from shopping at a Wal-Mart. The proprietor greets you, discusses your needs, presents options for your consideration, confers with you about what fits your purpose with the grave air of a Michelangelo choosing his next block of stone—even if it's just the purchase of a couple of oranges we're talking about. That's how I want you to treat each customer. A big part of life's joy comes from our simple interactions with each other every day. Try getting a joyful feeling shopping at a big box. You know why they employ greeters? Because they wish they had what you have: the personal advantage.

But this "P" isn't just about your customers. It's also about your staff. Support your employees like they were your kids. Teach them the skills and product knowledge they need, and teach them your values, too. Teach by example, as you work together. Motivate them with rewards.

Treat your employees and customers like the neighbors and friends they are, and you weave the fabric of community tightly together. That's a good defense against outsiders pursuing the cold corporate interests of their headquarters several states away.

Really!

Show your employees they're important to you by participating in their lives! Encourage them to join in community activities like team sports and service clubs, and participate yourself if you can. Even if you can't turn out for every game or the fundraiser, offer to support them with your dollars or donations of other goods, services, or time. Your employees will likely reciprocate with a kind of goodwill toward you and your business that customers will recognize and appreciate.

#3 Small Business Advantage: Partners

Five fingers alone are just a hand; five fingers together make a fist. You can accomplish more in your fight against the giants if you band together with other small businesses. Form a merchants' association with your neighbors and agree on common hours for opening and closing. Team up with other businesses for co-promotions and joint media buys. A car wash and a cafe could exchange coupons for discounts and leverage the fact that customers visit both with some frequency.

Take a look at Chapter 11's discussion of partners in social marketing and Chapter 15's advice on sales promotions. I think you'll find a small business advantage if you just ask yourself: Who are my friends, and how can we help each other?

There's another resource I'm fond of turning to when I need ideas for small town marketing. Check out Tom Egelhoff's website www.smalltownmarketing.com. On his site, you can purchase his self-published book *How to Market, Advertise, and Promote Your Business or Service in a Small Town* or browse many useful articles.

Marketing to Urban/Youth Niches: How to Reach Outlaws and Skeptics

There are some populations you can't or shouldn't even try to reach with advertising techniques. For the young, the hip, the disaffected, marketers must be as subtle in their approach as the guerillas who gave "guerilla marketing" its name. And I don't mean subtle as in "sneaky." The last thing you want to do with an already distrustful audience is to validate their distrust.

No, I mean subtle as in "characterized by skill or ingenuity." The marketing techniques you employ to reach these people must be carefully chosen and even more carefully pursued, for any misstep might trigger the opposite reaction from the one you seek.

Marketing to Children Is Big Business

There were more than 50 million kids born between about 1980 and 2000, and there will be an estimated 60 million under 18 by 2010. These kids spend anywhere from $160 billion to $258 billion annually, depending on whose estimates you believe. That's a lot of spending power. No wonder the marketing industry is focusing more and more on how to reach young people.

In some ways, because of their lack of experience with the world, these young consumers represent the last great mass market. Children tend to be as unsophisticated about marketing as the mass consumer society of the 1950s was as television entered their living rooms and ratcheted up the appeals to buy, buy, buy.

But children don't stay that unsophisticated for long. By age 10 or 12, they morph into media-savvy critical thinkers who know just what marketing is. They form strong opinions about what's truly cool and what's just a line to reel them in.

Marketing to children is controversial, and rightly so. Before I tell you how to do it, let me suggest you consider the ethics of bringing commercialism into children's lives too soon or too aggressively. I consider it appropriate to offer children products, ideas, and services that build character, teach skills, and model appropriate behavior. I consider it reprehensible to direct persuasion at young people for products, ideas, and services that do not meet that description. A Life of Faith dolls? Good. Joe Camel merchandise? Bad. In this situation as all others, ask yourself: Would you be proud to tell your mother what you're doing? No? Then change what you're doing.

Really!

Marketing to young people represents three distinct opportunities. You can go after them as a current market, talking to who they are today. You can view them as a future market, addressing them in ways that build loyalty so that when they are older, you're already an established brand. And finally, you can address them as an influence market, because young people wield considerable influence over family spending, on everything from breakfast cereal to vacation destinations.

With that understood, here's how to market to children. Segmentation is the key. When the population you're addressing is undergoing rapid transition through developmental stages, you've got many market niches with unique needs and interests. You can't treat "Under 18" as one market! Start by breaking them into three subsets:

- Children (under age eight)
- "Tweens" (8 to about 12)
- Teenagers (13 to 17)

Then segment even further. Children under age four are focused on their parents and enjoy anything that strengthens the parent-child bond (although they couldn't tell you that). School-age children tend to define their likes and dislikes along gender lines, so you'll target boys as one niche and girls as a different one if you're appealing to this group.

Mentor

For further advice on marketing to children, "tweens," and teenagers, I'll suggest you review the social marketing suggestions in Chapter 11 and then leave you in the hands of other authors, like Gene Del Vecchio in *Creating Ever-Cool* and Peter Zollo in *Wise Up to Teens*.

"Tweens" will likely resist anything that seems babyish. They prefer products and messages that help them make the transition into their teens.

Teenagers are going through the turbulence of defining personalities and projecting image—an exercise any marketer would recognize as positioning the brand! This stage leads many teens to adopt the pose of cynic or outsider. And that leads me to my next stubborn marketing situation: how to reach the disaffected.

Outlaws and Skeptics Resist Advertising But Follow "Buzz"

In a world where consumers are actively resisting advertising, the only smart choice is to stop advertising at them. Instead, work to create an environment where they market to each other. It's become popular to call this *buzz*.

People buzz to connect, to share information, to make sense of the world, to reduce risk, to let off steam. Buzz is how people replace advertisers' pitches with authentic information and recommendations. Buzz plays a major role in many purchasing decisions, not to mention behavioral decisions like which candidate to vote for or whether to engage in risky behavior.

What?

Buzz is something like what we used to call "word of mouth." But it's not quite the same. Buzz is a genuine and infectious excitement about a hot new product, person, or idea. A broader definition, given in Emanuel Rosen's *The Anatomy of Buzz*, says "Buzz is all the word of mouth about a brand. It's the aggregate of all person-to-person communication about a particular product, service, or company."

Buzz is a way to stop the battle for attention. In the face of the several thousand advertising pitches that assault us every day, most of us have developed excellent defenses. We tune out advertising by selectively focusing our attention. Consequently, your marketing messages have little chance of breaking through unless you have deep enough pockets to out-shout the other voices in the marketplace.

Will buzz work for you? The technique works better with some offerings than others. Products that are exciting or innovative get buzz because there's real news to buzz about. Products or services that include a personal experience get buzz—people talk about where they've traveled and how they liked their hotel. They also buzz about books, movies, and restaurants ... There's one thing all "buzzable" offerings share—they're best of class. An offering won't get buzz if it's not the greatest of its kind. Otherwise, the buzz you get will be the angry whine of dissatisfied customers!

Mentor

Buzz is something that can't be bought, so going after buzz is a good technique for the business with a low budget for marketing.

Like good publicity in the media, buzz is something you can't buy. But you can create the conditions that make buzz likely to happen. Creating buzz changes the focus from your interactions with customer niches to the interactions customers have with each other.

So what do you do? You talk to your customers. You find the ones who like to talk, the naturally gregarious "people people." You give them ammunition—plan special events that let you connect with them—and while you're connected, you give them a good story to tell.

A friend of mine went to Bob's Bottomless Boats' "Kaya Canoe Camp"—an action-packed weekend on and off the water, with demonstrations, whitewater obstacle courses, barbecue, and so on. When he returned home, he found he'd been mailed a videotape showing him paddling his craft through the whitewater course. You'd better believe he's out buzzing to his friends about his great camp experiences.

Charlee Bear Farms distributes a lot of free dog treats to veterinarians and trainers. They're hoping for buzz from these people, because the dogs have a hard time buzzing about their preferred brand of treats.

Really!

Buzz and marketing to young people go together like ice cream and a cone. I know two kids who are both 13 years old and skateboard masters. They share a part-time job for a maker of a certain brand of skateboarding shoes and clothes. They're paid to demonstrate skate tricks, talk about safety, and tell other kids about new skateboarding stuff. Why? That company hopes to keep its products popular with kids like these two.

Hit a Stubborn Plateau? Use Friends and Relatives to Extend Your Reach

Information drives sales. If you knew what your friends and relatives liked about your offering, you'd be on your way to a marketing strategy—and it might be one based on buzz, if they like your offering enough to talk it up to others.

What?

A **key informant** is an individual who has depth of experience in a specific area and is willing to share it. In this case, you're interested in individuals who have experience with your product or service offering. Ask your friends and relatives to participate with you in key informant interviews.

Finding out what people like about your offering is a form of market research. Usually a researcher will suggest a focus group to explore what people think of an offering, but that carries a hefty price tag. For businesses without the budget for focus groups, there's a low-cost option. Use the satisfied customers who will do you a favor if asked—your friends and relatives. Get them together or visit them individually and perform a *key informant* interview.

To do a key informant interview, prepare your questions in advance. Tell your informant(s) to be brutally honest. This isn't about being nice. It's about the details of their experience, positive or negative. The key informant interview requires that you remain neutral, even if what you hear indicates you or your offering has been misunderstood. You'll learn more by staying open to what's being said. Resist the urge to take the floor and try to set things straight. Learning *how* you are misunderstood has more value.

You might ask:

- What does this individual like or dislike about your offering?
- What problems does it solve and why?
- How does it compare to other competing or substitute offerings?
- What are the advantages or benefits it offers?

Probe deeper to get beyond their first responses; don't be too quick to move on to your next questions. You may uncover observations and often even the specific words to use as you frame your advertising's creative concepts. Keep performing interviews until you run out of friends and relatives or until the answers begin to repeat themselves. Look for patterns among those answers, such as an emphasis on convenience, or the experience of using the product … you get the idea.

The people you interview have characteristics that will help you discover your best target customer demographics. Take note of their gender, age, ethnicity, income, and so on. Slip in a few questions about their lifestyles. Each bit of information about them helps you draw a customer profile. If everyone over 30 hated your offering but everyone under 20 loved it, that's pretty important for you to know.

When the interviews are done and the answers have been analyzed, it's time to turn your friends and relatives from informants into mavens. Review your notes and see if there is anywhere an individual has misunderstood your messages or perceived your offering in a light that doesn't match your brand identity and positioning. Now you may revisit that individual and tactfully explain where you think they may have missed the boat. Reinforce how you'd like them to understand your offering. (Correcting a misunderstanding is different from rejecting a constructive criticism. If a person's perception doesn't match what you'd like them to perceive, but they're right, you've got to work on that problem yourself.)

Mavens are people who get a kick out of telling others what they're excited about. They collect information and can't wait to share it. Hopefully you'll number some mavens among your friends and relatives. Let them know how much you appreciate it when they buzz about you. You may even consider creating your own affiliate program to reward them when they are instrumental in bringing you new sales.

Mentor

For home-based businesses or lone operators, the key informant interview can be an excellent and inexpensive marketing technique, for reasons that go beyond research. If you're in this type of business, it probably doesn't make sense for you to spend a lot on advertising. Everything you can do to keep your friends and relatives informed about what you do and how much you'd like more of it to do helps you promote your business.

Niches for the New Millennium

It's easier to sell what people need than to generate desire for something they don't. I'm going to hand you five ideas for new products and services. Choose one, find a way to adapt it in your personal interests and expertise, and go get rich, with my best wishes.

Ethnically, America is becoming much more diverse. One in four Baby Boomers claimed a race/ethnicity other than "white" on the 2000 Census, the first to describe ethnicity in detail.

Regarding age, America's population counts are drawing a strange new shape. The "rat has moved through the python"—the Baby Boom that swelled the ranks of children, then youth, and then middle age, is now reaching (horrors!) retirement.

Following them, the "Baby Bust" takes center stage, while the "Echo Boom" children (equal or greater in numbers compared to the original Baby Boom) are coming up quickly.

Blend these trends and imagine what the new population will need. Here's what the experts see: demand for products and services related to education, health, finances, home, and leisure.

Let's take a closer look.

Lifelong Learning

School is no longer just for schoolchildren. We take courses to retool for changing careers or to fill in gaps we missed the first time around. Women and minorities in particular take classes to learn what the good ol' boys picked up in the corporate air around them: supervisory skills or assertiveness, for example.

In our spare time, we pursue knowledge about our hobbies and interests. We take classes to learn skills like boat building or tai chi. We also take classes to learn technical skills, like computer-aided drafting or engine repair.

As a marketer, how do you get in on the action? Think about what you know, and then turn it into training. Offer brush-up training in basic skills in your area of expertise, like "proofreading for secretaries" or "basic grammar refresher course." Take your technical expertise and offer to train in it. If you're a tree surgeon, don't just offer to trim trees—offer a "Learn Tree Surgery" class. Or take a distribution role. Package others as presenters and market a series of "brown-bag" luncheons to workplaces as an employee benefit.

You prefer to produce a product? Create training sessions in package form—foreign language tapes for children, books on tape for any age—you get the idea.

Really!

Dozens of publications forecast trends, from the delightfully named *Popcorn Report* to *American Demographics*. You can find them all at the library or find versions online (although don't expect access to be free). Browse them, and you'll see there's a strong consensus about where the next successful business niches are shaping up.

Two major demographic shifts are underway: one produced by changing immigration patterns, and the other by the aging of the post-World War II Baby Boom. These demographic shifts are rapidly changing the world in which you do business.

Good Health

There's a huge population out there on a mighty quest for youth and wellness, and it goes way beyond medical health. Any product or service that helps someone regain or retain a youthful feeling is finding consumers queuing up to buy. That applies to appearance, health, and mental outlook.

We buy low-calorie food and drink, we go to health clubs, we join weight-loss programs, we buy books and cassettes on health. As we age, we look for all of the above tailored to our changing physical needs. The Baby Boom built its identity on youth, and it isn't giving that up without a fight. If your product or service is a weapon against aging (vitamin supplements, cosmetic surgery, and so on), it's going to sell like hotcakes.

I think personal historians like Anita Hecht are targeting the intersection of these two trends: lifelong learning and good health. Reminiscing (a process researchers are calling "life review") is proving to fight depression and promote well-being in life's later stages. It's even being used in therapy with the elderly. Good health and lifelong learning result when an elder takes on creating a life history, guided by professionals like the members of the Association of Personal Historians.

Financial Products and Services

There's only one other thing Baby Boomers like me (and maybe you, too) value as much as holding onto our youth, and that's financial independence. The thing that makes us feel in control in the face of this awful aging thing is money. We maybe didn't start worrying about it soon enough, or hard enough, but it has become a major preoccupation for most of us.

> **Mentor**
>
> Are you a social marketer? Looking for funding for your nonprofit organization perhaps? Welcome to the boom town—Baby Boomers, that is. Philanthropic giving is predicted to increase substantially as affluent Boomers, ever an idealistic lot, find themselves with resources to give back to their communities and causes. (Or maybe they're just searching for a tax break.) Target the Boomer bracket with your fundraising appeals.

Living longer brings concerns about living well. Financial planning is a boomtown that's going to keep booming. Pick your financial products and use what you've learned about understanding customer behavior to market them. Financial products play well to geographic, demographic, and psychographic target marketing.

What kinds of products and services am I talking about? Prepaid insurance plans (especially long-term care) and savings/investment programs. Education funds for the children. Estate planning. Portfolio management and cash flow analysis.

For some of us, the problem will be stretching meager assets. For others, it will be managing (perhaps unexpected) wealth. Boomers are coming into inheritances at an unprecedented rate. Suddenly the problem becomes the search for tax advantages—a boon to nonprofit organizations looking for donations. Individualistic as ever, we want control over our money even after we've gifted it to someone else. Baby Boomers donate to causes that allow us some control over who receives our contribution and how it's spent.

Financial service businesses like University Credit Union can position themselves to serve emerging financial needs. Consultants can find fields of plenty here as well.

Feathering the New Nest

The retirement housing market is one of the fastest growing business niches, and if you can find a place in that market, you have a profitable opportunity. And that doesn't mean you have to build homes, either.

Remodeling is big business: kitchens and baths need adaptation to help an aging population continue living at home. Downsized housing will cater to the elderly, from "mother-in-law flats" behind larger homes to clustered "retirement communities." But this trend isn't all about aging. Everyone is moving. We're buying larger homes for our teenage families, and then smaller homes once the kids have gone. We buy amenities like Jacuzzis because we deserve them; we buy security systems to protect the loot we've gathered.

What?

Do you find yourself staying home instead of going out, enjoying movies on video instead of going to the theater, and cooking your own pasta primavera when you used to dine in restaurants? Then you're part of the trend toward **cocooning**, the same energy once directed toward outside entertainment now applied to enjoying the comforts of home.

If you sell anything that is used in the home, you'll sell some of it as people move. The old furniture might not fit in the new home—ditto the appliances and even the sheets and towels.

One business I know of, Tall Walls Inc., has staked out a niche providing super-size décor for the acres of walls in large-scale homes popular with the affluent. Their business is growing like Jack's Beanstalk.

You've probably read about the major home trends, *cocooning*, the home office, and the empty nest. Just think for a moment about the needs for products and services each trend predicts. Getting any ideas?

Enjoying It All: Travel and Leisure

As a population, we spend even more money on recreation than we do on clothing. It's hard to imagine a leisure or travel business that won't make money in the years ahead. Even acts of terrorism have been unable to stop this inclination. Those acts simply push travel/leisure aficionados to consider different destinations.

Again, it's Baby Boomers fueling the trend, with time and money to spend and a well-ingrained habit of spending both on recreation.

The product and service possibilities span cultural attractions, the performing arts, restaurants, travel, and leisure activities. How do you find any focus in such a wide field? It's tough, but I'll try.

It appears that Baby Boomers are particularly drawn toward activities that provide meaningful experiences. That may mean recreation that enhances our togetherness with our family, or travel to an offbeat destination. It means seeing performances that move us. It means dining together with friends, enjoying community.

We love our sports and hobbies, too. Bird watching, gardening, photography. These activities and more help us relax and at the same time provide that spiritually refreshing "meaningful experience" we seek. The demand for the Kaya Canoe from Bob's Bottomless Boats is a direct outgrowth of this trend.

If you offer a product or service that enhances leisure time, you're starting out in the right direction. Use customer behavior to segment the market, and you're on a profit trip.

The Least You Need to Know

- "Small town USA" succeeds despite "category killers" by leveraging their strengths in size, people, and partnerships.
- Some target markets actively resist traditional advertising techniques; others are just too young for such techniques to be appropriate.
- Use your friends and relatives as research subjects, and then encourage them to be mavens.
- Product/service niches that are bound to grow include lifelong learning, good health, financial products and services, home-related offerings, and travel/leisure.

Part 5 Here's a Part You Can't Pass Up! (Selling Techniques the Professionals Use)

What would it take to make you a more successful salesman? Maybe you need to experience the satisfaction of doing it well and of seeing results. Most of us have never had any training at the one thing that's more likely to increase our paychecks than any other professional skill.

In the following chapters, I'll explain the personal side of selling: how to match your offering to the way people buy, and how to make your selling process effective. And, a subject close to my heart, I'll shine a light on "rain making," the art of selling for professional service providers.

We all sell a lot of the time, no matter what our exact job descriptions may be. We convince others to buy our proposals, products, or buy into our beliefs. Let's take a look at the skills that can help you sell better.

Chapter 25

The Skills You Need to Sell

In This Chapter

- Your selling approach tools: cold-calling, sales letters, or personal contact?
- How to develop proven sales skills
- How to move from making contact to closing a sale
- Why selling doesn't end at the sale

Nothing happens until somebody makes a sale. Maybe you've heard that saying. The sales transaction gives a purpose to your business; without it, you're out of business. That said, here's something else to ponder: Nobody ever sells anything to anybody.

Do those statements sound contradictory? Well, here's the point: You don't really sell things to other people. What you do is help people sell things to themselves. As a good salesperson, you facilitate that process. That's really what selling is all about—helping people understand why what you offer is going to fulfill a need or solve a problem. When you do a good job of that, transactions happen. If you want to know how to help people sell themselves whatever it is you offer, read on.

Marketing Isn't Necessarily Selling

Many people use the words *marketing* and *sales* as if they mean the same thing. They don't. In fact, understanding of the difference between the two is essential to success.

Marketing consists of getting a mutually beneficial exchange to take place between a buyer and a seller. Marketing sees the big picture.

But marketing activity doesn't put money in the cash register. Sales activity does.

Sales is the personal side of marketing. Sales activity focuses on how people handle the buying exchange. It can be as simple as taking quarters at a lemonade stand or as complicated as writing an order for a custom computer program that hasn't been developed yet.

> **What?**
>
> **Marketing** and **sales**: two halves of a tough nut to crack! Marketing means planning and executing the pricing, promotion, and distribution of an offering so that a mutually beneficial exchange can take place. Sales means the personal effort of individuals who work to complete that exchange.

Sales and marketing are more than a little related, of course. Good marketing is important if you want to expect good sales results. Marketing activities provide the base on which you build sales activities.

Have you ever worked in sales? Then you know how important it is to have the right product at the right price and with the right promotional programs in place to help you get your message across. Each element of the marketing mix contributes to the success or failure of the sales force.

People in sales rely on marketing and advertising to bring in well-qualified leads. When you play the sales role, you appreciate having a good place to start—a list of people who have expressed interest or are predisposed to buy. Almost as important as good leads are good brochures to leave behind and persuasive sales presentation tools. It's the job of marketing and advertising to provide these.

With leads, advertising, and sales support materials in place, you can consider how to sell. So, let's take a look at the tools you can use for your *selling approach*, the selling process itself, and the skills you will need to succeed.

Choose Your Selling Approach Tools

How do you get in touch with your potential customer? You can use any or all of these *selling approach tools:*

- Cold-calling
- Personal letters

- Telemarketing
- In-person sales

Your choice will depend on several factors. First, there are probably norms for your industry. What do other people like you do? Then, there is your personality and what feels most comfortable to you. Let's look at an example.

Rich is a sales rep for a photography studio that specializes in catalog shooting. His customers are production managers and art directors. They might work at catalog houses, or they might work for the agencies hired to produce the catalogs. These are busy people and they can be tough gatekeepers.

What?

Selling approach tools are the methods you can use to approach your customers. The tools are cold-calling, personal letters, telemarketing, and in-person sales. In most cases, your sales approach will use a combination of these tools.

So, the question is, how does Rich use his selling approach tools to build a relationship—to go from total stranger to valued consultant?

It starts with cold-calling. Rich digs everywhere, from the Internet to the pages of *Catalog Age* to the local printers' client lists to create his prospect list. Then he cold-calls to prequalify the list, finding out as much as he can about each company he's targeted.

Mentor

There are ways to make your cold calls warmer. Read job promotions and trade journals, and pay attention to local gossip to build your house prospect list. The first time you pick up the phone, make it purely a fact-finding mission. Then when you make that sales call, you know they need what you sell.

Because the product he sells is visual, Rich relies heavily on a variation of the personal letter approach. Three or four times a year, he produces a postcard showcasing some recent work by the studio. These mailings act as a reminder and also provide an expanding collection of samples that art directors can keep and refer to when shopping for ideas.

Rich makes sure to spend a portion of his time on telemarketing as well. How is that different from cold-calling? Cold-calling gathers information to facilitate approaching a prospect. It can turn into telemarketing, or it can lead to other selling approaches.

Telemarketing is the specific activity of calling someone on the phone and asking for a sale. For Rich, this means keeping in touch with good prospects with regular phone contact. (Like most successful sales people, Rich uses contact manager software to maintain detailed records of his customer touch points.) He'll call to ask whether there's anything coming up that he can bid on, whether a recent proposal is still active, or whether samples are back from the printer on the last job. It doesn't matter so much what he's calling about, but that he calls. In some industries, and this is one of them, buyers like to feel sought after. When you're spending thousands of dollars for something, you want to be treated like you matter.

What?

Collaborative selling means selling like a consultant—not a salesperson. It means building a relationship of trust with your prospect. The prospect shares with you the details of his needs and trusts you to bring to his attention products or services that meet those needs—not waste time bringing those that don't.

That's one reason Rich spends a portion of his time on in-person sales as well. He knows the importance of "face time." Sometimes the reason for the visit is to show the work—to demonstrate a new technical capability, for example, or a new photographer's unique style. Other times the reason is a mix of business and pleasure—a lunch to brainstorm about a new project, or just to keep in touch. In-person sales offer Rich the opportunity to practice *collaborative selling*, pursuing genuine dialogue with his customers to make them partners in the selling process.

Rich's selling approach includes a little of everything. His success lies in the way he tailors the approach to each client's needs. While cold-calling helps bring in new business, letters asking key business associates for referrals are very effective, too. A combination of phone, e-mail, and in-person contact helps Rich reach his goals. Certainly a different marketer on a different mission would mix the ingredients differently.

The Selling Process: Think Big

The art of selling varies dramatically depending on the situation you find yourself in. A distributor selling business-to-business finds himself in a very different world than a retail store selling to local customers. Professionals selling their services experience a different climate, and for that reason, Chapter 26 focuses on the skills necessary there. The advice that follows in this chapter is more appropriate to the retail situation, although many techniques and concepts cross over.

The selling process begins with image, and image begins when you first make contact with your prospect. Your advertising should reflect your image. In fact, you should project a consistent personality (brand identity) through all your contacts, ads, stores, vehicles, and staff. It's a cliché that happens to be true: You never get a second chance to make a first impression. Control your image so that the first impression prospects form is a good one.

Advertise for Leads

Your advertising should contain enough hard information about your product or service to bring in well-qualified prospects. This is one of the strongest arguments in favor of long copy in ads. If the product you sell is complex or expensive, buyers will want information they can refer to for comparison shopping.

If your ads are not especially informative, make sure you have a brochure that spells out the facts. You'll waste less time explaining widgets to people looking for whatsits.

First Contact: Show, Tell, and Question

Okay, let's practice that image-establishing first contact. A prospect has turned herself in: She's called or come to your store. Now you can learn about each other to see if the relationship should go forward. The prospect wants information about the product or service. Give it to her. That's your opening—use it to determine as quickly as possible whether to work with this prospect or gently move on to one with greater potential.

What do you say to the customer who's out shopping and just walked into your store? Make a helpful, friendly greeting, and then watch and wait. That's not always easy! Don't hover, but don't disappear. When the customer seems comfortable, begin the selling conversation. Use this formula: show, tell, and question.

"I see you're looking at coffee makers. This one is particularly nice—it has a neat gizmo for mounting under a kitchen cabinet, which really saves space. How are you currently making coffee?" The answer will guide you to what benefits matter to this prospect and help you find out her personality style, too, if you listen carefully.

Present the widget, describe a benefit, and then ask a probing question. This simple formula works like magic. You can use it for any situation where you have a prospect's attention.

Build a Platform for Your Skills

You will need to base your skills on a couple of necessities: product knowledge and a persuasive personality. Now, don't start shuffling your feet. First of all, anyone can apply themselves to learn their products well enough to know everything prospects might ask. And yes, the sales personality thing is harder, unless you just naturally have it. But if you ground yourself in product knowledge and practice the skills that sales professionals use, you may just find yourself blooming into a sales charmer.

Base Your Skills on Product Knowledge

Make yourself an expert on the products you sell. Knowledge like this gives customers confidence both in you and in the product you know so much about. It makes you part of the value you offer and can give you a real edge over your competition.

How do you get product knowledge?

- **Ask your customers.** If they're using your products, they know what they like and don't like about them. Next time you see the coffee-maker lady, ask her how her purchase is working out. If she says, "It saves space but it drips all over the place," you've learned something important.
- **Ask your suppliers.** Study the printed literature your suppliers provide. Probe your sales reps for information. Listen to the language they use to sell these items to you. The same phrases will help you sell to your customers.
- **Study your trade sources.** Attend trade shows, join your trade association, subscribe to your industry's journals. Product knowledge is one of the main assets they have to offer.

Your job is to become the ultimate know-it-all where your products and services are concerned.

Mentor

All across America, from groceries to bookstores to hardware stores, small business people are facing competition from major chains and discount stores that offer low prices. They fight back with product knowledge and personal service.

Really!

There is a right way and a wrong way to show off a product.

To demonstrate a product effectively, handle it frequently and treat it like a star. Be an actor—project how much you like and want the product, and your audience will adopt the same attitude.

Whatever you do, don't abuse the product. It used to be popular to demonstrate durability with rough treatment, but this often backfires. You don't want to leave an impression the product is of little value.

Become Personally Persuasive

All right, I admit it. You can be a highly motivated person who believes in your product or service and still stink as a salesperson. Some people are born with persuasive sales ability. You probably remember them from your high school class—the people who were able to get their way about anything they wanted. Well, those people might very well be pursuing successful sales careers today. But what about you? Maybe you were a late bloomer? Or maybe you're one of those self-effacing types who feel uncomfortable praising yourself or voicing a strong opinion. Do a little personality weightlifting. Practice the skills top sales professionals use. You can bet a lot of them felt they couldn't sell when they started out.

Develop the Skills Professionals Use

When you're buying something, you don't want to deal with salespeople who don't have your needs in mind, and neither do your customers. When you understand what it is they're looking for, you're not going to waste their time and you're not going to waste your time either. So develop the skill of "reading" your prospects.

Sell the Way People Buy: Match Your Style to Theirs

Have you ever worked with someone who, no matter how hard you tried, just could never understand your approach to things or agree with you without a fight? You probably had mismatched personality styles. This can be worse for a salesperson than mismatched socks.

Researchers in human behavior have identified ways people act that actually create barriers to communication. You can reach across these barriers if you learn to identify other people's personality styles. Then you can choose successful ways to get your ideas across. In a management situation, this can lead to a smoother workplace. In sales, it leads to sales.

Your personality characteristics tell where you belong on this grid. Of course, not everyone is an extreme example. I find myself placing almost at dead center, and I use that to my advantage. I can adjust my style easily to sell my services—or my ideas—to all types of individuals.

Find yourself on the following table:

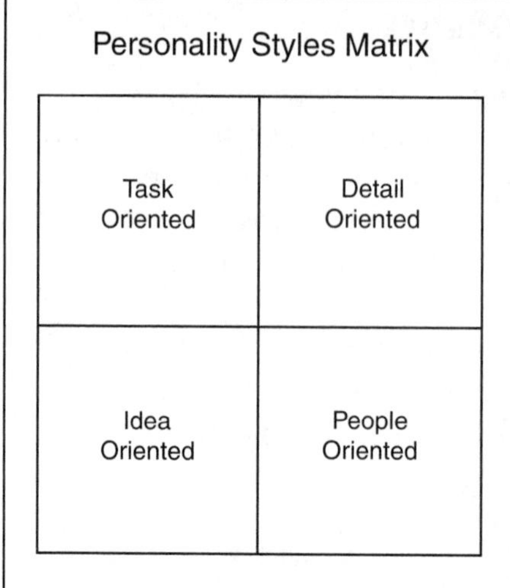

Personality styles matrix.

Personality Styles—Attributes

	Task-Oriented	Detail-Oriented	People-Oriented	Idea-Oriented
Your conversation is:	Straight to the point	Full of background	About feelings	Full of compliments
You make decisions:	Quickly	Never enough information	Consensus	Intuitive (flash)
Your strengths:	Dependable	Thorough	Team builder	Visionary
Your weaknesses:	Inflexible	Perfectionist	Never finished	Impractical

How do you find out the style of others? First, take a good look around his or her office. Look for clues like these:

Personality Styles—Decor

	Task-Oriented	Detail-Oriented	People-Oriented	Idea-Oriented
Decor:	Calendar, bulletin board	Piles: Everything is in sight	Homey: pictures, candy dish	Cluttered, especially with awards (likes recognition)

Next, mine for information that will let you place your prospects on this grid. Questions about families, hobbies, or recent changes in their business can bring out clues. Once you have a fix on the prospect, tailor your communication to their needs. This may require bending who *you* are quite a bit. Learn to be an actor—a good one. Phony salespeople are a plague on humanity.

A people person will appreciate your "just in the neighborhood" visits or an occasional invitation to lunch. Task-oriented people will appreciate it if you leave them alone but respond like lightning when they need price quotes. Even if your style makes it hard for you, adjust your approach accordingly.

Phrase your benefits in a way your prospects can relate to if you want to persuade them to buy what you're offering, be it a mail-order book or a creative idea. A detail-oriented person will be interested in dollars saved—and don't round the cents. A people-oriented person will enjoy hearing testimonial stories and will probably want to check references. An idea person will want to hear about new opportunities that this purchase will create. A task-oriented person will respond to hearing how this offering solves a problem.

Mentor

Knowledge of effective interpersonal communication will greatly improve your skills as a salesperson. Look for books on the subject or seminars you can attend.

Practice Active Listening

I have a hard time really listening to other people. My mind is always jumping ahead to what I will say next. I have to remind myself what's important instead: active listening.

Focus with empathy on your prospects' words. Ask open-ended questions, and really listen to the answers. To train yourself in this, repeat back what you are hearing, in your own words. If your prospect is saying, "I wish my copier didn't break down so often," you could say, "So you're looking for a copier that performs reliably." You are showing you understand his or her situation; you are building a bond of affirmation between you.

Make Use of People's Motivation to Buy

People make purchases when they perceive a need, have the ability to buy, and find a product that suits their expectations of function and value. In Chapter 4, you'll find a description of the purchasing process and the influences and motivations that color each exchange. Turn back to that chapter and have a look at what I said about the committee of six inside the head of every customer.

CAUTION

Pitfall

Are you selling features instead of benefits? Tape your next selling conversation, and study it. Have you fallen into the habit of talking about features, rather than probing for problems and offering solutions? Are you saying your widget features "dual wobbles" instead of saying your widget will make the sound fuller and clearer? If you want to increase your sales, focus on talking about benefits instead. Remember, this person is buying a solution to a problem—not just a product!

Sometimes you'll find buyers using rational reasons to cover basically illogical motivations to buy. "Because I like it," sounds so empty (although it's not) that many times we make up reasons to justify our actions. A woman choosing the pricier suit in a department store might insist it's because it goes with other clothes she owns—not just because she likes it. There's often a little guilt that goes with a purchase. A good salesperson will help people ease that guilt by helping them come up with good reasons this purchase is justified, such as "Because it's so well made, it will last longer."

Now You Are Ready for Advanced Skills

Okay, you know your product. You're a practiced listener and you know how to read your prospects. Confidence brims. So, plunge into the heart of the sales transaction: handling objections and closing the sale.

Overcome Objections

First, realize that not every question is an objection. On the other hand, treat each objection as a question that still hasn't been effectively addressed.

Learn to distinguish the two types of objections: product-knowledge questions and barrier-to-sale questions. The product knowledge ones are your cue to explain features and describe their related benefits. These questions are a valuable assist from your prospect and will help you make the sale.

Barrier-to-sale questions are the objections and hesitations your prospects raise. Real objections are the most interesting part of the sales process, if you're truly a motivated salesperson. Here's advice from the pros on handling objections:

- **Don't get angry.** You'll never make up the lost ground if you lose empathy with your customer.
- **Actively listen to the customer's question or concern.** Show it: Nod your head and use phrases like, "I see your point of view."
- **Clarify with questions.** Probe for the real reasons behind a customer's resistance. Break general statements into specifics that you can answer one by one.

Plenty of times in your sales career, you'll come up against tough customers—the skeptics who are never convinced or the moving targets whose needs you can never pin down. Know when to cut your losses, and end the conversation gracefully. Make sure this person walks away with a good impression of you and your offering.

Really!

The objection you're probably most worried about facing is price. When someone says, "It's just too expensive," or "I don't have that kind of money to spend," what can you say? The last thing you should do is lower your price at that moment. Instead respond by demonstrating the value delivered at that price. Explain payment terms or return on investment over the life of the product. If the price objection remains, *offer a different product* at lesser price. Never cut price on the original product. Even if you are selling services, offer a different package. Don't simply say you'll do the job for less. Once word gets out that you're negotiable on price, you'll never get top dollar again.

Closing Techniques You'll Take to the Bank

You don't want to waste your time selling to people who will not buy. We sometimes forget that the purchase exchange goes both ways: There has to be something beneficial for you in the deal, as well as something for your prospect. Answer these four questions as early as you can in the sales process. Gracefully shut the process down and get on with your life if the answer to any one question is "No."

- **Does your prospect need what you have to offer?** You can sell something for which there is no need, but later, at least one of that "committee of six" is going to be disappointed, and that will reflect on you. It is better for your long-term health not to press for this sale.
- **Is he or she the decision-maker?** You can sell to a nondecision maker, but you can't close. They can say no, but they can't say yes. Find out the decision process you're up against, and press for a meeting with the ones who can say yes.

- **Does he or she have money budgeted for this purchase?** If no money is available, you're being used. Someone is wishing for what you have but they're not going to say yes no matter what you do. Find out when money will be available—maybe next fiscal year.

- **Is he or she politically able to buy from you?** Often a deal will look good, but then at the last minute, you find out there's no hope for you. It happened to me all the time when I sold graphic design services. I'd be invited in to discuss a project because some parties in a company were frustrated with their in-house art department's capabilities. But ultimately, company policy overrides individuals' desires. I would submit my proposal, only to learn "we had to get that job done in-house."

What?

Closing means asking for a specific action on your customers' part. There are small closes, when the customer agrees with you on specific sales points, and there is the ultimate close, when the customer agrees to the purchase.

If you've ascertained that the prospect meets these four criteria, then you know it's worth your effort to work at *closing* this sale.

Closing a sale is the real test of your skill as a salesperson. To choose the right moment and the right words to say, you must be perfectly attuned to the state of mind of your customer. You must have perfect self-confidence, or the fear of failure will stop you from taking the risk. Sales requires a relentlessly positive state of mind and superb customer knowledge.

Here's how to close: Watch for the prospect to communicate strong interest through posture, facial expression, or gestures. Listen to the tone of voice in which questions are asked. Listen to the content of questions. Is the customer asking about delivery and installation? Then he has already made the purchase in his mind.

When the prospect shows signs of being ready to buy, make your move. Ask for the sale—directly or indirectly. Be very open to what happens next. If the customer raises an objection, return to your active listening mode until you've removed that concern. Then try to close again.

Here are seven tried-and-true closing techniques. Think about how these questions could be rephrased to fit your selling situation.

1. **Close on a small choice.** "Would you like that in peach or teal?" or "Would you like those by the dozen or by the case?"
2. **Close via small affirmations.** "Would you like to see a size larger? Isn't that more comfortable? Isn't the fit flattering? Would you like me to wrap it for you?"

3. **Close on a bargain opportunity.** "They're selling fast—we won't have them long at this price."
4. **Close on joining the club.** "We're selling a lot of these to people like yourself."
5. **Close on a method of payment.** "Will that be cash or charge?"
6. **Close on approval.** "Would you like to take this home and try it? We guarantee satisfaction or your money back."
7. **Close by asking for the order.** "We can begin work as soon as you sign here on the contract."

Mentor

Still not confident about closing the sale? Put the shoe on the other foot. Study the selling situations next time you go out to buy something. Analyze how salespeople lead you through the process. Learn from their examples, good or bad.

Try different closes, to see which work in your situation. It really helps to role-play with a friend or business associate. You may even want to write and rehearse a script that takes you through active listening, demonstrating the product, handling objections, and closing the sale. Not that you'll stick to the script in live selling situations, but the practice will make appropriate phrases come to mind when the situation arises.

Support After the Sale

After a sale, contact the decision maker and make sure everything is okay. This may be one of the toughest pieces of advice in this book. You absolutely have to make that post-sale satisfaction call. Resolve any doubts or misgivings if you can. Even after the sale takes place, there are still concerns for you as the salesperson. Remember that "committee of six" involved in the purchase? Two remain to be satisfied after the sale: the consumer (the one who uses the product) and the evaluator (the one who is able to say later whether the product satisfied the need).

Let's revisit the lady who bought the coffee maker that saved space but leaked on her counter. As a consumer she's less than happy, and as an evaluator she's likely to point out the

Pitfall

If you don't follow up on a sale to make sure your customer is satisfied, you're in trouble. A printer I used to know said, "I just send the boxes out the door and hope they don't explode." Heaven knows printing—a custom manufacturing process—is particularly prone to post-sale disappointment. But his approach was dead wrong, and he's not in the business today.

product's deficiencies to others, maybe even suggesting that your deficiency in product knowledge led to her bad purchase.

What should you do about it? Everything you can. Handle it like a complaint, and take action to make it work for you instead of against. Call your supplier and see if you can get some kind of "make good" for the defective coffee maker. Maybe a replacement, maybe an offer of free repair, or maybe a free supply of special coffee filters. Your effort will make the buyer feel better about you. Employ your empathy to make customers feel heard even if there's nothing you can do to resolve their complaints. Given what it costs to advertise and bring in new customers, you should realize what a valuable asset your current customers are. Your support after the sale is your insurance policy on that asset.

Remember, every company makes an occasional mistake. If your company does, admit it and then go all out to make it right. Over the long run, some of your most loyal customers are likely to be those where a mistake was made initially and then was corrected quickly and fairly.

How to Sell Services

When someone comes to you for your expertise and experience, he needs to believe that the result of your work together will be the solution for whatever problem motivated him to seek you out. To give him that belief, you need to focus on two things: the process by which you'll solve his problem and the results of that work, as tangible as you can make them.

Explain the Process

Your best approach is to demystify the process by which you do your work. When people can envision what you do (and what a pain it would be to do it themselves), they can place value on what you do.

> **What?**
>
> When you sell a custom product or service, you must define what will be delivered on each and every job. This definition of processes and outputs is called the scope of work. Once defined, it gives both client and service provider a means of verifying what's been done, what remains, and what the agreed-on budget is supposed to cover.

When I sold graphic design services, I would break the project down into steps: information gathering, concept development, and execution. I defined what inputs I would need—existing photographs, interviews with key management, or whatever. I described the process that would take place at each step. I defined the final deliverables of my work: a printed box of brochures, a graphic standards manual, or an electronic template for a catalog. Taken together, this description made up the scope of work to be performed, and that's the basis on which a customer contracted with me. This outline makes sense for any type of service. It will help you define inputs, describe process, and list outputs.

Promise Tangible Results

If you understand your customers' problems, you should have no problem phrasing tangible results you will deliver that will solve those problems. It's particularly important to be precise about what you promise to deliver. I used to get in trouble saying I would "edit copy to client's satisfaction." Now I say I will "provide one draft plus two editorial revisions."

You'll find the contracting process, and the job itself, will go much smoother if you describe any milestones, such as key approval and delivery deadlines, so that clients can tell when the work is finished. Specific language is the key to this stage of the sell. Use language to keep the prospect focused on tangible benefits.

Unlike retail selling, where hundreds of transactions might take place each day in your store, selling professional services requires pacing the prospect through several rounds of meetings and proposals and finally negotiating a contract. See Chapter 26 for a fuller discussion of this difficult task!

The Least You Need to Know

- Develop the selling approach tools (printed literature, telemarketing scripts, and so on) that you will need to get your sales work underway.
- Your success in sales will be based on your ability to balance product knowledge, empathy, and selling skills.
- Choose the right mix of selling approaches, and then tailor your activities to the personality styles of those you sell to.
- Study, practice, and rehearse your way through the selling process, from first contact to closing to support after the sale.

Chapter 26

Rainmaking: Selling for Professional Service Providers

In This Chapter

- How to generate leads and turn them into new business
- What works when it comes to presentations and proposals
- How to make you and your firm successful marketers

Skills are the sine qua non of professional services. Kai Miaka has a range of musical talents that make it possible for him to teach lessons, perform with a band, and write commercial jingles. Anita Hecht's Life History Services requires skills from interviewing to video editing to book production. To succeed, professionals like these need more than just skills in their field: They have to attract customers.

If you're a professional service provider, you have to market yourself and your business. The ideas I've been writing about all through this book will be useful to you in doing that. But to put them in context and make them even more applicable to the direct needs of professionals like you, you get a special chapter all your own.

Are You a Professional Service Provider?

In Chapter 10, I included retailers and consultants in the category of service providers. Here I'd like to focus on the professionals who negotiate a scope of work, deliver expertise, and most often rely on billable hours. This could include accountants, graphic designers, writers, lawyers, computer experts, architects, psychiatrists, and other such professionals. Of course, plumbers, house painters, electricians, and other professional tradesman could fit in this category, but they offer a mix of product and service that was well covered in Chapter 10.

The professional service provider addressed here is frequently a lone operator, but may also work for a firm of professionals.

Selling Your Services and Selling Yourself

Most professionals get started in business to practice their profession or to escape an organization that practices their profession in a way they consider ineffective. But they don't leave because they enjoy selling themselves. Some are lucky enough to work for firms that entrust marketing to a specialized staff member and have no personal responsibility for sales. But most professional service providers, and I'm in this boat, have to develop some skill at salesmanship just to stay afloat.

Really!

Going out as a lone operator requires some risk, loneliness, money worries, and confidence in the workings of good luck. There are, of course, the rewards of freedom, adventure, and independence. A friend of mine left a tenured professorship at a major university, where he taught recent American trends and literature, to venture out on his own with no real plan in mind. He was sure a new direction would reveal itself, and it did. He began offering training in creativity, trend reading, and writing. And this led him to whole new areas of income possibilities. As he learned about market needs, he found that he had expertise and skills that matched those needs. Luck and confidence served him well. Creativity, authenticity, and commitment kept him from falling into regrets.

There was a phase of my life wherein I built a graphic design and advertising practice. Once, in the early years, I picked up a book called the *A/E Handbook* that outlined selling skills for professionals. I thought "A/E" meant "Account Executive," and that meant me, so I began applying the suggestions in the book right away.

I found many of them insightful, but there was something kind of odd about the book. Two-thirds of the way through, I finally picked up on what it was. To the author, "A/E" meant "Architects and Engineers." I had been applying advice intended for a completely different industry.

The moral of this story? You guessed it. Whether you're selling architecture or advertising, legal advice or psychiatry, if you rely on billable hours for your income, there are specific techniques you should employ for marketing. To succeed, you've probably discovered you need skill in presenting yourself both in person and in writing. In fact, a weakness in either area will cost you. The strategies coming up in this chapter for generating leads will teach you the skills you need, if you adopt them. Writing an article hones your analytical, organizational, and writing skills. Public speaking and networking polish your ease of manner in presenting yourself to others. This, in turn, leads to strong relationships in your community, and that leads to a dependable stream of new business.

Pitfall

Are you intimidated by the thought of writing or public speaking? Do something about it. Don't tarnish your reputation by performing badly. Take a course in public speaking, or find a successful presenter and recruit him or her as a mentor. For writing, get yourself a reliable editor. You can then simply get your thoughts on paper, describe your audience and goals, and let the editor put it together. These are tax-deductible expenses and are well worth the investment.

Generating Leads

The following scenario is all-too-familiar to many professional service providers: A lull in your projects leads to a wild orgy of self-promotion, which results in new business. Then your efforts work *too* well, and you suffer a period of overwork. The quality of your process and your output suffers, and your hard-won clients experience disappointment. Meanwhile, you're so busy fighting fires you can't keep up with your new business efforts, and when the current clients walk out, there

Mentor

One of the best things about having prospects at every stage of development is that they help each other along. When your marketing activity is consistent, you'll be noticed. Your name will come up in conversation, and good referrals will come your way.

you are, downsized and demoralized. To avoid this ugly cycle of peaks and valleys, you need prospects at every step of development.

I wouldn't put this so strongly if it hadn't happened to me. So listen when I tell you to build marketing into every week of your professional life. This is a hard-earned lesson that most professionals try to avoid. Take it seriously.

Here's how you do it. First, study generating leads and pursue any of the techniques I'm about to present that are comfortable for you, mixing and matching to suit your situation.

Show Off in Print: Get Published

Clients hire outsiders like you because they need expertise. Demonstrate that you have it. Write articles that position you as the expert in your field or specialty.

Keep a file on topic ideas. Contact magazines that seem likely possibilities for publication and ask for their guidelines for editorial submissions. Make it part of your personal marketing plan to produce articles and place them in print.

Publishing is an oblique way to generate leads. Be certain your name and address will appear with the article. To give publishing more power as a lead-generator, end your article by offering something of value, like "Send for my free report, 'Important Facts about XYZ.'"

Show Off in Person: Be a Speaker

Speaking on a topic in public is just as big a credibility-booster as having an article in print. Identify potential audiences by searching online or asking at your library. Look at directories of associations and service clubs.

Attend a meeting or two if possible, develop your subject, and send your proposal. Include a letter explaining the subject's relevance to that group and a short summary focusing on how the audience will benefit. Also be sure to include your credentials, testifying both to your authority on the subject and your skill as a presenter.

Anita Hecht learned the hard way that targeting the right audience makes a difference. Early on, she sought speaking engagements at retirement centers—obvious places to find people at the right stage in life to be reflecting and recording memories. The engagements were easy to get, and her presentations were followed by warm complements, but the contracts for work didn't materialize. She realized she was reaching too few people who could combine an interest in her offering with an ability to pay for it. She now seeks presentations to referral sources (such as estate planners and attorneys) and to groups interested in history and likely to include affluent Baby Boomers who might become interested in contracting with her for work with their aged parents.

Once you have the gig, prepare thoroughly. Doing a bad job is worse than having done nothing in the first place. I'll leave the how-to's of public speaking to some other book, and settle for reminding you that if it's worth doing, it's worth doing right.

Mentor

Make your speaking and publishing activities work together. A speech can be recycled into an article, saving you research time and solidifying your position as the expert.

To get new business out of a public speaking engagement, make contact with your audience and sponsors. Follow up with as many people as possible with a letter. High-octane approach: Instead of giving the audience handouts, offer to mail materials to everyone who leaves you a business card.

Networking Is Better Than Not Working

Networking doesn't mean juggling soggy canapés at a business card shuffle. Proper networking means developing real relationships over time by giving real help to your network members, no strings attached. These attitudes will make you a successful networker:

- Identify network members and make a conscious effort to develop long-term relationships with them based on mutual business referrals and information sharing.
- Show your network members how your services add value to theirs. If they don't understand what you do, they can't help you. If they understand your work in terms of their own, they gain motivation to help you.
- Don't keep score. It's not tit for tat.
- Show gratitude for help you receive.
- Never break trust: Confidentiality is all-important.
- Don't begrudge time spent selling your network's services rather than your own.

Who becomes a network member? Be selective about whom you include. Are they good at what they do? Do they move in circles that are likely to produce leads for you? Would they say yes if asked these questions about you? Are they outgoing, unselfish, ethical, and involved in the community? Those are the people who make good members of a referral network.

Be prepared to drop network members who don't produce leads for you or those who call you only when they want something. If you like them, keep them as friends, but don't consider them part of your network.

Most important of all: Continue to network, even if your plate is full. A network that isn't expanding is contracting. People change jobs, leave town, retire. You must replace them.

Your business life is where you spend most of your waking hours—more (maybe much more) time than you spend with your family. Networking leads to fast friendships, one of the chief rewards of an entrepreneurial life.

Really!

Walking into a crowd of people and starting to network isn't as hard as it sounds if you can concentrate on relationships, not selling. Here's a simple routine that works. Introduce yourself to someone. Say something positive about that person's company and ask questions about things like busy seasons or growth trends. After the person responds, make comments that keep the ball rolling. Do not introduce the topic of what you do or sell, but respond if asked (and you probably will be, especially if this person is following this same formula). When the conversation lags, close it gracefully with an offer to exchange business cards. Move away and repeat the process. It works!

Position Yourself as an Expert

In addition to writing, speaking, and networking, there are other ways to help the world see you as an authority. One is to organize a seminar. These offer benefits to both you and your attendees. They get valuable information and a "free sample" of you.

Choose a workable topic, along the lines of "How to …" or "What You Need to Know About …." Choose something you can create a certain feel of urgency about. Be prepared to invest in making your seminar authentic, well-coordinated, useful, and polished.

Plan to fill about two hours, and start either early morning or late afternoon. Be sure to include a refreshment break so there's a slot for networking to take place. Put together a flyer that covers who should attend, a benefit-oriented description of the program, a schedule, and background on the speaker(s). Include logistics like place, registration fees, accommodations, parking, and a registration form.

Mentor

Online seminars ("webinars" some call them) offer a great way to give presentations without the time and expense—for you or your audience—that traditional seminars require. Your participants don't have to travel to your seminar location, so you've saved them time, and you don't have to feed them snacks or rent a meeting room—savings for you. Send a postcard invitation, hang a landing page out on the Internet with more information about the event, and even include e-commerce to accept registrations if you feel like it.

Before your first seminar, get nervous. You must get everything right—from a good prospect list to tasty snacks—to make this technique work for you. Take the logistics as seriously as the subject matter. This technique requires a lot of preparation, at least the first few times, but when done well, I've seen it reap spectacular results for many professionals. It's a perennial.

If you follow even a few of these suggestions, you will soon find yourself moving closer to working relationships with prospects you've met. You will then be asked to present yourself to potential clients in a way that will persuade them to entrust their projects to you. Traditional selling techniques must be modified. It's not time for selling: It's time for persuasion.

Pitfall

Don't try to carry the show if you don't carry any weight! If you're not comfortable presenting solo, or you're simply too early in your career to pass as an expert, assemble a panel discussion and bring in the heaviest hitters you know. Your role as moderator and producer of the event will give you a boost.

Persuading Without Selling: Your Presentation and Your Proposal

For most of us in professional services, our opportunities to persuade are twofold. We are usually asked to make our "pitch" both in person and in writing. A presentation and a proposal make up the two halves of our selling effort.

Presenting: Handling a New-Business Meeting

Plan your presentation from the prospect's point of view. You may want to review the skills of salesmanship in Chapter 25, especially active listening. The following are some tips on what to say:

- Use examples as you talk to make your ideas more tangible.
- Find out your prospects' objectives and link your services to their goals.
- Create an emotional bond. Encourage prospects to feel you're already on their team.

What?

The first time I heard the phrase **new-business meeting,** I thought it was silly. We're talking about a sale presentation here, a pitch, a dog and pony show. But, because "selling" is practically a dirty word in some circles, when a business seeks a professional service and schedules interviews with each potential supplier of that service, we call those interviews new-business meetings.

As you prepare for the *new-business meeting*, review your positioning. Your prospect is probably meeting with several firms, and the presentations will blur together. Make yours stand out by reinforcing your brand identity.

It might help you to think of yourself as an actor auditioning for a role. Project enthusiasm, sincerity, listening ability, confidence, subject knowledge, and an open mind. Use good props: Design your portfolio, PowerPoint presentations, or slides, handouts, and even your wardrobe to support the can-do image you're after.

The other half of the persuasion equation is the written proposal. In many types of professional practice, especially those of a consulting nature, your potential clients screen candidates by requesting detailed written proposals.

Writing a Proper Proposal

A written proposal isn't a test: It's an opportunity for you to capture your persuasive skills in writing. It helps your prospects stay persuaded of the points you've made in your presentation. It helps to sell yourself to other decision makers in the firm who haven't met you in person. Use this checklist to make sure your proposal is complete.

Complete Proposal Checklist

The proposal itself should be organized as follows:

Begin with a cover letter (either bound as first page of the proposal, or attached to the cover)

Follow with an executive summary (not more than three paragraphs)

State your understanding of the problem

Describe "deliverables," stressing benefits to the client

Describe the process that will result in those benefits

Spell out schedule and milestones by which progress will be measured

State fees and price structures

Explain payment terms and conditions

Describe the contract or letter of agreement that will initiate the job

Provide background on the firm

List credentials of key personnel

If the prospects have requested a certain format and organization for the proposal in their request for proposal (*RFP*), follow it. No variations. If they say they want three-ring binders and tab dividers, do it. If they say Question 1a. should cover your relevant capabilities, make sure you do exactly that—especially if you're dealing with engineers or the government. Trust me on this.

What?

RFP stands for Request for Proposal. In many industries, like construction and engineering, almost all projects are awarded on the basis of RFPs. Follow the instructions in detail.

And a last few words of advice: Take the effort to make your proposal a good piece of publishing. Design the pages to be visually appealing. Use simple language. Our instinct is to write inflated, passive bureaucratese when the stakes are high. Resist. Edit your first draft or hire a good editor, and look for ways to tighten and lighten the language.

Can We Talk About Money?

A proposal often doubles as a contract when it is accompanied by a signed letter of agreement that basically says, "I agree to everything spelled out in this proposal."

Your pricing strategy dictates the price you put on your services and how firm or negotiable that price will be. Review Chapter 12 for a full discussion of price issues.

There are really no hard and fast rules on how service professionals should set prices. It depends a great deal on your target, their expectations, market norms, and the perceived value of your services. Many maintain that you should set a price and not vary to meet the paying ability of your clients. Others recommend the exact opposite. Consider the norms in your profession as you decide where you stand on this issue.

Remember Anita Hecht and her solo service Life History Services. She is perceived as a valuable resource. She has good word of mouth. The cost of her services can be high, so she guards against disappointing potential clients of modest means by targeting only those whom she has reason to believe can afford it. She offers excellent quality and wonderful service. She uses the same price structure for all her clients. Since she seeks work by referral, a consistent price structure is important. Word gets around.

Some professionals, like our friend Kai Miaka the musician, do need to vary their prices. In Kai's case, because his band plays a variety of venues, he pretty much has to know the norms of the places he plays to know where his price will stand in his client's payment structure.

> **Mentor**
>
> When can you set your fee higher? You can ask a higher fee if you've nurtured a contact over some time, and the prospective client is in a hierarchical organization. The higher the position of the person you're selling to in the organization, the higher the fee you can ask. Press for a meeting early on with the highest level you can get access to, and make that person your ally.

> **Pitfall**
>
> Submitting your proposal without an in-person presentation is more likely to fall flat. If you can't be there in person, schedule an online meeting (I like www.placeware.com for these) or at the very least a conference call.

And a massage therapist I know varies her fee based on what her clients can afford. She sets the upper and lower fee limits and lets her clients pay on a sliding scale. She reports that it has helped earn her a loyal clientele. She also feels people honestly pay what they can within her limits.

An important question is: How do you present your prices when you're selling your services? An hourly rate doesn't tell a client how much the job is going to cost. A project fee without a complete description of process doesn't give a client any way to judge value. Obviously, how prices are presented is as important as the question, "How much?"

It's often a good idea to find out the prospect's fee expectations. Questions like "Have you ever commissioned a project like this before?," "What benefits are you expecting?," and "Why now?" give you clues to the value and urgency of the project and the prospect's familiarity with pricing.

Don't quote fees sooner than you have to, and when you do, do it in person. This is a difficult piece of advice! You probably don't like talking about money any more than the rest of us. But people are less likely to balk at your price while under the full influence of your persuasive presence.

Oh No! You Didn't Get the Job!

Too bad. Do you close the file and move on? Absolutely not! The ones you lose can provide more valuable information than the ones you win. Ask for a critique of your proposal. But news flash: Don't just start asking the person who called you with the bad news what was wrong. That phone call is as uncomfortable for him to make as it is for you to take, so respect his mental state. Respond with something like, "I'm disappointed, but I hope it works out well for you with the firm you've chosen. Could I ask a favor at this point? Understanding your decision could help us gain something from the time and resources we invested in the proposal. Could you meet with me for few minutes so I could ask some questions?" Press for a short meeting soon, rather than launching into your debriefing questions on the phone.

There are two key messages in what I just said. One is, "Ask a favor." You are subtly reminding the caller that you two have developed a relationship during the proposal process. The second message is, "Time and resources we invested." You are introducing the guilt factor, reminding the caller that their firm owes you something for your trouble, and it would be boorish to refuse your request.

When you get the meeting, this is what you want to ask:

- "Why did you select the other firm?" (What criteria were crucial in the decision?)
- "What impressed you about them during the proposal process?" (What can you learn from your competitor's salesmanship?)

Ask your ex-prospect to critique your sales presentation. Then review, section by section, their reactions to your written proposal. When you get to "fees," you'll find out whether price was the deciding factor. Probe for influences on the purchase decision. How has this person perceived your brand identity and your value proposition? Ask for comments on any visual aids or printed materials you've used. Are they helping or hindering?

> CAUTION
>
> **Pitfall**
>
> Don't believe what you're told—at least by the person who calls to give you the bad news. The caller wants to get this over with as quickly as possible. He doesn't want an argument, and he doesn't want to embarrass you. He may not even know the real reasons for the decision. So don't take what he says too seriously. Instead, press for a meeting.

Throughout the meeting, be brief and diplomatic—never disagree or contradict what you are told, even if they're just plain wrong. Take notes, and review what you learned with others at your firm. Be sure to send a thank-you letter showing your appreciation for the time. Now you can file that one and move on.

Selling Strategies for the Professional Service Provider

There are two ways to approach selling your services: marketing you, and marketing your firm. Which is right for you? Unless you are a lone operator, you'll probably use a balanced strategy including both.

Self-Marketing

Your professional reputation will follow you as you move from firm to firm or client to client. It pays to develop a self-marketing plan early in your career. Think for a moment about who your customers are. If you work in a professional firm, include the higher-ups in your firm as customers. For your career advancement, you need to impress them just as you do prospects outside the firm. Networking, publishing, and public speaking can work to increase your value to your current employer or to prospective clients if you're a lone operator.

> **Mentor**
>
> Balance your billable time with marketing time. Plan on 5 to 25 percent of any week going toward marketing. Being too busy with billable work is as dangerous as being non-billable. If you're always busy working, you're not out there maintaining your network, writing your articles, and hosting your seminars. You're invisible except to current clients, which means outside forces could rob you of your seeming success.

Your self-marketing plan begins with assessing your skills, experience, and training. Make lists of your assets in each area; these are your credentials. How can you leverage these credentials to position yourself successfully? (The principles of positioning apply to self-marketing, of course. Go back to Chapter 16 to brush up on positioning.) Follow the techniques for generating leads discussed earlier in this chapter. Again, be sure your prospect list includes the principals in the firm you now work for, and firms where you might like to work someday. And if you're the kind of self-starter who is or will be entrepreneurial, take heed! Self-marketing is crucial to the success of the self-employed!

Marketing the Firm

Make your firm shine, and the light will reflect on you. Time spent selling in the name of your bosses and associates is a good investment. The strategy you choose to pursue will be some combination of the techniques discussed earlier: publishing, public speaking, networking, hosting seminars, and getting quoted in the press.

You could choose to emphasize one technique over another, depending on your personal strengths, the philosophy of your firm, and the nature of the competition. You might emphasize networking, for example, laying the groundwork for relationships that will produce results for years. Or you might emphasize seminars, involving others in your firm as panelists, to spread your marketing halo over your co-workers. Your effort builds the reputation of the firm as a whole.

A Source of New Customers: Your Existing Clients

One marketing strategy not to be overlooked: Mine your existing clients as a source of new business! When your business works with clients on an ongoing basis, you don't have to think about asking current clients for new projects. But take a business like Anita's. If she does a life history book for an individual, that person is likely to think of it as "one per customer." The burden is on Anita to call from time to time, to remind that individual of other services, like commemorative books for important anniversaries or birthdays, or to suggest making a video as a companion to the completed book. She might also ask for referrals, or suggest a package of books about memories of each of that client's children.

You get the idea. Just as we all start as actors auditioning for the part, once we get the job, we're in danger of being typecast. Clients are more likely to send opportunity your way if you remember to ask for it.

Packaging Yourself

You can't use an unprofessional package to sell yourself as a professional or to sell a professional firm. That means your brochures, your presentation visuals, your office environment, and even your car all have to send the proper message about you and your firm. You must above all appear successful. That doesn't mean everything has to be lavishly expensive—although we do expect quality to come at a price! I mean most specifically: nothing outdated, nothing worn or shabby, nothing thrown-together-looking can be associated with you or your firm. Know your business environment well enough to know what is considered a successful appearance. That will be quite different for a tattoo artist and an attorney.

Proposals must be well-written, graphically pleasing, and professionally reproduced with the appropriate tabs, binding, and cover pages. Websites are increasingly being used to present proposals. Presentation graphics must follow conventions of legibility, good labeling, and clarity in reproduction. Hire a graphics professional to help you—don't chip around. As to your personnel, their style of dress, and so on, you be the judge of what's acceptable to your prospective clients.

Be aware of a psychological factor at play here called "matching." People like to do business with people who are somewhat like themselves. A CEO likes to deal with someone on a CEO level at your firm. This principle extends to the behavior and image you project. If employees of the client firm dress conservatively, you should, too. If their style is to talk socially for a few minutes before beginning the meat of a meeting, join in—don't tap your pencil and glance at your watch. Use your sales skills to match your prospective clients, and you'll quickly build a relationship of confidence and trust.

The Least You Need to Know

- The goal of marketing professional services is to develop skills that make it easy for you to maintain an ongoing marketing effort that takes on average from 5 to 25 percent of your time.
- Marketing a professional service means keeping leads moving down the pipeline toward signed contracts by balancing the time you spend marketing between developing leads and developing clients.
- How you persuade clients to favor you with their projects is a combination of your presentation in person and in writing.
- When you market, you're selling both yourself and your firm, so don't downplay selling the firm in favor of selling yourself. It won't take anything away from your personal success and can lead to good things down the road.

Part 6

Building Your Marketing Plan

You take on a lot of responsibility when you take on the role of "marketing manager." In fact, I know your head must be spinning with all that we've covered so far. There's just one more step to go. Get your marketing plan down in writing.

Begin with a business review and you're halfway done. Follow my suggestions for writing a marketing plan and you're nearly there. Think you're done? Sorry. Marketing, like doing the dishes, is never done. Which is actually a good thing. Why would we want to work ourselves out of such a fun job?

Chapter 27

Getting to Know Yourself: The Business Review

In This Chapter

- Why you need a business review
- What comprises the business review (hint: your "Five Ps" are involved)
- Applying the business review technique to your operation

The business review is a standard tool in anybody's marketing starter-kit. You'll find the same basic questions in most marketing textbooks, usually presented under such electrifying titles as "Internal Marketing Needs Assessment."

I've spent much of past two decades helping businesses improve their advertising and marketing methods. As I've met with businesses and assessed their needs, I've developed my own version of the business review. It changed a lot in the early years and then settled down into the outline you'll find in this chapter.

> **Mentor**
>
> How you respond to the business review is up to you. You can write essays, jot notes, or just think a bit about each one. However, you might want to choose the essay approach if your intention is to write a complete business plan. After all, sometimes you don't know what you know until you take time to write it down.

Reviewing Your Business

In this chapter, I'll provide you with the tools and concepts you need to perform your own business review. Notice that a blank worksheet is provided at the end of the chapter for you to fill in. To prepare you for that task, let's go through the review section by section, first discussing what's involved and then looking over the shoulder of an example business.

Remember how on *Dragnet* Joe Friday would always say, "Just the facts, ma'am?" That's where we begin.

Who You Are and What You Do

Each company is unique in its history, organizational structure, outputs, and goals. Defining these helps us all "get on the same page" as we begin our quest to understand a business. In this section, you'll recap your business's origin and describe where you are today concerning your product offerings and place/distribution issues.

Start Out with the Basics

To start out slow and easy, begin with the questions that describe a business the way a census-taker might. Only one question here is not demographically oriented. That's the one about your mission and vision. *Mission* reflects what problems your company helps your customers solve—what benefits you deliver to them. *Vision* is where you see your company being in, say, five years. It's a very good idea to have a mission and vision because they explain the purpose of your business and give direction for the future.

> **What?**
>
> When you talk about your business's **mission**, you mean its raison d'être: what it was put in the world to do for people. Your **vision**, on the other hand, has to do with your long-term objectives for the business (that is, where it's headed).

Summarize the following information in a paragraph or two:

- Year established
- Mission/vision
- Major milestones (incorporations, product launches, and so on)
- Number of employees

- Growth pattern
- Approximate annual sales today

In Chapter 9, I introduced you to Charlee Bear Farms, a business with one core product: an all-natural dog treat. In this chapter, we'll use Charlee Bear Farms as an example as we conduct a business review.

I interviewed Charlee Bear Farms' president Fritz Findley in the summer of 1996; this review is based on his description of the exciting growth Charlee Bear was experiencing. (At the end of this chapter, I'll reveal what happened next.)

The Basics of Charlee Bear Farms

Charlee Bear Farms (CBF) began operations in 1991, the brainchild of product developer and dog lover Steve Brown. Steve teamed up with Ava Olsen, who brought her background in art and marketing to the mix.

The company's mission: Enhance the bond between dogs and their owners by providing nutritious dog snacks. Its vision: Have national distribution of its products by 1998 and to be considered the leader in its market niche. Its success in those early years lead to phenomenal growth. The company projected sales of over $2 million for the end of its fifth year.

Reflecting On the Marketing Mix

To do a thorough business review, we'll look at each of the Four Ps of the marketing mix: Product, Place, Price, and Promotion. We'll also devote plenty of attention to that Fifth P I like to talk about: "People."

Maximizing your opportunities concerning each of these Ps is the prime function of marketing. As I said in Chapter 3, marketing involves a complex set of interdependent activities. We use the "Four Ps" to break that set of activities into components we can study. How you bring those components together is a recipe you'll continue to tinker with as your situation evolves.

Which Widget? Product Issues

Product issues—everybody's got them, even if you sell a service or simply promote a concept. Understanding what your company sells can help you identify problems and opportunities. You should be able to answer the following questions without doing any special research:

- What do you sell? (Describe physical characteristics.)
- What makes it unique/better than similar offerings?
- Where are your products in their life cycle?
- Do you have new products in the pipeline?
- How is your product packaged?

Many great product ideas come from individuals who discover a need for something that hasn't yet been brought to market by anyone else; Charlee Bear treats fit that description. A dog breeder and trainer developed this dog snack because others on the market were too big and too calorific for the frequent treating that training requires.

The Charlee Bear Product

Charlee Bear Farms produces one product: a dog snack that's not only made of healthy all-natural ingredients, but is sized small enough to use often without fattening your pet. This makes it a perfect training treat. (There's a whole science behind this called behavioral modification; it centers on doling out reinforcements every time the trainee performs the right behavior.)

Fritz Findley explained, "As people are more mindful of what they're eating themselves, they mimic their feeding patterns in their dogs."

Mentor

When your product is a service, the widget takes a little deeper reflection. Thinking about the attributes of services as if they were products can lead to interesting insights. In doing this, consider the benefits being offered and the problems being solved. This can even help you come up with ways to enhance service.

As soon as the product was launched, Charlee Bear Treats were eagerly adopted by pet owners and trainers. The treats showed potential to become a perennial strong seller for the company. The company has explored expanding into other pet products or a line extension, but is loath to leave behind its strong positioning as the makers of the tiny "pocket-perfect™" treat.

The packaging of Charlee Bear treats—in small bags and larger canisters—helps position the brand by showing clearly what's unique about the treats. A newsletter inside each package encourages customers to communicate with the company.

Where You Are: Place Issues

Place issues may be location issues or may be distribution issues. Like product knowledge, understanding how location and distribution affect you can help you identify problems and opportunities.

- Where is your product sold?
- What logistics affect distribution, like transportation and warehousing?
- What value does your location or distribution systems add to the product?

Place for Charlee Bear

For Charlee Bear Farms (CBF), the "Place" issue starts with manufacturing and ends with real estate: shelf space in grocery and pet supply stores. The treats are made under contract by a commercial pet food manufacturer. They are then shipped to a second supplier, inventoried, and distributed to the national chains' distribution centers. To reach other outlets, orders are packaged and shipped using over-the-road haulers.

Another stroke of Charlee Bear brilliance: The company discovered a creative distribution opportunity. CBF made a deal with a distributor of snack foods—people snacks, that is. CBF showed the distributor the advantages of reaching out into this new category with a high-margin product. This deal benefits both parties and allows CBF to avoid the high fees grocery brokers charge for shelf space. It also multiplies CBF's sales force many times over, as the snack distributors promote CBF's product.

Creating Value: Price Issues

Most purchasers (regardless of whether they are consumers or business buyers) are looking for an appropriate mix of the components that make up the Customer Value Pyramid. These are product quality, service quality, and reasonable price (value in relation to product and service quality). The value purchasers place on an offering—whether they consider it a good buy at the price it is offered—depends on how each of these components meets or exceeds their expectations. To summarize your pricing strategy for your business review, ask yourself these questions:

- How do you set your prices?
- How does price influence customers' perception of your offering's value?

Price for Charlee Bear

Gourmet/health food for pets is a niche that's still relatively new. There is little direct price competition, although the company learned quickly that people start to balk at purchasing pet-related indulgences when the price tag goes over $3. Charlee Bear's price is comparable by weight with other premium dog snacks. The fact that each individual treat is smaller than others on the market means that in a very real way, customers get more for their money. Combine this with the attention to nutritious ingredients and customer care (through encouraging feedback), and you'll find Charlee Bear Farms' product is an excellent value.

People: Know the Pack You Run With

You don't have to be the alpha wolf to know you have a place in the pack. In this section of the business review, we study the customers, competitors, employees, and suppliers who make up the environment in which you do business.

Really!

You'd like to think that whether you succeed or fail in business depends on how good you are, how apt at strategy, clever at finances, or creative at marketing. But who you are is only half the equation. The people with whom you do business are at least as important as the business you do.

Who your customers, competitors, employees, and suppliers are—their needs, desires, plans, and aspirations—influences you every moment of every day. What do you really know about these "business partners" of yours?

Customers: Who Are They and What Do They Want?

Summarize what you know today about your customers.

- Who comprises your primary target market niches? Secondary targets?
- What problems are you helping them solve?
- Describe the buying exchange. (We talked about this concept in Chapter 4.)
- How do your distribution channels figure as customers?
- What market research techniques do you use to learn about competitors, customers, and industry trends?

Charlee Bear's Customers

Of course, the real targets for Charlee Bear Treats are the dogs! But because dogs don't carry wallets, CBF concentrates on reaching their owners and especially the people who influence their owners' decisions. Dog trainers are a very important customer segment to CBF.

CBF exploits the fact that, just as we take our doctor's advice about what we need, we take our trainer's advice about what our dogs need. Free samples to vets and trainers have resulted in an enthusiastic customer base.

One key to the CBF success, I believe, is their understanding of the importance of distribution channels. The company concentrates on building relationships with customers at each step along the way, using both "push" and "pull" marketing strategies.

For customer knowledge, CBF relies on sales reports from their retailers to understand what products are moving where and why. From these reports, the staff can learn about usage rates, geographic distribution of their customer base, market penetration, and more. Contact with the end users (encouraged by the little newsletter in the package) fills in the details of the customer picture.

Mentor

"Primary and secondary targets" sounds like you're planning to drop bombs over your buyers. Don't be frightened by the military metaphors that lurk in marketing. Primary Targets are the good customers you already have and the people just like them you are hoping to find. Secondary targets are—you guessed it—purchasers without the clout of primary targets, but still worthy of your attention.

Your Competitive Environment

You probably have a good feel for the competitive environment just by going on gut instinct alone; most entrepreneurs do. Still, disciplined research can confirm those hunches or uncover new opportunities that give you a competitive advantage.

- What's your *market share?*
- What sort of competition do you face? Heavy/light?
- How do you keep up on what your competition is doing?

What?

Market share is a fancy way of asking, "If the dollars spent in your market purchasing things you sell could be seen as a pie, how big is the slice you're eating?" Typically, market share is expressed as a percentage of a total. Knowing your share, and that of your competitors, helps you design effective marketing strategies in response.

Charlee Bear's Competitors

Today, CBF has a little less than one half of 1 percent of the dog treat market, with a future target share of 4 percent. There is really no competition as yet, but the company is always vulnerable to a me-too knock-off when the "big boys" see the success of this product. CBF relies on relationships with industry insiders to provide information on its competitors' moves.

Promotions' Place in the Mix

The Promotion "P" is all about helping prospects realize a need and then becoming the one those prospects choose over other similar offerings when they set out to fill that need. Three types of activities come under the heading of Promotion: advertising, selling, and sales promotions. A quick summary of activities or plans in each area belongs in the business review.

Advertising: Getting the Word Out

You need to review what you're doing to get the word out about your offerings.

- What's your current media plan? (What?/Where?/When?)
- What's the goal of your current advertising?
- What's your advertising budget?
- How do you test or measure results of advertising?

Advertising at Charlee Bear

Charlee Bear Farms has found that mass-media advertising doesn't make sense. The company doesn't have the buying power of the national big-name brands, and its strategy points a different direction anyway. Its entire marketing activity goes toward developing relationships with distribution channels and influencers like trainers and veterinarians.

With no advertising budget, there is nothing to test or measure, but growth in sales revenues would indicate its strategy is working.

Sales Activity

"Nothing happens until somebody makes a sale," salespeople like to say (especially when they're fighting the advertising folks for a piece of the budget). Sales activity focuses on creating buying exchanges. Salespeople use an array of selling approach tools, including cold-calling, personal letters, telemarketing, and in-person sales.

- What is the role of sales in your organization?
- What kind of sales staff do you have, and how do they do their jobs?
- What selling approach tools do you use?

Sales Activities at Charlee Bear

The Charlee Bear operation is a small and efficient one—partly because, rather than employing a number of sales representatives, the company leverages its distribution strategy to fill this function. The sales staff at CBF consists of two people who spend a lot of time traveling and motivating store buyers. The distribution arrangement with a (people) snack food distributor carries most of the burden of sales for CBF.

Other Promotions

Promotions is a slippery word. Depending on the context, it might be referring to advertising, selling, or the use of incentives to stimulate short-term sales. Other activities, like getting stories about your activities in the press, can be lumped into this catch-all as well.

Answer this grab-bag of questions, and you're almost done with your business review:

- Do you use sales promotions, like coupons and so on?
- Do you go to trade shows?
- Do you pursue any public relations activity?

Charlee Bear's Other Promotions

Everything CBF does is geared to relationship marketing. When they use sales promotions, that's the approach they take. They've used coupons occasionally, but as a way to convince retailers CBF supports its products, not because they need a sales incentive. Special events figure, too, with appearances by founder Steve Brown and senior business dog Zach.

The people who do sales work for CBF don't go to trade shows; instead, they pursue another avenue unique to their industry—dog shows. Handing out free samples at these events has been an extremely effective promotional technique.

Because of the unique nature of the company and its product, getting coverage in the press has never been a problem for Charlee Bear Farms. Zach is an excellent on-camera talent; besides, what news crew could resist footage of a fuzzy black dog with the biggest brown eyes you ever saw? The clippings and light news footage that CBF has accumulated serve as a testimonial to the company's savvy in handling an interested press.

Conclusions and Observations

Many small businesses get interested in marketing activities as a result of a problem, like declining sales or the inroads of a competitor on their turf. Of course, there are some, like Charlee Bear, that take a more proactive approach. Whichever is true for you, describe it now. These will be the last entries in your business review.

- What negative consequence might result if no marketing action is taken?
- What opportunity could be exploited if action is taken?

Charlee Bear Farms' Conclusions and Observations

Several issues loom large when Charlee Bear Farms thinks about next steps. Whether these issues' effects turn out to be positive or negative will depend on how CBF faces these challenges.

One issue that has surfaced centers on distributors who are making suggestions about new products they'd like to see from CBF. This could turn into a classic case of the tail wagging the dog, pulling CBF away from its focused niche.

Another threat may be approaching in the form of me-too introductions from other manufacturers. CBF refuses to worry about this, relying on the marketing wisdom that it's "better to be first than best." Not that CBF feels anyone could make a better treat than the Charlee Bear cracker, but its prominence as first on the block gives it a nearly unbeatable market position.

For CBF, the real opportunity for new growth lies in exploiting the brand image it has already developed. CBF recognizes the opportunity to be exploited by line extension, a technique of using existing products as a springboard to new related offerings. Whether CBF goes this route remains to be seen.

Charlee Bear Farms: The Story Continues

As that interview with Fritz Findley back in 1996 drew to a close, I thanked him and switched off my little tape recorder. Then he leaned toward me and made one last comment. "The marketing side of Charlee Bear is interesting, but the real story here is financial. Too bad I can't talk about that."

I've seen rapid growth kill a successful business more than once, and I assumed he was alluding to the cash-flow problems of scaling up to meet the product demand CBF had created. As it turned out, my guess was right on the money. The original Charlee Bear Farms went out of business several years after that interview. The product line was purchased by Wixon Fontarome.

Charlee Bear treats are still on the shelf at my pet store (and yours, too, I hope.) Why? Because, with its carefully chosen guerilla marketing techniques, Charlee Bear Farms had built a customer base so loyal they would not let their preferred dog treat go away! That loyalty represented a salable asset.

Charlee Bear treats are still around because of a strong customer base and brand image built in those start-up years. The company now goes by the name of Charlee Bear Products and continues to be managed and marketed by founding partner Ava Olsen. Charlee Bear treats will (I hope) continue to be available as long as good dogs need rewards.

Applying the Business Review to Your Business

What have we learned from Charlee Bear Farms' example? You may have taken many lessons from this exercise, from the importance of distribution channels to a new way to train your dog. I hope you've learned how to apply the business review technique to your business.

Fill in the following business review questionnaire. As I said at the beginning, let anything that is difficult for you to answer be your guide to what to study next. The whole point of this book is to help you use this tool to improve your marketing.

"Now what am I doing this for?" I hear you thinking. "Why the exercise in stating the obvious?" The purpose of the business review is to provide background for subsequent marketing decisions. Take my word for it; you'll make better decisions if you can systematically review all the known facts from time to time. Do the exercise, and update it every year, or as your situation changes.

Business Review for ________________

Who You Are and What You Do

The Basics

- Year established
- Mission/vision
- Major milestones (incorporations, product launches, and so on)
- Number of employees
- Growth pattern
- Approximate annual sales today

Product Issues

- What do you sell? (Describe physical characteristics.)
- What makes it unique/better than similar offerings?
- Where are your products in their life cycle?
- Do you have new products in the pipeline?
- How is your product packaged?

Place Issues

- Where is your product sold?
- What logistics affect your distribution, like transportation and warehousing?
- What value does your distribution strategy add to the product?

People in Your Marketing Environment

Customers: Who Are They, What Do They Want?

- Who comprises your primary target market niches? Secondary targets?
- What problems are you helping them solve?

- Describe the buying exchange.
- How do your distribution channels figure as customers?
- What market research techniques do you use to learn about competitors, customers, and industry trends?

Your Competitive Environment

- What's your market share?
- What sort of competition do you face? Heavy? Light?
- How do you keep up on what your competition is doing?

Promotions

Advertising Activity

- What's your current media plan?
- What is the goal of your current advertising?
- What is your advertising budget?
- How do you test or measure results of advertising?

Sales

- What is the role of sales in your organization?
- What kind of sales staff do you have, and how do they do their jobs?
- What selling approach tools do you use?

Other Promotions

- Do you use sales promotions?
- Do you go to trade shows?
- Do you pursue any public relations activity?

continues

continued

Conclusions and Observations

- What negative consequence might result if no marketing action is taken?
- What opportunity could be exploited if action is taken?

The Least You Need to Know

- You need a business review to provide background for marketing decisions.
- The business review covers who you are and what you do, using the marketing mix's Four Ps plus the unofficial "Fifth P," People.
- By applying the business review technique, you discover possible directions you might take in the future.

Chapter 28

The Best-Laid Plans Are Written Down

In This Chapter

- What a marketing plan is and why you need one
- What topics a marketing plan will cover
- How to use the worksheets throughout this book to build your plan
- Tracking the effectiveness of your marketing plan
- Tips for documenting the plan in writing

It's easy for consultants like me to say you need a written marketing plan. We're the same people who tell you to document your employee procedures and keep your disaster plan up-to-date as well. You devote time to all these things, but you probably don't ever feel like you're finished.

The truth is, any kind of planning work is never done. But that doesn't mean you should put off starting. Once you get started, planning is a process that just keeps rolling along. Look at the arguments that follow in support of the written marketing plan. I'll know I've succeeded at my objective if I motivate you to start working on one of your own.

First Things First: Why Plan?

Why a marketing plan? What will it do for you? First, it will help you focus on overall business strategies. It's only logical to check your overall objectives whenever you want to start something new in your business. Doing a marketing plan has a freshening effect.

Second, when it's time to bring others in on your marketing activities, a marketing plan is the best way to help them find their roles. Send your plan home with your copywriter, and you'll get him up to speed in days, not weeks. Study it yourself when you need to switch into marketing high gear.

Third, a marketing plan is good for justifying expenses. It helps present your financial decision maker with a rationale explaining the dollars and other resources needed to get your job done. With a marketing plan you'll find it easier to get the resources you need. This advice applies even if you work for yourself: You know how tough it is to justify expenditures out of your own pocket.

Mentor

Having a marketing plan will keep you from making rash or impulsive decisions. You don't have to stick to it rigidly but it does give you a baseline that's been thought out by an expert on your business—you. Measure any emerging opportunities against your marketing plan.

A marketing plan helps define and organize your marketing functions. But just as critical as the planning and doing is the tallying after. How did your marketing activity pay off? I don't mean to suggest you can calculate exact gains derived from advertising or measure audience-perception shifts as precisely as units of production. Still, like humankind ever striving upward, you have to try. You take risks as you try different activities. You need to know what's in it for you. Are you finding and keeping customers?

Quiz: Do You Need to Write a Marketing Plan?

Do you need to write a marketing plan? Check those statements that apply to your situation.

- ❑ There is more than one person in your marketing department.
- ❑ The manager you report to likes written documentation.
- ❑ You are not getting the budget you feel is necessary to achieve what you'd like.

- ❑ You haven't thought much about your core products or current marketplace circumstances in a while.
- ❑ You are thinking about targeting multiple market niches.
- ❑ You have other job responsibilities besides marketing.
- ❑ You are often pressured to make hasty decisions about marketing.
- ❑ You have aspirations of getting promoted to a higher position in your current firm or elsewhere.

Score:

To find your score, give yourself one point for each box you checked.

1–3: A written plan would help, but is not critical.

4–6: A written plan is strongly indicated.

7–8: Get started documenting your plan in writing today.

The Marketing Plan Outline

If I've convinced you that a plan is needed, by now you're probably wondering, "What does one look like?" That's surprisingly hard to answer because each marketing plan is as distinctive as the business it's written for. A complete marketing plan will include some or all of these topics:

- **Objectives.** What do you intend this marketing program to accomplish?
- **Situation analysis.** What are the special circumstances of your organization, your offering, and your business environment? What are your special strengths and weaknesses?
- **Marketplace issues.** What's going on with your customers, competitors, and industry trends? Review any threats or opportunities relating to marketplace issues.
- **Strategies.** Introduce your strategic initiative(s) and explain how these will accomplish your objectives.
- **Implementation plans.** Describe the tactics you've chosen and any goals or milestones you expect them to meet. In a detailed marketing plan, each tactic

will be plotted out to include special promotions, an advertising plan, selling strategies, budgets, and timelines.

- **Measures of effectiveness.** No plan is complete without projections of results against which actual performance can be measured.

Don't be scared away from the planning process by the unfamiliarity of the terrain. Take a deep breath and get over it. Each part of this book fills in some of the perspective you need for successful marketing. After reading this book, you should find it reasonably easy to transform your notes and thoughts into a simple, practical, and achievable marketing plan. The rest of this chapter will follow this marketing plan outline as we look closer at each component of it.

In Appendix A of this book, you will find a Marketing Plan for Bob's Bottomless Boats. This is an informal plan prepared for internal review; it includes many of the components we'll talk about in this chapter.

CAUTION

Pitfall

Writing a marketing plan may sound like too much work, but look at what happens if you don't. It's harder to learn from each experience as you progress without before-and-after notes to compare. You'll lose valuable perspective if your advisors misunderstand things that a marketing plan would make clear. You'll forget your objectives and make impulsive decisions. Wouldn't it be wiser to do what it takes to write that marketing plan?

The Language of Planning

Objectives. Goals. Strategies. Tactics. We throw these words around until their meanings have all the impact of old tennis balls. But they're all we've got to work with, so let's try to put a little "oomph" back into them.

Here come my definitions.

An *objective* is what you're trying to achieve. It builds a bridge connecting your marketing plan to your company's mission and vision. Many use "objectives" and "goals" interchangeably, but I like to make a distinction. *Goals* are smaller. A goal is the end point of specific steps that lead toward an objective. You need a vision toward which to steer your little ship—objectives (the long view) and goals (the short view) describe that vision.

If objectives and goals provide the *where*, strategies and tactics provide the *how*.

A *strategy* is big—a concept of what you'll do to move toward your objectives. *Tactics* are specific tasks that step by step lead to accomplishing goals.

Your tactics meet goals in pursuit of strategies to accomplish objectives. (Oh no, I'm starting to sound like a business school professor.)

Here's another way to explain these planning terms. Think about making a road trip to California in your 1965 Plymouth Valiant. Your objective is a pleasurable driving vacation. As a strategy, you choose the northern route because of the numerous national parks along the way. Your time is limited, so your goal is to drive at least 700 miles per day, which will get you to California in under a week. Your tactic to achieve that goal might be to eat meals in the car, saving your stops for scenery rather than drive-in restaurants. Objectives, strategies, goals, tactics—nobody gets from Annapolis to Zenia without them.

What?

Objectives comprise the broad overview—a vision for the future. They carry you toward what you want to achieve in your business over the long term. That's a bit different from **goals**, which you could think of as the end points of the specific steps taken toward your objective. Goals need to be specific because they relate to more immediate activities. Your **strategy** outlines approaches to achieving goals, in pursuit of objectives. **Tactics** are the specific building blocks of your strategy.

Objectives: What Are You Setting Out to Do?

Way back in the beginning of time, or at least the beginning of this book, I presented you with five marketing techniques and examples of businesses using them. Now I'm going to reveal a secret: Those five approaches I outlined back in Chapter 2 actually make great underpinnings for marketing *objectives*. To save you flipping back to that chapter, I've listed those techniques again here:

- Promoting the end result
- Separating from the competition
- Anticipating change
- Becoming a valued resource
- Always doing something new

You could choose one of these techniques, make it your objective, and there you are, beginning your marketing plan. In fact, at the end of Chapter 2, I suggested you use the provided worksheet to jot down ideas about how these techniques might work in your situation. If you did as I suggested, you've got a head start. Just pull out that worksheet now.

Objectives should be simple statements that answer questions like, "What am I trying to accomplish?" Here's an example from Bob's Bottomless Boats: "Our objective is to get the new Kaya Canoe we've developed launched in the local marketplace."

A strong statement of objectives will meet this test: It will be feasible (it's doable), flexible (allows for ongoing modifications), understandable (people know what's expected), and relevant (directly related to your mission).

Don't put the cart before the horse as you write your objectives. Stay away from *how* and *why* and *when;* just concentrate on *what* to give your plan a direction to go in as you work your way through the upcoming sections.

Situation Analysis: What's So Special?

A situation analysis asks you to look in two directions: inward and outward. What do you bring to the party, and what's going on when you get there?

If you completed your business review as described in Chapter 27, you've done your situation analysis. Hopefully that process got you thinking about what you might change in your marketing.

The business review told you something about your strengths and weaknesses. It probably also revealed opportunities and threats in your environment. Both types of factors—those you can control and those you can't—are important to understand.

Mentor

The SWOT Analysis is a common tool taught in business schools and management seminars. SWOT stands for Strengths, Weaknesses, Opportunities, and Threats. Use this tool to consider your organization's internal situation (your strengths and weaknesses) and external situation (threats and opportunities in the environment).

Now it's time to go deeper, to look for information that will improve your understanding of your situation and suggest ways to maximize its opportunities. In your situation analysis, include discussion of your marketing mix of product, place, price, and promotions. The worksheet at the end of Chapter 3, entitled "Marketing Mix at Work in My Business," is a useful component of your situation analysis. When you get to that all-important (but unofficial) fifth "P" of People, you've arrived at the next section of your marketing plan.

Review of Marketplace Issues: Scanning Your Environment

Your next job is to discover what customers think about your products or services. You must also find out what competitors are up to and how your industry is changing. Everything I presented in Part 2 of this book is relevant to your work on this section of the marketing plan.

In Chapters 4 and 5, we explored your customers' perspective. We looked at influences on buying behavior. I preached the importance of using customer knowledge to develop target marketing strategies.

In Chapter 6, I encouraged you to use market research to unlock your customer imagination. Research can reveal hidden opportunities. One man uncovered an emerging consumer need and target market by simply asking, "What do I as a dog trainer like and dislike about training reward treats now on the market?" Your next new product or line extension might be revealed by the research component of your marketing plan. Chapter 6 concluded with a worksheet, "Starter Kit for Customer Research," that might be useful to you in this section of your marketing plan.

Chapter 7 delved into target marketing, the strategy of focusing your efforts on unique customer segments that are most likely to buy your product or service.

In Chapter 8, I advocated that you adopt a competitive strategy that plays to your strengths and protects the most profitable areas of your business. That chapter's worksheet, "Ranking Against Competitors on Key Aspects of Competition," will also be useful as you write about marketplace issues.

One input you'll need that research might provide relates to your customers' media habits. What do they read, listen to, or watch? Where do they turn for advice? As you scan your environment, watch for possible communication vehicles for your media plan.

Mentor

Paying attention to your competition is especially important when you're dealing with a declining market. The only way you or your competitors can succeed is by stealing market share from each other. And the way you usually do this is through price cuts, which can kill your profits as well your competitor's.

Strategies: Targeting a Market Segment

Research will reveal what market segments deserve your attention. Once you've identified them, develop strategies to approach them.

For instance, if you're in retail, you might want to analyze your offering by determining who your heaviest purchasers are. Look for a common demographic or geographic profile. Look for the heaviest user/purchaser concentrations. Do sales increase when bicyclists pass your ice cream stand? That might suggest certain promotional strategies like giving specially marked road maps to local cycling groups.

Pitfall

The largest segment doesn't always represent the best opportunity. Often the largest segment draws fierce competition, and consumers in that category may be perfectly happy with the competitors' offerings. In many cases, you'd do better to select a segment the competition has been ignoring. There you'll find consumers who are dissatisfied and underserved—and ready to switch to you.

Mentor

Not everybody will buy your products. But some segment will, and you can probably identify them by commonalities in their age, sex, or geographic location. Or you can use behavioral attributes such as lifestyle, interests, and opinions to define a market segment. Choose which segment to focus on, and you have a target marketing strategy.

In Appendix B, you will find 10 tactical steps in the segmentation process. Refer to this if you need help at this juncture. Once you've chosen the market segments that deserve your attention, you're ready to develop strategies to approach them.

Here's another example of analyzing heavy purchasers to discover strategic opportunities, this time from the world of business-to-business sales.

An office-products company engaged in an internal survey of recent client purchases and found its heaviest users were workgroups at companies upgrading their computer networks. These people generally moved their furniture around to accommodate new workflows, and this created a need for new partitions, work surfaces, and file cabinets. The office-products company targeted new customers by partnering with the firm that upgrades the computers in a cross-promotional strategy. With this strategy, they gained entree where they might otherwise have missed sales.

Perhaps studying how the product is used, rather than who its heaviest purchasers are, will reveal a strategy to you. Consider this example from the world of medical products:

A manufacturer of medical devices makes a respiratory monitor. As part of ongoing marketing research, the manufacturer examined the product's use in hospital settings. This research observed that nurses had to remain nearby to keep an eye on whether the monitor's display indicated a failure. With constant nursing shortages a fact of life in most health care settings, the manufacturer realized that this was a definite weakness in the product. By literally adding "bells and whistles" to the product (in this case, alarm tones), nursing staff were freed to do more while monitoring patients on respirators. This was a clear advantage and one the company drove home by adding a Nurse Advocate (in other words, a customer service representative) to provide support by phone.

A key to the strategies you cook up will be your brand identity. Branding helps differentiate your offering from competitors'. Brands build over the long term as a result of (hopefully) carefully chosen actions to position that brand in the target audience's hearts and minds. Positioning connects your overall brand strategy to your specific advertising campaigns and sales promotions.

Really!

The product's stage in its life cycle is very important to the strategies you choose. Needs disappear as often as they appear. Typesetting equipment became boat anchors the day desktop publishing arrived, but the need for software training for desktop publishers was born. Do you have new products in the pipeline to replace ones that are concluding their life cycle?

Positioning requires knowledge of the dimensions of competition that are top concerns to your target market, such as price or styling. Certain dimensions are going to be more important than others to any given market segment, and that's where key customer benefits come in.

Something about your product, the way you make it or stand behind it, gives it a benefit that makes customers choose your offering over others. That's your competitive advantage, or key benefit. Where does that perceived value come from? Sometimes it's nothing more than the cachet a brand name adds to a commodity, like the value added when the name "Levi's 501" goes on some fairly ordinary blue jeans. Sometimes it's value added as tangibly as the size and composition of the Charlee Bear dog treat we talked about in Chapter 27.

Listen to what customers are saying, and you'll find the key benefit you're looking for. You could make exploiting that benefit a marketing strategy. In Chapter 16, I suggested you use the worksheet "My Branding and Positioning" to record thoughts about you and your toughest competitor's branding and positioning strategies.

To write the Strategy section of your plan, go back over your marketing mix. As I've said before, these are the factors you control. You decide what each component will be, and each decision is in essence a strategic plan. How much you choose to alter the recipe depends on how your previous strategies are working out for you. Did the business review reveal challenges to be met? Perhaps your product has moved from a growth cycle into a stagnant one, or a competitor is making inroads on your turf. Examine each "P" and come up with a response.

Really!

Positioning is a perception your potential customers hold about you. You use advertising and marketing to influence how potential customers perceive your product or service relative to your competitors. Choose attributes to play up or to play down in response to the wants of your target customers and the positions claimed by your competitors. The goal? To be remembered for some advantage only you alone—and especially none of your competitors—can claim.

How Do You Get There? Implementation Plans

Every marketer needs a road map with enough detail to navigate by—that's the function of the implementation plan. Each objective should be supported by strategies and tactics that form a to-do list as you plot out the details of getting things done. Arrange the steps chronologically and attach deadlines. The implementation plan is where you describe the tactics you've chosen and any goals or milestones you expect them to meet.

Your implementation plan will include activities like planning special events, sending out press releases, and purchasing advertising time and space. I use spreadsheets to plot multiple activities over quarters, months, or weeks, depending on the goal. You'll need to find a format—calendars, lists, whatever—that works for you.

Part 4 of this book focused largely on implementation of different possible communication strategies, like using advertising, direct mail, or publicity to get the word out. Worksheets in those chapters are designed to help you write implementation plans.

Write Down Your Specific Short-Term Tactics

Now it's time to get concrete, specific, quantifiable, and focused on short-term results. Consider your objectives; for example, Bob's objective of launching the Kaya Canoe. He might write the following tactic: "We will host a 'Kaya Canoe Camp' event the weekend of June 20 through 22. We want to register 600 participants and to sell 30 boats of which we hope at least 20 will be the new Kaya Canoes." The nitty-gritty details of that promotional event, from the invitational mailing through to the contract for trash removal on Sunday night, could be included in this section of the marketing plan.

It's painful to go to this level of detail—I won't deny it! In defense of planning, I'll just say that the more carefully you map out the route, the more you'll be able to enjoy the journey once you hit the road.

Develop Your Advertising Tactics ...

You will use your knowledge about your competitors, your customers, and yourself to develop advertising tactics, including messages, strategies, and media plans. Are you going to buy radio commercials, TV time, or print ads? Develop a website and market it online? Maybe none of the above?

In Chapters 16 and 17, I explored advertising messages; the worksheet "Crafting My Ad Message" in Chapter 17 is relevant here.

In Chapter 18, I provided a framework for deciding when and where to advertise. The worksheets for a media calendar and a media budget in that chapter are intended to help you prepare this portion of your implementation plan.

... And Other Promotional Plans

You will likely also use your knowledge about your competitors, your customers, and yourself to develop tactical plans that do not involve the techniques we think of as "advertising."

Anita Hecht promotes her Life History Service mostly through publicity activities and networking. There is no advertising component in her marketing plan.

A tactical plan for a promotion might require publicity activity, mass media advertising, improved selling techniques, or all of the above. Bob's plans for Kaya Canoe Camp would be classified as a sales promotion event, one that requires advertising but also selling and publicity components.

Allocate Your Resources of Time and Money

Timelines and budgets are two unfortunate intruders who will invade your happy land of marketing schemes sooner or later. Like gravity, everything a marketer undertakes is pinned down by the realities of what it will cost and how long it will take.

Tomorrow comes before you know it. For that reason, when we talk about tactics, it's imperative that you state a timeframe in which these activities should fall. One reason for the timeline is the psychological motivation a deadline gives. Deadlines will help you organize and prioritize your day-to-day activities.

The other reason is that without a timeframe, it is impossible to measure the relative success of your activities. You need start and stop dates to quantify the number of responses to a mail piece. You also need time frames to claim a cause/effect relationship between marketing activities and sales trends.

And budgets? Remember those story problems in your math class? Well, business is the greatest story problem ever told. I was completely allergic to math before I began to see how it related to what I wanted to accomplish and what I had to work with. Gradually the poetry of profit and loss, markup percentages, and return on investment revealed itself to me.

Think of the budget documents in your marketing plan as a collection of poems, a highly stylized language for describing your plans in terms of the dollars they'll require and the dollars they will produce.

Mentor

Going into detail about budget planning for marketing is beyond the scope of this book. If this topic is unfamiliar to you, any good business planning book—such as *The Complete Idiot's Guide to Starting a Business*—should fill in the knowledge you're lacking.

Cost estimates, cash flow statements, and break-even analyses are among the financial documents that are a marketer's responsibility to develop and maintain. The completed financial portion of a marketing plan (if prepared by a masochist with an accounting background) will include budgets for all projected expenses, a cash flow calendar, a break-even analysis, projected profit-and-loss statements, and an estimate of current and potential sales and market share.

If this were a marketing textbook and you were a college student, this course would suddenly get tougher right now. We'd dive into a lot of math about calculating market potential, sales potential, and forecasts of both cost and sales over time. You'd work on a break-even chart to determine how much product you need to move in order to make money on your program. (How much is Bob's Kaya Canoe Camp going to cost, and how many new boats must he sell to cover those costs?)

Obviously, money is important. No marketing plan can go into action without some financial resources behind it. Financial projections help you believe in the benefit that will accrue.

Tracking the Effectiveness of Your Marketing Plan

Your financial projections have two important roles. In the beginning, the plan and its financial component help you decide on a course of action. At the end, they allow you to measure the effectiveness of your work.

Measuring results is the single most important thing you can do to earn marketing a favored place in your organization. Build in your control systems from the start, establish your performance standards up front, and put occasional "checkups" into the control system to make sure activities planned are actually taking place the way they should. Finally, evaluate performance against goals. This cycle gives you control because you learn when to continue doing what you've been doing and when to change the plan. If you're sliding off track, you'll catch it soon enough to take corrective action.

Mentor

Record the tactics you've planned before you begin, and track the tasks and expenses that actually take place. Your performance against projections is the most effective measure of your marketing plan.

Really!

Whenever it's practical to do so, keep a control group and measure whatever you do against it, whether it's putting a coupon in an ad or hosting a focus group to redesign your packaging. Remember your high school science project, when you planted two sets of lima beans and gave them different growing environments? One got the normal houseplant treatment and the other one got the best in fertilizer, sun, water, and new-age music? The houseplant beans were your control group. In marketing, control means comparing two sets of activities (advertising offer A in the east-side newspaper and offer B in the west-side edition) or comparing a time period before the activity against a time period during it (boat sales last July versus sales this July with the promotional prices in effect). The difference equals the measure of your marketing success.

The final rule of thumb in measuring is to mess with the mix. Whatever you're doing, keep doing it just a little differently. Explore in every direction, push every decision you make, and remember that in strange territory, we usually find our way by going too far and turning back. You'll never know where your most effective course of action lies if you don't actively hunt for it.

At Last! You're Writing Your Marketing Plan Document

I started this chapter talking about the written marketing plan, why you would need one, and what belongs in the one you write. It's time to close the loop and talk again about the written plan.

Return to the outline for a marketing plan at the opening of this chapter. I bet it's clear now what you need to do. Take this as an outline, or even just a starting point, and begin to create the structured report of objectives, strategies, and implementation tactics that will make up your marketing plan.

Really!

If you need to present a formal marketing plan as part of a business plan, add an executive summary up front that provides a quick read of the plan's main points before you launch into the meat of the marketing plan. After fleshing out the rest of the outline, return to the beginning and insert a short section stating why you believe in your success, what you need to accomplish your goals, and what return you expect from your project.

Double-check that your financial projections are accurate and appropriate in level of detail, and you're ready to present your plan to the world.

Let me make a suggestion about the format of your plan: I like to keep a three-ring binder going with current sections on each topic. Keep your plan up-to-date with the latest copies of your planning worksheets and notes. The formality of the presentation isn't nearly as important as the quality of the content. You'll be surprised how important this notebook will become to you.

If you pride yourself on being computerized, then keep your marketing notebook electronically. A set of folders or directories serves as well as a ring binder, with one weakness: It's tougher to integrate hard-copy material, like press clippings or notes. You'll quickly find the format that works best for you. The important thing is that your organizing keeps up with creative marketing ideas.

In Appendix A, you'll find a marketing plan for Bob's Bottomless Boats, written as the company is planning to launch the Kaya Canoe. Read that for inspiration (or just for giggles), and then dive into your own marketing planning process.

The Least You Need to Know

- A marketing plan documents your plans and processes; it will help you stay organized, avoid rash actions, and improve over time.
- A marketing plan covers objectives and goals, a situation analysis, marketplace issues, strategies, tactical implementation plans, and measures of effectiveness.
- Use the worksheets found throughout this book to help you build your marketing plan.
- Measuring effectiveness is the single most important thing you can do to make your marketing accountable to larger business goals like growth or profitability.
- Keep a three-ring binder going with current sections on each topic in your plan—or if you're married to your computer, keep it there—just promise me you'll look at it often and keep it up to date!

Chapter 29

Marketing Is Like Doing Dishes: It's Never Done

In This Chapter

- How and when to revisit your marketing territory
- Why customer imagination is the most important factor in marketing
- How to gear your advertising and promotions for long-term results
- What the future may hold for marketers
- Making marketing part of every day

If you made it to the end of this book, that means you're just about ready to start at the beginning. "What!?" you say?

The bad news is that marketing, like doing the dishes, is never done. The environment changes, or you change, and new responses have to emerge. That means you have to keep revisiting what you've done and exploring new ways to do it better.

Look How Far You've Come

The good news is, it's often pleasant to reflect on where you've been. It gives you a chance to measure your progress. It's nice to see increases in sales, in message awareness, and in profits thanks to the marketing work you've accomplished.

In that spirit, let's reflect on the territory we've passed through in this book. I'll bet you feel some nostalgia for early points of interest, like the "Four Ps" and the "Four Utilities," and later side trips into sales promotions, publicity, and online advertising. Who knows, perhaps you were intrigued by the suggestions for salesmanship. Just look how far you've come!

The Marketing Environment Is Changing

What do customers want? What are competitors doing about giving them what they want? These are good questions, and ones you need to know the answer to. Market research techniques, applied both to your customer base and your competitive environment, will help you learn the truth.

> **Mentor**
>
> The knowledge you gain through research can guide your new product development, positioning strategies, pricing, advertising plans, and many other aspects of your business as well—but only if you let the right people know about it. Spread the results of your investigations through every area of your business. Finance, human resources, and operations benefit from knowing "what the other guy is up to" just as much as marketing does.

I've said it before, but it bears repeating: Know the sea you swim in. Study your competitors. You don't have to be Agent 007 to be successful at spying. You don't even have to be unethical. What you do need is motivation because competitive research without follow-through is worthless.

Your customers are always changing, and so is the environment around them. Your sea is undergoing ebbs and flows all the time. Your goal is to spot the trends in time to ride them, rather than be carried like so much flotsam.

How you interpret the information you learn will affect your marketing mix, those "Four Ps" we keep talking about. Use them to take control of your direction.

Keep in Touch with Your Customer Base

Earlier in this book, I introduced a concept I call "customer imagination." It's that sixth sense that gives our creative work its edge when it comes to intuition about what would excite, incite, or invite our customers.

Description, understanding, and accurate prediction come together to make up this special skill. The most important factor is understanding, a quality acquired only when plenty of information is available, as well as plenty of time to digest it. Use your market research and competitor intelligence programs to gather the information, and the managerial skill you're famous for to carve out the time to think.

Your mission: Find out who wants what you sell, and then use advertising, sales promotions, and personal selling skills to move the goods.

Your Market Is a Moving Target

Some segment of the great masses out there is buying what you sell, but who and why? And what would encourage them do it again tomorrow? The answer isn't the same today as it was last year, and it probably won't be the same next year either. Niches emerge, bloom, and fade. You need market research and a good media plan to help you stay in touch with your market. Research allows them to talk to you. The media plan allows you to communicate back to them. This dialogue helps you stay in sync with each other.

The things you learn in the process bear considerable thought. Knowing your audience takes more than knowing their ZIP code or phone number. The successful marketer becomes a student of psychology, actively studying customer behavior, the buying exchange, and psychographics' impact on consumer motivations and desires.

All of this leads to a branding strategy, a way of creating awareness of some attribute that's uniquely you. That brand leads to positioning that drives the message development of your advertising, as well as the media plan for spreading that message.

Promotions: How Long to Ride the Same Horse

Ride it until it slows to a walk. In other words, don't change what's working, but do measure the effectiveness of your advertising. If the pace slows to a crawl, do something about it.

Take my word on this point: You will grow tired of your advertising and promotions long before your customers do. Keep your campaign running *at least* twice as long as you think you should. Nobody, but nobody, listens (watches, reads) your advertising half as closely as you do. So give them time to heed, grow familiar, and finally bond with the message in your ad.

Rejuvenating Old Campaigns

The time does come when a campaign needs to head for the barn. Check the message against the AIDA formula; check the style and fit of the message to the medium and audience it's planned for. If, in your opinion, it still has legs, the ad hasn't become irrelevant or out of date. So what's wrong with it? Put it to this test.

Big advertising agencies, with their national name-brand clients, do this test all the time. It's called the *A/B Split.* Run the same ad in several different media with one key change—a different headline, or promotional offer, or photograph, for example. (If your schedule doesn't permit simultaneous A/B splits, try it sequentially: Run the "A" ad for six months, and then run the "B.")

What?

The **A/B Split** is a technique by which one changes an ad one factor at a time, and then compares the relative results. By only changing one element at a time the effectiveness of each part of the ad can be measured and improved. More effective parts will add up to a more effective whole.

Ad "A" is the control group, the ad without revisions. Ad "B" is the changed version. You could try a different headline, photo, style of layout, or special offer in the coupon. Change only one thing. Like an optometrist zeroing in on your perfect prescription, keep trying A/B Splits until your ad is just right. Then keep on testing, because "just right" will always change.

Warning: Don't take this too far. You can run up ridiculously high advertising production expenses and confuse your market completely if you change your advertising messages too often. To avoid this, keep positioning in mind. Don't explore so far in your A/B tests that you leave your original position behind. Move slowly. And most importantly, keep track of what it's costing and how it's performing.

A Look into My Crystal Ball

A couple of shapes are floating in that hazy orb; let Madame Sarah gaze into the future and tell you what she sees.

First, if you work as a marketing professional, your job is not that secure—but your career is. Many a marketing department downsizes in response to a management shift. Acquisitions and mergers can change the lay of the land overnight. Marketing is not going to go away, however. The downsized division now uses outside contract labor more than it used to. Maybe you're about to open a new consulting biz from your home and charge those weasels who fired you $120/hour to tell them what they never thought to ask you when you worked there for much less. My point: Don't expect a huge amount of permanence in a marketing position, and don't let that upset you.

Mentor

Think of your work as a portfolio of projects that builds the marketability of "Brand You." Keep your resumé up-to-date with concise descriptions of your most successful marketing accomplishments. As you hone your marketing and selling skills, keep in mind you might one day need to use these skills to sell yourself. Don't worry—you'll be fine.

There's something else in that crystal ball. It's a vision of the future, with new market niches that offer exciting potential.

You don't need supernatural powers to guess that America is changing, and a big part of that change is (putting it bluntly) that Baby Boomers are about to get old. The market for products and services of value to older life stages is growing like Topsy. (Of course, these nouveau oldsters don't remember what that means.) Meanwhile, the Echo Boom is swelling—the U.S. Census Bureau predicts in the year 2010 there will be about as many individuals under age 20 as over age 65.

From strollers to wheelchairs, the population will welcome amenities and accommodations for individuals with a wide range of abilities!

There are other shifts afoot. The population is becoming more ethnically and culturally diverse. People of different ethnicities have different lifestyles, likes and dislikes, and learning to accommodate (or cater to) these new niches will reward the marketer who goes that route.

All of this means increased demand for offerings related to education, health, finances, home, and leisure in the near future. (In Chapter 24, I went into more detail about these guaranteed goldmines.)

Just like those people on the radio who want you to buy heating-oil futures, I'm going to encourage you to read all the fine print before you jump into anything I've recommended. Certainly, take everything I say in this book and hold it up to the experience you've already seen in the field. Use only what fits or what fine-tunes what you already do.

Make Marketing Part of Every Day

From my friends Michael and Irene Tobis, the Ducks-In-A-Row Efficiency Consultants, I've learned how important it is to schedule in routines for any project you seriously want to accomplish. This is absolutely essential for marketing.

Make time for marketing part of every day. Some days that activity should be long-range planning—remember the pilot of a ship watches the horizon, not the wave immediately ahead! Take a look at your overall objectives fairly often—once a month or once a quarter, depending on the pace of your marketing program. Check that you have the right tactical plans in place, and update your calendar with any upcoming goals or milestones you intend to meet.

But also include time for the grunt work of marketing. Consider the activities that, while small, require daily attention, otherwise your lack of follow-through will undermine your most brilliant bursts of effort. Failing to make a call-back on the promised date or to respond promptly to a request for proposal will sink your little ship faster than you can yell "iceberg!"

This whole book could be a self-improvement book as easily as a marketing text. It's all about making yourself as helpful and friendly as can be.

Making yourself "helpful" includes a whole range of activities, from focus group research to reengineering products and distribution channels. "Friendly" doesn't happen without sending the right message. You earn "friendly" by how your company communicates, in advertising, publicity, and in person.

The helpful and friendly company—wherever you are, whatever you sell—strives to get the right product offering to the right audience, in the right quantities, and with an extra measure of service. Are you taking steps to see that you are doing each of these things well? Then marketing success is just around the corner. I hope I've helped you find it.

How Can You Improve Customer Satisfaction Starting Tomorrow?

Follow these four steps:

1. Ask customers what's important to them. You might want to develop a survey tool and do this as market research. If so, look back at Chapter 6.

2. Encourage customers to rate the relative importance of the attributes they list. It's not enough to know what they care about—you have to know what they care about *most*.
3. Gather data to understand how you are the same or different from competitors, especially when it comes to the attributes customers ranked most important.
4. Develop action plans that will help you meet or exceed competitors' offerings in each important area.

You're probably suspicious, as I am, of anything that promises dramatic breakthroughs in a few easy steps. Notice I didn't say these were easy. They are, however, the fundamentals that will build your customer imagination—and help you act on it.

The Least You Need to Know

- The most important factor in marketing is "customer imagination," that sixth sense that gives us intuition about our customers' needs and wants.
- While jobs come and go with a merger here and a downsizing there, the demand for marketing expertise is steadily growing.
- The population is rapidly becoming more diverse, culturally and ethnically, and new marketing techniques will be needed to reach emerging markets.
- Make time for marketing every day, varying your focus from daily "grunt work" to long-range planning.

Appendix A

Marketing Plan: Bob's Bottomless Boats

This plan has been prepared for informal internal review; some documents are incomplete, and these are noted as "open items" for Bob's to-do list.

This plan draft has been prepared by consultant S. White based on an interview conducted with Bob, Bill, and marketing intern Kelly Kaghnoue in February 2003.

Feb. 13, 2003

Objectives/Goals

Bob's Bottomless Boats (BBB) plans to pursue a reasonable pace of growth in the next year, fueled by the launch of a new product developed to help address the ongoing objectives.

The company's ongoing objectives are as follows:

- To build loyal customer bonds, resulting in increased sales from current customers.
- To increase the potential market by introducing newcomers to water sports.
- To increase sales by lengthening the buying season.

This year, we've added a new objective:

- To profitably introduce our new Kaya Canoe product.

This marketing plan focuses on the next three months leading up to the introduction of the new Kaya Canoe.

Situation Analysis

Bob's Bottomless Boats is primarily a retailer of watercraft ranging from one-person canoes to luxury boats. In addition, the store carries boating aftermarket supplies like fishing gear. Secondary components of the business include the manufacturing of a proprietary boat and a thriving rental division. As the name suggests, the business positions itself by promoting its limitless selection of products.

Bob's Bottomless Boats faces no particular threats from competitors. This business "owns" the region's recreational-boating market, with close to 75 percent of market share. That doesn't mean BBB is not motivated to pursue greater sales, however, or to worry about competition. "Even an 800-pound gorilla has to worry about fleas," Bob quipped.

The owners see three opportunities for next-stage growth. One is to promote greater aftermarket purchases from current customers. Another is to grow the boat-buying market by introducing newcomers to water sports. And third, the business can increase sales by lengthening the buying season.

A major strength of Bob's Bottomless Boats is its management. Bob has a background in auto sales, while brother and co-owner Bill has gained national attention for his ingenuity in boat design and fabrication. The two brothers are ideally suited to build a broad-based commercial presence.

The breadth of their customer base may be the company's weakness as well. The boat-buying public to whom BBB appeals is made up of small target markets with differentiated and sometimes conflicting interests. Silent-sports enthusiasts—those who purchase sailboats, kayaks, and canoes—are quite different demographically from motor-sports boaters. The challenge for BBB is to appeal to a broad spectrum of distinct submarkets. His response is to build an image of a collection of boutique boat businesses in one convenient location, together enjoying the combined buying clout that guarantees a good value proposition for their offerings.

Marketplace Issues

BBB's customers range in age from early 20s to late 70s. More than three fourths are male, but the women in their lives figure heavily in the decision when and what to buy and how much to spend.

BBB faces immediate competition from three or four other boat dealers in the area, plus sporting goods stores and mail-order catalogs. The second-hand market represents a potential competitor that becomes more serious whenever the economy is tight and people start unloading their toys. And, of course, there are lots of other recreational opportunities that compete for people's spare time. BBB must consider bicycles, motorcycles, recreational vehicles, and sports cars as competitors for our customers' dollars. When asked, Bob says the main competition is television or "anything that keeps people on their butts and indoors."

Market research indicates that BBB's customers come from a fairly homogenous background, but are spread over life-stages that makes each submarket unique. The twenty-something cohort has smaller purchasing power but more ability to spend discretionary income on hobbies than the next cohort, the thirty-somethings with their growing families. For this group, boating is a shared family activity, desirable but perhaps difficult to afford. For the forty-something group, boat purchases fall in two categories: the upgrade family boat, or the midlife-crisis boat for one parent. Here the choice may be a return to the canoes and sailboats of the twenty-something, in a search for youthful adventure, or an investment in the exhilaration of speed and power through the purchase of motor craft. From fifty-something up, the boat is a comfortable part of family life, to be upgraded every few years just like the family car. Within this cohort, product features of the boat are chosen both for enjoyment and for the status they project.

Members of each of these groups can be identified by descriptive attributes such as age, sex, and geographic location, and by behavioral attributes, such as their lifestyle, activities, interests, and opinions. Bob's Bottomless Boats shows excellent potential for using target marketing to increase sales. In fact, we feel we must exploit target marketing, or we will fall into the trap of trying to be "all things to all people."

Opportunity for New Product

About a year ago, Bill (the boat designer) recognized an opportunity for BBB based in the relative maturity of the retail boat market. There hasn't been a lot of innovation in boat retailing; the addition of Jet Skis a few years ago is the most excitement we've seen in a long time. And Bob despises them.

We see this situation as an opportunity to take advantage of our competitors' sleepiness and our customers' evolving needs. Bill has been hard at work on a new product design that will ease the discomfort a middle-aged body feels when it tries to participate in a young person's sport. Bill has developed a hybrid Kaya Canoe.

Bill's new boat is a lightweight (35-pound) one-person craft with a unique new seat. The boat combines the comfort of canoeing with the mobility only kayaks have delivered. The boats are easy to maneuver both in and out of the water. They're broad in the beam, which makes them stable enough for bird watching, photography, and fishing.

By introducing a new product that's affordable, comfortable, and fun, Bob's Bottomless Boats plans to reinforce our leadership position in the market. Once again, we've proven that if you want bottomless inventory, innovation, and expertise, start your search at Bob's Bottomless Boats.

Strategies

Our strategic focus for the next few months will be aimed at our objective of profitably introducing our new Kaya Canoe via the product launch event. The following strategies are specific to that objective.

Product Strategy

Launch the new boat! Our craftsmen have met the demanding schedule over the winter and the first boats are nearly ready to bring into the showroom. We'll start showing our new product, the Kaya Canoe, sometime in April or May.

Price Strategy

Price the Kaya Canoes at a premium (about $1,200) and promote to current customers in target demographics as a fun upgrade or second craft. Later, once market is familiar with the new product, drop price to broaden prospect base ($600–$900 depending on promotional bundles).

Promotion Strategy

Use promotions targeted at market segments. Offer free demonstrations, contests, and giveaways. Host special "Kaya Canoe Camp" event, followed by other events and promotions to target markets later this summer.

Tentatively, we plan to hold a "Women on the Water" weekend to remove psychological barriers for those who perceive boating as a guy thing, and to host a "Singles Night" promotion. As we choose and execute promotions, we'll pursue publicity regarding the new boat.

A portion of our usual advertising spending will be earmarked to support the product launch.

Place Strategy

Install electric sign to exploit our high-visibility location. Use sign to announce special events.

Explore new distribution channels, including participation in recreational sports shows at shopping malls, fairgrounds, etc. Goal: Bring Kaya Canoe to where the new customers are.

Create demand that might lead to expanding the Kaya Canoe's distribution area and interest other dealers in carrying the product.

Implementation Plans

We will continue plans already underway addressing the objectives outlined in the beginning of this plan, with the addition of marketing efforts surrounding launch of the Kaya Canoe.

This plan focuses on the Kaya Canoe launch at the Kaya Canoe Camp Event in June.

The Kaya Canoe launch will receive marketing support in three tactical areas:

- Staff resources
- Advertising (media costs and production)
- Publicity

This event is going to be a "family reunion" in honor of our newest addition. We expect word of mouth to spread quickly once we begin the public side of our preparations.

We will pursue all possible publicity opportunities surrounding the introduction of the Kaya Canoe, especially demonstration events. Advertising will support those events, of course.

Promotional Plan

Promotional events targeted to market segments will always be part of our calendar. The next upcoming event is "Kaya Canoe Camp"—an action-packed weekend on and off the water, tentatively scheduled for June 20–22. This event will include several activities:

- Demonstrations
- Whitewater obstacle courses
- Barbecue
- Strolling "paddle pals" (customer service associates)
- Camping optional

Note: Bob needs to flesh out the promotional plan for this event. Tactical plan should be complete no later than March 15 for the June 20–22 event.

This event presents plenty of opportunity for publicity, which should be leveraged to our advantage, both to make the event a success and to reach our goals for the launch of the Kaya Canoe.

Advertising Plan

We will continue plans for advertising already scheduled in support of ongoing objectives. That advertising will be image-oriented, designed to augment our position as the ultimate authority on all things boating. To do so, we will sponsor the local TV show *Boats and Boating*. We will also produce and distribute an audio column featuring Bob and Bill, who will answer questions about water sports and boats.

One component of the overall ad schedule will be response-oriented, promoting the Kaya Canoe Camp. Print and radio will support this component.

The advertising plan for Bob's Bottomless Boats will include newspaper and radio advertising around a calendar of sale events, to raise awareness with both current and potential boaters. There will obviously be no co-op support for the Kaya Canoe Camp, as we are promoting the boat we're manufacturing. It's very important that we plan carefully and make sure this event is successful and profitable.

Note: Bob needs to flesh out this advertising plan.

Budgets and Timelines

Bob is responsible for preparing budgets and timelines for the product launch tactics. Note: This is high priority and must be completed soon if the June event is to be a success.

- **Media Schedule** (first appearances, esp. We need deadlines!)

  to come from Bob

- **Budget for Media Schedule**

  to come from Bob

- **Budget for Advertising Production Expenses**

  Bob has provided these estimates of advertising production based on prior experience. Advertising expenses related to the Kaya Canoe Camp should be tracked to the Silent Sportscraft Division.

Client: Bob's Bottomless Boats

Description: Simple black-and-white print ad, using stock photography

Size: 2 column by 8"	
Fees	
Creative development & copy writing	$400
Graphic design	$350
Production of camera-ready art	$200
Expenses	
Deliveries & misc.	$30
Stock photo use fee	$75
Negative + contact print	$265
Total Fees and Expenses:	$1,080

Client: Bob's Bottomless Boats

Description: Radio Commercial

Length:	**:30**
Fees	
Develop concept & write copy	$600
Producer (record voice, mix down)	$195
Announcer	$65
Voices (male + female giggle)	$85

continues

continued

Length:		**:30**
Expenses		
Tape	$15	
Sound effects (from library)	$20	
Dubs	$125	
Total Fees and Expenses:	$1,105	

- **Brainstorm: other budgets and timelines**

  In addition to the advertising plan, the Kaya Canoe Camp requires tactical plans for each component of the event promotion.

  The following notes were gathered informally as the planning group ate lunch. Bob, with Kelly's assistance, will develop this list into task descriptions with budget, timing, and person responsible.

Kaya Canoe Camp product launch event needs:

Publicity. Press release, photos, background pages on BBB and the Kaya Canoe, print invitations, gifts

Event Planning. Menu (barbecue!), staff (camp counselors and paddle pals), photographer, logistics (reception tents, parking control, etc.)

Collateral. Freebies for all, some prizes for contest winners; travel mugs, water bottles, Frisbees, duffel/stuff sacks, coolers, more?

Mentor

Note that Bob's Marketing Plan is incomplete—it's full of mentions of items to come, things to do, estimates to be prepared, and so on. I point this out to show you how to do a plan without getting frustrated. You don't have to have every detail worked out to the penny. Some parts of the plan will always be under revision. Think of it as a house you're always remodeling. Before Kaya Canoe Camp even takes place, the marketing plan will be moving on to cover the Women on the Water Weekend or the Singles Night promotion. It's not important that you consider the plan *complete*; it's important that you *consider the plan*.

Measures of Effectiveness

Bob has prepared an estimate of market potential for the "Silent Sportscraft" division, the group responsible for launching the Kaya Canoe. At the end of the year, we will compare actual performance to these estimates in order to measure the effectiveness of our marketing plan. Note that sales and expenses related to the launch of the Kaya Canoe should be charged to the Silent Sportscraft Division.

Bob's Bottomless Boats Market Potential

Silent Sportscraft Division (canoes, sailboats, kayaks, hybrids)

Time Period: One Calendar Year 2003

1. **Expected sales volume:** $600,000

   Assumption: .1% (one tenth of one percent) of 300,000 residents will purchase a boat at an average cost of $2,000.

2. **Expected sales potential:** $390,000

   Assumption: Given previous years' performance, maximum marketing over the time period could be expected to earn Bob a 65 percent share of all Silent Sportscraft sales.

3. **Actual sales volume:** $253,500

   Assumption: Actual sales volume will average 65 percent of sales potential. The reason for this is Bob's introduction of the Kaya Canoe, which will drain marketing excitement away from other established products. Bob is realistic about the lower sales he can expect during the new product's introduction.

Of course, we would like to have some measures of effectiveness for the upcoming Kaya Canoe Camp event. We intend to register 600 participants and to sell 30 boats, of which we hope at least 20 will be the new Kaya Canoes, generating sales of $20,000.

We understand that $20,000 is not likely to cover our event promotion costs, but that was never our goal. Rather, we are investing in awareness and enthusiasm about our new product.

We'll estimate costs associated with the event and monitor what actually happens. Bob has our marketing intern Kelly Kaghnoue to assist him in drawing up the necessary projections.

Conclusions

This plan indicates that a great deal needs to be done if the event in June is to be a success. Responsibilities were assigned, and Kelly's going to follow up with distribution and scheduling of the task group meetings in the next few days.

Appendix B

Resources

Books

Egelhoff, Tom. *How to Market, Advertise, and Promote Your Business or Service in a Small Town.* Eagle Marketing, 1998.

Godin, Seth. *Permission Marketing: Turning Strangers into Friends, and Friends into Customers.* Simon and Schuster, 1999.

Kaatz, Ron. *Advertising & Marketing Checklists.* NTC Business Books, 1995.

Kobliski, Kathy J. *Advertising Without an Agency.* The Oasis Press, 1998.

Mark, Margaret, and Carol Pearson. *The Hero and the Outlaw: Building Extraordinary Brands Through the Power of Archetypes.* McGraw Hill, 2001.

Novo, Jim. *Drilling Down: Turning Customer Data into Profits with a Spreadsheet.* Book Locker, 2002.

Peppers, Don, and Martha Rogers. *The One to One Future: Building Relationships One Customer at a Time.* Currency Doubleday, 1996.

Smith, J. Walker, and Ann Clurman. *Rocking the Ages.* Harper Business, 1997.

Taylor, Don, and Jeanne Smalling Archer. *Up Against the Wal-Marts.* Amacom, 1994.

Trout, Jack. *Positioning: The Battle for Your Mind.* McGraw Hill, 2000.

Trout, Jack, with Steve Rivkin. *Differentiate or Die: Survival in Our Era of Killer Competition.* John Wiley & Sons, 2000.

Underhill, Paco. *Why We Buy: The Science of Shopping.* Touchstone/Simon and Schuster, 1999.

Websites

Dr. E-Biz Ralph Wilson, www.wilsonweb.com
An excellent resource for small businesses interested in advertising on the Internet.

Ducks-In-A-Row Efficiency Consultants, www.ducksinarow.com
If you're going to increase your marketing activity, you'll need to get organized. Visit the Ducks' website for tips on personal productivity, managing multiple projects, and more!

Marketing Profs, www.marketingprofs.com
This website is an archive of well-written and informative articles from the free e-zine, which brings together marketing professors and professionals to share insights.

Microsoft's business resource site, www.bcentral.com
Some of the ideas I've included in this book, I first wrote about in my articles for the Demographics area on bCentral. You can subscribe to my monthly newsletter by registering at http://bcentral.thirdwaveresearch.com. Check the opt-in box for "The Bulletin."

Statistics Canada, www.statcan.ca
Similar resources to U.S. Census site but for Canadian population, economics, and industry.

The Advertising Show, www.theadvertisingshow.com
A radio program that does for local advertisers what Click and Clack do for cars. The nationally syndicated program airs on Saturdays. You can catch it in broadcast or via the Internet. Check the website to find out if the program airs in your area, and to explore other resources for local advertisers.

U.S. Census Bureau website, www.census.gov
Resources for population, economics, and industry research.

UCLA Rosenfeld Library of Competitive Intelligence
www.anderson.ucla.edu/resources/library/libcoint.htm
Research resources in three categories: corporate profiles, industry environment, and socio-political environment.

Associations and Advisors

National Federation of Independent Businesses (NFIB)
www.nfib.org

Canadian Federation of Independent Businesses (CFIB)
www.cfib.org

Direct Marketing Association (DMA)
www.the-dma.org

American Marketing Association (AMA)
www.ama.org

Small Business Administration (SBA)
www.sba.gov

Small Business Development Centers
www.sba.gov/sbdc/

Women's Business Centers
www.onlinewbc.gov

Index

A

B

C

D

E

F

G

H

I

J-K

L

M

N

O

P

Q

R

S

T

U-V

W

X-Y-Z